FEAST

A History of Grand Eating

ROY STRONG

JONATHAN CAPE
LONDON

Copyright © Oman Productions Ltd 2002

Roy Strong has asserted his right under the Copyright, Designs and Patents Act 1988 to be identified as the author of this work

First published in Great Britain in 2002 by
JONATHAN CAPE
Random House, 20 Vauxhall Bridge Road, London SW1V 2SA

Random House Australia (Pty) Limited
20 Alfred Street, Milsons Point, Sydney,
New South Wales 2061, Australia

Random House New Zealand Limited
18 Poland Road, Glenfield,
Auckland 10, New Zealand

Random House (Pty) Limited
Endulini, 5A Jubilee Road, Parktown 2193, South Africa

The Random House Group Limited Reg. No. 954009
www.randomhouse.co.uk

A CIP catalogue record for this book is available from the British Library

ISBN 0–224–06138–0

Papers used by The Random House Group Limited are natural, recyclable products made from wood grown in sustainable forests; the manufacturing processes conform to the environmental regulations of the country of origin

Designed by Peter Ward
Set in 11¾pt on 14½pt Centaur by
Palimpsest Book Production Limited, Polmont, Stirlingshire
Printed and bound in Great Britain by
Biddles Ltd, Guildford & King's Lynn

For

DAVID HUTT

friend, priest, gardener and cook

CONTENTS

CONTENTS

CHAPTER SIX

Dinner is Served

269

POSTSCRIPT

The Eclipse of the Table?

309

NOTES AND SOURCES

313

INDEX

343

LIST OF ILLUSTRATIONS

[xi]

PHOTOGRAPHIC SOURCES

Bridgeman Art Library, London: pages 61, 62, 72, 92, 168, 171, 182, 210, 234, 241, 261, 265, 266, 278, 282, 297. Angelo Hornak Library: page 271. Hulton Archive/Getty Images: pages 268, 302. Photothèque des Musées de la Ville de Paris: pages 117, 126. Scala, Florence: pages 2, 32, 44, 53, 56, 59, 60, 63, 64, 128, 178. Studio Fotografico Giovetti, Mantua: page 164.

I HAVE ALWAYS been interested in food, or rather (as who *isn't* interested in food?) in the history of food. Of course the practicalities appeal to me too. When, during my late twenties, I shared a flat with a colleague I chose to be the cook. I took this role with me into marriage, and over thirty years (and the perusal of several hundred cookery books) on, I am still cooking away most evenings with pleasure, having explored the cuisine of the majority of European countries. I also delight in laying tables and staging a lunch or a dinner as a flawless spectacle – or as flawless as such an event can be in an age when the cook is also the butler and the washer-up as well as the host. Still, I have never ceased to be keenly aware that to entertain well calls for a sense of choreography and an aesthetic eye, not only in respect of the table as a whole and its decoration, but also as to how each course is presented on the plate.

My interest in the history of food can be traced back to my days as a postgraduate student under the late Dame Frances Yates in the late 1950s. It was a time when the topic of pageantry and all kinds of festivals was being opened up as a matter of academic concern. But I think that the real turning point was a visit to the Nordiska Museum in Stockholm in 1966. I vividly recall rounding a corner and suddenly finding myself in a long darkened corridor containing a panoramic history of table-laying. I was mesmerised, fascinated to see how pottery, pewter and wood were replaced by porcelain and silver, how the scanty cutlery of earlier centuries gave way to the intimidating plethora that confronted the late nineteenth-century diner, how trestle tables made way for solid oak and then polished mahogany, how rudimentary benches metamorphosed into upholstered seats and then elegant sets of dining chairs.

It must have left a big impression on me, for it was a display format

I longed for but failed to introduce during my period as Director of the Victoria & Albert Museum. Yet from time to time the topic surfaced in exhibitions. In 1970 my wife, the designer Julia Trevelyan Oman, designed an exhibition on Samuel Pepys for the National Portrait Gallery in which she recreated his dining table, complete with game pie. During my last year as Director of the V & A I took soundings for a major exhibition on the subject and I recall the privilege of discussing it with the late Elizabeth David and the late Jane Grigson. Sadly, on my departure the project withered.

During the 1990s, however, I became increasingly aware of a rising tide of interest. There was the splendid exhibition at Versailles on the royal tables of eighteenth-century Europe, another on a similar theme devoted to the Danish court (which came to Kensington Palace), not to mention the innovative and pioneering exhibitions in this country at the Bowes Museum, Barnard Castle and at Fairfax House in York. I began to write a series of articles involving food history in *Country Life*.

All of which brings me to the present book. It stems from a realisation that no single volume exists in English that synthesises the enormous body of scholarly work on the subject of food and feasting that has been done in recent years by dozens of historians in a number of different countries. The information gathered in these pages lies scattered for the most part in hundreds of specialised articles, largely in French, Italian and English, given at conferences and colloquia over the past two decades. The likelihood of the average reader searching out and reading such material is remote, yet the subject is one that has a universal appeal.

A basic problem is the fact that the material tends to be compartmentalised, to deal with one or another particular aspect of what has happened through history around the table rather than the whole phenomenon. After all, the subject embraces not only food but etiquette, furniture, textiles, ceramics, glass, metalwork, architecture, interior decoration and music, to name but a few. I have attempted here to draw together information from all these often disparate – and sometimes obscure – fields. Certain aspects of research, it should be said, have received more attention from scholars than others. The Greek *symposion*, the medieval feast and the Renaissance banquet, for example, have given rise to minor academic industries.

Eating is a topic that all too easily can fragment and go off in many directions, so it would seem useful to outline the boundaries of this book. Its prime focus is the table and the main meal of the day. Each period produces what we may consider to be an archetypal meal of the era. Each chapter therefore opens with the description of such a meal and then moves on to analyse the political, social and other forces that shaped it. Although I deal with the development of cookery, in the main food production and supply are not covered, nor the development of the kitchen and cooking methods beyond what is necessary to explain the meal that appears on the table. Books on historic food with recipes from every period reinterpreted for today's cooks now exist in some number. Do not look for such things here. The choice of the word 'feast' for the title signals that our primary interest is in upper-class eating, although as power in society devolves, a fairly large part of the populace is eventually involved by the time the book ends, in 1914. This is therefore history from the top, somewhat out of fashion these days, but central to one of this book's themes, the interconnection of what occurs at the table and shifts in power and class.

Writing it has brought me back to the Warburg Institute, that great institution which first taught me to think and also preached that an educated mind can move in any direction it chooses. As the late Dame Frances Yates always used to say to me, 'You have an educated mind. Take the book from the shelf and read it.' And that is precisely what I have done. Next comes that mainstay of so many of my books, the London Library. I am more than grateful to Guy Penman and his colleagues who cheerfully dealt with my many requests for inter-library loans. So too am I to my editor, Charles Elliott, who has tolerated an author who has the habit of starting with chapter three of a book and writing chapters one and two last. My gratitude must be expressed to Richard Barber in respect of the medieval period, and to Professor Ken Albala who read the whole text, making several helpful suggestions. Any mistakes, of course, are mine. Once again I have to thank Juliet Brightmore for gathering in the illustrations for a book whose elegant design I owe to Peter Ward. Mention too must be made of my agent, Felicity Bryan, who has a sharp sense of the direction that my pen should next take. Finally comes the inspiration and enthusiasm of the publishers, Will Sulkin and his colleague Jörg Hensgen. In spite of all the pressures affecting their field today they still strive to keep alive the tradition, all too often absent, of cherishing the creators. After all there would be no books without authors.

ROY STRONG
The Laskett, Much Birch, Herefordshire

September 2001

FEAST

A History of Grand Eating

A Roman banquet from a Pompeian wall-painting.
A slave removes a guest's sandals while another proffers him a drink.
Another guest, the worse for drink, is helped away.

CHAPTER ONE

Convivium: When in Rome . . .

T HE MOST NOTORIOUS description of a feast ever written comes in what survives of a first-century satire, Petronius' *Satyricon*.[1] The host is a former slave, profiteer, food speculator, braggart, drunkard and wife-beater called Trimalchio. The book itself concerns the adventures of a homosexual couple, Encolpius, the narrator, and his friend, the younger Giton. In the episode known as the *Cena Trimalchionis* a third unscrupulous character is involved, Ascyltus, who sets out to divide the lovers. Encolpius and Ascyltus go as guests to Trimalchio's feast, while Giton is on hand acting as their servant.

The episode opens with all three visiting the baths. The two guests are already arrayed in 'dinner dress', and their host is pointed out to them playing ball with his slaves. What follows sets the scene for an extravaganza of tasteless vulgarity: 'Trimalchio clicked his fingers, and at this signal the eunuch supplied him with the chamber-pot as he continued playing. The host voided his bladder, demanded water for his hands, and after perfunctorily washing his fingers, wiped them on the slave's hair.'

On arrival at Trimalchio's house (which was probably at Puteoli, not far from Naples) the guests are met by a janitor and ushered along a colonnaded gallery decorated with allegorical scenes glorifying their host. At the entrance to the dining-room a slave exhorts them to enter right foot first, which they do, only to encounter a slave, stripped ready for flogging, grovelling in front of them and pleading to be rescued from such a fate. They do so.

From here on the text is one long catalogue of surprises. Inside the dining-room the rescued slave promptly showers them with kisses and reveals himself to be the butler, promising them good wine. Encolpius and Ascyltus settle themselves on couches, attended by slaves who resemble 'a dancer's supporting group'. Iced water (no mean feat in a pre-refrigerator age) is produced, in which they wash their hands, and wine. More surprisingly, their toenails are trimmed for them to the sound of the slaves singing in chorus.

The guests – there are several, including (on and off) Trimalchio's wife, Fortunata, and another wife, Scintilla – having taken their places, the meal begins. It opens with *hors d'oeuvres* (*gustatio*):

> In the entrée dish stood a donkey of Corinthian bronze, bearing a double pannier which contained white olives one side, and black on the other . . . little bridges which had been soldered on spanned the dishes; they contained dormice dipped in honey and sprinkled with poppy-seed. There were also hot sausages lying on a silver grill, and underneath were plums and pomegranate seeds.

At this point Trimalchio, bedizened in scarlet and jewels, enters in a litter to the salute of a musical fanfare. Without any apology to his guests for arriving halfway through the first course he proceeds to position himself in the place normally accorded to the most distinguished guest. Even then he ignores the company by continuing to play a board game. Slaves carry in a large platter on which sits a basket containing a wooden hen, her wings outstretched in the act of hatching eggs. To 'the blaring sound of music', the slaves rummage around in the straw beneath her and unearth large eggs weighing half a pound each. These are made of flour fried in oil. They are distributed to the guests who, on opening them, find little birds, fig-peckers, in spiced egg yolk.

The text indicates that the first course was accompanied by a glass of sweetened wine (probably the kind called *mulsum*), for Trimalchio is offering his guests a second glass 'when at a sudden musical signal the *hors d'oeuvre* dishes were all whisked away simultaneously by the singing troupe'. One of the silver dishes is dropped in the process, but the slave who picks it up has his ears boxed for his pains and is told to throw it back on the ground to be swept up with the rest of the rubbish.

A new excess follows: the guests' hands are washed not in water but wine, by two long-haired Ethiopians. Glass winejars containing 'hundred-year-old' Falernian wine appear. Then something weird occurs: a slave brings in a silver skeleton, and Trimalchio arranges it on the table in a series of different postures. The first course of the *cena* proper is a circular plate on which are arrayed foods for each sign of the zodiac – kidneys on Gemini, beef on Taurus, chick-peas on Capricorn, a barren sow's womb on Virgo and so on. A square of turf in the centre supports a honeycomb. Bread is now served by an Egyptian slave, apparently still singing, for Trimalchio joins in 'with a most scurrilous and tortured mime-song'. Encolpius and Ascyltus, who are aristocrats and busily scoffing at the vulgarity of everything the whole time, bridle at the prospect of having to eat plebeian fare. But suddenly four slaves leap forward and reveal the zodiac to be only a lid, which they lift:

> Inside we saw fowls, sows' udders, and in the centre a hare equipped with wings, a veritable Pegasus. We also noticed four representations of Marsyas at the corners of the dish; from their wineskins a peppered gravy was pouring over fish which were swimming, so to say, in the channel.

Everyone, including the servants, applauds and a carver appears who cuts the meat rhythmically to music.

Gossip follows. Trimalchio, parading a pretence to erudition, announces that 'even when we're dining we must advance learning' and embarks on an explanation of the symbolism of the zodiac lid. Everyone sycophantically applauds. Slaves then carry in coverlets for the couches depicting hunting scenes while Spartan hunting dogs bound into the room to herald the arrival of the second course:

> . . . a tray with a massive boar on it, wearing the cap of freedom. From its teeth hung two small baskets woven from palm-leaves, one filled with fresh dates, and the other with the dried Egyptian variety. The boar was surrounded by tiny piglets of pastry, seemingly crowded over the teats . . .

The piglets are handed around as gifts. A carver enters dressed as a huntsman and plunges his hunter's knife into the boar's flanks, whereupon thrushes fly out, circling the room until they are trapped. The meat is then distributed along with the dates 'in time to the music'. During this course a handsome slave boy disguised as Bacchus sings poems by Trimalchio, who vanishes into the lavatory promptly afterwards.

There is seemingly no end to this feast. It goes on to include a pig which, when slashed open, gushes sausages and black puddings; acrobats; actors performing in Greek; golden crowns and jars of perfume descending from the ceiling; presents for everyone; cakes that spurt saffron at the guests; and, at last, the dessert (*secundae mensae*):

> It consisted of pastry thrushes stuffed with raisins and nuts; quinces followed, with thorns implanted in them to make them resemble sea-urchins . . . a fat goose surrounded by every kind of bird.

Slaves bear in pitchers from which oysters and scallops cascade. Snails arrive on a silver gridiron and long-haired boys wash the guests' feet in liquid perfume and festoon their legs with garlands. By then everyone is drunk and the whole affair winds up with Trimalchio, reclining like a corpse lying in state while the musicians play the dead march, reading his will aloud. At this point Encolpius, Ascyltus and Giton make their escape.

What are we to make of the *Cena Trimalchionis*? How accurate a picture does it give, allowing for the distortions of the satirist's pen, of a Roman dinner party or *convivium*? The answer, surprisingly, is that the *Cena Trimalchionis* is probably far closer to reality than a first reading would suggest. The author is generally accepted to be Petronius Arbiter, a politician and *arbiter elegantiarum* at the court of Nero, who was forced to commit suicide in AD 66; the *Satyricon* can thus be dated quite closely to the years AD 63–65. Anyone familiar with Suetonius' account of the excesses of Nero will find many of the characteristics of that notorious emperor embodied in Trimalchio. And even allowing for satire, a *convivium* in this period might well be a matter of extremes.

The grand dinner party was a defining event in first-century Roman society. Trimalchio is one of the aspiring classes, a freedman, out to impress his guests by the sheer opulence of his hospitality. By the middle of the first century such a meal had already reached a high pitch of ritual and artifice. Special clothes had to be worn. The visit to the baths as a prelude establishes that such a feast took place in that part of the day dedicated to *otium* (leisure) as against *negotium* (business). Guests took servants with them and were placed on couches (for the Romans dined reclining) in a certain order denoting status (Petronius makes a point of the way the host usurped the place — *locus consularis* — that should have been assigned to the most distinguished guest). The meal, which was divided into three sections, resembled a theatrical performance involving musicians and a large cast of servants who sang in chorus as they served, washed hands and feet, cut guests' toenails and distributed garlands. The cuisine was lavish and elaborate, involving figurative food such as the winged hare and quinces in the guise of sea-urchins. It was also calculated to astonish the guests with constant surprises, like the pig stuffed with sausages and puddings. Some kind of learned dialogue as well as performances by singers, dancers, acrobats and actors also played a part. In short, this meal came to epitomise the aspirations of an age, and provided a perfect target for a satirist intent on exposing its inanities.

Yet such biting mockery of foolishness implies of course that the opposite sort of *convivia* existed, gatherings reflecting the essence of ordered society as the Romans defined it. As I shall demonstrate, each age has produced its own archetypal feast. The *convivium* was as defining for the Romans as the dinner party for the Victorians. From its inception, the act of eating together transformed a necessary bodily function into something far more significant, a social event. It assumed the acceptance of guidelines as to how such a gathering should conduct itself. In the world of classical Antiquity this was one of the first actions distinguishing civilised men from semi-savages. Conviviality, to both the Greeks and Romans, was seen as one of the cornerstones of civilisation, though an ambiguous and complex one. The table and those bidden to gather round it and share its pleasures could be a vehicle for social aggregation and unity; but equally it could encourage social distinctions, separating people into categories by placement or, even worse, exclusion. Eating together by the chosen few was an expression of the principle of oligarchy; a meal for the masses of democracy. If a meal was given in honour of a superior it expressed humility and subservience on the part of the host. If it was a gathering of equals it demonstrated the communality of the group. The meal and everything connected with it has been and, to a very large extent still is, a vehicle determining status and hierarchy — and also aspiration — no matter what pattern of society prevails. This was clearly true by the time of the *Cena Trimalchionis*, and had already found a highly sophisticated form of expression. Yet it was a tradition that the Romans had taken over from the Greeks, and before them the ancient Near Eastern civilisations. It is with these more ancient cultures that we must begin.

The Greek inheritance

ALREADY BY THE second millennium BC the sharing of food and wine as the social counterpart to a written contract – such as that occasioned by a marriage or a treaty – was established among the Babylonians. The Mesopotamian monarchs staged stupendous banquets for important events such as military victories or the arrival of an embassy, the inauguration of a new palace or a temple. Etiquette for such occasions was elaborate: the king sat apart, reclining on a couch, with his queen close by, and guests were placed in groups according to their status. The role of cupbearer involved much ceremonial. There was ritual hand-washing, and guests received a phial of oil perfumed with cedar, ginger and myrtle with which to anoint themselves both at the start and the finish of the meal. Grilled and stewed meats were served on flat bread, followed by a dessert of fruits and pastries sweetened with honey. There was entertainment too: music, song, clowns, wrestlers, jugglers and actors.

Such feasts took place on a vast scale. Assurnasirpal II (883–859 BC) inaugurated his new palace with a ten-day feast for no fewer than 69,574 guests. Events of this kind played a major role in dynastic politics. The provisions consumed vividly expressed to all present how the ruler could command tributes from all over the vast Persian kingdom. The food and drink brought from such remote regions emphasised the government's prepotence, and the meal itself made manifest the alliance of the monarchy with the great aristocratic families. One aspect of such grand shows is especially significant to the history of the table. Those parts of the royal domains anxious to curry regal favour would deliberately send delicacies to tempt the royal palate and the appetites of the powerful guests. Thus here, at the very beginning of our survey, one phenomenon is evident: the use of rare ingredients and the development of *haute cuisine* as the children of hierarchy, clearly related to the manipulation of one group by another for sociopolitical aims.

Similarly in Ancient Egypt, the banquet served as a significant social ritual. Wall-paintings in tombs provide the evidence. We see female guests proffered flowers, probably on arrival, the entry of food in procession, the presence of innumerable servants and music and dancing. The banquet, even in these remote times, was already an aesthetic experience far beyond the mere consumption of food, embracing elegance of dress, some kind of manners, ceremonial, and every form of theatrical entertainment.[2]

All of this was to have profound influence on Greece as it evolved into a major civilisation from the land of isolated farmsteads and small walled towns that the *Iliad* and the *Odyssey* record. Already, however, even in Homeric society the banquet was a place of display and prestige. In the words of the hero Odysseus:

> For myself I declare that there is no greater fulfilment of delight than when joy possesses a whole people, and banqueters in the halls listen to a minstrel as they sit in order due, and by them tables are laden with bread and meat, and the cupbearer draws wine from the bowl and bears it round and pours it into the cups. This seems to my mind the fairest thing there is.[3]

There we have all the elements of the ceremonial feast already in place: music and singing, placing by status and the symbolic role of the cup-bearer. But Ancient Greece was to go on and develop a far more complex culinary culture, leaving it as a legacy to Rome.

Greek cuisine was based on the sea.[4] The range of fish in its waters was huge: tunny, angler-fish, grey mullet, blue fish, pike, catfish, conger eel, skate, sturgeon, carp, swordfish, bream, shark and dogfish. To these add octopus, squid, cuttlefish, oysters, crab and lobster. Meat was highly valued but relatively scarce. In any early society domesticated animals were needed far more for their milk and wool, and to work the land, than for consumption. But the Greeks ate sheep, pigs, goats and game, and also animals less appealing to most modern sensibilities, such as dog and horse. Game included hares, boar, goats, asses, foxes, deer and lion, as well as such feathered prey as thrushes, chaffinches, larks, quail, moorhens, geese, pigeons, mallards and pheasants. There was domesticated poultry. For vegetables the range was considerable too as horticulture improved: celery, cress, asparagus, beet, cabbage, capers, kale, cardoon, chicory, endive and fennel. For fruit they had olives, quinces, plums, cherries, melons, apples, figs, cucumbers, pears and grapes, as well as a range of nuts. Grapes furnished wine and olives oil. Both of the latter products were basic to the evolution of Greek gastronomy. To all of these ingredients were added prestige imported spices, especially pepper, from China, India, Arabia and Africa.

What little we know about Greek cuisine comes from a work by Athenaeus of Naucratis in Egypt entitled *The Deipnosophists* (The Sophists' Banquet). It was probably completed in the year immediately following the death of the Emperor Commodus in AD 192. Running to fifteen books, it takes the form of a series of fictional dinner conversations which are set in Rome and which discuss a vast range of topics, including gastronomy in Ancient Greece. Thanks to the author's habit of incorporating large chunks of other people's writings, *The Deipnosophists* is fairly informative about an era that would otherwise have been wrapped in obscurity. In particular he incorporates extracts from the world's earliest known food and cookery writer, Archestratus, a fourth-century BC Sicilian Greek.

Greek gastronomy developed out of the practice of sacrifice. Meat, as I have already indicated, was relatively scarce, available mainly following the sacrifice of a domestic animal to the gods. On such occasions the meat would be divided into equal portions and roasted. (The fact that it was divided equally and apportioned by drawing lots meant that there was no such craft as that of butchery. But in any case the consuming passion of the Greeks, certainly of the Athenians, was for fish which, since it was never part of religious ritual, was free to be a wholly secular food.) With the invention of that gastronomical cornerstone, the cooking pot, meat or fish could be boiled or stewed. Then the more sophisticated began adding other ingredients to the pot, like salt to heighten the taste or honey as a sweetener, or the fragrance of herbs and spices. In such a manner the art of cookery was born and, in the case of the Greeks, quickly became quite sophisticated. Athenaeus' text contains references to no fewer than thirty Greek cookery books, the earliest datable to the fifth century BC. Much of the culinary skill they record seems to have come to Greece with cooks from Sicily in the fourth and third centuries. By that date, too, the wine trade had fully developed, with geographical differences already being recognised. Cookery by then included a large range of complex meat and fish dishes as well as a repertory of biscuits, breads and cakes.

The aim was to achieve a balance of the sweet with the bitter, of sour with very unusual flavours. It involved the use of a vast array of fresh and dried herbs and spices together with honey and vinegar, and an ingredient which was also to be basic for the succeeding cuisines of Rome and Byzantium – the fish sauce called *garos* in Greek, *garum* in Latin.[5] *Garos* was made by mixing whole fish with salt, leaving it to ferment for up to three months, then straining off and bottling the liquid. Its production was along factory lines at a very early date.

Only fragments survive of these fifth- and fourth-century cookbooks, but they make plain that by the close of the fifth century BC Greek civilisation had given birth to a complete interconnected literature covering diet, health, exercise and hygiene as well as cookery. The Greeks, moreover, were the first to recognise cookery as one of the basic skills and arts of human life.[6] Diet in the ancient world was seen first and foremost as a means of preventing and curing illness. It was based on the virtually universally accepted view of the human body as composed of four humours: blood, phlegm, yellow and black bile, each of which had its own characteristic: hot and dry (blood), cold and dry (phlegm), hot and moist (yellow bile), and cold and moist (black bile). All foods were categorised as embodying one or more of these attributes. The perfect balance, which was central to maintaining a healthy disease-free body, depended on eating food capable of correcting any existing imbalance in the system.

That imbalance was not only an inbred characteristic of the individual given human being, but also one that varied with age and the seasons of the year. So, for example, old men had to avoid starches, cheese or hard-boiled eggs. And the foods consumed in winter should be hotter, stronger and drier than those in the summer. The whole of this theory was later to be codified in the work of Galen (AD 129–?199/216), court physician to the Emperor Marcus Aurelius, whose works on medicine, diet and hygiene spelled out exactly what each person should eat according to their humoral disposition. Galen was to remain the ultimate authority on diet in late Antiquity and throughout the Middle Ages into the Renaissance.

* * *

As I have said, buried within *The Deipnosophists* are large extracts from earlier writing. Two of them give us rare detailed glimpses of banquets in Greece. A feast that can be dated to the late fifth or early fourth century BC is described in a poem entitled *The Banquet*, written by Philoxenus of Leucas.[7] It is an elaborate affair, of a kind that might have been served in a city like Athens in the early fourth century. Only men were present. Each reclined on a couch, with a small table to hand. The feast opened with hand-washing and the distribution of wreaths of myrtle. Then came 'snow-white barley-rolls in baskets' followed by a succession of handsome fish dishes: eel, skate, huss, ray, cuttlefish, squid and honey-glazed shrimps. There were also 'baby birds in flaky pastry'. Next came meat: pork, kid, lamb, both stewed and roasted, sausages, baby cockerel, pigeon and partridge. 'Croissants,' he writes, 'flaky and soft, were served with clotted cream.' After all of this, slaves again washed the guests' hands, and presented them with wreaths of violets. Then more drink, we are told, and what would be termed by the Romans 'second tables' (*secundae mensae*): 'sweet pastry shells', flapjacks, cheesecake, cheese and sesame, sweetmeats, almonds and walnuts.

The second text is a lengthy quotation from a letter written by one Hippolochus describing the wedding feast of Caranus, king of Macedonia, in 275 BC.[8] About a century has passed since Philoxenus and the escalation in opulence and spectacle under Eastern influence is almost startling. This banquet was for twenty men, each of whom brought his slaves with him. There is an abundance of gold and silver tableware, and indeed the guests are twice presented with golden circlets to wear. After the opening course, which was shared with the attendant slaves, floral wreaths were distributed. Then a surprise: 'In rushed flute-girls and singers and some Rhodian harp girls, I seem to think that they were naked, only some have been saying they had tunics on . . .' After this frisson more girls appeared, this time bearing gold and silver flasks filled with perfume for the guests. The meal resumed with the arrival of a roast pig on a vast silver charger which, like the one at Trimalchio's banquet, disgorged 'thrushes and wombs and an infinite number of *beccafici* [literally fig-peckers, i.e. tiny birds], and yolks of eggs poured over them'. The menu went on to include barbecued oysters and scallops, whole kids (along with individual containers so that overstuffed guests could take them home if

Dining in Ancient Greece. The food lies on the diner's table
as he calls for a drink. Vase-painting, *c.* 480 BC.

they wished), grilled fish, and a boar roasted on a spit. Hot wine was
served in large golden bowls and there was much hand-washing between
courses, the whole event winding up with the usual 'second tables' of fruit,
nuts and cakes. But accompanying this culinary marathon was what
amounted to a full-scale theatrical production that included 'phallic
dancers', buffoons, naked female acrobats and a one-hundred-strong
male voice choir which sang a wedding paean followed by dancing girls in
disguise as nymphs and nereids. In this account we see that the banquet as
theatre was fully fledged by the second half of the third century BC.

Wealthy Greeks ate one main meal a day, in the early evening.[9] Formal
eating of any kind was the preserve of men; women and children were
excluded. Older boys were allowed to be present but sat on their father's
or a friend's couch. This was above all a patriarchal society. The meal
was known as the *deipnon* and was separate from the *symposion*, devoted
solely to communal drinking, which followed. The room would have been

lit with hanging lamps and perfumed with oils and sweet-smelling leaves. The meal would be served by slaves who began by offering wheat and barley loaves in baskets. Then would come something resembling *hors d'oeuvres* – fresh fruit, shellfish, roasted small birds, salt sturgeon and tuna along with meat delicacies in highly flavoured sauces. Fresh fish followed, and the meal culminated in stewed or spit-roasted lamb. Then everything was cleared for the 'second tables': cakes, sweetmeats, nuts, dried fruit and cheeses. The ritual mixing of wine with water signalled the beginning of the *symposion*.

So far I have barely touched upon the role of the meal in Greek society. Its inner meaning was profound, and fundamental to the operation of the *polis*.[10] In Ancient Greece eating and drinking together was an expression of equality – equality, that is, between members of a distinct group sharing the same values, and also political power. Whether in their oligarchic or democratic phase, Greek cities were ruled by larger or smaller coteries of exclusively male citizens. Women, children, foreigners and slaves had no part in this scheme of things. Within the power structure, the civic banquet emerged at an early date as a strong communal expression of unity among the citizens of the *polis*. Such an event had as its central element a blood sacrifice made to the gods, after which the meat was divided equally between the citizens, cooked and eaten together. Admittance to the banquet certified citizenship, and though such feasting assumed the nature of a liturgy of state, it was nevertheless highly pleasurable for those who took part. No one, in fact, until the advent of the classical moralists and later the Early Church Fathers, wrote a single word in condemnation. Civic banquets were seen to be a necessity, a means of sustaining the political order of the city-state. Eating together thus became an important activity of the ruling classes, so much so that in Athens *c.*480–460 BC a special building was erected in which the standing committee of fifty-eight governing the city ate together daily.

The form of such communal feasts of course changed through the centuries. They were always held, however, on public holidays honouring a god or in conjunction, for example, with games. Euripides in his *Ion* provides a vivid word picture of such a celebration. The banquet was held in a tent whose decor, incorporating themes from Athenian myths, suggests that the description may reflect reality:

> Straightway the youth on uprights, sheet by sheet
> His tent erected, careful not to meet
> The burning rays of noon or westering eve;
> One plethron square he made it, to receive
> As guests if need be, the whole Delphian folk.
> Then weavings from the sacred store he took
> To clothe the frame, things marvellous to the eyes
> first, for the roof, a wing of broderies
> He spread . . .
> On the sides, too, were other broderies
> Of eastern art, warships with prows that ran
> To pierce Greek ships, and shapes half-beast, half-man
> And stags pursued on horseback, and the chase
> Of lions ravening in the wilderness . . .
> Then midway in the tent
> He stood great mixing bowls, and forth was sent
> A herald who, to full height straining, cried
> That Delphians all who would should come inside
> And share the banquet. When the room was full
> They crowned them with flowers, and bountiful
> The feast was.[11]

There were in fact many forms of communal dining in Ancient Greece, but all began with a blood sacrifice, followed by eating and, finally, drinking. The division between the latter two elements, between the meal and the drinking party, is perhaps most striking. It was an arrangement inherited by the Romans and lingers even today in England, where in some households the women leave the dining-room and the men are left to indulge in hard drinking and hard talk. In Ancient Greece that part of the action, the *symposion*, was by far the most important, calling for observance of elaborate rules and ritual.

The word *symposion* first appears in the seventh century BC.[12] By the fifth, rooms were being specifically built as feasting or dining-rooms,

A *symposion* scene with slave-boys waiting on the guests.
Vase-painting, *c.* 420 BC.

square in shape and designed at first to take seven but latterly eleven couches. Each couch accommodated two men. The room customarily had three couches to a wall, with one couch omitted from the front wall, allowing for an off-centre door. The couches could be of stone or wood. It is crucial to remember that such rooms were the prerogative of an elite. Suites of them still exist today in sanctuaries in which the blood sacrifice would be made prior to the *deipnon* and then the *symposion*. Those down the social scale merely picnicked outside on the ground.

A *symposion* was a drinking party, but by no means a debauch. Wine occupied a central place in Ancient Greek society. It was seen as a divine gift and blessing from the gods, one whose power was such that it could cure sorrow, induce sleep, encourage forgetfulness of cares and relief from misery. As a consequence the god of wine, Dionysus, was accorded great power. But wine was never drunk unmixed with water. That practice again was a feature distinguishing a civilised man from a barbarian.

The separation of the *symposion* from the meal was emphasised by the cleaning of the floor, hand-washing and the arrival of cups and floral garlands. Men reclined on couches, youths sat; passage to manhood would eventually entitle them to recline. The positioning of the couches around the room meant that each guest could see the others. The first act was the choice of a *symposiarch*, whose duty was to set the agenda and – most important – to decide the balance between the water and the wine in the *krater* standing in their midst. Proceedings then began with a libation dedicating the *krater* to Zeus and the Olympian gods, while two paeans in honour of heroes and three more in honour of Zeus Soter (Zeus the saviour in time of need) were sung in chorus to the accompaniment of a double flute.

It was a little world apart, a men's world. The *symposiarch* decreed what was to happen: the subject of any discourse, the types of music to be played, what sort of mime or dance was to be presented or contest take place among the participants. It could also be an arena for homosexual courtship; Plato in his *Symposium* (*c.* 385 BC) in fact describes Alcibiades' attempts to seduce Socrates during a *symposion*. It might be enlivened by the incursion of *Akletoi*, hungry people who would be fed and made to 'perform', thereby revealing (or rather being forced to reveal) their social inferiority. The party might well wind up with an inebriated procession of participants singing through the streets.

Xenophon's *The Banquet* (421 BC) offers by far the most vivid evocation of one of these occasions. The dinner and *symposion* is given by Callius in honour of the hero of the Panathenaic games, Autolycus. Among the guests is Socrates. The conversation is witty and fast-flowing and the evening is enlivened by the japes of a professional buffoon and a flute player, a dancing girl, who juggles, and a boy who is able to play the lyre, sing and dance, brought by a Syracusan. Out of the badinage, with its homo-erotic overtones, comes a lottery whose prize is to kiss Autolycus, and the event ends with a dramatic interlude in which Ariadne and Dionysius, to the strains of music, are united as lovers.[13]

The *symposion* was always occasioned by some event – public games, a festival, the welcome of visitors. What makes these gatherings so significant for us today is that it was here that the great epics were sung to the lyre by professional bards. In the sixth century this gave way to sung choruses and new poetic genres, lyric poetry, elegiac poetry and popular song. Still later these would be replaced by intellectual and philosophical discussions of the Platonic kind. The *symposion* functioned, in short, as a ritualised expression of the passions, a psychological and cultural micro-universe, a world set apart in which wine relaxed inhibitions and released the imagination to preserve old and create new poetic forms.

Such was to be the legacy of Greece to Rome: a male-dominated bipartite structure of feasting in which eating and drinking were seen as two quite separate if connected events. Yet there was more. Any type of formal eating had already come to involve ceremonial, hierarchy and spectacle, to say nothing of the arts – not only culinary arts but those associated with the theatre: music, dance and song. Even the intellectual arts expressed in the learned debating society had found a place there. The Romans were to preserve the essential structure of the Greek feast, what went on within it was, as we have already seen at Trimalchio's banquet, to be something of another order.

The age of Apicius

THE ROMAN DIET too was Mediterranean, but with a difference.[14] Whereas the basis of Greek cuisine had been the sea, the Romans looked to the land, where their attitude to food and eating was dominated by a duality. Foodstuffs were divided between *fruges*, products of the soil (and therefore basically vegetarian), and *percudes*, those foods derived from animals linked, as for the Greeks, to ritual sacrifice. Cattle, sheep and pigs were the subjects of public sacrifice, while lambs, piglets and pullets were employed privately. Likewise in common with the Greeks, the consumption of sacrificial meat – confined to the upper classes – identi-fied the properly civilised members of a community. Those like the German tribes, whose diet consisted largely of indiscriminate meat-eating, were therefore deemed to be barbarians.

The Roman duality about food manifested itself in several other ways, perhaps the most marked being the contrast between the two ideals of personal frugality and lavish hospitality. This contrast is perfectly epitomised in the nature of the two main meals of any Roman day. *Prandium*, a kind of midday snack, was often little more than left-overs from the day before, eaten standing up. The *cena*, on the other hand, or its grander form, the *convivium*, was a substantial meal, and might well involve a lavish spread of cooked dishes eaten while reclining alongside guests. *Prandium* was intended merely to replenish the stomach so one could get on with the business of the day, *negotium*. The time for *cena* was *otium*, the period of leisure that followed, when one might legitimately find satisfaction in titillating the 'gullet' with rich foods taken for pleasure alone.

As Rome evolved from a republic into the capital of a vast empire the contrast between these two approaches to food was seized upon by moralists who saw modern luxuries as a sign of decay compared to the noble frugality of times past. Indeed indulgences were freely available to those who could afford them. As the empire reached its height the delicacies of the known world flowed towards Rome. Aulus Gellius in his *Noctes atticae* (Attic Nights) describes a satire by Marcus Varro (116–27 BC) which illuminates just how far this kind of imperial gourmandising could go. The poet in his satire 'treats of exquisite elegance in banquets and viands' and goes on to list those delicacies that gluttons seek:

> . . . these are the varieties and names of the foods surpassing all others, which a bottomless gullet has hunted out and which Varro has analysed in his satire, with the places where they are found: a peacock from Samos, a woodcock from Phrygia, cranes from Media, a kid from Ambracia, oysters from Tarentum, cockles from Sicily, a swordfish from Rhodes, pike from Cilicia, nuts from Thasos, dates from Egypt, acorns from Spain.[15]

That such culinary refinement reflected reality we know from the accounts of banquets given by Licinius Lucullus (died 57/56 BC), whose name has passed into history as synonymous with the most extreme forms of sybaritic repast.[16] In his case delicacies could include sea-urchins from Capo Miseno, snails from Taranto, Chalcedonian tuna, oysters from Locrino, prosciutto from Gaul, sturgeon from Rhodes, prawns from Formia, hazelnuts from Nola, almonds from Agrigento, Sicilian grapes and Egyptian dates.

That appreciation of quality extended equally to wine.[17] Interest in good wine begins in the last century of the Republic and in 121 BC, in the consulship of Opimius, came the first famous vintage. Falernian and Nomentanum wines were those most prized. Connoisseurs gradually realised that the best wines would improve if kept for five to fifteen years, and the concept of dated vintages took hold. Trimalchio's hundred-year-old wine is a tilt at this. And, as in the case of Greece, only a sparing intake of wine accompanied a meal, with the serious drinking beginning after the eating was finished.

The Romans, of course, associated particular foodstuffs with the humours in the same way as the Greeks. But they were also bound by another belief, that only fresh ingredients were absolutely pure and uncorrupt.[18] In its most elemental form this theory regarded, for instance, an olive as purer than olive oil, because the pressing required to produce the oil was a step towards corruption and rottenness. The notion applied especially to meat, which was never hung; anything remotely resembling the decay of flesh being seen as a cause of bad breath, vomiting and dysentery. Here again we come up against Roman duality. The frugal meal of raw vegetables, bread and a piece of streaky bacon stewed in a cauldron was viewed as the ideal meal in terms of health. The *cena*, by contrast, with its elaborate cooked dishes, was regarded as potentially dangerous. It exposed the internal system to delicious, soft foods achieved by cooking methods analogous to what happened within the stomach, which was viewed as a cooking pot. Thus tender cuts of meat which required least cooking, like entrails or sexual organs, and which could merely be quickly grilled, were much more desirable than meat with gristle calling for long stewing – another step along the path towards rottenness.

So in respect to his diet every Roman had two faces. For the soldier, orator or man of affairs there was the frugal repast of the *prandium*. For the gentleman, a citizen who reclined in a loose robe on a couch eating dishes potentially dangerous to his system, there was the *cena*. Yet the same man – or woman – might be involved in both.

The subtly dubious safety of the *cena* sheds light on the question of why women and children, both regarded as weaker vessels, were at first not allowed to recline but had to sit. Reclining was thought to loosen the system, which only grown men could withstand. It also helps to explain why from time to time the authorities became obsessed with trying to control the *cena* and what people ate.

From the *lex Orchia* of 182 BC onwards there was a steady stream of laws attempting to regulate the number of guests that could be entertained and what could be served to them.[19] The senatorial decree of 161 BC, for example, laid down the amount that could be spent on a dinner, limited the number of guests outside the family to five and banned the consumption of fattened hens. Legislation of 115 BC prohibited the eating of dormice, shellfish and imported birds. All of this, however, was of no avail. What people ate and how many guests they had to dinner was clearly outside the control of the state. Opulence escalated, along with the horrified laments of the moralists preaching restraint and republican frugality as a model for public and family life.

Yet though it may have been honoured in the breach, there was a genuine and widely held belief that Rome's greatness had been built upon the cultivation of an austere frugality. Moreover, these attempts to control rich living styles during the imperial period were aimed at trying to prevent the gap between the haves and the have-nots widening and thus threatening social stability. The truth is that for most of the population food consisted of a thick soup of meal and water with bread supplemented by turnips, olives, beans, figs, cheese and, from time to time, pork.

The ability to draw on the wealth of a mighty empire inevitably left its imprint on Roman cuisine. Apicius' *De re coquinaria*[20] makes use of Numidian chickens, includes an Alexandrian sauce for fish, and even offers Indian-style peas. At its apogee Roman cuisine was the first international cuisine in the history of Western Europe, and it was practised, with regional variations, the length and breadth of the Empire, from the shores of North Africa to the fastnesses of the island of Britain. What began as a rustic and vegetarian cuisine under the Republic became under the Empire increasingly sophisticated in response first to Etruscan and then to Greek influences. The latter filtered northwards from Sicily and southern Italy. Then, via the mediation of Carthage, came the impact of the East. Under the late Republic and Early Empire Roman gastronomy achieved richness and refinement, and this was fortunately recorded by Apicius. The High Empire was to take that tradition, which for all its elegance still displayed a degree of restraint, and carry it in the direction of decadence and excess. Finally, with the disintegration of the Empire in the fifth and sixth centuries AD, Roman gastronomy gradually fragmented and broke down, gone with the civilisation that spawned it.

* * *

De re coquinaria (*On Cooking*) by Apicius is the earliest cookery book to survive. Who was he? We know of three Romans bearing that name, but undoubtedly the Apicius of the cookbook was M. Gabius Apicius, a wealthy gourmet who taught *haute cuisine* during the first half of the first century AD in the reigns of the emperors Augustus and Tiberius. Many of his recipes were famous and, in addition, dishes not by him were named in his honour. We know he wrote two cookery books that do not survive, and that he founded a school for teaching cookery. It is understandable, therefore, that his name became attached to *De re coquinaria*.

This collection of recipes has come to us in the main through two ninth-century manuscripts, one written in Tours between 844 and 851 and the other in Fulda, also during the ninth century. Both manuscripts go back to lost earlier ones, and what we have is far from complete. There is a virtual absence of any recipes for sweet dishes and none for bakery, both essential aspects of Roman cuisine. To these two manuscripts must be added a third which contains far fewer recipes and which was compiled by a certain Vinidarius, an Ostrogoth living in northern Italy in the early fifth century. The copy which exists of that version was written in the eighth century. The Latin of Apicius suggests that the original dates from a late fourth- or early fifth-century source, although it has been placed as early as the third century.

De re coquinaria contains four hundred and seventy recipes in all, divided into eleven books with titles like 'The Gardener', 'Of Birds' and 'The Sea'. Like most cookery books it is an accumulation, and draws on a tradition stretching back centuries to the cuisine of classical Greece. Book Ten, 'The fisherman', which deals principally with fish sauces, is so different from Books One to Eight that it is thought likely to be a Roman version of a Greek treatise on fish sauces (Athenaeus records that there were many). Certain recipes clearly have a particular group of users in view, like farmers anxious to learn how to preserve food. There is also a nucleus of recipes deriving from medical sources. Overall the picture it presents is by no means one of excess, although it does include the infamous stuffed dormice. To this day Apicius remains an exciting, confident and joyous document to read.

The book takes a large labour force for granted. Poultry, game and domestic animals are mainly stuffed and half-stewed and then finished in a sauce allowing for its slow permeation. Gravies are thickened with starch or flour, ragouts with eggs, breadcrumbs or crumbled pastry. What Apicius reveals is that, in spite of their theoretical taste for simplicity, the Romans disliked any ingredient in its pure form. There is hardly a recipe without a sauce, one that radically changes the taste of the principal ingredient.

The object of these sauces was varied. They could disguise or enhance flavour, colour or discolour, make sweet or sour, thicken or thin the mixture. Sweet sauces predominated in meat dishes, sweet and sour for fish. A single dish could involve adding up to as many as ten different herbs and spices, while 90 per cent of the recipes called for expensive imported spices. As with the Greeks, pepper heads the list, followed by cinnamon, ginger, nutmeg and cloves, shipped from India, Ceylon, the Bay of Bengal, the Spice Islands and China. This obsession with exotic spices was indeed to be Roman cookery's greatest legacy to the Middle Ages. Apicius, we know, was studied at the court of Charlemagne.

Garum retained its place, along with two other popular flavourings – *silphium*, a spice from Libya which became extinct during the first century AD, and *asafoetida*, the resin of the plant *Ferula asafoetida*, a relative of fennel, which replaced it. As for herbs, lovage and rue head the list, both wanted for their sharp, bitter flavour. Then come coriander, cumin, oregano, celery seed, parsley seed, bay leaf, aniseed, fennel, mint, caraway, mustard seed, wormwood, chervil, rocket, sweet cecily, thyme, sage, pennyroyal, pellitory, elecampane, saffron and mastic.

Although Apicius includes much that we would now regard as decadent, like larks' tongues, parrots and flamingos, his is a refined and tasteful cuisine fully reflective of a sophisticated and cultured upper class. What this corpus of recipes illustrates is how the Romans, who discovered Greek cuisine towards the end of the third century BC, took it over and changed it by greatly increasing the use of exotic spices and herbs. What it does not tell us, and what we shall never know in spite of our possession of this amazing document, is just how Roman food tasted and exactly what it looked like.

Cena and *convivium*

THE ROMANS divided their day into two – twelve hours of day and twelve of night. It was punctuated by three meals. The first, *jentaculum* (breakfast), was eaten immediately upon rising and consisted of little more than a light snack of bread and fruit. The second, *prandium* (lunch), had no fixed time or indeed fixed place of consumption, and consisted, as we have seen, of simple food designed to sustain the eater through the active business of the working day.[21] Its very frugality was regarded as the epitome of the Roman virtues.[22]

The only proper meal of the day was the *cena* or *fercula* (supper or dinner), normally taken at the ninth hour. In midsummer this meant between about 2.30 and 3.45 in the afternoon, and in winter between about 1.30 and 3. In the past, the *cena* had taken place even earlier in the day, followed by a second frugal repast called the *vesperna*, some time in the evening. But as the use of artificial light became widespread, it – like the dinner party in the nineteenth century – moved later and later, becoming the most important culinary and social event of the day. When the *cena* was lavish and included guests it was a *convivium*, the Roman version of a dinner party. The orator Cicero regarded such events as lying at the heart of Roman civilised life: 'For it was a good idea of our ancestors to style the presence of guests at a dinner-table – seeing that it implied a community of enjoyment – a *convivium*, "a living to-gether".'[23]

The Roman *convivium* differed from its Greek predecessor in that, thanks to Etruscan influence, it could include women among the participants. Its centrality to Roman life stemmed from its function as a complex essay in the achievement of perfect balance.[24] Those who did not give *convivia* were labelled as *avarus* (miserly), while someone who went to too many of them was castigated as a *parasitus* (parasite). As host, the aim was to avoid equally an appearance of stinginess and of unnecessary ostentation. The writings of Cicero, Seneca, Tacitus and Pliny the Younger are filled with accounts of the educated upper classes dining with each other, both in the city and at their villas in the country or beside the sea. To such people, the *convivium* was an elegant ceremony of civility, an occasion for the private man to savour his accomplishments and, to an extent, display these to his peers in the setting of his own home and family. As a social mechanism, the *convivium* was thus as important to the Romans as the salon to eighteenth-century France or the dinner party to Victorian England.[25]

By the late Republican period, in fact, the *convivium* even called for special clothes.[26] The *synthesis* combined a tunic with a smallish cloak (*pallium*), both made of the same material, brilliantly coloured and elaborately embroidered. The *pallium* might be light or heavy depending on the season and the weather. Its size and the manner of its draping varied according to personal preference and the occasion. The *synthesis* was equally worn by women. Unlike the familiar toga, however, it was a form of dress worn only in private, never in public. Dandies could go through several changes of *synthesis* during the course of a single dinner. Martial ridicules Zollius for changing his costume no fewer than eleven times.[27]

In mid-fourth-century Rome Ammianus Marcellinus, the last great Latin historian, bemoaning the indulgence and decadence of the nobles, wrote: 'Their ideas of civility are such that a stranger did better kill a man's brother than send an excuse to them if he be asked to dinner.'[28] The Roman dinner party began as a pure expression of an elite republican society, essential to its social cohesion. In the absence of an imperial court they served to bring together powerful people who were equal, while of course also often including dependants and hangers-on. During the imperial period, however, the dinner party was seen as the survival of a format from a vanished era, an occasion in which host and guests of various ranks could behave as equals around the table. At least that is the way the old Republican *convivia* were viewed in retrospect, as pleasant class-less affairs where social barriers were lowered and normal conventions relaxed, with inferiors allowed to indulge freely in sharp wit without fear of recrimination. 'I serve the same to everyone, for when I invite guests it is for a meal, not to make class distinctions,' wrote the younger Pliny. 'I have brought them as equals to the same table, so I give them the same treatment in everything.'[29] The reality was very different. Dinner parties in Rome worked as they still do, on the basis of who gets asked and who does not. As ever, there were those invited to be judged for their suitability and as often as not then never asked again. A well-known *graffito* on the walls of Pompeii sums it up: 'The man with whom I do not dine is a barbarian to me.'[30]

The truth of the matter is that as we cross into the Imperial period, although lip-service continued to be paid to the notion of equality, these events were hierarchical exercises in precedence, with those of senatorial or equestrian rank or local councillors or magistrates enjoying positions unattainable to the merely rich.[31] The Emperor Augustus gave what were called *cenae rectae* (formal dinners) 'with strict attention to social rank and to individuals'. The Romans were class-obsessed, deeply concerned with concepts like *dignitas* and *existimatio, liberalitas* and *munificentia*, all patrician virtues. The Emperor Domitian may have invited all the different *ordines* (orders) to his *cenae rectae* and indeed also to his *cenae publicae* (state banquets), but it is clear that there was not only a rigid segregation of the guests in terms of rank but that distinctions were also made in the food served to them. Even before the close of the Republican era, guests of different rank were being served different food.[32] When Cicero entertained Julius Caesar at Puteoli during the Saturnalia of 45 BC the guests dined at three separate tables. All of them ate well, but those at the second and third tables rather less well than the others.[33] Pliny is scathing about such behaviour, sending a description of just such a dinner party as a 'warning example' to a young friend: 'The best dishes were set forth in front of himself and a select few, and cheap scraps of food before the rest of the company. He had even put wine into tiny flasks, divided into three categories . . . One lot was intended for himself and us, another for his lesser friends (all his friends are graded) and the third for his and our freedmen.'[34]

How such a party was put together was both calculated and unpredictable. Men of superior rank, for example, didn't hesitate to turn up with a friend in tow who was not on the guest list. And then there was always a sprinkling of guests who were asked to fill in any gaps, people widely referred to as *umbrae* (shadows). Dependants, or *clientes* as they were called, came as paid guests.

At grand dinners the differentiation in food from one table to another could be considerable. Martial captures the anguish of one demoted guest:

Since I am no longer invited to dinner at a price as formerly [i.e. as a paid guest], why don't I get the same dinner as you? You take oysters

fattened in the Lucrine pool, I cut my mouth sucking a mussel. You have
mushrooms, I take pig fungi. You set to with turbot, I with bream. A
golden turtle dove fills you up with its outsize rump, I am served with
a magpie that died in its cage.[35]

The advent of Christianity with its communal feasts highlighted the
problem of food hierarchy in another way. The apostle Paul had to solve
the problem of how to avoid gatherings where the rich and their friends
had better food and drink than those present of lower social status. He
did so in the end by deciding that the wealthy had better eat privately.

Such an assembly of guests could be the recipe for a certain edginess,
but that would have been as nothing compared with the tension between
the host and his guests and the small army of slaves ministering to their
every need. A single household could have as many as four hundred slaves
and a *convivium* might require the services of every one of them.[36] The menu
was often chosen by a freed slave, an *obsonator*, who was familiar with the
tastes of both his master and those invited. Slaves known as *nomenclatores*
arranged and delivered presents to the guests on departure. A *vocator* kept
an eye on the behaviour of the staff during the proceedings and probably
also supervised the dining-room slaves. That team included the *ministri* or
pueri a cyatho, who were chosen on account of their looks and were allowed
to keep their hair long. Splendidly dressed, their task was to serve wine and
cut up food into bite-sized pieces. (Particularly pretty wine waiters might
also be employed to serve the sexual needs of the diners.) A specially
trained slave acted as carver or *structor*. Lower in rank came the shaven-head
scoparii, who wore coarse clothing and cleared the floor of debris.

Slaves saw everything, but were required to contemplate it in silence.
They were underfed, repressed and subject to the most brutal retribution
for the slightest shortcoming. Twice during Trimalchio's banquet savage
punishment was threatened. That was the norm. If the game was under-
done or the fish poorly seasoned the cook (who actually ranked fairly high
in the slave hierarchy) would be stripped and beaten. Any slave who stole
or destroyed a valuable object was killed, mutilated or thrown into chains.
The cruelty of the era is typified in the notorious case of a *cena* given
by P. Vedius Pollio, a friend of the Emperor Augustus, during which the
cupbearer who broke a crystal goblet had his hands cut off and hung

around his neck. He was then forced to parade among the diners before being thrown to the lampreys in the fishpond.

The setting for the *cena* or *convivium* was the *triclinium*.[37] In the early Roman period meals had been served in the *atrium* and later in a room called the *cenaculum*, but when the fashion for reclining came in, this special room was developed. Many *triclinia* survive in the ruins of Pompeii and Herculaneum. Such rooms were designed to hold three couches, each accommodating three diners, surrounding a central round or rectangular table. In great houses and villas there could be several *triclinia*, warmer ones for dining in winter and others placed to attract cool breezes and shade in summer. Some might be set up for alfresco meals in the gardens. The siting of the rooms frequently took advantage of fine views of the country-side or the sea. In such *triclinia* the couches could be of wood or stone, elaborated with every kind of luxurious decoration. *Triclinia* at Pompeii include some where a jet of water spouted from the central table and cool-ing rivulets were made to trickle in front of each diner. In the so-called house of Loreius Tiburtinus guests took their food from dishes floating in a large basin in front of them. While most *triclinia* were essentially small rooms, the rich would also have had larger banqueting halls with clusters of couches accommodating many guests.

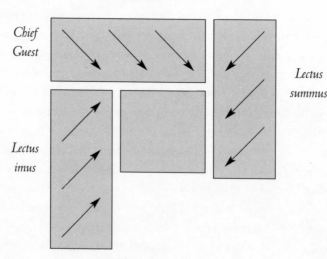

Lectus medius

Chief Guest

Lectus summus

Lectus imus

Plan of a *triclinium*.

Banquet scene, fourth to fifth century AD, the guests reclining on a *stibadium*.
One servant proffers wine from a jug, the other carries a water-jug
and basin for hand-washing. Illumination.

That arrangement of the dining-room was to change late in the
second and early third century AD. Instead of three rectangular couches
there was one large semicircular one called a *stibadium, sigma* or *accubitum*
where seven or eight guests could recline. Evidence suggests that this was
a form first developed for eating outdoors, and later adapted for use
indoors in response to the more elaborate entertainments introduced by
hosts at *convivia*. The *triclinium* itself changed shape, becoming a room with
up to three alcoves, each containing a couch facing the unoccupied floor
space in the middle. In effect, the dining-room was transformed into an
arena theatre.

Even in its most primitive form, the *triclinium* was replete with symbolic overtones.[38] The ceiling could be equated with the heavens, the table and its contents with the earth and the floor with the abode of the dead, Hades. That view of the *triclinium* as a kind of microcosm of the universe is reinforced by the subject matter of surviving mosaic pavements. At the entrance to the room, for example, Cerberus, the canine guardian of the Underworld, is often depicted. In Nero's notorious *Domus Aurea*, recently excavated in Rome, the ceiling portrayed the heavens and could even be made to move. Its roof revolved day and night, Suetonius records, in time with the sky. Other dining-rooms in the *Domus* 'had ceilings of fretted ivory, the panels of which could slide back and let a rain of flowers, or of perfume from hidden sprinklers, shower upon his guests'.[39]

Every Roman house had an altar for the household gods, the *lares*, in its *atrium*; at a particular moment in the *cena* the gods would be ceremonially carried in and placed on the table. The still-life decoration which figures so prominently on the walls of so many *triclinia* at Pompeii and Herculaneum is in fact food for the dead. Not that it put a damper on festivities. Frank and pithy advice suggesting anything but gloom is also found there: 'Spare thy neighbour's wife lascivious glances and ogling flatteries, and let thy modesty dwell in thy mouth'; 'Be amiable and abstain from odious brawlings if thou canst. If not, let thy steps bear thee back again to thine own home.'[40]

On arrival at a dinner party, a guest first took off his outdoor shoes or sandals, passing them to his attendant slave for safe keeping, and donning slippers supplied by the host. He then joined the others in the *atrium* or some other room close to the dining-room. This would be an occasion for conversation; only during the principate of Tiberius, early in the first century AD, did drinking before dinner become the norm. Grand houses would have had a master of ceremonies who was in overall control of the choreography of such an entertainment.

At a given signal everyone would enter the *triclinium* and take their places on the couches, removing their slippers. This was the time for slaves to wash the guests' feet, a ritual spelled out in another inscription at Pompeii: 'Let the slave wash and dry the feet of the guests, and let him be mindful to spread a linen cloth on the cushion of the couches.'[41] In the earlier pre-*stibadium* period the three couches were designated the *lectus summus,* the *lectus medius* and the *lectus imus.* The host would recline on the last, generally with members of his own family. The place of honour or *consularis locus* could vary but was usually situated in the middle of the *lectus medius* – *imus in medio* – where it was apparently convenient for transacting business if necessary. In the case of the *stibadium* the place of honour was at first in the centre, but by the late empire had become the position on the viewer's left-hand edge. The couches sloped, with the head higher than the foot, and the diners were separated one from another by ridges of cushions. A coverlet spread over all.

A man's right to recline came with his assumption of the *toga virilis* at the age of seventeen.[42] With rights, of course, came hazards. In the eyes of both pagan and Christian moralists, this passage into adulthood opened boys to a trinity of vices: eating, drinking and sex. The danger of homosexual seduction was particularly acute. Quintilian, the authority on rhetoric, threw his hands up in horror. What should anyone expect, he wrote, in view of what young people were already exposed to before they were even old enough to recline for dinner: 'We taught them: they hear us use such words, they see our mistresses and our male concubines; every-dinner party is loud with foul songs and things are presented to their eyes which we should blush to speak.'

So much for the non-gustatory temptations of the couch. On the table in front of each diner stood a salt cellar, *salinum,* and a vinegar bottle, *acetabulum.* To hand were two buffets, one for wine, the *cilibantium,* and the other for food and to hold plates, the *repositorium.* There were wine-containers, *oenophorus,* and vessels for hot water, *caldarium,* and mixing bowls, *cratera* – the Romans drank their wine warm and watered. The room was lit by candelabra and lamps hung from the ceiling on chains. Censers released the fumes of aromatic oils, for part of the pleasure of dining lay in smell. The mosaic floor too was spread with aromatic foliage – bugloss, verbena and maidenhair fern – while vases of flowers, especially roses, decorated the room. Guests received floral wreaths, and perfumed oils for their body and their hair.

The diner reclined at an angle with his left arm supported by a cushion and his feet turned to the right. Any meal began with hand-washing, and this ritual was repeated at regular intervals throughout the meal. Slaves were constantly bringing fresh perfumed water along with towels to the

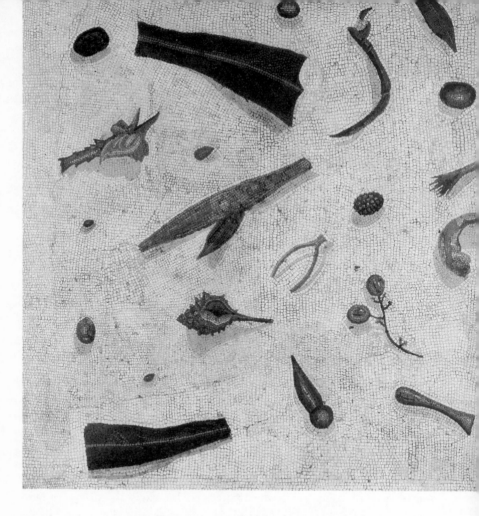

Roman mosaic depicting the debris typical of a *triclinium* floor
before it was swept away.

guests. By the first century AD a napkin, *mappa*, was provided by the host,
although some guests brought their own, capacious ones at that, so that they
could scoop up and take home any unconsumed delicacy. Food was eaten
from a plate (*patina*, *patella* or, if deep, *catinus*) which the diner would hold
in his left hand. Slaves cut up awkward bits into small pieces to make
consumption easier. Guests generally ate with their fingertips, taking great
care to besmirch neither hands nor face. Food could also be taken to
the mouth on the tip of a knife, and there were spoons, which came in a
variety of forms from the ladle, *trulla*, to the *cochlea* or *ligula* for small items like

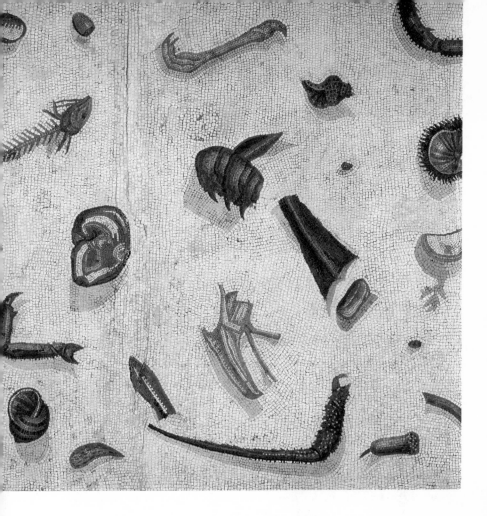

eggs or shellfish. Only late in the imperial era did forks make an appearance. Toothpicks were also provided. Individual dishes and those from which food was served could be astonishingly rich and luxurious, as the numerous hoards of silver unearthed all over Western Europe bear witness. Cups could be of crystal, gold, electrum and murra, an expensive opaque stone said to improve the bouquet of the wine. They could come in any number of shapes, with or without handles, embossed and even set with precious stones.

The meal opened with the *gustus* or *gustatio*, a variety of *hors d'oeuvre*, largely consisting of vegetables and herbs, olives, slices of hard-boiled egg, snails and shellfish washed down with the honeyed wine known as *mulsum*.[43] If the meal was grander there could be other dishes, such as oysters, thrushes and stuffed dormice. Then followed the *cena* proper, usually

[33]

of three courses — *cena prima* or *ferculum*, *secunda* and *tertia* — but the courses could run to many more. The most important dish was always that which made use of the sacrificial meat, possibly a pig or a pregnant cow. Young kid was considered a great delicacy. There could be pheasant or goose, ham or hare together with a variety of fish, lamprey and turbot being the favourites. The guests selected what they wanted from among the offerings. Then, after the last course, the table was cleared and the floor swept. (In the greater houses, this process might involve coloured sawdust.) Then came dessert, *secundae mensae* or *bellaria*, which consisted of apples, pears, nuts, grapes and figs, sometimes accompanied by shellfish and young birds.

Very few precise menus of a Roman meal have survived. Macrobius in his *Saturnalia* provides us with an account of a lavish *cena* given some time between 74 and 69 BC by the college of *pontifices* ('priests') of Rome on the inauguration of a *flamen martialis*. There were eleven priests present, including Julius Caesar, as well as the wife and mother-in-law of the new *flamen* and four Vestal Virgins. The men were disposed in two groups, the women in one, and the dinner was as follows:

> There were served, for the preliminary service, sea urchins, unlimited raw oysters, scallops, cockles, thrushes on asparagus, fattened fowls, a dish of oysters and scallops, a corn fish (both black and white), then another service of cockles, mussels, sea nettles, figpeckers, haunches of venison and boar, fattened fowls cooked in pastry, more figpeckers, murex, and purple fish. For the main dishes were served sow's udders, ducks, boiled teal, hares, fattened fowls roasted, creamed wheat, and rolls of Picenum.[44]

In the case of the Romans the drinking that followed the *cena*, the *comissatio*, had none of the complex resonances of its Greek predecessor, but it did involve a certain amount of ritual formality. Before it began the *lares* were brought in and placed on the table. Libations were poured and words of omen uttered. The party selected a *rex convivii* or *magister* or *arbiter* to decide, as his Greek prototype had done, the proportion of wine to water. During the *comissatio*, guests donned garlands of flowers and scented themselves with perfume. The main activity was often toasts — to those absent, to the ladies, to the imperial armies. The commonest way to toast a fellow guest was to fill one's cup, drain it, have it refilled and then pass it to him to drink in turn.

Of this part of the evening, Macrobius says that 'the conversation at table will of course take a more jovial turn, as having pleasure for its aim rather than some earnest purpose'.[45] Cicero in his *De officiis* advises the guest not to talk too much about himself, or pass on the wrong kind of gossip but, rather, to focus on domestic matters, politics, the arts and sciences and never to give way to passion or anger.[46] 'The Emperor invited us to dinner every day,' Pliny the Younger writes in a letter, 'a simple affair if you consider his position. Sometimes we were entertained by recitations, or else the night was prolonged by pleasant conversation.'[47] Roman dinners involved the services of both readers and singers who represented a continuation of the Greek belief that the pleasures of feeding the body should not be divorced from the higher pleasures of feeding the mind. Cicero, when trying to coax a disaffected friend into coming to dinner parties again, argues: 'You have deprived yourself of a great deal of amusement and pleasure . . . conversation is at its most agreeable at dinner parties. In this respect our countrymen are wiser than the Greeks. They use words meaning literally "co-drinkings" or "co-dinings" but we say "co-livings", because at dinner parties more than anywhere else life is lived in company.'[48] That was the ideal. Such gatherings could of course veer in quite another direction, dissolving into tasteless orgies of stuffing, sexual licence, vomiting and drunkenness.

In any household there would be one or more readers, *lector* or *anagnostes*, among the slaves or freedmen. Generally the selections read were chosen for their educational or entertainment value – passages of Greek or Roman history, lyric poems both in Greek and Latin, in particular the works of Virgil and Homer.[49] The worst thing that a host could do was inflict his own compositions on his fellow guests. Let Martial have the last word on that one:

> This and no other is the reason why you invite me to dinner, Ligurinus: to recite your verses. I take my slippers off: immediately a bulky volume is brought in among the lettuces and the sharp sauce. Another is read through while the first course hangs fire. There is a third, and the dessert is not yet come. And you recite a fourth and finally a fifth roll. If you don't serve me

boar this often, it stinks. But if you don't consign your damnable poems to the mackerel, Ligurinus, in future you will dine at home by yourself.[50]

As the opulence of empire burgeoned during the first century AD, the rich increasingly hired professional performers of every kind to provide entertainment. They included lyre players, singers, actors, fools and jesters, not to mention transvestites, dancing girls, gladiators, clowns and half-idiot dwarfs.[51] Suetonius records that even the frugal Augustus had dinners which included pantomimes, players from the circus, and frequently story-tellers. The Roman emperors' tastes ran the whole gamut from the harmless to the utterly horrendous. Caligula liked his dinners to be enlivened by torture or decapitations by an adept soldier. Hadrian's bent was theatrical, for tragedies, comedies and farces, *sambuca* players, as well as readers, poets and those expert in mime. Lucius Verus chose to watch gladiatorial displays.[52]

What must strike the contemporary observer about the *convivium* in its restrained form, devoid of the later decadent excesses, is the modernity of so much about it – its order, its culinary excellence, its sense of style and ceremony, to say nothing of its delight in all the appurtenances of civilised living: conversation and music, the reading of prose and poetry, what in effect often amounted to a cabaret attached to a meal – what we would now call dinner-theatre. But that modernity was underpinned by a vast substructure of slavery, which was in turn based upon brutality, violence and every form of cruel subjection. At no other period in the history of eating does such a startling and frightening polarity occur.

Public and imperial banquets

PUBLIC BANQUETS were almost as important to the Romans as to the Greeks. In both cases they took place within a frame of reference that was both sacred and secular.[53] In Rome, private sponsorship of such events began during public feasts in the second century BC when the rich, nervous about possible public unrest, saw them as a means of placating and pacifying the masses. Public feasts punctuated the Roman year. March the

17th, for example, was the feast of father Liber (equated with Bacchus and Dionysus) when the whole population banqueted in the streets. Other feasts celebrated the birth of a child, the coming of age of a youth at seventeen, a marriage. Marriage, in fact, involved two feasts – a *cena* on the day of the nuptials staged in the bride's house, and what was called the *repotia* the next day at their new marital home. The *cena funebris* was consumed at the tomb of the deceased before the last rites of purification.

Such meals were thus entwined into the very fabric of Roman life. But nothing matched the spectacular banquets staged under the emperors. They have become a part of culinary legend. These *convivia publica* brought together key people from every level of Roman society. The Emperor Claudius invited as many as six hundred guests at a time, and a thousand tables were counted at another of his dinners.[54] Yet it is not merely the imperial scale that left such an indelible impression on the imagination of subsequent ages, but the excesses so often involved.

In the case of Elagabalus, for example, the banquets held in summer had to change colour on each occasion. He was the first to indulge in massive displays of silver, the first to have fish sausages, along with sausages made from molluscs, prawns, oysters, squid and crab. His guests dined off such exotica as camels' feet, the combs from live chickens and peacocks' and nightingales' tongues. Vast chargers filled with mullets' livers, flamingos' and thrushes' brains, parrots', pheasants' and peacocks' heads might enliven a banquet; couches were scattered with lilies, violets, hyacinths and narcissi, while overhead mechanisms deluged the diners with violets and other flowers in such vast quantities that guests were sometimes suffocated.[55]

The Emperor Vitellius' greed was to reach epic proportions, as recounted by Suetonius:

> He banqueted three or four times a day, namely morning, noon, after-noon and evening – the last meal being mainly a drinking bout – and survived the ordeal well enough by taking frequent emetics. What made things worse was that he used to invite himself out to such meals at the houses of a number of different people on one and the same day; and these never cost his various hosts less than 4,000 gold pieces each. The most notorious feast of the series was given him by his brother on his entry into Rome; 2,000 magnificent fish and 7,000 game birds are said

to have been served. Yet even this hardly compares in luxuriousness with a single tremendously large dish which Vitellius dedicated to the Goddess Minerva and named 'Shield of Minerva the Protectress of the City'. The recipe called for pike-livers, pheasant-brains, peacock-brains, flamingo-tongues, and lamprey-milt; and the ingredients, collected in every corner of the Empire right from the Parthian frontier to the Spanish straits, were brought to Rome by naval captains and triremes.[56]

The extravagance of imperial banquets knew no bounds. Tigellinus, the commander of the Praetorian Guard, organised a dinner for Nero, probably in the summer of AD 64, staged in the middle of an artificial lake. The emperor and his cronies reclined on rugs and cushions on a great raft which was in turn towed by barges adorned with gold and ivory and crewed by *exoleti* ('joy-boys') deliberately chosen for their lascivious abilities. The wooded park surrounding the lake had been stocked with exotic birds and animals, while pleasure pavilions and brothels stood at the water's edge. The historian Dio Cassius describes the goings-on:

> Thus Nero and Tigellinus and their fellow banqueters occupied the centre, where they held their feast on purple rugs and soft cushions, while all the rest made merry in the taverns. They would also enter the brothels and without let or hindrance have intercourse with any of the women who were seated there, among them were the most beautiful and distinguished in the city . . . Every man had the privilege of enjoying whichever one he wished, as the women were not allowed to refuse anyone.[57]

Nero was the most flamboyantly theatrical of all the Roman emperors and, as a result, the populace adored him. His behaviour was a good deal less admirable. In AD 54, at a banquet on the occasion of his seventeenth birthday, he attempted to mock Britannicus, the youthful natural son of the Emperor Tiberius, by demanding that he sing to the assembled company. Britannicus, however, not only performed well but sang a song alluding to his own expulsion from his father's house and throne. At the next banquet Nero had him poisoned at table.

Perhaps the weirdest of all the imperial banquets was that staged by the Emperor Domitian with the theme of Hell. The guests were asked to come unaccompanied by the usual slave. Beside each diner stood a gravestone-like stele bearing the guest's name. The banquet was lit by votive lamps of the kind hung at tombs and the food, all black, resembled the sacrificial viands offered to the *manes* of the departed at funerals. The slave boys who waited and danced were painted black and during the entire macabre proceeding only Domitian himself was allowed to speak. His subject was death. At a certain point in the dinner the guests were suddenly dismissed and escorted home by strange slaves, leading them to suspect with sinking hearts that they had been chosen to be further victims of the emperor's bloodthirsty rule. Instead, however, they were summoned back to a second banquet, and at its close loaded with costly gifts.[58]

The splendour of Roman imperial banquets would be remembered. When the texts describing them were rediscovered and entered the domain of learning in the fifteenth and sixteenth centuries, it is at least tempting to suggest that their sheer extravagance and sense of spectacle must have had some influence on the Renaissance court banquet. Yet, unbelievably, a thousand years were to pass before anything remotely resembling the Roman spectacles was re-enacted at the humanist courts of Mantua and Ferrara.

Disintegration and survival

THE ROMAN EMPIRE proved mortal. Attila the Hun sacked Rome in 410, and in the aftermath of this catastrophe the seat of empire shifted to the capital of the Eastern Empire, Constantinople. The last Roman Emperor in the West, Romulus Augustulus, was deposed in 476 by the German Odoacer, who then proclaimed himself king of Italy.

That event is generally taken as the end of the Roman Empire in Western Europe, but in fact the daily framework of Roman life, including that surrounding the *cena* and *convivium*, was to linger on into the sixth century and, in a far smaller way, to survive in some form into the eighth.[59] In the scattered villas of Gaul life went on more or less as before. In the middle of the 460s, for example, the patrician Sidonius Apollinaris, later bishop of Avernus, paid a visit to his friend Tonantius Ferreolus at his villa near Nîmes in southern Gaul. Sidonius describes how the guests

gathered in the library, the women seated at one end and the men standing at the other, both deliberately positioned within reach of books on
subjects considered appropriate to them, the women to devotional works
and the men to 'works distinguished by the grandeur of Latin eloquence'.
The time passed in conversation and gaming before a slave entered
announcing luncheon. Elsewhere Sidonius describes the dining-room in
the villa of a friend named Leontius. It had folding doors which opened
on to a vista to a courtyard framed by colonnades and a well-stocked fishpond. In the distance diners could see a panorama of the Garonne valley.
Thus in some parts of the old empire, at least, civilised life continued.
On the whole, however, Sidonius' writings reflect the conflict between
the traditional Roman way of life and the new realities imposed by the
presence of the Germanic tribes.

When Sidonius visited Theodoric the Ostrogoth (d. 466), he notes with
surprise the fact that his host sits rather than reclines at table. It is a symbol
of change – and of resistance to change. In the late sixth century another
Roman aristocrat, Gregory of Tours, describes a private dinner where
the guests reclined, except for the host's wife who sat. At the end of that
century Bishop Venantius Fortunatus refers to his friend Bishop Leontius
reclining to eat in what was a Roman villa. So we see that the old Roman
way of dining lingered on in these crumbling and disintegrating buildings.
But beyond the sixth century, reclining survived only in the most exclusive of
contexts, in the great imperial and papal palaces of the early Middle Ages,
revived, it is said, by Pope Leo III at the close of the eighth century.

The culinary tradition likewise falters and fragments. With the collapse
of the Empire ingredients taken for granted by cooks raised on Apicius
ceased to be available. Trade routes were not, however, totally abandoned.
Even when Gaul shattered into a jigsaw of barbarian kingdoms in the sixth
century, the port of Marseille still maintained trade with Egypt, North
Africa and Spain, importing spices, salt and *garum*. But the culinary tradition
was inevitably breaking down as the social context of Roman villa life gave
way to that of the new barbarian courts, and classical education crumbled.
Classical gastronomy would survive mainly through the medical tradition, for
the barbarian courts recruited physicians trained within the Galenic system.
One such was a Greek doctor called Anthimus. He had studied in
Constantinople, but in the early sixth century was condemned to a life of

exile in the court of Theodoric the Ostrogoth, king of Italy. Theodoric sent him as ambassador to Theuderic, king of the Franks, who reigned in the area around Metz between 511 and 534. It was for Theuderic that Anthimus wrote *On the Observance of Foods*, the key documentary source for the transition between the classical culinary tradition and that of the Middle Ages.[60]

Anthimus works from the Galenic principles of the humours and is clearly aware of the traditional prescriptions for cooking as a means of ensuring good health, but he does not dwell on it; in the West the Galenic tradition had almost been lost by this time, and would only return in the Middle Ages via Arab scholars in Spain. He mentions exotic spices and such unusual ingredients as peacocks, although by that time such items must have been very rare. More notably, he captures the shift to indigenous ingredients – butter instead of olive oil, or salmon instead of red mullet – at the same time as he preserves certain Roman predilections – the taste for sweet-and-sour (mixing vinegar and honey, for instance), or eating eggs while they are still runny. All through the text it is plain that he is writing about and for meat-eating barbarians; he constantly uses phrases like 'the Franks have a habit of eating . . .'

It was to be the Byzantine Empire that inherited the Greco-Roman culinary tradition. This is plain from rare glimpses of the imperial court recorded by visitors from the West. Bishop Luitprand of Cremona led an embassy in 968 from Otto III to the Emperor Nicephorus Phocas.[61] The food, he writes, was 'fairly foul and disgusting, washed down with oil after the fashion of drunkards and moistened also with an exceedingly bad fish liquor . . .' (That must have been the once indispensable *garum*, which as we have seen was still known and used in Gaul in the sixth century, but three centuries on had become repulsive to the Western palate.) Later he writes: 'The sacred emperor sent me one of his most delicate dishes, a fat goat . . . richly stuffed with garlic onions and leeks, and swimming in fish sauce.' Although by the period of Luitprand's visit the emperor and his court sat rather than reclined for most meals, on certain important ceremonial occasions old traditions were observed. One such was the great feast on Christmas Day:

> There is a hall near the Hippodrome looking northwards, wonderfully lofty and beautiful, which is called *Decanneacubita*, the House of the Nineteen Couches. The reason for its name is obvious: *deca* is Greek for

'ten', *ennea* for 'nine', and *cubita* are couches with curved ends, and on the day when our Lord Jesus Christ was born in the flesh, nineteen covers are always laid here at the table. The emperor and his guests on this occasion do not sit at table, as they usually do, but recline on couches: and everything is served on vessels, not of silver, but of gold. After the solid food, fruit is brought on in three golden bowls, which are too heavy for men to lift and come in on carriers covered over with purple cloth. Two of them are put on the table in the following way. Through openings in the ceiling hang three ropes covered with gilded leather and furnished with golden rings. These rings are attached to the handles projecting from the bowls, and with four or five men helping from below, they are swung on to the table by means of a movable device in the ceiling and removed again in the same fashion . . . As for the various entertainments I saw there, it would be too long a task to describe them all, and so for the moment I pass them by.[62]

The world of Nero and Trimalchio was clearly alive and well in tenth-century Byzantium, a fact corroborated by a second account by a Syrian prisoner of war held captive in Byzantium in 911–12. He too gives a description of an imperial feast at Christmas:

If you lift a curtain and enter the Palace, you will see a vast courtyard, four hundred paces square, paved with green marble. Its walls are deco-rated with various mosaics and paintings . . . To the left of the entrance is a room two hundred paces long and fifty wide. In this room are a wooden table, an ivory table, and, facing the door, a gold table. After the festivities, when the Emperor leaves the church, he enters this room and sits at the gold table. This is what happens at Christmas. He sends for the Muslim captives and they are seated at these tables. When the Emperor is seated at his gold table, they bring him four gold dishes, each of which is brought on its own little chariot.

One of these dishes, encrusted with pearls and rubies, they say belonged to Solomon . . . the second, similarly encrusted, to David . . . the third to Alexander; and the fourth to Constantine. They are placed before the Emperor, and one may eat from them. They remain there while the Emperor is at table: when he rises, they are taken away. Then, for the Muslims, many hot and cold dishes are placed on the other tables and the imperial herald announces: 'I swear on the Emperor's head that there is no pork at all in these dishes!' The dishes, on large silver and gold platters, are then served to the Emperor's guests.

Then they bring in an organ. It is a remarkable wooden object like an oil-press, and covered in solid leather. Sixty copper pipes are placed in it . . . and each pipe, according to its tuning and the master's playing, sounds the praises of the Emperor. The guests are meanwhile seated at their tables, and twenty men enter with cymbals in their hands. The music continues while the guests enjoy their meal.[63]

In many ways we are not so far from where we started; imperial Rome lived on in the East. But in Western Europe a whole new civilisation was in the throes of emerging.

CHAPTER TWO

Interlude: Fast and Feast

O N TRINITY SUNDAY in the year 1180, the Welsh monk and scholar Giraldus Cambrensis broke his journey back from the mainland of Europe at the great Benedictine abbey of St Augustine at Canterbury in Kent. On that occasion, as a guest, he was placed at the prior's table and later wrote (in the third person) a vivid account of the monastery's one main meal of the day:

> He noted two things, the multitude of the dishes and the excessive superfluity of signs which the monks made to one another. For there was the Prior giving so many dishes to the serving monks, and they in their turn bearing these as gifts to the lower tables; and there were those, to whom these gifts were brought, offering their thanks, and all of them gesticulating with fingers, hands and arms, and whistling one to another in lieu of speaking, all extravagating in a manner more free and frivolous than was seemly; so that Giraldus seemed to be seated at a stage-play or among actors and jesters . . . And as to the dishes and the number thereof, what shall I say, save that I have oft heard Giraldus himself declare that sixteen very costly dishes or even more were placed upon the table in order, not to say contrary to all order [i.e. to the monastic Rule]. Finally, potherbs [that is, vegetables] were brought to every table but were little tasted. For you might see so many kinds of fish, roasted and boiled, stuffed and fried, so many dishes contrived with eggs and pepper by dexterous cooks, so many flavourings and condiments, compounded with like dexterity to tickle gluttony and

Opposite: Nuns dining in a convent refectory while one reads from a pulpit. Scene from *The Life of the Blessed Umiltà* by Pietro Lorenzetti, 1341.

awaken appetite. Moreover you might see in the midst of such abundance 'wine and strong drink', metheglin and claret, must, mead and mulberry juice, and all that can intoxicate, beverages so choice that beer, such as is made at its best in England and above all in Kent, found no place among them.[1]

In this account we are six centuries on from the Gaul of Sidonius Apollinaris, well into the period generally categorised as the early Middle Ages. The so-called Dark Ages, running from about the fifth to the ninth centuries, had long since passed, and the late Middle Ages were yet to come. But in terms of the history of the table, this entire span from the fall of the Roman Empire until the fourteenth century is largely a mystery, a huge gap in the record. That is what makes Giraldus' eyewitness description of dinner in the second greatest Benedictine abbey in Europe of such extraordinary importance.

It tells of communal eating of a new kind. Here are Christian monks assembled in a refectory, no longer reclining but seated. New standards of behaviour have been established; in spite of the fact that Giraldus is painting what he clearly regards as a picture of decadence, the norms are discernible beneath the overlay. Such a meal was meant, of course, to be eaten in silence while a monk read uplifting works aloud. That practice had been got around by a quite outrageous exploitation of sign language and whistling. The meal was also meant to be frugal. That it certainly was not, indeed far from it given the lavishness of the spread, emphasises the fact the culinary skills of classical Antiquity had not been totally lost. Only fish and vegetables were served – the flesh of quadrupeds was forbidden – but this apparently did not discourage the cooks from producing a repertory of fine seafood dishes. From Giraldus' description we glean that the prior sat apart, and thus can assume that the seating was hierarchical.

Giraldus goes on to give a second anecdote to demonstrate further the lack of discipline into which the order had sunk. This time it involved the monks of St Swithun's at Winchester. They had prostrated themselves before Henry II, he reports, complaining that their abbot, who happened to be the bishop, had deprived them of three dishes. 'And when the King inquired how many dishes were left them, they replied "ten". "And I", said the King, "am content in my court with three. Perish your Bishop, if he does not reduce your dishes to the number of three." [2] The monks, who seem not to have been at all fazed by this burst of Plantagenet rage, defended themselves by saying that all of those dishes were necessary because they were in fact distributed to the needy as alms.

'What would Paul the hermit say to this?' Giraldus asks. 'What Anthony, what Benedict, the father and founder of monastic life?' What indeed. And yet the communal meal in a monkish refectory was, in its original austere guise, one of the two archetypal dining experiences of these obscure centuries. The other was the secular feast, one very different from the Roman *convivium*. Both are quintessential expressions of the two great forces shaping Western civilisation during these centuries: the institutions of Christianity, and the traditions of the tribes that dismembered and replaced the Roman Empire. For the first time we have two conflicting visions of the table, the holy one in the refectory, whose purpose was less to nourish the body than the spirit, and the secular one in the hall, which focused upon the deployment of power.

During these centuries the two approaches went more or less in tandem, but only one of them had any real potential for development. The monastic table was essentially a static and unchanging phenomenon, bound by exact rules which, although evaded from time to time, sooner or later reasserted themselves. In sharp contrast, the secular table had almost unlimited potential as a vehicle for the display of pomp, power and magnificence. All of this would be realised, even among the barbarian tribes, although seven centuries would pass before anything remotely resembling the excesses described by Petronius re-emerged.

Cuisine: the silent centuries

THERE ARE FEW cookery books between Apicius and those of the fourteenth century, yet Giraldus' description of dinner at St Augustine's provides evidence that skilled cooks capable of producing interesting cuisine were active at the close of the twelfth century. They worked within an oral tradition, for it is clear that the earliest written collections of recipes, the *Viandier de Taillevent* and *Le Ménagier de Paris*, to which I will come in the next chapter, contain recipes that went back a very long way in time.

These obscure centuries saw shifts in food habits that profoundly affected the history of the table.[3] Barbarian food culture was not based like the Roman on agriculture but on the exploitation of natural resources – livestock raising in the wild and hunting. The Mediterranean trinity of bread, oil and wine had its barbarian counterpart in meat, milk and butter. In the long run, however, the collapse of the Empire and the rise of the barbarian kingdoms resulted not so much in culinary confrontation as in synthesis. The turn to food derived from forests, pastures, streams, lakes and rivers was matched by barbarian fascination with the Roman traditions that survived in the conquered territories. That fascination was to be reinforced by the progressive conversion to Christianity, a faith rooted in the classical tradition, with bread, wine and oil utilised in its most important sacraments – above all the re-enactment of the Last Supper in the mass.

At the same time food became more and more linked to rank.[4] Such differentiation already existed in Antiquity, but it was to be continued and indeed increased as medieval feudal society gradually assumed its pyramidal structure. Dietary science, as expounded by Anthimus, had already recommended meat, the staple of the barbarian diet, as essential to physical strength. And strength was of course of direct concern to the new feudal nobility, whose role in society was to fight and, if not fighting, to hunt as a training for it. Inevitably, therefore, meat, from being the source of bodily prowess, came to be regarded as an attribute of power and hence command. It is in this context that we must place, for example, the eulogy of Henry I of England for being 'an excellent mete-gever'. Similarly, the denial of meat to high-ranking wrongdoers in the Carolingian period emphasised its significance as a source of aristocratic strength and power. Such an equation of meat and power accounts too for the utterly prodigal quantities consumed by the ruling classes. To eat more was literally a badge of true nobility.

The division between an upper class that ate meat and a peasant class denied it became further marked during the tenth and eleventh centuries as landowners acquired fresh administrative and judicial powers. They made use of these to enact legislation progressively excluding the peasant classes from any access to wild meat through the imposition of restrictive game laws. As time passed, the self-sufficient economies of the ninth and tenth centuries gave way to a market-led economy, with large-scale farming aimed at supplying food for increasing numbers of urban dwellers. So it was that over a period from about 1050 to 1280, the royal and aristocratic diet became firmly based upon meat and poultry. Meat was boiled with spices and aromatic herbs and other condiments to make it tender and flavoursome. It was also braised, fried and, above all, spit-roasted. Drink for the upper classes was wine and its derivatives.

The earliest evidence of the emergence of a more sophisticated cuisine comes in the thirteenth century.[5] By then the trade routes across the Mediterranean were once again active and the crusades had brought direct contact with the cuisine of Islam. In the eighth century the Arabs were established in Sicily and in the ninth they had footholds in southern Italy. They also occupied most of the Iberian peninsula. Not only did they have their own highly developed cuisine, making abundant use of spices, but they also served as transmitters, via the writings of the Arabic philosopher Avicenna (Ibn Sina) in the late tenth century, of the Greco-Roman medical and dietary traditions of Galen and Hippocrates. In these traditions sugar, spice and saffron were cast as having crucial medical virtues, offering relief from melancholia and other ills. One of Avicenna's shorter treatises, *De viribus cordis* (Powers of the Heart), for example, prescribed exotic cordials to strengthen the heart and generate food for the *spiritus*, thus averting melancholia. Into such cordials went not only spices, pomegranates, rosewater, yolks of eggs, saffron, sandalwood, citrus peel and wine but gold, silver, precious stones, coral, pearls and even silk. Sugar was particularly lauded for its salutary effects, a harbinger of much that was to come.

Such considerations precipitated a culinary revolution on the grounds of health alone. Another influence was the linkage between food and alchemy and astral magic. As outlined in the twelfth-century Arabic treatise *Picatrix*, each terrestrial substance was linked to some planetary deity. Such principles and beliefs set the scene for the brightly coloured and sweetly fragrant food that we find in the earliest substantial cookery books when they first appear in the fourteenth century.

The Christian table and the birth of manners

ALTHOUGH FOOD WAS closely connected to religion in Greek and Roman culture, in neither case did religion attempt to control when and what people ate. From the time of Homer until the Christian suppression of pagan sacrifice in the late Empire, the role of food in worship and associated feasting remained basically the same: the solemn slaughter of an animal followed by division of the meat, with a portion for the god placed on the altar and the rest equally shared out, cooked and consumed at a feast – at which the god was deemed present as guest of honour. On the conversion of the Emperor Constantine in 312, when Christianity became the official state religion of the Roman Empire, all of this was doomed to change.

Christianity inherited from the Judaic tradition the practice of regulating what and when people ate.[6] Along with sex, food became subject to God-given rules and thus a matter of ethical conduct. But that took time to evolve. The Gospels along with the Pauline Epistles had no overt concern with food. Their approach was natural and matter-of-fact and, if anything, encouraged ease among diners, with numerous instances of communal eating as a means of engendering brotherhood and conviviality. Although fasting had a place in both the Greco-Roman and the Jewish religious traditions, there was no attempt to promote fasting in early Christianity, other than as a pious supplement to prayer. The earliest evidence for Christians being exhorted to fast comes in the late second and early third centuries. In this case fasting was seen as a self-imposed 'martyrdom' during a period of persecution. The development of fasting as a sign of holiness drew on both Jewish traditions and the writings of those pagan philosophers who were advocates of temperance and sensual austerity. It also involved to some extent repudiation of Antiquity's cult of the strong, healthy and beautiful body, something that could be achieved partly through the careful observance of dietary rules. Tertullian, the late second- and early third-century African Church Father, cast fasting as one of the marks of a Christian elite, a practice which set the elect apart. The long-term effect of this was a form of Christian asceticism in which self-starvation became one aspect of the pathway to perfection.

By the sixth century food was seen as a temptation leading to the sin of gluttony. Gradually, fasting under the aegis of the Church was systematised. In the Western Church, Wednesdays and Fridays became fast days. Fasting also preceded baptism and accompanied any prolonged penance. The fast which initially had run only from Good Friday to Easter morning was extended first to embrace all of Holy Week and then, by the fourth century, the whole forty days of what came to be called Lent. Fasting involved less an overall reduction in quantity of food for the laity than a total abstinence from meat, here cast in its role as a symbol of violence, death and every form of physicality and sexuality. Another consequence of this attitude towards meat was the development – as we have already witnessed at St Augustine's – of a non-carnivorous cuisine equal in every way to the meat-based one.

The determining document for the diet in Christian religious institutions is the Rule of St Benedict (480–543), which dominated Western monasticism from the ninth until the twelfth century.[7] It is a remarkable document, not least for the information contained in it about meals and how monks should behave at them. In Rule XLIII we witness the circumscription that binds a monk at table: 'He who does not come to table before the verse [that is Grace], so that all may say it, and praying together sit down to table at the same time, must be corrected once or twice if this be through his own fault or bad habit. If he do not after this amend he is not allowed to share in the common table, but he is to be separated from the company of all the rest and eat alone. Until he makes satisfaction and mends his ways let his portion of wine be taken away from him.'

What we have here are table manners in the making. The rules include a number of other dos and don'ts. A monk should be neither 'a wine bibber' nor 'a great eater'. Meals are to be taken in silence, listening to whatever is being read, those who wait on table taking care that each monk lacks for nothing; if he does, he is to communicate only by sign language. Two meals a day are to be served: 'there shall be in all seasons of the year two cooked dishes, so that he that cannot eat of the one may make his meal of the other . . . if there be any fruit or young vegetables these may be added as a third dish'. Each monk had a daily ration of a pound of bread and a pint of wine. All except the weak and sick had to abstain totally from the flesh of quadrupeds. From Easter to Whitsun the first meal was to be served at the sixth hour (counting from sunrise), and therefore generally about noon, and the second, supper, just before nightfall, as candles were not to be lit. From 13 September to Lent the main meal was eaten at the ninth hour from sunrise, and through Lent to Easter at eventide.

Monastic records provide us with the only detailed account of food and the table during these centuries. In some ways we witness the monastery picking up where the villa left off. The celebrated plan from about 820 for an ideal complex at Saint Gall resembles that of an ancient villa, with its inner courtyard abutting the church and its sides accommodating a wine cellar, food stores, a bakery, a kitchen and refectory. Beyond lay a whole range of other buildings necessary for the sustenance of the monks and the agricultural activities upon which they depended. Such an arrangement was adopted in Carolingian monasteries during the eighth and ninth centuries. What is striking is that it is the monastery which preserves through the Dark and Middle Ages a feature which was only to re-emerge with the Renaissance villa, a room whose sole purpose was dining.[8]

In many ways the great Benedictine house at Cluny in Burgundy under Odilo (abbot 994–1048) resembled an aristocratic house. This is hardly surprising in view of the fact that the reformed Cluniac order drew so many of its monks from the nobility.[9] Although the abbot lived, slept and dined with his brothers, he was accorded a degree of deference great enough to affect the basic ritual of the refectory. With two candles burning before him, he ate alone, and was provided with more sophisticated dishes and better wine. Meals at Cluny were ceremonial occasions. Monks washed as they entered the refectory and sat in a prescribed order. The linen on the tables was changed once a fortnight and before each monk was set a knife and a loaf. The bowls from the kitchen arrived in portions for two, as did the wine from the cellar. No one started to eat until grace had been said and the abbot gave the signal. This was the meal as a form of spiritual communion, with the mind lifted heavenwards by the text being read aloud, away from any consideration of what was being eaten. Deference, courtesy and consideration for one's fellows, all attributes essential to the evolution of table manners, are in fact already in place in the refectory at Cluny.

Fountains Abbey, in the remote valley of the river Skell in Yorkshire, was a Cistercian house, built at the close of the twelfth century.[10] The Cistercians were a reforming order living by a strict interpretation of the

The abbot dines, before him fish, bread, a knife,
a jug of wine and a beaker.
Detail from *The Supper of San Guido*, 1318.

Benedictine Rule and a section of it, *De Refectione*, provides us with detailed information about a refectory meal and its consumption. The refectory stood within the south cloister range, its imposing entrance flanked by a series of blind arches which housed pewter basins or lavers in which the monks washed their hands before meals. The refectory itself was lofty with two aisles dominated by the *pulpitum*, the stone balcony for the reader. There were five long tables, the supports stone, the tops wooden, one against the southern wall and two flanking it either side. These were all raised on to platforms, the southern high table raised more than the four others. The walls were lime-washed in off-white and painted in imitation of stonework while the large windows were filled with non-figurative graisaille stained glass. The horseshoe arrangement with the diners facing into a central arena was to be the format for the medieval secular feast.

To signal a meal a bell was rung. The monks gathered, washed their hands, and then entered the refectory, bowing towards the high table and arranging themselves in order of precedence standing in front of their tables. The prior then entered processing to the high table, bowing before he reached it, a bell was rung and prayers and a psalm were recited, parts antiphonally, followed by grace. Then all sat. Before each monk there was a knife, a cup and a piece of bread covered with a cloth. According to the will of the abbot the food might already be on the table or, at this point, was immediately carried in. Reading began and the meal was eaten in total silence. Service was easy as the monks sat with their backs to the walls leaving the front of the table free. No one began eating until the signal was given by the prior. The etiquette was strict and any breach of it called for the offending monk to prostrate himself on the step of the high table until the prior tapped his knife bidding the monk to rise. Cups had to be held with both hands and not cleaned with the fingers but a cloth. Fingers and knives should be first wiped on a piece of bread and then on the table-cloth; salt was to be taken on the tip of the knife; nothing was to be passed without a mutual bow of respect. Dishes were collected in strict order of precedence and the end of the meal was signalled by a bell bidding everyone to rise. That was followed by a second bell and then the monks processed in order, the youngest monk first, the cantor singing, towards the church. In the order and choreographed ceremonial of the monastic meal we can see much that the secular world was to borrow and develop.

By 1300 art in the West began to depict the natural world with accuracy of observation, and we consequently have depictions of monks and nuns at table. We also have the long series of Last Suppers with which it became customary to adorn in fresco form the refectory walls and which were to culminate in Leonardo da Vinci's fresco in Santa Maria delle Grazie in Milan. The scene they present is an unchanging one. As the refectory was not used for anything other than dining, the tables could be permanent rather than removable trestles. Over each is spread a white cloth adorned with a sparse still life: loaves of bread, small dishes for salt, jugs filled with wine, tumblers from which to drink, knives, one or more large dishes containing fish and slices of bread to act as trenchers. Moving the event forward or backward a few centuries would offer us much the same picture. The same, however, would not be true of the secular table. It was to take a very different direction.

Feast as power

IN ANOTHER WAY, Christianity also affected the secular table. The Bible was able to offer a plethora of examples, from the marriage at Cana to the miracle of the loaves and fishes, in which eating together constituted a profound expression of love, communion and fellowship.[11] Such texts gave sanction to the barbarian tradition of celebrating any major event – a treaty of peace, an installation, a marriage – with a feast. During the Dark Ages, in response to the tribal rituals of the barbarian tribes, the Roman *convivium* gradually changes its form to emerge as the fully-fledged medieval feast.

In both Nordic and Anglo-Saxon Dark Age literature the feast-hall was at the heart of society, the place in which victories were communally celebrated and social bonds formed.[12] Anglo-Saxon had an extensive vocabulary of terms to denote the feast-hall and its furnishings. The lord

Overleaf: The Last Supper was often depicted on the walls of refectories. This one by Domenico Ghirlandaio, dated 1480, is in the refectory of the convent of the *umiliati*, Ognissanti, Florence.

was *hlaford* (bread-guardian) and his dependant a *hlfaeta* (bread-eater). Neither bread nor any other form of food, it should at once be said, was the prime focus of a feast. The main purpose of barbarian feasting was to get drunk, hence the expressions *beorsele* (beer-hall), *ealusele* (ale-hall) and *winsele* (wine-hall). The prime duty of the king and queen or lord and lady was to provide drink. The hall for the Anglo-Saxons was the setting in which bonds were forged between a lord and his followers through the dispensing of drink, gifts and pledges. It was also to be, for some centuries, a shared space for more or less primitive communal living, a far remove from the refinements of a typical upper-class Roman villa with rooms devoted to specific activities like eating. Simultaneously, as we know from the great epic *Beowulf,* such gatherings for feasting in the hall were the occasion for the performance of music and poetry celebrating the deeds of heroes.

Drink was also at the heart of Viking feasts.[13] Accounts of banquets in their sagas never describe the food, only the drink. The offering of drink had been an integral part of sacrifice in Scandinavian paganism. Even after the conversion of the Vikings to Christianity, the object of any banquet continued to be getting drunk. Drinking on such occasions started as soon as host and guests had taken their place at table. The host opened with a toast, one which in pre-Christian times would have been a libation to the pagan gods, but which in the new dispensation was in honour of Christ, the Virgin and saints. A drink once proffered could not be refused, and any man worth his salt had to be capable of downing an ocean. Moreover, guests were expected to respond to such toasts with a short recital or with poetic strophes. The table was a round one and everyone therefore faced inwards, the drinking horn passing from hand to hand around it.

A major development during these centuries was the change from a reclining to a sitting position at table.[14] It is possible to date this switch by reference to pictures of the Last Supper. In a sixth-century mosaic in S. Apollinare Nuovo in Ravenna the *stibadium* is still firmly in place, with Christ sited in the place of honour and the apostles reclining in a circle around a table with a plate with two large fish on it. Already, however, in the fourth century Martin, bishop of Tours, recalls an imperial banquet at which the priest reclined and his superiors sat upright, reversing the Roman practice. The new preference for sitting at table probably had

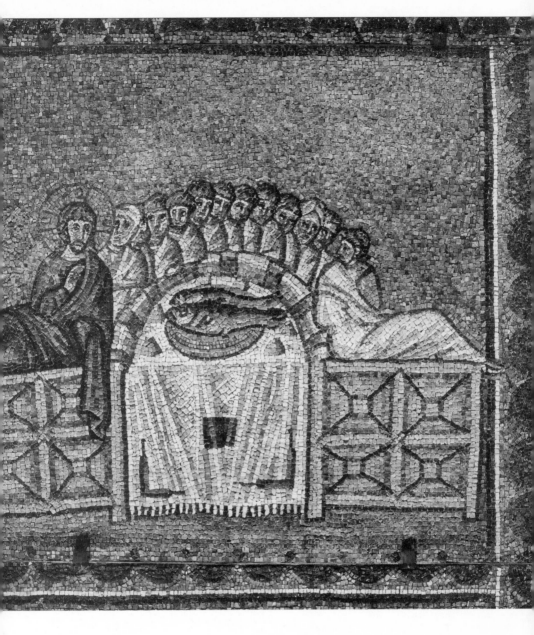

The Last Supper with Christ in the traditional Roman place
of honour on the *stibadium* to the left.
Mosaic, sixth century AD.

The survival of the curved table of
Antiquity into the late twelfth century.
Illumination from
a French *Life of Christ*.

some connection with barbarian inauguration ceremonies, in which whoever was to succeed as king, lord or chief was lowered or ceremonially placed in some kind of upright seat or throne-chair in the feast-hall. With Christianisation, that rite was transferred to the Church and with the addition of anointing and crowning became a coronation. Certainly by the Carolingian period the image of a monarch seated upright enthroned was symbolic of his rule. Inevitably, sitting and the exertion of power became inextricably entwined.

If the position of the diner changed, so did the shape of the table, although this process was slower. The round table can still be seen in the late eleventh-century Bayeux Tapestry. Bishop Odo, raising his hand in blessing, is saying grace, while a servant on the other side of the table kneels, napkin to hand, proffering water for the ablutions. The round table is still there – in a late twelfth-century French illumination of the Last Supper, for example – but by then it is exceptional. By about 1100 the rectangular trestle table is universal. A miniature datable between the years 1285 and 1291 shows the arrangement that, following the custom in the monastic refectory, was to be the norm for the medieval feast: a long trestle table behind which the guests sat on a bench. The advantages of the trestle

Opposite: A banquet as recorded in the late eleventh-century Bayeux Tapestry.
A servant kneels proffering water and a towel for ablutions to Bishop Odo
and William the Conqueror seated at a curved table.

The advent of the rectangular trestle table.
Illumination in a French romance, between 1285 and 1291.

table were obvious – it could be set up or dismantled and stored easily, leaving room for other activities in the great hall that was the focus of medieval courtly life.

One other change takes place by 1300, and that concerns the place of honour.[15] In Antiquity that position on the *stibadium* had initially been at the centre, but by the late imperial period it had moved to the extreme left edge of the couch (when looking towards it), as in the S. Apollinare Nuovo mosaic. Medieval representations of feast scenes waver between the two. In Duccio's *Feast at Cana*, painted early in the fourteenth century, Christ and the Virgin are placed on the far left in accordance with antique practice. In his *Last Supper* Christ is at the centre. Both positions were to

The place of honour at the left transferred from the *stibadium*
of Antiquity to the medieval rectangular trestle table.
The Feast at Cana by Duccio di Buoninsegna, 1308–11.

retain their dignity into the sixteenth century, and this was only to be
resolved when, with the universal adoption of perspective as a means of
ordering space, the centre finally won.

It was the patterns established at the Carolingian court of the eighth
and ninth centuries that were to shape the form of medieval eating.
Charlemagne created the first great concentration of power in Western
Europe since the fall of the Roman Empire, imposing common styles of
thought and behaviour on most of continental Europe. In the Carolingian
era three activities were seen as binding a king and his magnates: joint
Christian worship, the hunt and the feast. The banquet thus became one
of the prime means whereby kings and magnates maintained and

The place of honour as the centre of the table.
The Last Supper by Duccio di Buoninsegna, 1308–11.

expressed their feudal ties. This is no better demonstrated than in the
evolution of the coronation banquet.[16] At the two great feasts held
for the coronations of members of the Ottonian dynasty in 936 and
986 the German dukes acted as cupbearer, steward and marshal, providing
a vivid demonstration to all present that the highest expression of
feudal fealty was to act as a servant to the emperor at his inaugural
feast. That role was to be re-enacted again and again at imperial and royal
coronations throughout Europe. It was not a part that everyone accepted
readily. When, in 1290, Albert I of Austria compelled Wenceslas, king
of Bohemia to serve as his ceremonial cupbearer as a public acknowledgement of Albert's superior position, Wenceslas at first refused. Later,
in company with a thousand of his knights, he performed the function –
on horseback!

Detailed descriptions of eating habits during these centuries are so rare that it is worth quoting Charlemagne's biographer, Einhard, on the emperor's own:

> He was temperate in eating and drinking, but especially so in drinking; for he had a fierce hatred of drunkenness in any man, and especially in himself or in his friends. He could not abstain so easily from food, and used often to complain that fasting was injurious to his health. He rarely gave large banquets, and only on the high festivals, but then he invited a large number of guests. His daily meal was served in four courses only, exclusive of the roast, which the hunters used to bring in on spits, and which he ate with more pleasure than any other food. During the meal there was either singing or a reader for him to listen to. Histories and the great deeds of men of old were read to him. He took delight also in the books of Saint Augustine, and especially in those which are entitled the City of God. He was so temperate that he rarely drank oftener than thrice during dinner.[17]

In this narrative we seem to be present at a cultural synthesis: reading during meals as in a monastic refectory and in classical Antiquity, songs or tales of heroic deeds as in the sagas sung at barbarian feasts.

The Carolingian dynasty multiplied feast days in monasteries and cathedrals in honour of members of the reigning family.[18] No mention of feasts in the sense of the lavish consumption of food and drink occurs in the Rule of St Benedict, but a steady stream of royal charters from the mid-eighth to the mid-tenth centuries record a long series of such feasts in memory of members of the dynasty. To feasts of the Church like Christmas and Easter were now added commemoration of an important abbot and birthdays of members of the royal family. Five generations of emperors and kings accumulated feast days with such zeal that in the case of a great monastery like Saint Denis they were to total eighty-eight in all. Feasts of this kind were a tradition which came out of pre-Christian Germanic custom, here transferred into the new Christian framework. They were to be swept away in the tide of monastic reform emanating from Cluny in the tenth century. But what is remarkable is the premise underlying these monastic banquets. Feasting under the aegis of the king spoke for the victory of the king's armies and for the good of the kingdom. Thus a monk's full stomach became a form of prayer.

Through the eleventh century and into the twelfth, the feast became a quintessential part of the fabric of feudalism, a massive periodic culinary event celebrating the relationship between a lord and his vassals, and the power this relationship engendered. Then, as the twelfth century gave way to the thirteenth, there was a shift in atmosphere. Drunkenness ceased to be the main aim of such gatherings. We sense the first stirrings of the courtliness that was to transform the feast from a ritual of feudal dependence into a manifestation of friendship. The household structure which had begun its existence at the Carolingian court found imitators all across the aristocratic classes. At the court of Charlemagne there had been three major household officials: the grand seneschal, the grand butler and the grand chamberlain. The first two served the hall, the latter the private chamber. Such arrangements obviously affected how meals were staged, and documents exist making it possible in two instances to trace how far they had developed by the thirteenth century. The first describes practice in the household of the count of Hainault in 1210; the second consists of a set of rules drawn up by Robert Grosseteste, bishop of Lincoln, for the widow of the earl of Lincoln. This was compiled in 1240 or 1241.

The count of Hainault, in common with every other aristocrat, moved between several residences, in his case three. At each he was served by a seneschal and butler for the hall and a chamberlain for the private chamber.[19] Reporting to the seneschal there was a buyer of foodstuffs, three cooks, a concierge to take care of the fires both in the kitchen and in the hall, a cutler in charge of the salt and cutlery, a butler with a staff who looked after the wine, and a pantler who, together with a staff of four, produced the bread necessary for the trenchers at each meal. Eating was regarded as a solemn act in which the whole household took part. A minor chamberlain looked after the candles and also provided the water and towel for the ablutions of the count and countess which prefaced every meal. This chamberlain also brought water for the clerks and knights who made up the upper echelons of the household hierarchy. Candles stuck into loaves of bread provided illumination for what was clearly a high table served by knights, at which sat the count and the countess. The seneschal sat near to them, and also qualified for salted bread to eat with his meat.

The arrangements were not so different in the case of the countess of Lincoln, judging from Grosseteste's advice to her on how to conduct her household.[20] What it reveals is that meals had become increasingly choreographed events of a kind reminiscent in our own age of school dinners. 'Command your knights and all your gentlemen who wear your livery, that the same livery which they use daily, especially at your meals, and in your presence, be kept for honour,' he begins somewhat grandly. Freemen and guests should not be allowed to dispose themselves in desultory groups just anywhere, but should sit together. The grooms should enter and leave en masse. 'And you yourself,' he continues, 'always be seated at the middle of the high table, that your presence as lord or lady may appear openly to all, and that you may plainly see on either side all the service and all the faults.' The countess — somewhat resembling a disapproving headmistress presiding over an unruly girls' school — should have two overseers placed in the main body of the hall to see that good order prevailed. The result of this would be that 'you shall be very much feared and reverenced'.

Service in the hall was to be under the supervision of a marshal, with servers who carried the food from the kitchen in procession followed by the seneschal. Food was borne first to the high table and then down into the main body of the hall. Each day at dinner two types of meat were to be served 'large and full, to increase the alms' (what was not consumed was distributed to the poor), along with two lighter dishes for all freemen present. At supper there was one substantial dish along with more light dishes, followed by cheese. Grosseteste is insistent on the crucial role played by public eating, constantly re-enacted, in maintaining the harmony and order of the household: 'As far as possible for sickness or fatigue, constrain yourself to eat before your people, for this shall bring great benefit and honour to you.' The fact that he makes such a point about the countess's presence suggests strongly that the withdrawal of the lord and lady to eat privately in their own chamber was already being practised.

As the staging and structure of medieval secular meals took shape, table manners began to emerge.[21] The roots of good behaviour at table lay as we have seen in the monastery's refectory, but its appearance in the secular world owed much to the courtesy tradition. This comprised a series of ideals grounded in religion which included chivalry and its

expression in terms of courtly love, benevolence, kindliness and cheerful-
ness of disposition. Etiquette of some kind must have existed in the
twelfth century, but until someone set the rules down on paper we have no
way of knowing. That they were written down, however, demonstrates
their importance and the demand for such guidance. The earliest treatise
covering table manners dates from about 1215, and is called *Der Wälsche
Gast* (*The Italian Guest*). It takes the form of a didactic poem some fifteen
thousand lines long by Thomasin of Zerclaere (Tommasino di Circlaria),
an Italian from Trieste writing for Germans. Many manuscripts of this
type survive from the following years, testimony to a demand.

Thomasin writes for the instruction of young gentlemen, and in his
verse we are at the fount of a tradition that runs down the centuries to our
own age:

> When he begins to eat,
> He touches nothing but his food
> With the hand: that is doing things well.
> One must not eat the bread
> Before the first dishes are brought.
> A man shall be very careful
> Not to put [food]
> On both sides in his mouth.
> He shall at that time be on his guard
> Lest he drink or speak
> Whilst he has something in his mouth.
> Those who turn with the beaker to their companions
> As if they were about to give it,
> Before they take it from their lips,
> Them the wine has bound thereto,
> Who, drinking, looks over the beaker
> [Does that which] is not fitting to courteous men.[22]

And so it goes on. But Thomasin is not alone. Another author, this time
from the mid-thirteenth century, also provides rules in his treatise on
Courtly Breeding. What Tannhäuser writes gives some insight into what this
new courtliness of behaviour was meant to replace:

Those who like to eat mustard and sauces,
Let them be very careful
To forbear being dirty,
And not to push their fingers into them.
He who belches when he is to eat
And blows his nose into the table-cloth,
Both these things are not befitting,
As far as I can understand ...
You are not to clean your teeth
With knives, as some do,
And as still happens here and there:
He who does so, it is not good.[23]

To a hierarchy of food was now added a new element. By adopting the code of courtliness at table, diners had another way of setting themselves apart – and above. The ascent of manners had begun.

A reconciliation of opposites

I OPENED THIS chapter with a vision of two tables and of the two ways of eating, one set within the refectory of a monastery, the other within the hall of a castle or great house. In moral terms, the first was clearly more acceptable, while secular consumption fell short of the ideal – it could lead to sin, initially to gluttony and from that onwards to who knows what else. Could the two ways of life ever be reconciled? One person tried to, Louis IX of France, Saint Louis, who was canonised by Pope Boniface VIII in 1297. Louis IX's life straddles much of the thirteenth century. He came to the throne at the age of twelve in 1226 and died forty-four years later in 1270. He was the archetypal medieval king, living an exemplary private life of austerity and prayer, leading a crusade to the Holy Land in 1248 and building the Sainte-Chapelle to house the Crown of Thorns which he had acquired from Emperor Baldwin II in 1239.

The French royal table was bound by rules, first by those of abstinence as laid down by the Church and second by the conventions of ceremonial.[24] Louis abstained from meat on Wednesdays and Fridays, and then added Mondays. He confined himself to bread and water on the principal vigils of the Virgin, also on Good Friday and on the eve of All Saints and other saints' days. During Advent and Lent he gave up both fish and fruit on Fridays until his health broke, at which point his confessor intervened and convinced him to take one piece of fish and fruit on those Fridays henceforth. On his return from the crusade in 1254, his piety intensified. He refused the large fish that he had previously enjoyed, eating only small ones with sauce that had been watered down to the point of being ruined. In general he deliberately chose inferior food and drink. Moreover, whenever he visited a monastery he waited on the monks, whose way of life was, of course, the source of all this regal self-denial. The picture we are left with is one of an exhibitionist ascetic.

Yet the secular table in the midst of all this kingly austerity remained intact. Meals were still framed in the kind of magnificence both tradition and popular opinion demanded of a medieval ruler. Louis might drink common beer as a token of his high humility but it was drunk from a jewel-encrusted goblet. The king's biographer, Joinville, who was close to him for most of his life, makes it clear that royal splendour was maintained whatever his master's idiosyncratic privations. In 1241, when the king was twenty-seven, a great court was held at Saumur. Joinville was an eyewitness:

> I was present and I can witness that the arrangement was the finest I ever saw . . . Facing the King, his brother, the Count of Artois, served him with meat, and the good Count John of Soissons carved with the knife. As a guard for the King's table were my Lord Humbert of Beaujeu, later Constable of France, my Lord Enguerrand of Coucy, and my Lord Archambaud of Bourbon. Behind these three barons were at least thirty knights, in velvet tunics, as their attendant guards; and behind them was a great number of men-at-arms, wearing the arms of the Count of Poitiers embroidered on satin. The King wore a tunic of dark blue satin, a surcoat and cloak of scarlet velvet lined with ermine, and a cotton cap, which did not suit him at all well, for he was then a young man.[25]

The feast was a great spectacle, with tables around the cloister, one accommodating the queen's mother and another at which twenty archbishops and bishops sat. 'Many folk,' Joinville writes, 'said that they had never seen so many surcoats or other garments of cloth of gold and silk at one feast, and that there were at least three thousand knights present.'

Perhaps the key to interpreting the event lay in the little cotton cap which Joinville thought so unbecoming a young man. Was this the king's solitary gesture of humility amidst the splendour? If so it would fit in with the nature of the king's rule, which mirrored that of his approach to food at the royal table. On the one hand he was devout, holding both Church and clergy in great respect, yet on the other he stoutly resisted any encroachment on royal power by the papacy or the bishops.

To some degree the formal splendour diminished after his return from the crusade in 1254. Joinville records that Louis's clothing henceforth was only 'of undyed or dark-blue wool' and that 'he was so temperate at table that he ordered no dishes beyond what his cook prepared; it was placed before him and he ate it. He mixed his wine with water in a glass goblet . . .' None the less the traditional royal ceremonial remained unchanged, nor was he any killjoy, for when he dined in 'the houses of the great' he listened to the minstrels who came after dinner before he rose and grace was said. And, again in another rare glimpse of life at the royal table: 'When any great men from abroad dined with him he was good company.'[26]

In the culinary habits of St Louis two opposing approaches to the table are reconciled, but the synthesis would not be repeated again. The future lay with the secular feast, which was henceforth to take a very different path.

The escalation of dining in splendour.

Jean, duc de Berri at table. Above the duke floats a canopy while before
him stretch dishes of food nibbled by pet dogs and a ceremonial nef.
One servant carves, another cuts up food, while a third, close to a
plate-laden buffet, deals with wine. The whole exercise comes under the
direction of the man with a wand of office to the duke's left.
Illumination in *Les Très Riches Heures*, 1416.

CHAPTER THREE

In the Eye of the Beholder

W HAT IS PROBABLY the best and most complete account we have of a late medieval banquet describes the dinner given by Gaston IV, comte de Foix, at Tours in 1457.[1] It was staged in honour of an embassy from the king of Hungary, a mission which included not only Hungarians but Germans, Bohemians and Luxemburgers. To that cosmopolitan guest list of a hundred and fifty must be added the whole of the French court. The guests were seated in strict order of precedence at twelve large tables with the host, together with the leaders of the embassy and the most important French notables, served separately, as was customary, at a high table.

The feast was exceptional, not only for the number of courses involved — no fewer than seven — but also for the fact that the account actually describes the food served. Up until now, such details were normally passed over in silence or, if mentioned at all, simply remarked in terms of splendour and abundance. The meal opened modestly with pieces of toast that the diner dipped into the spiced wine called hippocras, but then swiftly moved on to 'grands pates de chapons [capons]', 'jambons de sanglier [hams of wild boar]', and seven different kinds of pottage, all served on silver. Each table bore a hundred and forty silver plates, a feat of ostentation that was to be repeated in the courses that followed. Ragouts of game came next: pheasants, partridges, rabbits, peacocks, bustards, wild geese, swans and various river birds, not to mention venison. These ragouts were accompanied by several other kinds of dishes and pottage. Then came a pause.

Although there is no reference in our account to the placement of the tables, they must have been arranged in a horseshoe forming an arena at the centre. Into that space came what was called an *entremet*, the first of a series. Twelve men wheeled in a castle on a rock. Whether the men were concealed inside the rock or not we do not learn, but the castle itself had four corner towers and a large keep at the centre with four windows, at each of which could be seen a richly attired lady. The central keep was adorned with heraldic banners bearing the arms of the king of Hungary and those of the other great lords who made up the embassy. At the top of each of the four towers a child sang like an angel (though what they sang we do not learn).

After this display the feast resumed with a dish called 'oiseaux armes', which has defied definition by culinary historians, served with yet more pottages. But the real distinction of this course was that 'tout ce service fut doré' – all the food was apparently gilded, or at least given the appearance of being golden. Then came the second *entremet*: six men, dressed in the regional costume of Béarn, carried in a man disguised as a tiger wearing a collar from which was suspended the arms of the king of Hungary. The tiger spat fire and the Béarnais danced, to great applause from the onlookers.

Following a fifth course which included tarts, darioles (small moulded dishes, sweet in this case) and fried oranges, another *entremet* came forth. In terms of sheer spectacle this must have eclipsed everything that went before. Twenty-four men were needed to bring it into the hall, an indication as to both its size and weight. It was a mountain containing two fountains, one of which spouted rosewater, the other 'eau de muscade'. Suddenly out of this rocky promontory rabbits scampered while live birds emerged to fly around the hall. Four boys and a girl, all dressed as savages, descended to dance a morisco. Then the count distributed largesse to the various attendant heralds of arms, the one from Hungary receiving, in addition to the two hundred écus bestowed on the others, a fine length of velvet.

The sixth course consisted of dessert, red hippocras served with certain kinds of wafer called 'oublies' and 'roles', after which came a final *entremet*. A man attired in embroidered crimson satin appeared astride a similarly caparisoned horse. In his hands he carried a model garden made of wax which was filled with roses and a variety of other flowers, and set it before the ladies (an indication that they must have been seated separately from the men). This, we are told, was the most admired of all the *entremets*, although what followed in the way of food as a finale must have been equally extraordinary. It involved a heraldic menagerie sculpted in sugar: lions, stags, monkeys and various other birds and beasts, each holding in paw or beak the arms of the Hungarian king.

Unbelievably, the banquet was not yet over. In came a live peacock with the arms of the queen of France encompassing its neck and the arms of the ladies of the French court draped over its body. In response, all the lords present advanced and pledged to support the cause of the Hungarian king (it was customary to make vows of chivalry on birds). Our account closes with one other important detail. In the middle of the room there was apparently a platform, an *estrade*, from which singers and an organ provided music during the dinner.

In a description of this kind we are suddenly, for the first time, made aware of the extreme complexity of the late medieval table on great occasions. Certain aspects are already familiar: the setting, the arrangement of the tables, the stress on hierarchy, the presence of music and the association of a feast with a political event. But little at the close of the thirteenth century would seem to signal such an unprecedented escalation in terms of food, richness of presentation and dramatic spectacle. This feast at Tours therefore makes an invaluable point of departure for developments which at times will leave the reader almost bewildered.

In the first place the food is certainly far more elaborate than before. One whole course is described as being golden while another takes the form of a menagerie in sugar; these are strong pointers to an increasing interest in appearance, in colour and figurative presentation. And then there is the use of silver in vast quantities, on a scale that renders the tableware of earlier centuries positively stingy. Eating has become an element in a vast theatrical production. The simple *chansons*, jugglers and acrobats who enlivened earlier feasts appear primitive compared with the mobile scenery, costumed actors, singers, musicians and dancers who took part in the *entremets*. And, although we do not know what was sung, the description makes it clear that these eruptions into the hall were designed not only to surprise and delight but to convey a political message. Why else the arms of Hungary atop the castle keep? Yet we also seem to have struck upon a line of descent leading from the medieval feast to the birth of opera and ballet.

A royal banquet.

The king and his honoured guests are placed to the extreme left while the rest
are huddled down the table which is covered with dishes, cups and beakers.
This is a break between courses during which a dwarf and musicians
entertain the diners. Illumination, German, late fourteenth century.

But that is to anticipate. From the historian's point of view the greatest
change is the unfamiliar abundance of material. From the fourteenth
and fifteenth centuries we have menus; accounts of feasts; household
regulations, both royal and noble, which lay down the ritual of the table;

the earliest cookery books (which contain recipes that can, albeit reinterpreted, still be cooked today); not to mention a plethora of visual evidence. The latter, thanks to the increasing obsession with realism in Netherlandish art, provides us with a vast amount of information on late medieval dining, though for the most part only as experienced by the upper classes.

At this juncture it is wise to sound a note of caution. What is confusing and to a degree complicating is that the documentary evidence dating from 1300 to 1500 often refers to what had been standard practice for up to two centuries before. Much of the food and its attendant ritual described in the fifteenth century might have been found in the thirteenth century, but went unrecorded. As a consequence this chapter must be Janus-faced. At times the material will enable us to describe for the first time what happened earlier, while at other times it will point to what was a whirlwind of change, particularly from the close of the fourteenth century onwards. Our best point of departure is through two quite new phenomena, identifiable cooks and cookery books, and the cuisine which they record.

Cooks, cookery books and cuisine

THE VERY EMERGENCE of such a thing as a cookery book pre-supposes a food-conscious upper class.[2] For the medieval cook, sweating in the kitchen and probably illiterate, written recipes were unnecessary; his art was passed on orally. Manuscripts, laboriously written out by hand, were by their nature expensive, and those that do survive certainly did not belong to practising cooks but to those for whom they worked. The earliest of these date from the very end of the thirteenth century, and their preoccupation with diet places them in the field of medicine rather than the kitchen. None the less, as the manuscripts multiply we have evidence of a genuine lay interest in cooking. Scholars have pieced together what can only be described as large family trees of manuscripts whose contents overlap and interrelate in such a way as to establish the existence, give or take regional variations, of a Europe-wide late medieval courtly culinary art.

Of the hundred or so surviving manuscript collections of recipes, what is known as the *Viandier de Taillevent* was the medieval bestseller.[3] Taillevent was Guillaume de Tirel (*c.* 1310–95), cook to Charles V and Charles VI of France. Probably of wealthy bourgeois origins, Taillevent was to rise socially to the rank of squire and gain a coat of arms, appropriately incorporating three cooking pots. Although he was billed as the author of the *Viandier*, one version of the book can now be dated to around 1300, at least ten years before his birth. This demonstrates that what passes under Taillevent's name was actually a later reworking of an existing collection of recipes. Indeed by the time that the *Viandier* first appeared in print about 1486, a century after Taillevent's death, it had changed considerably from the original. It was to go on changing through no fewer than fifteen editions during the sixteenth century, and was still being modified and used at the opening of the seventeenth. The second great corpus of late medieval recipes, *Le Ménagier de Paris*, also drew upon it heavily.

The recipes of *Le Ménagier* occur in a book of household management compiled about 1393–4, once thought to be by a mature rich Parisian bourgeois for his new bride of fifteen but recently argued to be the work of a certain Guy de Montigny, who was in the service of the duc de Berri.[4] Its compiler, although educated, was not of the royal court; indeed he specifically refers to some food fashions as appropriate only to the royal household and censures such excess. Eighty-five out of its three hundred and fifty recipes – which cover pottages, roasts, pâtés, fish (both fresh-water and sea fish), eggs, *entremets* (here meaning desserts) and sauces, as well as food and drink for the sick – are taken from the *Viandier*. To the same period belongs another large collection embodying the English tradition, *The Forme of Cury* (i.e. the proper method of cookery), 'compiled of the chief Master Cooks of King Richard the Second King of England . . . the which was accounted the best and royalest "vyaundier" of all Christian kings'. It was assembled with the advice of the 'masters and [i.e. of] Physic and Philosophy that dwelled in court'.[5] This book was to remain at the heart of a fifteenth-century proliferation of English recipe collections.

The sudden plethora of cookery manuscripts suggests an increasing interest in food around 1400 in the courts of late medieval Europe. This is reflected a little later in a volume compiled about 1420 by the cook for twenty-five years to the ducal family of Savoy, Master Chiquart.[6] *Du fait de cuisine* was written at the request of Duke Amadeus VIII, and in it we can see Chiquart's own attitude to his task, for he describes cookery both as an art and as a science. The dukes of Savoy were connected directly by marriage to the dukes of Burgundy and the book is filled with recipes of a kind that would have impressed that wealthiest and most ostentatious of all the late medieval courts. (Oddly enough, no major manuscript or cook seems to be directly associated with fifteenth-century Burgundy. By the time Gaston de Foix gave his banquet for the Hungarians, the Burgundian court was staging feasts on a scale and with an innovative magnificence that set the pace for the rest of Europe. It may be, of course, that the absence of a Burgundian master chef and book of recipes reflects the fact that the focus was not actually on the food and how it tasted but what it looked like.)

Medieval food historians have argued that these cookery books, which incorporate so many earlier recipes now being written down for the first time, make clear how much of the medieval attitude towards food was based upon ancient theories of a healthy diet. These stemmed from Greco-Roman ideas about physiology and the effect of the four humours upon the body. The aim was to correct, through diet, any imbalance in the humours (sanguine, warm and moist; choleric, warm and dry; phlegmatic, cold and moist; and melancholic, cold and dry). Every person was believed to have a predisposition towards one or other of the humours, but its malign effects could be reduced by the consumption of the appropriate food. Not for nothing did a convocation of six doctors stand beside the duke of Burgundy at table advising him what to eat.

But the humoral factor was more complicated than simply choosing what to eat. Each type of food was itself categorised according to its humoral quality and had to be brought into balance by means of the cooking method employed. This explains why beef (moist) was roasted (dry) or why fish (cool and moist) was generally fried. The endless chopping, grinding, sieving, straining and filtering were all processes designed to rectify humoral imbalances (as well, probably, as providing soft food for those whose teeth were in a poor state). Sauces provided another means. A camelin sauce based on cinnamon and vinegar brought a warming and drying effect to moist baked salmon or trout. A green sauce, whose principal ingredient was parsley (warm and dry), was regarded as appropriate for a cold and moist pike or turbot. Humoral considerations also played a part in deciding which foods were suitable for a given season of the year. Moist foods like cucumbers or marrows were, for example, viewed as the right thing to eat during summer, which is hot and dry. Always most important was to match the elemental qualities of the food with the humoral disposition of the consumer.[7]

These cookery manuscripts, along with the surviving menus, provide us with the first clear idea of the range of the medieval diet.[8] Not, it must added, quite the full range; vegetables and fruit appear only if they are cooked. Meat, of course, was central – this category embraced pork, veal, lamb and beef, as well as game like venison and boar. Occasionally meat was simply roasted or boiled, carved into pieces and served, but more often it was cooked in a complex mixture of wine, vinegar and mustard along with spices and herbs, making use of egg yolks, breadcrumbs and liver as thickeners. Birds included not only poultry such as chickens, geese, ducks and pigeons but gamebirds – swans, cormorants, herons, pheasants, bustards, peacocks and plovers. Chicken came every possible way – roasted, stuffed or made into pâtés. The *hétoudeau*, a year-old chicken, was roasted and served with the famous *sauce jaune* made of ground almonds, ginger, wine and milk thickened with bread. That sauce could also accompany roasted goose or gosling; so too could *sauce poivre noire* based on pepper, ginger, roasted breadcrumbs, vinegar or verjuice. Pheasants and partridges were usually baked and then hashed, with the resulting *bouillon* thickened with breadcrumbs or grated cheese plus a last-minute addition of beaten egg perfumed with white ginger crushed in verjuice. The litany of small birds sacrificed to the table is unending: larks, quails, sparrows, blackbirds, starlings, thrushes and more. Nothing escaped.[9]

Fish, essential because of the large number of days of abstinence laid down by the Church calendar, might be fresh from the sea or river or dried, smoked and salted. Freshwater fish were generally cooked in a *court bouillon*, although perch could be roasted. Sauces again were varied and precise. Lamprey, for example, was served with a sauce made from the blood of the fish, spices, verjuice and burnt bread.[10]

Apart from the ubiquitous roasts, the dishes for which recipes are given fall into a number of set types.[11] There was the universal White Dish, *blanc mangier*, which began its life with chicken, rice starch and sugar (and occasionally almond milk) and which may originally not have been white (*blanc*) at all but *blant* (bland) *mangier*. There was a whole range of egg dishes, boiled and baked or made into omelettes. There were the *brouets* and *civets*, pottages in which either meat or fish was the principal ingredient, and the various sops, broth in which the diner dunked his bread. Pies of all kinds were also universal and filled with every sort of filling. So too were meat pâtés. Galantines and jellies, in which pieces of meat or fish were embedded, were hugely popular set pieces. So also were dough or batter *crêpes* or *crespelli*, not to mention the endless varieties of wafers or biscuits which accompanied the spiced wine ending any major meal.

When it came to drink, wine was universal, as only spring water was deemed safe. Although its general availability may sound democratic, wine had its own hierarchy of quality descending to vinegar. From the fall of the Roman Empire, French wines dominated the European market. By the fourteenth century those from Bordeaux and Burgundy were seen as the best, *de rigueur* on every aristocratic and rich bourgeois table. They included white, *clairet* (actually light red or pink) and red wines, all of which were drunk young and which had a low alcohol content. Italians drank their own regional wines. There was no notion that wine should be chosen to match particular foods. Instead it served to reinforce the class structure, the choice reflecting the social standing, constitution and occupation of the drinker. This cast the white and *clairet* wines as appropriate for the brainier upper classes, with red fit for labourers.

Cologne and Bruges were the axes of the German wine trade until Antwerp took over at the close of the fifteenth century. England remained the market for the wines of Bordeaux. The wine business was already highly complex, with pricing dependent greatly on quality. Beer, ale and cider were favourites in northern Europe. And, among the upper classes, there was an ever-growing taste for the sweet wines of Greece as well as those imported from Crete, Tyre and Cyprus. The Cyprus wines were expensive, but cheaper sweet wines were made from the Malvasia grapes grown in southern Italy, Sicily and Sardinia. There was also a taste for spiced wines. The famous hippocras, usually a red wine, was sweetened with honey or sugar, strongly spiced, and consumed with various kinds of wafer.[12]

So remarkably intensive has been the study of medieval food and cookery in the last twenty years that it is now possible to trace the history and evolution of particular dishes. To take a single example, look at the dish of Arab origin called 'mawmene'. It is first recorded in the twelfth century in an Anglo-Norman version, when it consisted of boiled beef or mutton with some fried onions in a sauce of wine-based almond milk thickened with ground capon seasoned with cloves and a little sugar.

Three centuries later it had evolved into something quite different – shredded poultry in a sauce of ground raisins seasoned with several spices, sweetened with dates and sugar and garnished with sugar candy.[13] Such opportunity for detailed analysis of recipes means that we can for the first time chart shifts in taste and fashion in late medieval food. What were those shifts?

The principal one was to greater complexity. The existence of recipe books in itself reflects the fact that cooking was becoming so sophisticated that it called for written transmission. The enormous elaboration in cuisine recorded in recipe collections is an index both of an increasing interest in food as an important aspect of court culture and of the arrival of a new class of *nouveaux riches* who regarded the arts of the table as one aspect of a new art of living. That Charles V and Charles VI of France had more cooks than Louis XIV three centuries later, forty-eight in all, illustrates how much food meant to the medieval court.[14] Recipes reveal three tastes as fundamental to the medieval palate: 'forte', which depended on the use of spices; sweet, reflecting the ever-escalating use of sugar; and sour, a penchant for sharpness and a tang in food. The latter was attained in the north of Europe by the addition of vinegar or verjuice and in the south by lemons. The *Viandier* deploys a sour element in 70 per cent of its recipes and the same element combined with spices in 50 per cent. This reveals the strong predilection of the French for piquant food, for in addition they made a great use of ginger. In contrast the Italian and English preference was for the bitter-sweet, or the just plain sweet.

Late medieval cuisine also incorporated considerable regional variations. These developed not only through the use of local ingredients but as a result of influences from neighbouring countries.[15] The French and the Italians, for example, depended on olive oil, while the Germans cooked with poppy oil; local production decided the matter. Dairy products were another sharp divide. The butter region bordered the North Sea and the Channel running from Normandy to Denmark. Not until the fifteenth century did the use of butter begin to spread south, first from Flanders into France and then, thanks to the Angevin kings of Naples, to Italian cuisine. In addition there were regional variations in cooking technique. This is caught in a passage in Hall's *Chronicle* where he describes Francis I supping with Henry VIII at the Field of the Cloth of Gold in

1520: 'The French King was served iii courses, and his meat dressed after the French fashion, and the King of England had the like after the English fashion . . .'[16]

The full impact of Arab cuisine, which came north via Sicily and Christian Spain and also by way of the crusades, still remains little understood. That cuisine had its own multiple traditions. The only thing certain is that Arab influences from Catalonia were already reaching southern Italy by the early fourteenth century, and moving northwards into the peninsula with major consequences. The effect can already be traced in the recipes of the man billed as the first Renaissance cook, Maestro Martino, in Rome in the 1450s (to whom we will come in the next chapter). More profound was the impact further south on the cuisine of the Neapolitan court, for there the synthesis of Catalan and medieval Italian traditions was to give birth to Renaissance gastronomy.[17]

To these culinary currents moving across Europe we must add major developments in technique. Master Martino can be associated with two of the most significant advances: the clarification of jelly through the use of beaten egg whites, which improved the appearance of what was always deemed a prestigious dish; and the development of edible shortcrust pastry. Up until then pastry was merely a container in which food was cooked, and not intended to be eaten. The arrival of shortcrust pastry made possible the whole range of *tourtes* and *tortes* that was to be the pinnacle of culinary sophistication in the sixteenth century.[18]

Another noticeable change took place in the use of spices. Pepper, the commonest and most widely used spice until the fifteenth century, gave way to the more costly 'grains of paradise' (malaguetta pepper), a far more exotic condiment, which was adopted enthusiastically by the upper classes.[19] To that we must add the growing taste for sugar. Until the close of the fourteenth century, sugar had been used in the main medicinally and only sparingly in cooking, more as a spice than as an ingredient. Because it had to be imported from the East and the south of Spain it was expensive, but the taste for it took a firm hold in Italy, England and the Netherlands, and gradually permeated French cooking during the fifteenth century. The fashion for sugar in food echoed the fashion for sweet wines in drink, leading to a large market for malmsey.[20]

Even more striking than any of this was the desire to endow food with form and colour. Suddenly what was eaten was called upon to assume a shape that would not only flatter the status of the eater but affirm it. Cooks set out to transform the food they cooked into a mirror of all that was most admired in late medieval society, converting it by means of shape, colour and pattern into a vision of superabundant riches, beauty and nobility. That aspiration is enshrined in the *Ménagier*. Whenever it refers to a dish as being 'bonne' or 'belle' it refers not to its taste but to its appearance. We are witnessing here one of the great revolutions in food history: where the physical side of eating is being displaced by the aesthetic pleasure of looking. In a phrase, emphasis has migrated from the mouth to the eyes.[21]

Colour makes a spectacular entrance.[22] In the earliest version of the *Viandier*, dating from about 1300, there are forty references to colour, among them fourteen to shades of yellow, four to white, two to green and three to gold. The early fifteenth-century version in the Vatican library, in sharp contrast, has no fewer than ninety-seven references to colour, including twenty-two to gold alone. Yellow was to be the most favoured colour in the fourteenth century, gold in the one which followed, both reflecting the same quest. This was food as an indicator of social status, for according to sumptuary legislation the use of gold was reserved for the upper classes. Gold was equally the colour of paradise reflected by its use in every aspect of Gothic religious art. By the fourteenth century green came next in popularity and third – more surprisingly – brown or russet, a colour associated with the peasantry (and symbolically with duplicity). Yellow was derived from saffron or egg yolks, green from herbs like parsley or sorrel or from vine buds or gooseberries. Uniquely the English had a passion for red, extracted from sandalwood, which they paired with yellow, combining at table the two dominant colours in late medieval heraldry. The deployment of colour in food can be traced to Arab cookery, where its origins lay in medical and alchemical lore. According to Arab medical lore, gold prolonged life; it was therefore regarded as desirable to eat gold itself or its nearest visual equivalent, yellow saffron. Red and white were connected with cinnabar, mercury sulphide, and mercury. These incidentally had alchemical associations, cinnabar serving as the starting material in the alchemist's quest for gold.

Mercury was first extracted from cinnabar, and then, with the help of sulphur, transmuted into gold – at least theoretically.

Indeed, late medieval cooking overall had, as has been noted, strong links with astral and alchemical medicine, which itself was derived from Arab sources. The cordials which were its principal focus employed an extraordinary variety of unusual and often expensive ingredients to strengthen the heart and avert Saturnian melancholy, among other bodily ills. Similarly, consuming coloured or sweetly fragrant foods had medicinal value. Colouring food yellow made it 'noble' like gold, and the diner eating it might hope to avoid physical decay just as if he were eating actual gold. Gilded and golden food remained a medieval obsession, for reasons of health and to attract the right astral influence on such great occasions as a wedding banquet.

Gaston de Foix's golden course for the Hungarian embassy was thus hardly a solitary manifestation. On 15 June 1368, for example, Galeazzo II Visconti staged a dinner on the occasion of the marriage of his daughter, Violante. It opened with two gilded sucking-pigs spitting fire and went on to include gilded hares, a gilded calf and a gilded carp.[23] Henry VI's coronation banquet in 1429 featured a 'Viaunde royal' decorated with golden lozenges, a 'Custard royal' with a golden leopard sitting on it, boars' heads in castles of gold and a baked meat fashioned in the form of a shield quartered red and white and set with gilt lozenges. The second course included 'A white leche planted [sic] with a red antelope; a crown about its neck, with a chain of gold; flampane powdered [decorated] with leopards and fleur de lys of gold. A fritter garnished with a leopard's head, and iii ostrich feathers.' How these dishes must have glistened and glittered on the table in the torch and candlelight.[24]

Such dishes point up the other significant shift, the move to figurative food. Gaston de Foix's banquet ended with an array of heraldic birds and beasts sculpted in sugar. As we shall see, that form of food soon develops into the sweet course, but everywhere as the fifteenth century proceeds representational food multiplies. By the opening of the following century it has come to dominate the banquet. Just how all-pervasive an obsession it was can be seen from George Cavendish's unforgettable account of the feast staged by Cardinal Wolsey in October 1527 for the French ambassadors at Hampton Court:

Anon came up the second course, with so many dishes, subtleties and curious devices, which were above a hundred in number, of so goodly proportion and costly, that I suppose the Frenchmen never saw the like. The wonder was no less than it was worthy indeed. There were castles with images in the same; Paul's church and steeple . . . There were beasts, birds, fowls of divers kinds, and personages, most lively made and counterfeit in dishes; some fighting, as it were with swords, some with guns and crossbows, some vaulting and leaping, some dancing with ladies, some in complete harness, jousting with spears, and with many more devices than I am able with my wit to describe.[25]

Yet by then figurative food was but one aspect of an all-pervasive drive towards ostentation and elaboration in everything connected with the table.

The triumph of conspicuous consumption[26]

THE FRENCH COURT at the close of the fourteenth century employed between seven and eight hundred people in the task of feeding members of its vast household.[27] During the same period Richard II fed some thousand people a day with a kitchen staff of three hundred.[28] Princely households could almost rival royal ones in terms of numbers. The duc de Guyenne, for instance, fed two hundred and fifty a day. The ordinances of Edward IV from the 1470s give the figures for the number of mouths demanding to be fed in a range of households: about two hundred and fifty for a duke, two hundred for an earl, seventy for a baron and twenty-three for a knight. Against this we have actual figures – two hundred and ninety-nine for the duke of Clarence in 1468 but only a hundred for the duke of Norfolk fifteen years later.[29] Catering every day on such a scale called for what was almost a small army to secure sufficient supplies of food and drink, not to mention the cooking and serving of it.

What this entailed for the various household departments is vividly captured in accounts of great feasts, although it must be borne in mind that such feasts were exceptional events. Chiquart, the Savoyard master cook, gives the astonishing quantities required for a two-day feast held in about 1420. For each day he required a hundred fat oxen, one hundred and thirty sheep, one hundred and twenty pigs, two hundred piglets, sixty fat pigs (for larding purposes), two hundred kids and lambs, one hundred calves and two thousand poultry. These were all supplied locally. When it came to game, four hundred horses were needed to transport it from across the ducal domains. Six thousand eggs a day were used. The orders for ginger, grains of paradise, cinnamon and pepper were huge. Even in the case of the so-called lesser spices it was bulk ordering: six pounds alike of nutmegs, cloves and mace and a gargantuan twenty-five pounds of saffron. Fully reflecting the century's obsession with gilding everything, in addition to the saffron Chiquart demanded eighteen pounds of gold leaf. Three thousand six hundred pounds of flour and cheese were used, not to mention two hundred boxes of glazed almonds (*dragées*) for garnishing. The kitchen equipment required ranged from two great kettles and oven shovels to a thousand cartloads of wood and a barn full of coal. No fewer than four thousand dishes in gold, silver, pewter and wood had to be requisitioned in which to serve everything.[30]

Accounts of this kind tend to leave the reader with a sense of numerical fatigue. Nevertheless they are necessary to an understanding of the scale and grandiosity of such displays. Moving back in time to the coronation feast of Pope Clement VI at Avignon on 19 May 1344, the figures are just as daunting. This time they included eighty *saumées* (each of five hundred loaves) of bread, a hundred and eighteen cows, one thousand and twenty-three sheep, one hundred and one calves, nine hundred and fourteen kids, sixty pigs, sixty-eight barrels of lard and salted meat, fifteen sturgeon, three hundred pike, fifteen hundred capons, three thousand and forty-three fowls (*poulets*), seven thousand four hundred and twenty-eight chickens, one thousand four hundred and forty-six geese and fifty thousand tarts using three thousand two hundred and fifty eggs. For the same event three hundred jugs, five thousand five hundred pitchers, two thousand five hundred glass flagons, five thousand glasses and two thousand six hundred *écuelles* (drinking bowls) were hired. And in addition the pope co-opted all the cardinals' cooks and eighty boys to fetch water and serve.[31]

Chiquart's feast called for a lead time of six weeks. This was of course an exceptional event, but even on ordinary days the supply and cooking of food was a major preoccupation of any great household. Every large establishment had departments dedicated to the making or acquisition of bread and the supply and care of tableware and related textiles (the Pantry), the purchasing, supply and serving of wine, beer, ale and other drink (the Butlery or Buttery), the acquisition, preparation and cooking of food (the Kitchen). These, in turn, needed the support of other household departments such as the stables in the case of transport or the cellar for storage. In the grandest households the numbers could be substantial. The officials who headed the Buttery and Kitchen at the Burgundian court, for instance, each had fifty assistants, while the fifty attached to the Pantry – headed by the Chief Pantler – included a saucier, eight valet bakers, two hall ushers, a bread-bearer, a waferer, a linen-keeper and a launderer.[32]

All of this household machinery had to be in working order before serving could take place. And that daily act in any palace or great house called for a whole department of its own. Give or take a little, the procedure was the same or very similar throughout Europe. As we have just encountered Cardinal Wolsey's gastronomic plenitude we might begin our exploration of consumption itself with George Cavendish's account of dining in the cardinal's household.

Now to speak of the ordering of his household and offices, I think it necessary here to be remembered; first you shall understand that he had in his hall, daily three special tables furnished with three principal officers. That is to say, a Steward, who was always a doctor or a priest; a Treasurer, a knight; and a Comptroller, an esquire; these always carried their white staves within his house. Then had he a cofferer, three marshals, two yeomen ushers, two grooms, and an almoner. He had also in the hall-kitchen two clerks of his kitchen, a clerk-controller, a surveyor of the dresser, a clerk of his spicery. Also in his hall-kitchen he had two master cooks, and twelve other labourers and children, as they called them; a yeoman of his scullery, with two others in his silver scullery; two yeomen of his pantry, and two grooms.

Now in his private kitchen he had a master cook who went daily in damask, satin, or velvet, with a chain of gold about his neck; and two grooms with six labourers and children to serve that place; in the Larder there, a yeoman and a groom; in the Scalding-house, a yeoman and two grooms; in the Scullery there, two persons; in the Buttery, two yeomen and two grooms with two other pages; in the Pantry, two yeomen, two grooms, and two pages; and in the Ewery [the department concerned with supplying water for washing] likewise; in the Cellar, three yeomen, two grooms, and two pages – beside a gentleman for the month; in the Chaundery [the department responsible for supplying candles], three persons; in the Wafery [where cakes and biscuits were made], two . . .

And in his chamber, all these persons; that is to say, his High Chamberlain; his Vice-Chamberlain; twelve gentlemen-ushers, daily waiters – besides two in his private chamber; and of gentlemen-waiters in his private chamber he had six; and also he had of lords nine or ten . . . Then had he of gentlemen, as cupbearers, carvers, sewers [those responsible for arranging seating and serving], and gentlemen daily-waiters, forty persons; of yeomen ushers he had six; of grooms in his chamber he had eight; of yeomen of his chamber he had forty-six daily to attend upon his person; he also had a priest there, who was his almoner, to attend upon his table at dinner . . .[33]

Cavendish is describing the arrangements during the first and second decade of the sixteenth century. They record a late medieval household system, but one supplemented by functions resulting from the new division between the hall and the chamber. Wolsey himself ate in his own chamber, and that now called not only for its own staff but its own kitchen.

The Boke of Curtaysye, written about 1460, describes more fully the operating spheres of the various officers connected with the service of food at table. At the summit of the pyramid in the majority of households came the marshal, to whom all others were answerable and who was in charge of placing the diners. This demanded a person with an encyclopedic knowledge of precedence. Beneath the marshal came the usher; his task was to order the grooms to set up and dismantle the trestle tables, chairs and benches for each meal. The usher was usually in charge of the wardrobe and hence would have access to any tapestries to be hung on the walls, a task that fell to the grooms. The steward's role was to consult with the kitchen staff on the menus. It was he, followed by the sewers, who headed the procession bearing each course into the hall. (In some houses it was the marshal who headed this procession, which could in grand instances include squires and sergeants-at-arms.) The sewers' job was to arrange the dishes on the table, seeing that each group of two or three persons had the serving which was their due. In some instances it was the sewers who also put up and took down the trestles. The role of the almoner was a fixed one: to preside over the alms dish and to deliver, after the meal was over, any surplus food to the poor.[34]

What seems obvious is that the tasks to be done were all alike, but who did them and the degree of elaboration with which they were done varied according to the household and its wealth. Yet whatever the variations, the general drift is clear: as the fourteenth century drew to its close, among the upper classes everything to do with eating was increasingly ritualised. That we know so much about it reflects the fact that it had to be written down, because it was so complicated. More and more people needed – and wanted – to learn the 'right' way of doing things. Their interest was manifested in a burgeoning literature both in the form of household regulations and in books of instruction. These began to proliferate during the fifteenth century, and one example is Olivier de La Marche's account of the etiquette of the Burgundian court under Charles the Bold. It embodies an extreme of elaboration at one end of the spectrum. Hugh Rhodes's *The Boke of Nurture*, written in the reign of Edward IV, on the other hand, describes practice in the house of an ordinary knight or gentleman. We will look at both to catch the flavour of late medieval food ritual.

At the Burgundian court, every meal became a spectacle whose resemblance at times to the liturgy of the mass cannot have been coincidental (much other late medieval secular ceremonial – for example the canopy placed over a royal or princely person – owed its origin to ecclesiastical ritual). In any case there is a ritual stateliness. The opening sequence is sufficient to suggest vividly what the whole procedure must have been like. It began with the entry of a parade headed by the hall usher. He was followed by the pantler bearing the great nef or salt, who was in turn followed by the hall porter. The latter directed the pantler where to place

the nef on the ducal table. The chosen position was deliberately to one side so as not to hide the duke from onlookers, because the sight of his dining had developed into a public event fit to be witnessed by ambassadors and other dignitaries. Then came the first of innumerable assays to test for poison. The pantler gave the porter some of the salt to taste, after which he set the duke's personal salt in place and filled it. A unicorn's horn had already been employed to check the safety of the table-cloths and the rich tapestry covering the bench on which the duke sat. At this point a serving valet carried the piece of unicorn's horn, which was in a small vessel, to the porter at the hall buffet. The porter poured water into a basin over the horn and then over his own hands. The towel with which the duke was to dry his hands was likewise cleared: the pantry porter kissed it and gave it to the pantler, who arranged it over his left shoulder so that a section of it touched his skin and demonstrated that it was uncontaminated. He then draped it over a dish containing the unicorn's horn used to assay any drink for poison. When the time came for the duke to dry his hands, the pantler passed the towel to the first master of the household, who then passed it to the first chamberlain, who passed it in his turn to someone of higher rank who finally gave it to the duke! And all of this was but a preliminary foray before the duke had even reached the table. What followed was a multiplication of such rituals extending over the entire meal and beyond. Little wonder that those who looked on were overawed. That was precisely the effect that the display was calculated to achieve.[35] The dukes of Burgundy were, after all, aspirants in search of a crown.

Rhodes's *The Boke of Nurture* is far more prosaic. What he describes is not inflated court etiquette but the routine of a household in the English shires. He opens by saying that in the houses of some knights and gentlemen the butler and the pantler could be the same person. Here the

Opposite: Feasting at the Burgundian court.
The L-shaped table preserves the place of honour for the bride at the extreme left and guests include recognisable members of the ducal family.
The humble bread trencher has graduated here to one of silver decorated bands of silver-gilt.
Detail from a painting of the Wedding at Cana, *c.* 1500.

pantler's task was to check that the bread was 'chopped and squared' for trenchers (which were to serve as edible 'plates') and that the napery was clean. He then prepared the hall cupboard for the lord's ablutions by putting a cloth upon it and laying in order a basin, ewer and towel. Next he laid the high table with salt, bread and trenchers, making sure that everyone who sat there had a napkin and a spoon. These opening sequences are practical and matter-of-fact, far removed from the choreography of the Burgundian court. One senses that much the same kind of thing had gone on for a century or more before. Evidently there were infinite gradations stretching up and down the social hierarchy that affected how a meal was actually served. Yet procedures were of central importance and the grander the personage the more likely it was that even the most mundane of actions would be ritualised.[36]

There is, however, one significant difference between these two accounts. In the case of the duke of Burgundy the description is of a meal served to him alone in the presence of onlookers. Wolsey too ate on his own or with a few honoured guests at most. Rhodes describes, on the contrary, a meal consumed by the whole household, as had been the practice earlier in the Middle Ages. The taste for greater privacy became pronounced by the close of the fourteenth century and is captured in an oft-quoted passage of Langland's *Vision of Piers Plowman*, written about 1362:

> Wretched is the hall . . . each day in the week
> There the lord and lady liketh not to sit.
> Now have the rich a rule to eat by themselves
> In a privy parlour . . . for poor men's sake,
> Or in a chamber with a chimney, and leave the chief hall
> That was made for meals, for men to eat in.[37]

Increasingly, royalty and great lords ate in public only on certain occasions – great feast days of the Church, for example, or banquets marking a marriage or a visiting embassy, like that of the Hungarians to France in 1457. In France this development shows in the multiplication of private rooms. The first of these, called the *chambre de parement*, contained a richly decorated but non-functional state bed, a symbol of rank. It was there that the lord often ate, rather than in the *grande salle*.[38]

Great feasts often demanded that tables proliferate into other rooms, again reinforcing little by little what was a drift towards separation. When George Neville was enthroned as archbishop of York in 1467, the two thousand five hundred guests were spread through the great hall, out into the great chamber and into the gallery.[39] The decision as to where each person sat was governed strictly by his or her position in the social hierarchy. Indeed the migration of the grandest to separate rooms to eat is less evidence of a desire for privacy than a ploy to reinforce rank during a period when the upper classes felt threatened both by the newly ennobled and the rich bourgeoisie. Royalty and great aristocrats gradually reduced their eating in public so that when it did occur it was a major epiphany to be contemplated with awe by lesser mortals. By retreating from view they acted in line with the old adage that familiarity bred contempt.

We can see the change, for instance, in the complicated arrangements made between the French and English at the Field of the Cloth of Gold in 1520. At the first exchange of feasts between the two courts, Henry VIII went to the castle of Ardres, where he was seated with the French queen and queen mother, the king's sister, the duchess of Alençon, and the duchess of Vendôme along one side of a table. In a second room the 'princes' of England were feasted by the duke of Alençon, while in another far larger one, where music and dancing were to take place later, there was a public banquet. Meanwhile, Francis I was dining in the temporary palace erected by the English at Guisnes. He sat opposite the English queen while Cardinal Wolsey and Henry VIII's sister, Mary, duchess of Suffolk, sat at the ends of the table. In the hall twenty gentlemen waited on a hundred and thirty ladies, and in another hall in the town of Guisnes itself, two hundred gentlemen were feasted.[40] In all of these arrangements the principal concern was the visual enactment of hierarchy through acts of separation.

The temporary palace erected by the English in 1520 is a reminder of another development, the creation of elaborate temporary decor for great banquets. This could take the form either of a *mise-en-scène* superimposed on to an existing hall or the construction of a special room for the occasion. When Philip the Good married Isabella of Portugal in 1430, the courtyard was transformed into a banqueting hall complete with a minstrels' gallery for sixty, a stag and a unicorn spouting rosewater and hippocras, and golden trees supporting the arms of the lands over which the duke ruled.[41] Almost four decades later, in 1468, this arrangement was repeated when Charles the Bold married Margaret of York, but with the addition of a gallery from which the ladies could observe the feast. The ceiling was of blue silk, the walls appropriately hung with the story of Gideon and the fleece, and both behind and above the high table there was a rich length of grey cloth of gold embroidered with the ducal arms.[42]

The adornment of the containing walls provided a backcloth on which to embroider a further, even richer display. The fourteenth century saw the emergence of *dressoirs de parement* – buffets intended purely for the display of plate. They had already become an established feature in France by the second quarter of the century.[43] This cupboard, which had started life with the simple purpose of serving as a place where beverages could be kept in large pitchers, food deposited before it went to the table or utensils usefully stacked, began to assume a life of its own. In less grand households, the buffet of course continued to be functional. *Le Ménagier de Paris* recommends that the 'escuiers' should stand by the *dessouer de sale* in order to give out and take back spoons, hanaps (fancy goblets) and other plate. At the same time they should pour out and serve the wine from it. But in the palace the dresser had already become something very different, basically a vehicle for the display of plate. At the banquet that Charles V gave for Emperor Charles IV in 1378, there were no fewer than three dressers laden with plate. Each one had a barrier around it and a guard to protect the display. In the next century this trend towards dazzling display was unremitting. At the 1429 Burgundian wedding there was a dresser on either side of the room, each twenty feet long, with five tiers of plate.[44] For the 1468 wedding the buffet was in the form of a lozenge rising in tiers, the lower shelves banked with large pieces of gold and silver plate, gradually ascending upwards and culminating in smaller items studded with precious stones. The guests feasted off silver, not one piece of which came from the buffet.[45]

The Burgundian court codified the system of display, specifying exactly how many tiers of plate persons of each rank were allowed to show. A sovereign or his consort was permitted five, a prince four, a countess three, the wife of a banneret two or one, and those devoid of title had no right to even a single 'gradin'.[46] The rules in England, if they existed, must have been different, because Henry VIII had eight and Cardinal Wolsey six. Indeed Wolsey's flashy display of plate for the French ambassadors in 1518 prompted tart comment from the Venetian ambassador, who remarked that it would have been more appropriate for a banquet given 'either by Cleopatra or Caligula; the whole banqueting hall being so decorated with huge vases of gold and silver, that I fancied myself in the tower of Chosroes, where that great monarch caused divine honours to be paid him'.[47]

Such a display can be compared to exhibiting one's bank balance in public, for plate of this kind was the first to be melted down in time of financial need. Nor did the obsession with plate end with the *dressoir*. The fourteenth and fifteenth centuries witnessed the rebirth of secular plate on a large scale in the West for the first time since the collapse of the Roman Empire.[48] The contrast with the austerity of the table could hardly have been more striking; it remained a simple affair of boards glued together and resting on trestles. It was narrow, for guests generally sat only along one side, being served from the other. When a table was erected in a lord's chamber it was often, as in the famous illumination for January in the *Très Riches Heures* showing the duc de Berri dining, placed in front of a fire-place for warmth with a screen protecting the diner from too direct heat. In the hall the arrangement remained the old one of a high table on an elevated dais, with two others at right angles to it forming a horseshoe shape framing an arena. As was customary earlier, the table could be dressed with as many as three cloths.

The Hungarian banquet was served on hundreds of silver dishes, forty a course for each table, a quantity unthinkable in the early Middle Ages but an accurate mirror of the huge expansion of regal and aristocratic collections of plate for the table by that date. Already by 1364 Louis d'Anjou, king of Naples and Jerusalem, had a thousand pieces, nine-tenths of which were new. Charles V of France had two thousand five hundred pieces, including ten golden cups set with precious stones. At the same period a number of rich Parisian bourgeois also boasted large collections, proving that Philippe le Bel's sumptuary decree of 1294 – which laid down that those whose income was less than six thousand *livres tournois* 'may not use, within their dwelling or without, vessels of gold or silver either to drink or eat' – had been ineffective.[49] Inventories reveal that by far the largest number of items were drinking vessels, hanaps or standing cups. The latter were recognised as status symbols, and might well be made of speckled and grained mazer (maple gall) wood with the addition of silver or silver-gilt mounts. These were used on great occasions, whereas short and squat goblets were used for ordinary dining. Of all the drinking vessels the most spectacular survival is the Royal Gold Cup, embellished in enamel with the story of St Agnes and her foster-sister, St Emerentiana. Recorded in an inventory dated 1391 of the plate of Charles VI, it is far too heavy to have served any but ceremonial purposes.[50]

By the close of the thirteenth century other items of plate appeared – the *pot à vin* and the *pot à eau*, which stood either on the table or the dresser. Gradually such vessels came to be made of either silver or gold, particularly in the case of the one known as a *temprier* (i.e. temperance). In fact, for those who could afford it, many table items previously of earthenware or wood made the transition to precious metal. By the fifteenth century the universal bread trencher began to be made of gold and silver for royal or princely tables. With this item we are within reach of the dinner plate. Even the egg cup existed as early as 1363, when the inventory of Charles V, then still duke of Normandy, recorded 'a little vessel of silver for eating eggs'. By 1403 these pieces had acquired lids to keep the eggs warm.[51]

Late medieval plate was a riot of imagery, much of it droll and witty, designed to amuse as much as to instruct: birds and beasts, figures from romance and legend, rustics and sirens, flowers and heraldry as well as the whole gamut of Christian symbolism. Use was made of jasper, chalcedony, glass and crystal as well as exotic shells, nuts and ostrich eggs, all embellished with gold, silver, enamelling and precious stones.

On the mainland of Europe the most important of all these new pieces was the nef.[52] This was a container associated only with kings, cardinals and great lords. As with the trend towards separate dining, its appearance reinforces the new emphasis on hierarchical gradation, for at table it was always placed in the immediate vicinity of its owner. The form of the nef (whose name, like the word nave, comes from the French for 'ship') was owed to the incense boat. It was often used only for display purposes, but sometimes it carried necessary tableware. Charles V's contained his serpent's tongue (used for detecting poison), a spoon, a little knife and – a great rarity – a little fork. Sometimes the newfangled metal trenchers were kept in it and in 1484, at the coronation feast of Charles VIII, the nef contained napkins. A century earlier, in 1395, Louis d'Orléans's golden nef is recorded as having a tableau of the Annunciation on the fo'c's'le and poop, with the twelve apostles around the deck and the four Evangelists on the bridge. A sail bore a cross of blue enamelled with golden fleurs de lys and surrounded by eight angels, while God the Father hovered above. In the jewel-besprinkled waters surrounding the ship there were two more figures of God the Father together, somewhat unaccountably, with eight of Adam and Eve as well as the pope and the emperor! Nefs were widespread, not only in France but in Spain, Germany, Italy and the Low Countries. Survivals – like the nef belonging to Anne of Brittany, which was given by Henry II to Rheims to convert into a reliquary – are nevertheless rare.

In England, the role played by the nef on the Continent was taken by the great salt.[53] These too were vehicles of costly fantasy, but they rarely used maritime imagery (although Edward II is supposed to have had a salt like a ship on four wheels). One of Richard II's salts was in the form of a crowned falcon wearing a collar of 's' shapes and another represented a dragon issuing from a whelk shell. Henry VI possessed one shaped like a castle with salt containers in each of its four towers. Another came in the form of a man wearing a kendal hood. These were grand salts, attributes of sovereignty and rank, table markers indicating that the person seated here was at the apex of the dining hierarchy. That these grand salts were actually used very much is doubtful, because smaller and more obviously practical salts of gold and silver multiplied. Piers Gaveston, Edward II's notorious favourite, had no fewer than thirty in his luggage when he was captured in 1313.

Ironically it was not the salt that was destined to be the greatest of all the display pieces but the table fountain.[54] These were not only *chefs d'oeuvre* of the goldsmith's craft but items of extreme ingenuity, involving the movement of liquids, wine or perfumed waters, which spurted or spouted and whose pressure caused figures to move or bells to jingle. We know that they already existed in the thirteenth century, and they begin turning up in inventories during the fourteenth. In 1311 Louis, count of Flanders, already had several. So did Queen Jean de Bourgoyne. She died in 1348, bequeathing a number of fountains, including one 'in the guise of a castle, with pillars of masonry, with men-at-arms around . . .' Seventeen years later Louis of Anjou also had a castle fountain, this time a Château d'Amour resting on the shoulders of twelve little men. The fortress itself was assailed by six knights and defended by ladies who manned the battlements, while minstrels trumpeted above the gates. The surviving example in the museum at Cleveland (Ohio), despite its missing basin and foot, gives some impression of the magnificence of these pieces, whose sole purpose was to amaze. In this example, eight columns support a crenellated tier bearing gargoyles, on which stand four nude men holding balls decked with bells and jets. Above, on a second tier, two dragons propel a bell-decked wheel, while at the summit there is a gathering of recumbent dragons and lions. Although scholars argue as to when exactly in the fourteenth century this extraordinary aristocratic toy was made, there can be no doubt about its impressiveness at a banquet, spurting and tinkling away.

Such a tour de force epitomises the new extremes of sophisticated luxury stratifying the classes, for even quite far down the social scale the table became crowded with artefacts as never before. At lower levels vessels would be of pewter, copper, iron or wood. But increasingly, anyone with pretensions to status would have had a few silver spoons or a hanap. Nor is it only in metalwork that standing could be displayed, for as ceramic production in Europe took off in the thirteenth century vessels *de luxe* emerged for the first time, pieces worthy to be exhibited on the buffet.[55] As in the case of plate, new forms emerged in response to the increasing elaboration of eating. Glazes came to reflect not only regional variations but also function. In Franche-Comté or the Nord-de Pas-de-Calais, for instance, grey was for the kitchen, red or white for the table. But earthenware was to fall from favour as the brilliantly coloured *faience*, which was originally of Spanish origin, took over after 1450. These were *de luxe* pieces for exhibition rather than use. Drinking vessels and flagons of course went on being made of glass. At the bottom of the social pyramid the peasantry found that turned wood provided all they needed in the way of plates, bowls, spoons and knives. Even these, however, often represented an advance on what they had used before.

Together all these artefacts add up to a consumer revolution, one aimed at defining a diner's position on the ladder of society. This was true even in the case of royalty. When Francis I was first feasted at the Field of the Cloth of Gold he was, significantly, served on gold plate. Katharine of Aragon and the duchess of Suffolk – the English king's wife and sister – along with Cardinal Wolsey, had to make do with silver gilt.[56] A fine distinction it may seem to modern eyes, but not to those present.

Manners maketh man[57]

THE FEAST was to increase in importance during the two centuries before 1500, its role as an ideal image of society heightened by the ever more elaborate ceremonial enveloping it. In late medieval chivalrous romances the feast always figures as a symbol of joy and harmony, an occasion for the display of the virtues stemming from good breeding and the exercise of courtesy. For the first time we have an abundance of visual depictions of secular meals based on such biblical prototypes as the banquet of Herod, the marriage at Cana, and the Last Supper. These sacred associations served to increase the power of other, non-religious symbolism connected with dining. The most bitter injury that could be inflicted on a knight, for example, was to cut through the tablecloth to his left and right, thus signifying that he had been false to honour and was therefore severed from society. This treatment was instituted by that flower of late medieval chivalry, Bertrand du Guesclin, in the reign of Charles V.[58] We can see such ignominy in action in an illumination in *The Statutes of the Neapolitan Order of the Holy Spirit* dated 1353. Before a frieze of feasting knights and their ladies sits a solitary black-clad knight at a black table eating the equivalent of humble pie.[59] What humiliation that must have been.

Again, in common with so many aspects of the table as we cross from the fourteenth into the fifteenth century, there is a new stress on etiquette and precedence, both reflections of a deep craving for order.[60] In France this was a response to the Hundred Years' War and a weak monarchy. In England the monarchy was also weak by mid-century, and the country was subsiding into the Wars of the Roses. As has been noted, the old aristocracy felt itself under threat both from newly ennobled families and from the proliferating rich bourgeoisie. Their response was to escalate pomp as a means preserving caste. The prime exemplar of this tactic was the court of Burgundy, whose style would be exported to England under the aegis first of Edward IV and then of Henry VII. By descent of the Burgundian inheritance to the Habsburgs, it would reach the rest of Europe in the following century. This was the era that gave birth to phrases that remain with us today: sitting 'below the salt', 'the upper crust', and being 'born with a silver spoon in one's mouth'.

Coronation banquets are touchstones for this obsession with precedence. Here great aristocrats themselves took on the roles of servants — marshal, pantler, carver, butler or almoner. At the coronation banquet of Henry IV in 1399, the earl of Warwick acted as pantler, the earl of Westmoreland as marshal, the earl of Somerset as carver, the earl of Arundel as chief butler, and Lord Latimer as almoner. Although in this case the king sat at a table with the two archbishops and seventeen other bishops, the monarch increasingly on these major state occasions sat alone.[61] Such was the practice at the banquet given on the consecration of a pope in Rome. The new pontiff was led to a table by two cardinal-deacons, and ate alone there. To his right there was a table for the cardinal-bishops, to his left one for the cardinal-deacons, and further away stood tables for other clergy and nobility.[62]

Woe betide anyone who violated precedence during a public manifestation of the body politic. In 1464 the Lord Mayor of London arrived at a feast given in his honour by the Sergeants of Coif to discover the earl of Worcester seated in his place: 'For within London he [the Mayor] is next unto the King in all manner of things.' Seeing this usurpation of his rightful place the Mayor and his entourage promptly went home and staged their own feast. Abashed, the offending Sergeants of Coif hastily sent a peace-offering of 'meat, bread, wine, and many diverse subtleties'. Thus, the City chronicle concludes with satisfaction, 'the worship of the City was kept and not lost for him'.[63]

Manuscript illuminations and other pictures of secular feasting provide more information than ever before about seating arrangements. Where a couple is shown, the woman always sits to the left. If the group is made up of three men and two women, they are not seated alternately but as

Daily dining in hall in England in the fifteenth century.
In the centre sit the lord of the manor and his wife with, to her right, two
clerics, and, to his left, two sons and a daughter. A servant kneels to serve.
Illumination from the *Luttrell Psalter*, *c.* 1420–40.

three men in a row next to the two women. When the number of diners
rises above six or seven, alternation of the sexes may occur, but men and
women may just as likely be segregated, particularly at wedding feasts.
On the latter occasions, the bride presides. Pictures of the marriage at Cana
often show a presiding bride seated beneath a canopy, flanked by two female
attendants.[64]

Hierarchy not only determined where a diner sat, it also determined
his allocation of food. An ordinance of the dauphin Humbert II of Valois
(reigned 1333–49) divided his household into five categories: the dauphin
himself, barons and upper knights, lower knights, squires together with
chaplains and clerks of the chapel, and finally servants and valets. It then
stipulated what each rank was to receive for daily rations, working from the
premise that the higher up the social ladder, the greater the diner's share. (A
corollary of this was the principle that he who got the most was expected
to give away the most in alms to the poor at the gate.) Fowl was never to be
served to the humblest guests or to the servants, capons and chickens being
reserved to the upper orders. Lamb and fresh pork were also regarded as

appropriate only for the higher classes, while beef and salt meat were good enough for the servants. Everyone, however, had fresh vegetables.[65]

This association of food with rank was universal. The records of the Confraternity of All Saints in Seville detailing their feasts for the years 1438–69 show that although members and their poor guests sat at the same table, they were served different food.[66] The household regulations of the 5th earl of Northumberland make it equally clear that capons and lamb, when they were at their dearest, were to be served at his table alone. On feast days it was the earl's table that consumed the plovers, mallards, cranes and pheasants.[67] An analysis of fifteenth-century English menus echoes this. Game birds like pheasants, herons, swans and peacocks were strictly reserved for the high table. Sumptuary legislation indeed recognised a direct correlation between food and social status. In 1363, for example, an English law specified one meal a day of flesh and meat for 'servants of lords, as they of mysteries and artificers', the other meals to consist of butter, cheese or whatever according to rank.[68] Fifteenth-century legislation in north German towns dictated not only the number of courses but the number of guests allowed at a banquet.[69]

A sense of hierarchy permeated dining. At Richard III's coronation feast only the king's table had three courses; the lords and ladies had two and the commoners only one. The lords and ladies got the lesser delicacies, the king alone ate peacock.[70] At a feast given by Henry V for the Order of the Garter at Windsor in 1416, at which the Emperor Sigismund was present, the three pictorial dishes or 'subtleties' were served only to the high table: 'And all these subtleties were served before the Emperor and the King and no further; and other lords were served with subtleties after their rank and degree'.[71] By 1517 excessive fare at banquets in England had got so out of hand that a proclamation attempted to control it. It decreed that the number of courses should 'be regulated according to the rank of the highest person present': nine courses for a cardinal, six for a lord of Parliament and three for a citizen with a yearly income of £500.[72]

In any household, two meals a day continued to be the norm — dinner and supper, a lighter meal, just after dusk. During the fifteenth century, however, slight changes began to occur. Supper came later, at seven or eight o'clock, and breakfast began to appear, but only rarely.[73] In the 1478 *Black Book* of the household of Edward IV, breakfast was allowed

The ceremonial of hand-washing.
Guests enter right and have water poured over their hands by a servant. At table
the same action is undergone by royal personages served on bended knee.
Illumination, Italian, c. 1320–50.

only to those above the rank of squire. The same source also gives the
dining times of 10 a.m. for dinner and 4 p.m. for supper when the king
and queen ate in hall; when, as became more and more common, they ate
privately in chamber, both meals were served an hour later.[74]

The ritual of eating was more or less the same all over Europe, the
ceremonial depending on the rank of those involved and the grandeur of
the occasion. Every meal started with hand-washing (though as a rule far
less formal than the ablutions of Charles the Bold described previously).
The rite of assay – testing practically everything and anything for traces of
poison – was standard only for monarchs and other nobility down to the
rank of earl (at least in England).[75] Various household officials were
empowered to carry out this duty, but in general the butler would assay
the drink and the pantler or steward the food.[76] Unicorn's horns (usually
narwhale tusks) played a role in these tests, but far more common were
fossilised shark's teeth – 'serpent's tongues' as they were believed to be –
which were often attached by little chains to the cup or salt. Bezoar-stone,
a concretion found in the stomach or intestines of some animals, was also

used as an antidote to poison. Such objects were rare and highly prized, and thus regarded as handsome gifts. In 1318 Philippe le Long gave Pope John XXII 'a beautiful *languier* of gold, sown with rubies and emeralds and fine pearls, containing six serpent's tongues'.[77]

At the grandest banquets, food entered in procession. In 1490, at the marriage feasts of Alfonso, son of John II of Portugal, a burst of trumpets, tabours, shawms and sackbuts signalled the entry of kings of arms, heralds and pursuivants, all with their hats doffed except for the chief member of the parade, the grand chamberlain. On reaching the centre of the hall they all bowed deeply to the king's table. In this manner each of the courses was ushered in, including one consisting of a golden chariot bearing a roast ox and sheep, both with gilded hoofs and horns.[78] At a feast given at the Bastille in 1518, the procession opened with eight trumpeters. Twelve archers and their captain followed, then five heralds, eight household officials, and finally the grand master. Twenty-four pages of honour bore in the dishes for the high table, while the archers carried the rest.[79] The food, as the illuminated manuscript evidence reveals, was served kneeling.

The fifteenth century also saw the rise to prominence of the carver, an officer whose duties were limited to the high table.[80] His basic task continued to be the cutting of trenchers for each of the diners from loaves of bread laid on the table by the pantler. Hierarchy controlled even the bread, with the finer fresh bread going to the host and his guests. This was what was called a manchet loaf or *pain de main*, of which the best part, shorn of its crust, was always assigned to the lord. Those who sat further down in the hall received three-day-old bread. The trenchers would be replaced all through the meal as required, and then scooped up at the end for distribution to the poor.[81] The carver also dealt with other viands. We can see him at work in, for example, the miniature of January in the *Très Riches Heures*, where his knives are neatly laid out in front of him and he

Opposite: A pantler at work at a wedding feast with the bride
enthroned beneath a canopy flanked by maids of honour. He hands a
dish to the carver, his own work finished. Before him lie the three knives
he has used to cut bread into trenchers, some of which are before
the diners and others stacked to his left.
Illumination, Flemish, late fifteenth century.

Dining alfresco during a hunt.
The lord and his guests have a high table, the rest eat from
cloths spread out upon the grass.
Illumination, French, early fifteenth century.

is applying his skill to a dish of birds. His role included cutting up food
and delivering morsels to the diners, making sure to dip them in the
appropriate sauce beforehand. In the case of pies, he had to open the crust,
lift out what was within, and carve it; only venison was left inside the crust.

The carver also boned fish. Strict rules governed how he was to do his work. No food was to be touched with the right hand at all, while only the thumb and two fingers of the left could be used. Each item, moreover, had to be carved in a particular way. Yet despite these constraints expert carvers developed a style and grace that was almost balletic.

The late medieval menu continued to be dictated by the Church calendar. Four days a week were meatless, and the whole of the penitential seasons of Advent and Lent. A cook like Master Chiquart lists menus for meat and meatless days side by side, yet the meal's structure was the same no matter what was served. We know this because the plenitude of written evidence enables us for the first time to view a medieval meal in detail.

The banquet for the Hungarian embassy has already introduced us to the format, which was one of successive courses. The *Ménagier de Paris* gives twenty-four types of menus divided between those involving meat and those designed for fish days, some of which consisted of only two courses (or, as the *Ménagier* calls them, *mets* or *assiettes*), others of three or four. But even a two-course menu could have a first course of twenty-four dishes and a second of thirty-one.[82] Food was served in 'messes' – that is, in quantities to be shared between two or three people in the same way as utensils like hanaps and goblets. Many dishes of each course might be placed on the table at the same time, from which the host helped himself and his guests. This practice eventually became known as *service à la française*.

While the number of courses and dishes varied, the standard sequence, being based on established theories about the human body, was fixed. Medieval man viewed his stomach as a cooking pot that demanded warming to function properly, and, at the end of a meal, to be 'closed'.[83] All foods fitted into this regimen. Roasts, for example, called for the stomach to be fully operative, so they were placed at the centre of the sequence. A dinner might open with fresh fruits, or salads dressed with salt, oil and vinegar, together with confections containing anise or caraway seeds in honey or sugar. The drink at this point would be spiced wine. Such foods prepared the stomach for the broths and pottages to follow (although since these were 'warm and moist' and hence easily digested, they often as not began an ordinary meal). Now, with the stomach well warmed, was the time for roasts and their various sauces. Then came an intermission, the *entremets*, an occasion for the presentation of such spectacular food as a peacock cooked and reassembled in its own feathers, or pageantry like that in the Hungarian banquet. The aim, whatever the scale of the event, was a pause in the eating before the dessert arrived. This consisted of such things as sweet tarts or fritters, followed by what the French called the *issue de table* – cheese, candied fruits, and light cakes or wafers served with hippocras or Malvasia wines. These 'closed' the stomach. Regardless of the number of courses, this, according to food historians, was the general order that was followed. However, this may not always have been the case, for among medieval physicians there raged a fierce debate over the exact sequence in which food should be served: whether light or solid food should come first. From them came a litany of complaints that the sequence they regarded as medically correct was in practice ignored.

Let us examine two short English menus dating from the fourteenth century, which will make clear better than any generalities just how the system worked:

On flesh days:

Boar's head enarmed [i.e. armed], brouet [broth] of Almain to pottage, therewith teals ybaked and woodcocks, pheasants and curlews. The ii partridges, coneys, and mallard [all presumably roasted], there with blandesire [a blancmange pudding containing ground poultry], caudel ferre [sweetened, thickened wine, heated with beaten egg yolks] with flampoyntes [pork-filled pastry decorated with fried pastry] of cream and tarts. The iii course plovers, larks and chickens farsed [i.e. stuffed], and therewith mawmene [in this case a meat dish of minced poultry in a sauce of wine and ground almonds].

On fish days:

The first course oysters in gravy, pike and baked [?smoked] herring, stockfish [dried cod] and merling [whiting] yfried. The ii course porpoises in galantine, and therewith conger and salmon fresh endored [i.e. gilded] and roasted and flampoyntes. The iii course, rosy to pottage [coloured to resemble rose petals] and cream of almonds, therewith sturgeons and welks, great eels and lamphreys, dariole [custard tarts],

lech frys of fruit [tarts with spiced chopped fruits in almond milk],
therewith nyrsebake [a fritter].[84]

Another striking fact about this era is the emergence of books of
instruction on etiquette, largely to do with table manners.[85] It might seem
that eating at a medieval table called for nothing more than knowing how
to use a knife, spoon and fingers (forks had yet to come). In fact the process
was as fraught in terms of proper behaviour as any Victorian dinner party.
Far more than today, eating and drinking provided a primary framework
for conversation and conviviality, and the importance of every gesture at
table was thus enhanced. Quite apart from major feasts, the daily dinner
table was an instrument to be used for the lord's business even at a humble
level. A cameo has been drawn of the widow Alice de Breyne dispensing
hospitality at her manor of Acton, twenty miles north of Colchester in
Essex. Between Michaelmas 1412 and Michaelmas 1413 she served more
than 16,000 meals, an average of 45 a day, of which only 24 were for her
own staff. The rest were for guests. She gave a New Year's feast for five
hundred each year, a great event for which she employed a harper, but
the vast majority of her daily guests were business contacts – estate staff
from her other manors, bailiffs, auditors, trustees and tenants.[86] The
business lunch was certainly not a twentieth-century invention.

Treatises on manners multiplied during this period, demonstrating the
spread of literacy among the laity as much as a keen desire to climb the
social ladder. One of the most influential fourteenth-century etiquette
books was Bonvesin de la Riva's *Cinque volgari*. It was, significantly, addressed
not to an aristocratic audience but to the aspiring Italian bourgeoisie.
Cinque volgari covers everything. The diner must enter the hall well-dressed,
alert, cheerful and affable at all times. He must be gracious in his conversation both before and during the meal. At table he must not slouch,
squirm, lean on his elbows, cross his legs, overstuff his mouth, criticise
the food or dunk his bread in the wine. He must remember to turn aside
when sneezing or coughing, and always to cut up a lady's meat for her. Such
strictures – and this is just a handful of those included – appear here for
the first time, and are destined to be reiterated down through the centuries
to our own time.

Books and verses on these themes emerge earlier in Italy and France than they do in England. In England and Northern Europe there is also far more emphasis on hierarchy, a feature summed up in the title of one fifteenth-century English book: 'To teach every man that is willing for to learn to serve a lord or master in everything to his pleasure.' Most upper-class young men, like Chaucer's squire, who acted as carver to his father, learned courtly etiquette as a matter of course. At the court of Edward IV it was the task of the Master of the Henchmen to teach youths a wide range of social skills including 'how mannerly they eat and drink'. *The Babees Boke*, written about 1475, is typical of the genre. It opens with the arrival of the lord at noon. Be ready, it says, with water for him to wash, and a towel. Wait for grace to be said but do not sit down until bidden by the lord. Then be quiet and do not tell stories.

> Cut with your knife your bread and break it not;
> A clean trencher before you eke ye lay,
> And when your pottage to you shall be brought,
> Take your spoon, and sup by no way,
> And in your dish leave not your spoon, I pray,
> Nor on the board leaning be ye not seen,
> But from embrowing [making dirty] the cloth ye keep clean.[87]

The poem continues with a long list. Don't lean your head over the table, don't drink with your mouth full, don't pick your nose, teeth or nails, don't stuff your mouth, don't hold the upper part of a cup (they were shared), don't dip your meat into the salt, don't put meat into your mouth with your knife, and, most important, don't eat like a peasant. Speak only when spoken to, wipe your mouth before drinking, share any good food with guests, stay seated until the final hand-washing, and attend to the washing of any lady nearby.

That manners emphasised social division is made clear by the Sienese Gentile Sermini's account of an urban cook complaining about the unrefined conduct of a country person at table:

He fills his bowl with long slices of bread which he cuts by holding his loaf against his chest . . . When his hands are greasy, he has no idea what to do, for he is used to wiping them on his chest or his side to avoid soiling the white napery or his clothes. Anyone but a villager would be pained by his manners.

It is his custom to devour everything in his big bowl before taking even a mouthful of meat; then he grabs everything together: meat and sauce and huge slices of bread. He doesn't merely lick his fingers; he looks like he is sucking *fiedoni* [a pastry with a soft filling] . . .[88]

Some meals were not an occasion for talk, especially when they were taken in the chamber privately. Christine de Pisan tells how Jeanne de Bourbon, wife of Charles V, 'according to ancient royal custom' had a learned man placed at one end of the table to read to her throughout the meal from books describing virtuous deeds from times past.[89] In this we see the practice at the court of Charlemagne still going strong six centuries on. Froissart similarly records that he used to read his romance *Méliador* to Gaston de Foix, interspersing songs composed by Wenceslas of Bohemia: 'These things, thanks to the skill with which I inserted them into the book, pleased the Count greatly . . . while I was reading no one presumed to speak a word . . .'[90]

That sense of increased social division already suggested by the practice of dining in the chamber also found expression on more public occasions. At the end of a feast in the hall the host would select guests to accompany him to his chamber where, in the words of *To serve a lord*, 'they must have cheer of novelties as the time of year requireth', along with sweet or spiced wines.[91] In aristocratic houses this was the signal to bring out the *drageoir*, a box containing sugared spices or sweetmeats. These would be handed round with ceremony. At the papal court in Avignon in the fourteenth century, a set ritual developed whereby the pope distributed the delicacies personally to his chaplains after Christmas or Easter banquets.[92] At the Burgundian court the *épicier* or one of his staff entered the ducal chamber bearing the *drageoir* with its spices. The duke and duchess were then served by their nephews and all the other princes and counts of the family. After that the first chamberlain or the duchess's *chevalier d'honneur* took the *drageoir* and served the ducal nephews and nieces.[93]

Not all royal and princely dining was so decorous. Charles VI of France loved women as well as the good life, and his feasts with cronies led around the year 1400 to a spate of moralising literature that sheds considerable light on the importance of royal eating practices in the medieval period.[94] Charles never as a rule rose until noon, often neglecting to attend mass; he ate dinner at noon and supper at six. The king's midnight suppers, moreover, were not taken in the royal palace, but at the Hôtel St Paul, to which Charles invited his favourites. They were expected to outshine each other in extravagance of dress. Hierarchy at table was ignored here, the conversation was fast and mannered, courtly dalliance between the sexes often went too far, and too much was eaten and drunk. Worse, to the sin of gluttony was added that of gaming, strictly forbidden by the Church, with lust and luxury lurking in the wings. Such behaviour by a monarch came in for heavy criticism and was, of course, blamed on evil courtiers, parvenus who had led the king astray. The outcry, however, stemmed from something deeper than mere revulsion from sin. The king was regarded as the head of the body politic; the peasants were its feet. It was the king's duty to enact his role as ruler by being seen to eat, seated in a way reflecting his hierarchical significance, the food that the 'feet' had produced. Charles's failure to do so represented a violation of established order, an abdication of responsibility.

The king's midnight feasts were symptomatic of another historical shift. By 1400, the aristocracy was increasingly at a loose end, with some of its former military and administrative duties being eroded and taken over by professionals. They had money and time and they were bored. More complex food and fashionable new ways of eating it, like every other form of extravagance from outré dress to obsessive collecting, gave purpose to the vacant hours.

This was high living and high style, and inevitably it is what we know most about. What about lower down the social ladder? For the first time, thanks to manuscript illuminations, we are able to gain an impression of bourgeois and peasant households at table. Those in the middle range, who would have a cook and perhaps a servant or two, would eat in one of the rooms of their house. Often the table is round and is usually covered with a cloth. The atmosphere is distinctly homespun. There are knives to cut bread and roasts, spoons to eat with, and a pitcher and goblets for drink, though often shared.

Lower down the class ladder, despite the culinary explosion taking place above them, the peasants dine much as they always have. Cooking

Bourgeois dining.
A merchant and his wife eating in the bedroom with a bench
and a trestle table set up before a fire.
Illumination, Flemish, *c.* 1440.

and eating goes on in the same room; a single dish, from which all the diners help themselves (often as not with their fingers), stands in the centre of the table. Meals are of bread, a simple pottage followed by fish or meat if good fortune shines, a lump of cheese washed down with ale or cider or poor wine. Only on feast days – and then not always – poultry, rabbit or hare might come their way.[95]

Enter the *entremets*

FEW AREAS OF study in the history of food are more perplexing than the period of intermission that preceded the arrival of dessert and was graced by the word *entremet*.[96] Today, *entremets* in French means nothing more or less than dessert, or the sweet course itself, but in medieval times the matter was much more complicated. By 1457, the date of our banquet for the Hungarians, *entremets*, which in its rudimentary sense means nothing more than between courses, referred to what were in effect a series of spectacles that punctuated a feast. They could involve pageant cars, musicians and singers, actors and dancers – in short any kind of visual effect. Yet the first appearance of the word may be traced to the close of the twelfth century, when the chronicler Servion described a feast given by Humbert, duke of Savoy: ' . . . grant feste tant de services, d'entremes, de mumeryes, de danses'. That means the feast had included dancing and mumming (mime), consisted of several courses, and featured *entremets*. What were they?

The general consensus is that the word *entremet* began life as descriptive of certain coloured dishes such as *brouets*. That at least ties it to the advent of exotic food and the rise of the cult of colour. It also suggests an association with the other distinctive culinary development of the fourteenth century, the delight in forming foodstuffs into strange figurative shapes. An Anglo-Norman recipe book of the late twelfth century includes a dish of spiced meat sweetened with honey and worked with cheese and almonds, called 'teste de tourk'. Was it in fact moulded into a Turk's head? The earliest version of the *Viandier*, of about 1300, contains a number of dishes that in later versions of the manuscript are termed *entrèmes*. One is for a fairly elementary dish of ground meats with spices boiled and thickened with a little bread and given a yellowish hue with saffron. The whole thing was sprinkled with cinnamon and given a tang of verjuice. Apart from its colour, however, it is difficult to see this kind of dish as the ancestor of what became major theatrical productions.

By the early fourteenth century, these *entremets* began to develop into something far more exotic. The *Liber de coquina* of that date gives a recipe for a *capite monachi* (monk's head) of pastry, fruits and spices which had a

Figurative food as an *entremet*.
A peacock with its feathers displayed is borne in to a feast.
Illumination, French, fifteenth century.

battlemented crown; the book also gives recipes for pastry figurines of a
musician and a juggler. During the same period the earliest recipes appear
for cooking a peacock and serving it recased in its feathers. By the close
of the century, in the *Viandier*, the bird could be gilded and served with
its tail outspread. As we cross over into the fifteenth century with the
Vatican manuscript of the *Viandier*, however, a new type of *entremet*
appears, one which seemingly has nothing to do with the cook and everything to do with the medieval equivalent of prop-maker and scene-painter.
These include a castle, St George, St Martha, and a knight riding on a
swan. They are apparently a series of pageant floats intended to enter
the dining arena.

From this it is clear that by 1400 the word *entremet* referred to various manifestations appearing in the intermissions between courses at great banquets. There was the solitary dish borne in triumph. There were collections of these, assembled as parts of a pageant car on wheels that could include actors and singers. And finally there was a purely theatrical event in which food played little or no part. The types moreover intertwine and overlap.

In September 1317, Pope John XXII gave a feast at Avignon for his nephew. This featured an *entremet* made from twenty capons and other birds mixed with flour, sugar, confitures and honey, and shaped like a castle.[97] It was clearly meant to be eaten. Nearly thirty years later, in 1343, Cardinal Annibale de Ceccano gave a reception for Pope Clement VI, also at Avignon. This time the castle was inedible but much larger, big enough to form a setting for a full-grown stag, a boar, some roebucks, hares and rabbits (which must have been meant to be eaten). After the fifth course a fountain appeared, surmounted by a tower and a column from which flowed five kinds of wine. As with the castle, it was festooned with edible decorations: peacocks, pheasants, partridges, cranes and other game birds. Between the seventh and eighth courses, two trees were carried in, one of silver hung with golden apples, pears, figs and plums, the other green and spangled with multicoloured candied fruits. The latter were plainly dessert.[98]

At the fashionable papal court at Avignon, the *entremets* had already moved a long way from the simple dish of swan or peacock dressed in its feathers, or another favourite, the boar's head breathing fire. But a distant court like Scotland's lagged behind. The boar was still regarded as the acme of sophistication there as late as 1449, when a daughter of the duke of Guelders married James II: 'The first dish to be brought in and presented to them [the king and queen] was a boar's head, on a huge plate. Round the head were a good thirty-two banners, with the arms of the king and the other lords of the country. Then the stuffing was set on fire, to the great joy of everyone in the room.'[99] Elsewhere, for example at the Savoy court, such things were strictly passé. Twenty years earlier Master Chiquart had described how to make the flaming boar's head before moving quickly on to a far more interesting and complicated construction in the Avignon manner – 'a raised castle in the middle of which is the Fountain of Love', borne in on a litter by four men. The castle's perimeter walls were of paste made of meat painted with waves and galleys and ships full of men coming to attack the fortress. Inside, three or four young men were to sit 'playing very well on a rebec, a lute, a psaltery and a harp; and they should have good voices and be singing melodious, sweet and pleasant songs'. Within the walls the castle itself was to have four towers filled with model archers and crossbowmen. From each tower a tree was to arise bearing flowers, fruit and birds. And then comes what pinpoints the linkage very neatly: at the foot of the towers would appear a culinary menagerie of beastly edibles — the boar's head breathing fire, a large pike cooked three different ways, a glazed piglet and a swan in its feathers (also breathing fire). Earlier (and even then in backwaters like Scotland) each of the latter items would have appeared one by one on their own. And there was more: the Fountain of Love within the castle was to spout rosewater and mulled wine, while cages of doves and other live birds were suspended above; a peacock with its tail outspread and stuffed with roast goose (possibly an admission of just how nearly uneatable peacock really is) stood near the fountain; the castle courtyard was to be filled with figures sculpted in meat paste — hares, hounds, stags, wild boars and huntsmen — as well as comestibles like partridges, chickens disguised as hedgehogs, lobsters, and glazed meat balls. The summit of the castle demanded a forest of heraldic banners, standards and pennants. An imposing load for four men and a litter.[100]

The Burgundian court would take all this further yet, choreographing food into one sustained overwhelming spectacle intended to exalt the ducal dynasty. When, in 1435, the duke staged a feast in the aftermath of the treaty of Arras for King René of Anjou, its decor consisted of two large tables on each of which stood a hawthorn tree covered in gold and silver flowers, the greenery enriched with gold tinsel and adorned with the heraldic arms of France and of the other guests. Eighteen smaller trees bore the ducal arms. This decor framed the entry of an *entremet* involving a peacock surrounded by ten golden lions, each holding a banner bearing the arms of all the ducal lands.[101] Such a display epitomises the super-imposition of heraldry on to food for political purposes, a *leitmotiv* of all Burgundian banquets and one which other courts were swift to copy. In actual fact, the dukes ruled no kingdom but a group of scattered domains, and by constantly parading the conjoined coats of arms in this way they attempted to forge a unity that never really existed.

The drive towards making the state banquet into a political tableau may have reached its apogee in the festivals that marked the marriage of Charles the Bold to the Yorkist princess, Margaret of York, in 1468. Two feasts on that occasion attempted dynastic apotheosis by means of metamorphosed food. On the first occasion guests entered to find fifteen gilded and six silver swans, each wearing a collar of the Order of the Golden Fleece and the arms of an individual knight. The table was further populated with an array of elephants bearing castles, camels with panniers, stags and unicorns all in gold, silver and azure, and filled with sweetmeats. Each figure carried a banner with the arms of a province of the duke.[102] A few days later there was a rerun in a final banquet. This time the tables were laden with thirty plates, each bearing miniature gardens bounded by golden hedges. In the middle of the hall rose a golden tree with meats piled up around it; the tree itself was decked with fruits and flowers and the arms of the thirty abbeys in the ducal domains. Close to where the duke was seated stood a model palace enlivened with mechanical figures and a fountain that spurted rosewater as if it were watering the miniature gardens.[103]

Unlike the European mainland food as allegory in England in the fifteenth century took a quite different direction in the phenomenon known as the subtlety.[104] It is difficult to establish whether these subtleties were edible, but they were certainly made to be placed on the dining table. We have already seen them mentioned in the account by George Cavendish of the figurative food presented by Cardinal Wolsey to the French ambassadors at Hampton Court in 1527. The earliest reference comes in the description of a banquet given by the bishop of Durham on 23 September 1387, where at the end of each course appears the phrase 'And a subtlety', but it is not until 1417 that we hear a description of one. At a feast celebrating the enthronement of John Chaundler as bishop of Salisbury in that year, the bishop is presented with a sequence of subtleties – an *Agnus Dei*, a leopard, and an eagle. Four years later we get a slightly amplified description at the coronation banquet of Henry V's queen, Catherine of Valois. The first subtlety was said to be a pelican in its piety; the second the queen's namesake, St Catherine, patroness of learning, disputing with learned doctors; and the third St Catherine again, this time with her wheel. The final subtlety was a heraldic tiger holding a mirror and a man riding away from it carrying the tiger's whelp, and casting down more mirrors as he fled. It was believed that a tiger could not resist looking at its own reflection, so here surely was an allegory of Henry V carrying away his Valois bride.[105]

Such items were devised not merely as courtly flattery but as profound statements couched in late medieval terms. Those created for the coronation of the child king Henry VI in 1432 attempted to establish an entire new regal iconography for what was hoped would be the dual monarchy of France and England. Each sublety had its meaning spelled out in verses by John Lydgate. The series culminated in the young monarch being presented to the Virgin, who proffered a crown, by the patron saints of both countries, St George and St Denis. The verses read like an invocation:

> O blessed lady, Christ's mother dear,
>   And thou St George, that calléd art her knight;
> Hold St Denis, O martyr most entire,
>   The sixth Henry here present in your sight . . .
>   Both by descent and by title right
> Justly to reign in England and in France.[106]

The English tradition of the subtlety remained vigorous throughout the following century. That subtleties were not confined to royal and episcopal circles can be gathered from the surviving record of a fifteenth-century series described as appropriate to a wedding feast. The feast was to consist of four courses, and the final subtlety depicted 'a wife lying in child-bed, with a scripture saying in this wise: "I am coming toward your bride if ye durst look me ward, I ween ye needs must." '[107] One ponders the poor bride's reaction.

The *entremet* as showpiece was only one aspect of a huge expansion of all kinds of entertainment associated with festal dining. Music and song had long been a part of any banquet, but from around 1300 they assumed a much more prominent and complex role. In 1306, at the knighting of the

Entremet staged at a banquet given by Charles V of France in honour of
the Emperor Charles IV, 1378. A pageant ship enters left while, to the right,
crusaders led by Godfrey de Bouillon storm and capture Jerusalem.
Illumination, French, late fourteenth century.

eldest son of Edward I, the guests brought their own minstrels to sing *chansons de geste*, those tales of ancient chivalry involving Arthur, Alexander, the Trojan Wars, Godfrey of Bouillon, and Jason and the Golden Fleece. Edward I had twenty-seven minstrels, Edward III sixteen.[108] They would have played harp, psaltery and lute, as well as wind and percussion instruments. Music-making became much more highly developed and international as the century progressed, with troupes of musicians moving from one court to another and minstrel schools during Lent. A distinction now emerged between music which was appropriate for the hall and that for the chamber. In the hall it was *haute musique*, itself divided between *musica alta* for wind bands and *basse musique* for soft instruments accompanied by voices. Recent research has suggested that some of the surviving French polyphonic *chansons* with symbolic texts were in fact intended for *entremets*. From what is known about the Burgundian court, that suggestion would seem to be correct; the great *entremets* demanded not only the services of the duke's own musicians and chaplains but also local talent in whatever town the duke happened to be.[109]

The most extraordinary of all the developments related to eating during the late Middle Ages is the emergence of the theatrical *entremets*. It represented an imaginative leap from merely reciting the dramatic events described in romances to actually staging them in the arena of the hall. The first record we have of such an attempt comes in 1378 at a banquet given by Charles V for the Emperor Charles IV. We are fortunate that there is a manuscript illumination of this amazing spectacle, which acted out the story of the crusader Godfrey of Bouillon taking Jerusalem. Christine de Pisan describes it as follows: 'The city, large and splendid, made of wood and painted with the scutcheons and arms of the Saracens (very well executed) was brought in front of the Dais. Next came the ship with Godfrey on board: and then the assault began and the city was taken which was very enjoyable to watch.'[110] Fourteen years later, at the feast celebrating Isabella of Bavaria's entry into Paris, the siege of Troy was the subject matter. That *entremet* included a miniature castle as Troy, a pavilion for the Greeks and a ship, but it all ended in disaster when the press of people was so great that a table tipped over, and the royal party had to retreat to its rooms.[111]

Such dramatic interludes soon became standard, as the idea spread remarkably quickly. It had already reached Barcelona in 1399 when a series was staged at the coronation of the queen of Pedro IV of Aragon. This time each course was prefaced by a little drama – men-at-arms killing a dragon, musicians on a rock bearing a wounded lion, actors imprisoned in a castle.[112] At the marriage of the duke of Savoy's son in 1434 at Chambéry, a fully-fledged ship flanked by sirens singing advanced to the high table and disgorged the fish course. At supper a horse disguised as an elephant with a castle on its back ambled in. Cupid, attired in peacock's feathers, emerged from the castle to shoot red and white roses at the diners. At another feast a huge pie was wheeled in and a man dressed as an eagle leaped out flapping his wings and releasing a flock of white doves.[113]

Although Lydgate wrote scenarios for modest mummings earlier in the fifteenth century,[114] it was not until 1502 that spectacles of the Burgundian kind graced the banqueting halls of the kings of England. The fêtes staged in November of that year lasted a week and marked a triumph of early Tudor policy, the marriage of Henry VII's son to Katharine of Aragon. They utilised the whole *entremets* repertory: castles, mounts and fountains. But what is so striking is the participation of members of the court. Professional musicians, actors and singers played and spoke and sang, but the central roles in the dramatic interludes were assigned to lords and ladies. In one *entremet* two mounts, one verdant symbolising England, the other sun-parched symbolising Spain, were linked by a golden chain. On the English mount sat twelve lords, on the Spanish twelve ladies, with one of the latter dressed like an infanta. They descended and danced what must have been some kind of choreographed display.[115] Such a performance would clearly lead in time to the Stuart court masques.

No discussion of late medieval banqueting would be complete without some account of the most famous of them all, the Feast of the Pheasant staged in his castle at Lille by Duke Philip the Good on 17 February 1454. It was a year after the Turkish capture of Constantinople, and the purpose of the feast was to launch a European crusade. Gathered in the hall to witness this event were not only five hundred guests, including members of the ducal family, the aristocracy and representatives of trade and industry, but also onlookers accommodated on five specially constructed platforms known as *estrades*. It was a display of hierarchy on the grand scale, the duke attired in black and grey adorned with jewels worth a million *écus d'or*, his servants dressed to match. The feast lasted until 4 a.m. the next day, and to it the whole household contributed – poets, artists, musicians and craftsmen, not to mention the cooks of the ducal kitchens, each course having no fewer than forty-eight dishes.[116]

The overwhelming effect of the event is summed up in a letter written by a member of the audience:

> The dishes were such that they had to be served on trolleys, and seemed infinite in number. There were so many side dishes, and they were so curious, that it's difficult to describe them. There was even a chapel on the table, with a choir in it, a pasty full of flute players, and a turret from which came the sound of an organ and other music. The figure of a girl, quite naked, stood against a pillar. Hippocras sprayed from her right breast and she was guarded by a live lion who sat near her on a table in front of my lord the duke. The story of Jason was represented on a raised stage by actors who did not speak. My lord the duke was served at table by a two-headed horse ridden by two men sitting back to back, each holding a trumpet and sounding it as loud as he could, and then a monster, consisting of a man riding on an elephant, with another man, whose feet were hidden, on his shoulders. Next came a white stag ridden by a young boy who sang marvellously, while the stag accompanied him with the tenor part. Next came an elephant . . . carrying a castle in which sat Holy Church, who made piteous complaints on behalf of the Christians persecuted by Turks, and begged for help. Then, two knights of the Order of the Golden Fleece brought in two damsels, together with a pheasant, which had a golden collar around its neck decorated with rubies and fine large pearls. These ladies asked my lord duke to make his vow . . . that, if the king [of France] would go on a crusade, the duke would follow him in person . . . Everyone was amazed at this, but Holy Church was overjoyed, and invited the other princes and knights to vow . . . I believe that nothing so sublime and splendid has ever been done before.[117]

To that one adds amen.

* * *

Regal dining becomes ritual.
The royal table is elevated and approached by a flight of steps.
The king is in solitary splendour beneath a canopy. Servants ascend
and his carver administers to him.
Illumination, French, fifteenth century.

Central to what would happen in the coming two centuries was the
deliberate elevation in status of the wearer of the crown. The process was
already well under way by the late fifteenth century. In Burgundy it was
bound up with the hope of recreating the old kingdom, but elsewhere
it was aimed simply at widening the gap between the monarch and the
magnates immediately beneath him. Ceremonial and festival, of which
eating was a crucial part, was one means of achieving this. 'The king's
[table] at the far end of the hall and taking up most of its width,' wrote
someone in 1428 regarding a feast given by the king of Portugal, 'was on a
wooden dais several steps high. The king's place, in the centre of the table,
was six inches higher than the rest and a canopy of cloth of gold was

stretched over it.'[118] In the late fifteenth-century *Roman de Jehan de Paris* the hero is based on Charles VII of France: 'He sat at table alone, the people attendant upon him silent and those to whom he spoke knelt.'[119]

But again it was the court of Burgundy that developed ceremonial to its highest pitch during the ritual of the feast. 'We went to see my lord of Burgundy dining,' wrote one of the ambassadors from Metz in 1473, 'and we saw all the pageantry and pomp which is arranged at his dinners.'[120]

Clearly, this was the place where food first assumed the grand role it would play in the service of the Renaissance and baroque monarchies to come. The duke at his table has already taken on an almost cult-like aura. Each meal is coming to resemble a secular version of the mass. The table is laid like an altar, bread and wine are consumed, the scene is the focus of ceremonial processing, ritual washing, the kissing of objects as though they were relics, genuflections as if before the sacrament. Even the ducal cup is elevated when carried in procession, a gesture that echoes the elevation of the consecrated chalice.[121] Everything is in place; regal dining is assuming the dimension of an act of state.

CHAPTER FOUR

Renaissance Ritual

O N 20 MAY 1529, the future Cardinal Ippolito d'Este entertained
his brother Ercole II, future duke of Ferrara, together with his
duchess, at the Este palace of Belfiore.[1] Ippolito was destined
to be one of the richest and most prodigal of Renaissance cardinals,
creator of the legendary Villa d'Este at Tivoli with its riot of sculpture and
sparkling fountains. In 1529, however, he was still archbishop of Milan, a
position given him at the age of ten a decade before. Belfiore lay within
the so-called 'Herculean addition' to the city, a vast new quarter added
in the 1490s which in effect tripled its size. The palace, surrounded by
marvellous gardens and a park, was among the most magnificent of the
Este *delizie*, its walls adorned with frescoes depicting the elegant life of this
wonderfully sophisticated court. On that occasion there were fifty-four
guests in all. The event began in the cool of the early evening with the
chivalrous exercise of running at the ring, in which mounted men charged
a target with lances. This ended at nine o'clock, after which the company
adjourned into one of the great frescoed halls of the palace for the
performance of a farce followed by a concert described as 'una divina
musica di diverse voci e vari strumenti' ('a divine concert of diverse voices
and instruments'). That was over at ten. Then came the supper.

A table had been erected in the gardens with, to its right, two *credenze*
or service tables, one for food, the other for wine. On the other side an
arbour had been constructed festooned with greenery, flowers and coats of

Opposite: A new dining ideal.
A servant lays a table beneath a shady pergola in the gardens
of an elegant palladian villa.
Painting by Benedetto Caliari, late sixteenth century.

[129]

arms. In it sat the musicians, for music was to be the meal's uniting theme. The tables bore four tablecloths, one on top of the other, for the supper would be punctuated from time to time by the removal of a cloth to reveal yet another beneath. Normally two cloths were used, one for the main part of the meal and a second for the final fruit course. But the cardinal had planned a surprise for his guests, doubling the number of cloths – and courses. When the ninth course was finished, they suddenly found themselves starting all over again with another nine, making eighteen in all.

Napkins were 'variously placed and folded in a divine way' on tables 'marvellously decorated with different flowers and arms, with salt cellars and knives' and fifteen sugar sculptures of Venus, Cupid and Bacchus, deities symbolic of gardens, love and wine. 'Above,' the description continues, 'was beautiful foliage with festoons and variously crafted trophies.' The guests were led to the table from the palace by musicians and young men and girls dancing a lively galliard, which they continued to perform while the diners washed their hands in perfumed water. On the table as a first course awaiting them were not only the customary bread rolls by each diner's place but antipasti – cold dishes and salads from the *credenza*. Each course consisted of eight different dishes. The second course alone is enough to give the flavour of the court's cuisine. It consisted of trout patties, halved and spiced hard-boiled eggs, sturgeon roe, pike spleens and other fish offal fried with orange, cinnamon and sugar, a boiled sturgeon with garlic sauce emblazoned with the cardinal's device, fried bream, wheatstarch soup, pizza with flaky pastry Catalan style and small fried fish from the river Po. No meat, for the day was one of abstinence. But if the food and the decor were striking, it was the music and the accompaniment that made the feast truly remarkable. The cardinal's sturgeon arrived at the table to the sound of three trumpeters and three cornets. Each course had its own particular music or form of spectacle, all perfectly integrated into the serving of the food in a way that we would categorise in modern parlance as a happening. There was a courtier playing a lute solo, a girl singing madrigals, 'songs *alla Pavana in villanesco* which was a wonderful thing to hear', country folk who executed a *morisco*, buffoons who performed *alla Bergamasca* and *alla Veneziana*, a man dressed as Orpheus singing to the lyre, a sonata *alla alemanna* and four French girls who sang *canzoni di gorga* (the duchess was French). In this way the whole musical resources of the Este court were deployed in contrasting vocal and instrumental display interspersed with choreographed dances. The evening was brought to its close at five in the morning. There were gifts of perfumed gloves, earrings, compasses and rings for the guests. As a grand finale twenty men dressed in livery and bearing torches in their hands erupted upon the scene from the arbour and danced one last *morisco*.

This is just one account of a private court supper, albeit a splendid one. Many others could be chosen.[2] But it makes a perfect point of departure for our exploration of eating style during the Italian Renaissance, when not only the cuisine but the way of presenting it was to embrace a refinement and elegance as yet unknown to the medieval north. Significantly, the fact that we know about the meal in such extraordinary detail reflects the wide contemporary interest in such events at the sophisticated and fashionable Este court. Cristoforo da Messisbugo's landmark book *Banchetti, composizioni di vivende e apparecchio* (1549), which provides the description, went into no fewer than thirteen editions between 1549 and 1626.

What sets this supper apart is the fact that it was a private, not a state, occasion. We have encountered similar concerns with decor and figurative food at the Burgundian court but only in feasts of great political significance. And such events were always staged within the palace walls. Here in the warm south, with weather so benign and predictable, a meal can be staged within a bower of greenery out of doors. We have admittedly met the sugar sculptures before, but not as adornments to the table at the opening of a meal. Here, moreover, they are figures from classical mythology sculpted, no doubt, in emulation of the antique. The elaborately folded napkins are also new, and the account of the antipasti and first course suggest that we are in the presence of a far more refined cuisine. Above all, one is aware of witnessing a meal conceived as an experience to be enjoyed by all the senses without any sense of guilt. The eye is ravished by everything from the decor to the arrangement of the edibles. The nose may appreciate the delicate scent of the perfumed water proffered for hand-washing no less than the aroma of the food which, being eaten with the hand, also satisfies the sense of touch. And throughout the ear is delighted by the sweet sounds of music. In short, the simple act of eating has been transmuted into an expression of sensual art.

[131]

The duchy of Ferrara was to play a key role in that transmutation.³
The Este had established themselves as rulers of this city-state during the
thirteenth century, but it was not until the first half of the quattrocento
that they began to assume dynastic pretensions and develop the apparatus
of a court. This accelerated during the reigns of three successive brothers,
Borso, Lionello and Ercole I d'Este, and the family's rule was to continue
until 1598 when, on the death of Alfonso II with no direct male heir, the
city reverted to the papacy. But for two centuries, until that catastrophe,
Ferrara was to be a major and innovative centre of Renaissance civilisation, a
court whose artists included Francesco Cossa and Ercole Roberti together
with the architect Biagio Rossetti. To these can be added, as visitors who
worked there, Pisanello, Mantegna, Jacopo Bellini and Roger van der
Weyden. It was also in the forefront of musical innovation, importing from
the Low Countries as court musician the renowned Josquin Du Prez. To
this court was due the revival of classical comedy and some of the earliest
attempts to recreate the antique stage. The culture of Ferrara was unique
in fusing the humanism of Ancient Greece and Rome with the cult of
northern romantic chivalry that gave rise to its two great literary masterpieces, Ariosto's *Orlando furioso* and Tasso's *Gerusalemma liberata*.

The Este court modelled itself on that of Burgundy. Both were new
dynasties out to prove their importance, which they ventured to do
by means of the splendour and ceremonial of their courts. Eating was
a central aspect of this undertaking, and it was the Ferrarese court
where that most distinctive form of Renaissance food consumption,
the banquet, was developed and refined. Already under Borso d'Este
the officers pertaining to the ducal table had begun to multiply. Under
his successor, Lionello, the Burgundian *entremet* tradition gained a foot-
hold and assumed a classical guise. Another source of influence was
the Neapolitan court. Ercole I had not only been educated in Naples
but, in 1473, married the king's daughter, Eleonora of Aragon. The
Neapolitan court was to play a crucial role in gastronomic innovation, and
was equally important in respect of the orchestration of meals, for in
Naples the carver – the *trinciante* – was established as the controlling officer
in charge of the order and presentation of banquets. Eleonora brought
with her to Ferrara a certain 'Iohn da Napoli' whose influence on the
Este court may well have been considerable, although there it was to

be the *scalco* or steward and not the *trinciante* who emerged as the presiding genius.

A description of what became an annual event in Ferrara each Maundy Thursday conveys a sense of the degree of elaboration achieved by 1491:

> At the end of the great hall was the head table, where there were thirteen poor citizens who were reduced to the status of paupers. One of them was a priest who sat in the middle, in most holy and divine memory of Christ at the Last Supper; and the others up to the number of the apostles. The other tables were placed along the sides of the hall, and at them sat all the other assembled poor. At the first table [was] Your Excellency [the duke]; at the others your sons and your brothers; according to the established order of your Religion they served the seated poor.[4]

The meal was magnificent, being served on the finest linen in silver dishes. It included sturgeon prepared in different ways, as well as other fish, all consumed with white wines. There was a roast course, including wild boar and other meats accompanied by red wine. After the feast everyone adjourned to another hall where the Este family, headed by the duke acting the part of Christ, washed the feet of the poor. The public was admitted to view the spectacle.

Such increasing ritualisation could also be seen in late quattrocento Este wedding feasts. These served on an even grander scale to exalt the dynasty through ostentatious display. Following a celebratory tournament on the occasion of Ercole's marriage in 1473 to Eleonora, for example, a procession brought the new duchess and her ladies 'one hundred very large plates full of sugar confections, all different, namely castles, columns of Hercules, birds, four-footed animals, the devices of the lord, and other confections . . .'[5] In this instance the sugar sculptures were detached from the banquet, thus anticipating what was to become a major feature of the sixteenth century, the separate sugar banquet.

For a later Este marriage, in 1491, the effect was repeated with a procession of a hundred and three men bearing 'tigers, unicorns, bucentaurs, foxes, wolves, lions . . . mountains, dromedaries, lobsters [?], castles, saracens, children, the Columns of Hercules, Hercules killing the dragon, lynxes, sheep, bucks, elephants, men at arms, large lilies, eagles, chained hounds, vases and many other things . . . all painted and made life-size and of solid sugar'.[6] This time each confection was destined for a particular person and the subject matter was both heraldic and emblematic. The sculptures cannot have been meant to be eaten or, at least, only in part; apart from sugar their ingredients included gum arabic, lake, white wax, incense, turpentine and cinnabar. Indeed the chronicler makes a clear distinction between these display items and other silver dishes laden with sweetmeats for consumption. Sculptors from Mantua, Padua and Venice were brought in to make them from designs by court painters. To crown the event, the duke himself, baton in hand, stood at the head of the stair-case leading down to the banquet 'in order that everything should go in its correct order'. This time, unfortunately, the audience got out of hand, plundering and breaking up the sculptures, much to the duke's fury.

As the quattrocento turned into the cinquecento every element was in place to enable the Este court to transform the medieval into the Renaissance banquet: the highly organised ritual, the exaltation of the ruler, the role of the court musicians and the presence of the public as onlookers. The greatest innovation, however, was to be the emergence of a new major court official to supervise all aspects of such events – the choice of location, the decoration of both room and table, the menu, the mechanics of food presentation and the selection of music and other forms of entertainment to enliven the meal. In Ferrara this man was the *scalco* or steward. His eye was on everything, from the large effects to the smallest detail – the shapes into which the napkins were folded, the costume of the servants, the choice of serving dishes, the parting gifts for the guests. Although the earliest short treatise on the role of the *scalco*, Eustachio Celebrino da Udine's *Opera nova che insegna apparechiar una mensa a uno convito*, appeared in Venice in 1526, Ferrara is recognised as perhaps the first court with an official devoted to the orchestration of major feasts. The *scalco* was already established as one of the three great household functionaries under Ercole I, the first duke to admit the public to watch banquets. Ercole's *scalco* was Sotio Bonleo, and we know little about him. But the man he taught, and who succeeded him, achieved considerable fame.[7] Cristoforo da Messisbugo came from an old Ferrarese noble family, and was of a social status high enough to have entertained the duke twice in his own house. In the service of Alfonso I by 1515, Messisbugo four years later became *sottospenditore ducale* and in 1539 *provveditore ducale.* That he was close to the duke and a trusted servant can be gauged by his role in the duke's foreign negotiations with the French, the Venetians and, in particular, with Emperor Charles V, who visited Ferrara in 1529. In 1533 the emperor made Messisbugo a count palatine. Although Ercole died in 1534 nothing was to dislodge Messisbugo from his position as the Este court *scalco* until his death in November 1548.

His book, the *Banchetti,* was published posthumously. Its second part is a recipe book with dishes for both ordinary and fish days, which fully reflect both the international nature of the court's cuisine and the late medieval and continuing Renaissance obsession with figurative food. Here are pastry castles and coats of arms as well as descriptions of wooden and iron moulds capable of turning out the eagles and fleurs de lys of the Este family arms. The book's real originality, however, resides in its descriptions of fourteen banquets and suppers, private and public alike, that Messisbugo had staged during his years in office. Staged is the appropriate word, too – he names the location and the guests, describes any temporary decor and the table ornaments, notes the food served course by course and its quantity, and gives an account of any music or entertainment presented while the guests were eating or between courses. A highly innovatory first chapter lists absolutely everything needed to put on one of these events, from beds for guests to cutlery, from tableware to seating, from kitchen equipment to the waiters, not to mention a gigantic litany of foodstuffs embracing every kind of meat, fish, game, dairy produce, fruit, vegetable and salad greens. The meal, Messisbugo makes plain, is only one aspect of what should be a whole sequence of experiences, usually opening with a play, a poetry reading, a concert or games and, in most cases, winding up with the removal of the tables and dancing. The great *scalco* emerges from his book as a man of wide culture, with a keen eye, considerable aesthetic taste and a genuine passion for music. In his own way he was a minor theatrical genius endowed with high organisational skills.

✳   ✳   ✳

Messisbugo was not a solitary phenomenon, nor was his book. He had two outstanding successors. The first was Giacomo Grana, *scalco* to Luigi d'Este, cardinal of Ferrara. In 1565 Grana was responsible for the banquet the cardinal gave in honour of his brother Alfonso I's marriage to Barbara of Austria.[8] This was staged in the cardinal's urban palace, the Palazzo Diamante, and is an index of how, by the second half of the sixteenth century, court banquets had become still more complex productions designed to astonish the guests and amaze the mere onlookers. For this affair, the room was transformed into a garden with branches suspended from the ceiling hung with lights and the walls swagged with tapestries bearing the arms of the royal families of Europe to which the Este were connected. Stucco figures bore torches, and around the sides of the room, well out of the way, there were boxes for spectators. The high table was elevated by three steps and carpeted. On it there was a table covered in a crimson velvet cloth edged with gold fringe. Two fine cloths were laid over that, and on them stood a tableau of napkins arranged in the form of the towers and crenellations of a castle. The table in the main part of the hall was a hundred and five feet long and at it sat a hundred and forty ladies and the knights who had escorted the bride from Germany. At the high table were the bride and groom, flanked by princes and princesses and cardinals to the number of twenty-two. These were attended to by four stewards, four carvers and four servers, all attired in the duchess's colours of dark crimson fringed with gold and silver and all wearing Hungarian hats. Each course was borne into the hall to the sound of trumpet fanfares by twenty-four gentlemen divided into groups of six, each answerable to a steward. The plates, four hundred of them, all silver, changed with every course. Dinner over, the company retired while the room was cleared for a concert followed by a collation of sweetmeats and sugared water served by pages and other youths dressed as nymphs and shepherds.

Even more important than Grana was the last duke's own *scalco*, Giovan Battista Rossetti.[9] He worked for Alfonso II from 1557 to 1576 and then served the duke's sister, Lucrezia d'Este, the estranged wife of the duke of Urbino. In 1584 Rossetti published *Dello scalco*, in which he developed this officer's role far beyond that described in the *Banchetti*. The attributes of the *scalco* are listed. These include a fine presence, elegance of dress, learning, attentiveness and eagerness of response, especially to the demands of the employer. By now his empire is very large indeed, taking in the control of all supplies, the kitchen, the selection of menus and the placement of the tables and *credenze*. It was the *scalco's* role to seat guests in strict hierarchical order, supervise the sequence of courses, the changing of tablecloths and napkins, indeed every detail of an occasion which had become increasingly ceremonious. His domain also took in a room where the gentlemen who had acted as waiters ate separately from the common servants. Rossetti praises the Este dukes for combining at their court the post of major domo with that of the *scalco*, thus ensuring obedience to the principle laid down in the *Ordini* of the duke, that at all times his magnificence and dignity be preserved.

Rossetti's capabilities are typified in another banquet for the 1565 ducal wedding.[10] In this instance the guests were presented with the illusion of eating beneath the sea. The ceiling was painted with waves and marine monsters, the tablecloth had waves upon it, the napkins were folded like fish, the salts were marine beasts, even the majolica plates were seashells. Its finale took the form of a triumph of Neptune with ninety sugar sculptures attendant upon the deity. No one in 1565 would have believed that all this was to be swept away with the death of the last duke thirty years later.

The innovations in food ritual at Ferrara set the scene for what is first and foremost the age of the courts. Whether in a small Italian state like that of the Medici grand dukes of Tuscany or a mighty empire like that of the Habsburgs, the court in its full-blown Renaissance form was a new phenomenon. It was a city within a city, one bound together by its own rituals, ceremonial and etiquette. It depended on a host of new officials – including the *scalco* – to maintain its exclusivity, and was inhabited by a new social type, the professional courtier. Every aspect of such an institution was deployed only to one end: to exalt the ruler as a being set apart, the representative of God on earth presiding over an earthly paradise, if you like, or a terrestrial Jove over a pagan Olympus. The act of eating could not help but be subsumed in this world of stupendous artifice. The actual food sometimes threatens to vanish from sight, sunk beneath the weight of ceremony. Yet of course it never does. It is to a consideration of what that food was and how it changed from that of the previous century that we must now turn our attention.

The refinement of cuisine

THE RENAISSANCE was about the rediscovery of the world of classical Antiquity combined with a keen desire to recreate it. That can be seen everywhere one looks in quattrocento and cinquecento Italy, whether it is in the cultivation of a Ciceronian literary style, the quest to resurrect the repertory of the Vitruvian classical orders, or the revival of the forms of classical theatre. But how did this affect food and its presentation?[11]

The desire of the courts to emulate the banquets of Antiquity was fuelled in large part by the recovery and printing of texts which either relate directly to ancient cuisine or which included graphic descriptions of meals. The classical texts previously known to the Middle Ages were limited to Virgil's *Georgics* and the like, which spoke of the rustic diet of those living close to the soil – peas and lentils, leeks and lettuce. One can therefore imagine the impact when, in 1498, the earliest-known edition of Apicius' *De re coquinaria* appeared, making widely available a text until then only available in manuscript to humanist scholars. Suddenly there was revealed a very different cuisine, that of a highly sophisticated society which cultivated the pleasures of the table and surrendered willingly to the temptations of the appetite without any feelings of guilt. Apicius was a world away from the centuries of fasting and self-denial institutionalised by the Christian Church. More, its recipes (dormice cooked in honey, for example) were incitements to cooks to compose ever richer and more recherché dishes. Then there were texts like Book XIII of Martial's *Epigrams*, full of references to food, and *The Deipnosophists* by Athenaeus, which was published in 1514; this discusses gluttons and famous cooks, along with the customs and manners of guests and the suitability of various foods.

Overall, this abundance of classical texts altered cuisine or, rather, made it more eclectic, for the new tastes never completely displaced the golden spiced and fragrant food of the late Middle Ages. The two styles in fact lived side by side. Yet the introductions – or reintroductions – were sweeping and numerous. To the humanist revival of the foods of Antiquity we owe the use of truffles and fungi; the elevation of sea fish over freshwater varieties, along with oysters and caviar; dishes making use of entrails and cartilaginous and bony bits like brains, sweetbreads, ears and feet; chopped meats and sausages; a predilection for pork and suckling pig; and such vegetables as artichokes, cardoons, asparagus and members of the cabbage and onion family. Some of these were, of course, known to the Middle Ages but now they were endowed with the aura of Antiquity. Added to this was an enormous increase in the number of kinds of fruit. There was also a new interest in taste, the salt–acid, a taste already known to the Middle Ages with its pickled foods, whose popularity owed much to the reverence for salt as a sacred substance in Antiquity. So too did the increased use of salt in cooking, and the consuming passion for hams, salt fish and caviar. Finally, rediscovery of the classic texts brought about the rediscovery of a long-lost social type – the gastronome, a person whose whole object in life was to delight in the joys of the table.

By the middle of the sixteenth century the world of Renaissance learning was remarkably knowledgeable about the food and eating habits of the classical world. Books on the subject appeared – like Johann Wilhelm Stucki's *Antiquitatem convivialium libri III* (1582). For the first time in more than a millennium, food was worthy of a learned pen. Not that approval was universal; the Renaissance was equally receptive to the alternative position, going back to Socrates' *Gorgias*, that the art of cookery was a form of deceit and that gastronomy led to the sin of gluttony. A similar distrust of food was to be found in Plato and within the Neoplatonic tradition whose revival was also central to Renaissance culture.

But academic chatter and the realities of court and kitchen are two very different things, and there is no doubt that food underwent a significant transformation during the Renaissance. It is moreover clear that the change began in the south of Italy at the court of the Aragonese kings of Naples.

In 1443 Alfonso V of Aragon took over Sardinia and Sicily. Naples became a separate kingdom ruled by his son, Ferrante. Southern Italy had already been subject to Arab influences and, under its Angevin kings, French. To those were now added influences from the Iberian peninsula, which were at the same time strengthened by the advent of a Spanish pope, Alfonso Borgia, Calixtus III, who brought his own cook to Rome with him. Within a century Rome was universally recognised to be 'il teatro del mondo' when it came to the gastronomic arts.

That great mid-fifteenth-century transition is summed up in the works of two people, one a practising cook named Martino de' Rossi – Maestro Martino – the other a humanist librarian, Bartolomeo Platina. Maestro Martino, of Swiss origin, was early in his career cook to the dukes of Milan but passed into the service of the Venetian Cardinal Trevisan, patriarch of Aquileia, who lived in attendance on the papal court in Rome.[12] About 1460 Maestro Martino compiled his *Libro de arte coquinaria*, a book which signalled a new era in the history of cookery. It was a landmark on account of the clarity, organisation, and exactitude with which the recipes are for the first time presented. Some are derived from Spanish sources. Martino's order of courses is also new; he does not open with fruit and sweet things but goes straight into what Platina calls the *pietanze*: meat of all kinds, roasted, stewed, in pies, in jelly, made into sausages or varieties of mortadelle. What is striking is the signs of a move away from imported spices in favour of using native aromatic herbs such as mint, marjoram, parsley, garlic, fennel, bay, sage and rosemary, although spices were still to reign supreme until the middle of the seventeenth century. There is also a greater deployment of sugar, rosewater and saffron, and of ground almonds and sugar for thickening and sweetening sauces. In this work we can see the first stages of the steady rise of sugar.

Yet Maestro Martino's cuisine would never have had the European impact it did if it had not been for its wholesale plagiarisation by the classical scholar Bartolomeo Platina.[13] In his book *De honesta voluptate*, the new culinary culture born of the synthesis of Spanish, Arab, French and Italian traditions meets the new impulses of Renaissance humanism. Gregarious, voluble and impetuous, Platina was never an easy character. His background was the Gonzaga court at Mantua at the school established by Vittorino da Feltre, but most of his career was spent in Rome, and in 1475 he became papal librarian. The *De honesta* was probably written in 1465, two years after he first acquired a copy of Maestro Martino's *Libro de arte coquinaria*, two-fifths of which he was to subsume into his own publication. (He tactfully referred to Martino as 'the chief cook of our age', perhaps by way of apology.) Combined with that contemporary source was a more traditional dietetic system, the Greek theory of humours as transmitted to the Middle Ages via the Arabs, the *regimen sanitatis* of the School of Salerno.

But this marriage of the new cuisine to the medieval medicinal tradition is not what marks Platina's book as epoch-making in the history of gastronomy. The clue to its originality and influence lies in the work's title, 'On right pleasure'. *Voluptas*, in medieval terms, was nothing more or less than sin. Platina instead promotes the idea that the physical pleasure of eating could in the right circumstances be honourable or *honesta*, which roughly translated means virtuous. In this way he legitimises the consumption of food and drink beyond dietary necessity to embrace both the physical and emotional pleasures it can bring. He does this, moreover, without any allusion to the Christian tradition. (In this he is likely to owe a debt to his humanist friend, Giulio Pomponio Leto, whose interests included the Roman cook Apicius.) As a result the book is both modern and secular, discoursing on the basics of food in terms of healthy living but also discussing its aesthetic and psychological dimensions – for example the importance of clean tableware, spotless linen and attractive decor. He also touches on the sequence of food, stating that everything which is light and slight, including lettuce, whatever is served with vinegar and oil, eggs, and certain sweets, should be served first. In effect Platina transforms what might have been an artisan's practical manual into a full-blown revival of the antique kitchen, utilising a battery of quotations from Apicius, Varro, Cato, Virgil and many others.

De honesta was to have influence all over Europe. It was probably published first in Rome in 1475, followed by a second edition in Venice the next year. Editions then came in Germany, Switzerland and France. It was translated from Latin into Italian (1487), French (1505) and German (1530). Platina in fact ennobled the cookery book and brought food writing into the world of letters, making food an acceptable subject for debate among the educated classes. Beyond that, the book precisely met the needs of a burgeoning educated Italian bourgeois elite.

The publication of Platina's book triggered a stream of successors that set Italy apart from the rest of Europe as pioneering a new gastronomic literature. This was encouraged not only by the radical new attitude to eating which Platina promoted and the increasing ostentation of the courts, but by the peninsula's abundance of raw ingredients. The meal structure in *De honesta* is tripartite: a first course of fruit, salads and sweet things, a second of meat, fish or vegetables served with an abundance of aromatic sauces, and a third of fruit, nuts, cheeses and, on grander occasions, dragees and sweetmeats. To appreciate just how wide a net for ingredients could be cast when it came to a major court banquet along these lines we need only refer back to that given by the cardinal of Ferrara on the marriage of Alfonso II.[14] Not only were the resources of all the ducal estates called upon, but freshwater fish came from Garda, sea fish and ten thousand oysters from Venice, artichokes, cardoons, fave, fruit, carnations and roses from Genoa (the event took place in December) and confectionery, candles, sugar, spices and sugar sculpture again from Venice.

This sense of plenitude is caught everywhere in the gastronomic literature of Renaissance Italy and, indeed, gave birth to the first book which can be described as a gastronomic tour, Ortensio Lando's *Commentario delle piu notabili e mostruose cose d'Italia e altri luoghi* (1548).[15] Lando describes such dishes as Sicilian macaroni with cheese cooked in chicken stock and spiced with sugar and cinnamon, and eels in Sorrento prepared with thyme, rosemary, marjoram, mint and other herbs. He sings the praises of Lucca for its sausages, Como for its trout and Piacenza for its gnocchi (so marvellous, he writes, that they would revive a corpse).

That delight in variety is similarly captured at the opening of the seventeenth century in the work of an Italian Protestant exile in England, Giacomo Castelvetro.[16] Poor man, he desperately missed the fruit and vegetables of his native land! Here he found, as another contemporary put it, vegetables 'either unknown or supposed as food more meet for hogs and savage beasts to feed on than mankind'. Italy, Castelvetro writes in his *Breve racconto di tutte le radici, di tutte l'herbe . . . che in Italia si mangiano* (1614) is 'la patria di tutte le gentilezze'. No other country prized fruit and vegetables so highly or grew them so well. Lyricism and nostalgia haunt this catalogue of Mediterranean delights, and it is impossible not to sympathise with a man who can write, at the close of a recipe for eating artichokes raw: 'We love these tasty morsels; just writing about them makes my mouth water.' Alas, his words of advice fell on deaf Jacobean ears, but his text reflects exactly the spirit that drove the changes in the gastronomy of cinquecento Italy.

Simultaneously wine begins to be accorded serious appreciation. Sante Lancerio, *bottigliere* to Pope Paul III (1534–50), produced a record of the best Italian and foreign wines drunk in Rome, awarding the palm to Malvaglia from Candia.[17] But in his text we witness the emergence of the vocabulary of the *sommelier* in terms like *tondo, asciutto, fumoso, odorifero, crudo* and *delicato*.

Equally consideration is given to colour in terms such as *verdeggiante, colore incorato* and *dorato*. Wines now begin to be carefully matched to courses, light white wines for the antipasti, red for the roasts, and on through fortified and intoxicating wines for dessert, to end with hippocras.

But what was distinctive about Renaissance food?[18] Basically the old medieval core remained intact, but it was enlarged, refined and enriched as the sixteenth century progressed. The same spices continued to be used, although reduced in range. Their presence, indicating expense, was central to the parade of wealth which was the essence of court cookery. So too the old medieval sauces continued to be made, and the passion for roasts, pies, tarts and figurative food remained unabated. But there were many new ways of cooking these items. One cookery writer, for instance, gave 227 recipes for cooking beef, 47 for tongue and 147 for sturgeon alone. No medieval cookery book could compete with that number. The renewed interest in fruit and vegetables has already been touched upon, but the sixteenth century also witnessed the arrival of new ingredients from America: pumpkins, tomatoes (but only used for cooking much later), maize and beans, not to mention the turkey. There were shifts too in taste in the case of some of the traditional ingredients. Beef, for example, regarded in the Middle Ages as appropriate for the retainers but not for the high table, now along with veal enjoyed greater status. Under the influence of classical sources parts of animals and fish which today we would find repugnant to eat were regarded as the summit of epicurean delight: noses, eyes, cheeks, livers, bowels, heads, kidneys, tripe, tongues, sweetbreads, cockscombs and testicles of animals, along with a parallel list of fish parts. And, harbinger of what was to come, butter became increasingly used in cooking, although not as yet cream.

Menus were still dominated by the liturgical year, even in Protestant countries like England where legislation continued to enforce the observation of fish days in the interests of the fishing industry. Indeed in Catholic countries in the second half of the sixteenth century, as the tide of the Counter-Reformation began to encroach ever deeper, there was a renewed emphasis on the observance of days of abstinence and of piety that could lead to fasting excesses. The irony is that the most important gastronomic work of the century, Bartolomeo Scappi's *Opera* (1570), was dedicated to a pope, Pius V, famous for the extreme abstemiousness of his diet.

Scappi was the most influential cook of the Renaissance.[19] Probably of Bolognese or Venetian origin, he began his career in the service of a Venetian, Cardinal Marin-Grimano, a member of the papal Curia in Rome. Subsequently he worked for Pope Paul III and Pope Pius V, whose coronation banquet he managed and whose 'secret [i.e. personal] cook', probably a sinecure, he became. His masterpiece, the *Opera*, appeared in 1570, probably after his death. It is a landmark publication, the summation of over forty years of cooking at the most prestigious court in Europe. Nothing quite like it had ever before been written, for in the *Opera* we encounter for the first time a true theoretician of the kitchen. It is the first cookery book that works from a notion of the centrality of taste and, above all, the first work which establishes cooking firmly as a science. Running to nine hundred pages divided into six books, it is illustrated with twenty-eight engravings providing a visual repertory far in excess of Messisbugo's *Banchetti*; they cover everything from cooking utensils to arranging a table as a fishpond composed entirely of comestibles. Scappi opens with a discussion of the kitchen and how it operates, and a consideration of ingredients. He moves on to deal with meat and fish, eggs and sauces, then gives a hundred and thirteen seasonal menus covering suppers, collations, dinners and banquets. There is a book devoted to the work of the pastry cook and finally one dealing with food for the sick. What he writes is lucid and precise, fully living up to his own definition of the cook as being like 'a judicious architect, who, building on his exact design, lays a strong foundation, and on that gives the world practical and marvellous things'. What Scappi records is international court food, dishes that can be described as *alla francese*, *alla tedesca* or *alla spagnola*, although national cuisines did not exist as such in the late sixteenth century. His influence was to be considerable, particularly in areas subject to Habsburg rule like Spain and the Empire. In Spain more than half of it was taken over by Diego Granado for his *Libro del arte cozina* (1599) and in Germany it was similarly plagiarised by Max Rumpolt for his *Ein neues Kuchbuch* (1581).

Scappi's book was a bid for social status on behalf of the cook, but it was one made in vain; the obsession with ceremonial ensured that the Renaissance would be the age of the *scalco* and the *trinciante*. Slightly shorter than Scappi's, running only to eight hundred pages, Domenico Romoli's

La singolare dottrina dell'ufficio dello scalco (1560) is the work of a Florentine steward.[20] Romoli, or Il Pununto as he was known, had also been a cook and 'secret cook' in the service of both aristocrats and cardinals. His book thus records the cuisine of the Roman Curia in the middle of the sixteenth century, containing hundreds of recipes and a second half devoted to diet. He also describes the roles of the *scalco*, the *trinciante* and the *credenziere* (the officer in charge of the *credenza*). Of the latter two, by far the most important was the *trinciante* or carver, who also sought to outbid the *scalco* as the controlling officer of upper-class ritual eating.

The origins of the emergence of the *trinciante* lie in Spain in a work on carving by Don Enrique de Aragon, marquess of Villena, compiled in 1423. Its premise, that the art of carving was worthy of those of noble birth, was exported to the Neapolitan court, where the king's *trinciante* was always selected from the aristocracy. In Italy the *trinciante* makes his debut in a work by Robert di Nola, the *Libro de cocina*. He was cook to Ferdinand I of Aragon, king of Naples, and in his book, compiled in the 1490s,[21] he describes the roles of the cook, the dispenser and the *trinciante*. The latter was to transform himself from a man who simply served and put food on people's plates to a senior court official responsible for turning what was a mundane operation into an elaborate ritual, a pyrotechnic display of strength and dexterity. Robert di Nola cast the *trinciante* as a kind of *scalco*, a choreographer of banquets. The description of a feast held in Naples in 1517 in honour of the coronation of Bona of Savoy as queen of Poland paid tribute to the precise and delicate carving of the meat 'by a dextrous and attitudinising carver'. The *trinciante* had arrived.

Hardly surprisingly, he next turns up at the Este court in a work written by Francesco Colle called *Refugio del povero gentilhuomo* (1520) dedicated to the duke, Alfonso I.[22] This treatise sets out to exalt the work of the carver at table as an aspect of princely magnificence, a skill that could be only exercised by a man of noble, albeit impoverished, birth. A far more important statement to this effect was to be Vincenzo Cervio's *Il trinciante* (1581). Cervio had been in the service of Guidobaldo II, duke of Urbino, and then, after 1540, in that of Cardinal Farnese in Rome.[23] He had also travelled widely in Northern Europe, where he was unimpressed by the abilities of carvers. His exemplars were to be found in Spain, in Naples and, more than anywhere else, in Rome (although, it has to be added, some of those were finding themselves out of work thanks to the renewed asceticism of the Counter-Reformation). Like Scappi and Colle, his was a bid for social status in a hierarchy-driven society and also an attempt to take over the role of the *scalco*, or at least to challenge it. The book's preoccupation with class is reflected vividly in the description of the style of a gentleman *trinciante* who doffs his hat before he performs but then firmly puts it back on his head again to demonstrate his equality with those at table.

The carver, according to Cervio, should be a gentleman of handsome presence, well dressed (in white, surprisingly), ready to please his master but careful to deport himself in such a manner as to set himself apart from the surrounding menials. The carving catalogue that follows is daunting, covering everything from game to a melon, with a blow-by-blow account of every gesture to be made in the process. Then comes the distribution, which must be strictly in order of rank, both in terms of priority and in judging which part of the animal carved is appropriate. The whole exercise in manual dexterity is deliberately designed both to entertain and astonish the diners. 'Carving in the air' it was called.

In 1593 there was another edition of Cervio, updated by Fusorito da Narni. By then the *trinciante*'s rise in status relative to the *scalco* was established, for descriptions are now included of the decor and food of a series of elaborate banquets. Needless to say, carving north of the Alps remained unelaborated in this way. In England in 1508 Wynken de Worde issued the old medieval *The Boke of Kervynge*, which continued to be reprinted down to 1613. The printing revolution meant simply publishing older cookery books which already existed in manuscript.[24] But the result of this was that late medieval court cuisine became accessible to a growing bourgeoisie. Although the earliest printed cookery book after Platina appeared in 1485, the real rise in production came only after 1530, in a clear response to a vastly expanded market anxious to learn aristocratic ways. That first book was *Kuchenmeisterei*, published in Nuremberg; it was to go through fifty-six editions. In France the *Viandier* went through fifteen editions between 1490 and 1520. Robert di Nola's book was translated into Catalan in 1520, running into seven editions, and then into Castilian with a further twelve. In England some twenty cookery books were published between 1500 and 1620.

What becomes clear is that the advances in cuisine and dining which had already taken place in Renaissance Italy were slow in percolating northwards, only making an impression in the second half of the century. That is certainly the case with France. The story there is one of stagnation, the only change being an increase in the number of sweet dishes and in those that made use of dairy products.[25] Platina was translated into French in 1505, going through many editions, and transmitting what was in effect Italian cooking of half a century before. In 1542 what would be later called *Le Grand Cuisinier de toute cuisine* appeared, in which only a third of the recipes were medieval. It was a cookery book with structure, a chapter for each course and a separate section on banquets.

The old view that French cuisine sprang to life when Catherine de' Medici brought Italian cooks with her to the Valois court on her marriage to Henry II in 1533 has long since been discounted. The only hint indeed that the new courtly style of a Scappi had arrived comes as late as 1604 in Lancelot de Casteau's *Overture de Cuisine*.[26] But then the author was cook to the bishop of Liège, whose see lay within the orbit of the Habsburg empire. All the old medieval favourites such as roast swan and peacock are there, alongside things that were certainly part of the new international court repertory, such as Bologna sausages and Parmesan cheese, moulded multicoloured jellies and sugar sculpture. Overall there was what can only be described as a north–south divide. Climatic factors, however, should never be discounted, for they continue even today to affect what is consumed in the sunny south as against the icy north. And those factors too were to play an important part in determining where people ate.

Pliny relived and the reinvention of the dining-room

THE LETTERS of Pliny the Younger (AD 61–c. 112) draw a vivid picture of a lifestyle that the Renaissance sought to revive and emulate, that of the rural villa. Pliny had two of them, one near the sea at Laurentium, the other in Tuscany. In his letters he not only describes their setting within the landscape, their architecture and their gardens but goes on to evoke the leisured life led within them, in which the rigours of the intellect were balanced by a whole-hearted response to the delights of the senses. The impact of these letters on eating was to be revolutionary.

One wing of the seaside villa contained a feature unknown to the Middle Ages, a dining-room: '. . . it is exceedingly warmed and enlightened, not only by the direct rays of the sun, but by their reflection from the sea'. There were two other dining-rooms as well, one which commanded 'a very extensive prospect of the sea, together with the beautiful villas that stand interspersed along the coast', a second in a turret with views down 'upon the garden, and the *gestatio* [the exercise ground]'.[27] The Tuscan villa similarly boasted a whole series of places for eating, and it too was sited on an eminence affording panoramic views. What Pliny designates as the 'grand dining-room' looked out upon 'a very extensive prospect over meadows up into the country'. It was positioned to catch the sun and therefore was for use in winter. In his own suite of apartments there was a dining-room 'which I use when I have none but intimate friends with me'. The third was close to the summer portico and therefore used during the hot months of the year; it was sited so as to catch 'the salutary breezes from the Apennine valleys', afforded vistas over vineyards, and was clearly open on at least one side. Finally, at the end of a walk of pleached trees there was a marble alcove shaded by vines where water gushed into a basin. 'When I sup there,' Pliny writes, 'this basin serves for a table, the larger sort of dishes being placed round the margin, while the smaller ones swim about in the form of little vessels and water-fowl.'[28]

From the first-century BC Roman architectural writer Vitruvius, Renaissance antiquaries could glean further information – that a dining-room should be twice as long as its width, that there should be two of them, one for spring and one for autumn, the former facing east, the latter north, in response to the movement of the sun. Vitruvius advises against decorating the ceiling vault of the winter dining-room, because it would be blackened from the smoke of the fire.[29]

With such sources to draw upon, the urge to recreate the antique villa and its life must have been overwhelming. What a different world they conjured up, so pleasingly remote from the moated castle or claustrophobic town house of the Middle Ages, with its communal great hall or lordly parlour. Here instead were rooms devoted solely to the joys of dining, rooms designed to be comfortable in summer and winter or placed in garden settings, rooms providing vistas to link civilised life to the beauties of nature. They could be enclosed for winter warmth or open to cool refreshing breezes – after all, this was Italy.

What thus occurs here during the fifteenth and sixteenth centuries, inspired in part by antique texts but equally by a desire for private as opposed to communal dining space, is the emergence of the dining-room used only for family and friends. It was variously called a *saletta* or *salotto*, or, more rarely, a *triclinio*, and represented the first move away from a living style that gave privacy only in the bedroom or *camera*, the other room being the public *sala*, a shared living and dining area. It was also the initial step towards the apartment system that lies at the heart of all architectural domestic interior planning in the Renaissance. A new sequence came into being: a major room, the *sala*, accommodating family and guests for receptions, dinners and entertainment; the *saletta* opening off it, for private use; and then for each family member a *camera*, preceded by an *anti-camera*.[30]

The great Renaissance architect Alberti's *De re aedificatoria* was composed some time around 1450. It was the first treatise on architecture to be written since Antiquity and was published in 1486, subsequently being translated into Italian in 1546 and French in 1553. The emergence of the villa as a new architectural type during the quattrocento may be largely laid to its influence. In it the dining-room makes its debut in a passage that reads as follows:

> The dining-room should be entered off the bosom of the house. As use demands, there should be one for summer, one for winter, and one for middling seasons, you might say. The principal requirements of a summer dining-room are water and greenery; of a winter one, the warmth of a hearth. Both should preferably be spacious, cheery and splendid.[31]

To this he adds Vitruvius' warning against decorating the ceiling of the winter dining-room for fear of smoke damage.

Although Platina, writing soon after in the 1460s, does not recommend a series of separate rooms he clearly has the idea in mind when he suggests that meals should be staged in different places according to the season:

> One must set a table according to the time of the year: in winter, in enclosed and warm places; in summer, in cool and open places. In spring, flowers are arranged in the dining-room and on the table; in winter, the air should be redolent with perfumes; in summer, the floor should be strewn with fragrant boughs of trees, of vine, and of willow, which freshen the dining-room; in autumn, let the ripe grapes, pears and apples hang from the ceiling.[32]

We have already seen the response to this recommendation in the banquets staged by the Este court, but by the close of the fifteenth century, new villas began to be built in the Italian countryside incorporating special places for dining.

Reviving the villa life of Ancient Rome required not only architectural knowledge but a changed attitude towards the countryside, epitomised by the humanist terms, *negotium* and *otium*. The former represented the busy life of the city, the latter the life of the country estate to which overstretched urban dwellers could retreat to indulge in philosophical contemplation and the pursuit of leisure. That villas could be built in the countryside to fulfil this new ideal was made possible by the political stability of the peninsula. This came to a close in 1494 when the long Italian wars began, but even conflict did not seriously constrain the new lifestyle except for a period after the Sack of Rome in 1527. After the treaty of Cateau-Cambrésis in 1559 brought peace again, the peninsula was undisturbed by battle, and villas proliferated.

One of the earliest villas boasted quite the most extraordinary dining arrangements. In 1487, the Florentine architect Giuliano da Maiano designed it for Alfonso II of Aragon at Poggio Reale outside Naples.[33] Let the Jacobean translator of Serlio, in which the plan of this pleasure palazzo appears, take up the story:

> . . . in the middlemost place . . . men go downe a payre of Stayres into a fayre eating place, in which place the King and his Lords vsed to banquet and eate at pleasure; in which place he caused certayne secret

places to bee opened, whereby in the twinckling of an eye, the place
was full of water: likewise at this Kings pleasure, all ye water voyded
out of the roome againe, but there wanted no shifts of clothes to
put on, nor yet rich and costly beds for them to lye in, that would rest
themselves.[34]

It was only later in the cinquecento that this combination of dining and
giochi d'acqua (water jokes) was to become an essential feature of every villa.
First to be developed was the loggia.

Although early suburban villas, elaborated from farmhouses, had
already featured primitive types of loggia, it was to be Bramante's Villa
Belvedere that recreated for the first time the summer dining space of
classical Antiquity.[35] The Villa Belvedere, which arose about 1485, began its
life as a recuperative pavilion for Pope Innocent VIII. By degrees, however,
it grew to incorporate many of the delights of the ancient Roman villa. Its
siting on the summit of Monte S. Egidio behind the Vatican was in
response to the classical texts and afforded magnificent views. The earliest
structure, a loggia-like pavilion, was intended for afternoon or early evening
repasts. Vasari records that it was decorated by Pintoricchio: 'full of landscapes and portrayed there Rome, Milan, Genoa, Florence, Venice, and
Naples, in the manner of the Flemings'. In this way a precedent was set for
the decoration of the Renaissance villa dining loggia. Its walls should
be frescoed with landscapes and topographical views, illusionistic vistas
complementary to the panoramas of the natural landscape seen through
the side of the loggia that was open to the countryside. The choice of
subject matter was in direct response to the newly published texts of
Vitruvius and Alberti. The former, issued in Venice in 1486, records
that covered walks in villas were adorned with landscapes 'copying the
characteristics of definite spots. In these paintings there are harbours,
promontories, seashores, rivers, fountains, straits, fanes, groves, mountains,
flocks, shepherds . . .'. Alberti endorsed this repertory.[36]

There is a vivid picture of eating in the Villa Belvedere loggia in a
letter to Isabella d'Este, duchess of Mantua. In 1510 her young son,
Federico Gonzaga, left as a hostage at the papal court, was accommodated
here. The Mantuan agent in Rome wrote to Federico's mother describing
how her son lived there and how 'he eats in a very beautiful loggia looking

out upon the whole plain, which can truly be called the Belvedere . . .'
Later, in June 1511, he reported on a banquet at the villa:

> Every sort of food was brought to the table. One came forward
> who was presented to Signor Federico . . . and recited some verses for
> every course . . . After dinner there was presented one who played
> the monochordo very well; then there came a musician and they
> played violins and sang. After this lovely diversion they rose from
> the table . . . and went out to enjoy those pleasant greenswards.[37]

Even more striking than the Villa Belvedere was its successor, the Villa
Farnesina, built by the papal banker, Agostino Chigi, from designs by
Baldassare Peruzzi.[38] This stood on the banks of the Tiber and went up
between about 1505–8 and 1510. Expense was no object. Here too there was
a dining loggia, this time in the north-east corner of the garden and
detached from the villa. In some respects it resembled a loggia erected
nearby by Cardinal Farnese a decade before, in that it was also an open
arcaded pavilion. But there was a difference. Now the antique dining
venue was situated atop another Renaissance recreation of the classical
past, a grotto. In 1520 Chigi entertained Pope Leo X and the cardinals in
it, grandly showing off his wealth by having the silver plate from each
completed course tossed into the river. (He did not let on that nets were
concealed underwater to catch it.)

The villa itself had a loggia forming part of the main entrance,
and that too must sometimes have been used for dining – its decoration
tells the story of Cupid and Psyche, culminating in their nuptial banquet.
Villa Farnesina was the setting for many of the most lavish entertainments
staged in Rome in the years preceding the Sack of 1527. In August 1512,
for example, Leo X and twelve cardinals were feasted in the *Sala delle
Prospettive*, after which the pope married the host to his mistress. On another
occasion the pope and his retinue were entertained in a tapestry-hung
room which, at the close of the event, was revealed to be the new stables
designed by Raphael. (On this occasion, some of the silver plate vanished
during the feast. Chigi gave orders that this was not to be mentioned.)

By the mid-cinquecento the dining loggia had become an essential
feature in any villa. We find it, for example, in such major landmarks both

in Rome and in North Italy as the Villa Madama (1516–27), designed by Raphael and Giulio Romano, in the Palazzo del Tè at Mantua (1525–32), also designed by Giulio Romano, and in the Villa Giulia (1550–9), built by Vignola and Ammanati for Pope Julius II.[39] In some instances, however, dining facilities were elaborated so far beyond this that they deserve separate consideration.

The Villa Farnese at Caprarola is a case in point.[40] In 1556 Cardinal Alessandro III Farnese commissioned Vignola to resume work on the palazzo. It was lavishly frescoed by members of the Zuccari family and completed in 1573. Here what was specifically a dining loggia occupies the centre of the entrance façade on the first floor – the *piano nobile* – from which the diners could look down through five large arches on to the small town below and out on to the country beyond. The inner wall has a matching set of illusionistically painted arches framing landscapes depicting the four seasons, while the rest of the room, again picking up from Bramante's Belvedere, contains topographical views of Farnese territories with the towns of Parma and Piacenza as focal points. At one end of the loggia there is a feature taken over from the monastery refectory, the *lavabo* or washbasin, but this one is surrounded by putti and a sleeping Cupid with, above it, a stucco relief depicting Aeneas and Rome, through which the Tiber flows. Interestingly, when Pope Gregory XIII paid a visit to the villa in September 1578 he dined in state in the *Sala della Cosmografia* immediately adjacent rather than in the loggia. The weather was no doubt at fault – the day had been bedevilled by downpours.

The decorative format of Caprarola was replicated not far away during the 1560s in the Villa Lante at Bagnaia, also designed by Vignola. The owner was Cardinal Francesco Gambara, bishop of Viterbo, who was related to Cardinal Farnese.[41] Lante had a dining loggia in a pavilion at ground level, but the walls are decorated in the same manner with topographical views. Lante was a modest statement. Far more interesting are the grandiosities of the Villa d'Este at Tivoli,[42] a stupendous pile designed by the archaeologist Pirro Ligorio for Cardinal Ippolito d'Este II, patron of the arts and avid collector of antiquities. Work began there in 1565 and went on for two decades, incorporating dining facilities on the grand scale. Begun in 1565 at the south-west end of the terrace in front of the palace, the dining loggia consisted of three large arches, each one of which framed stupendous views either of the famous garden with its incredible fountains or of the countryside. On the terrace side a door led along a corridor directly to the kitchens. At the Villa d'Este painted illusionism was reserved for the interior dining *salotto*, which was decorated with a scheme exactly echoing that of Caprarola. It also included a *lavabo*. In this case twisted Ionic columns and fruit and flower garlands framed views of the cardinal's various villas, while on the ceiling there was a Feast of the Gods. The villa was intended for summer use, so there is no fireplace.

The sheer multiplicity of places in which to eat associated with the new villa life has no equivalent in the rest of Europe. It went on to include tree houses, grottoes and casinos dotted through the grounds or surrounding woods of the villa. The architect of the Villa d'Este, for example, designed a casino for Pope Paul IV incorporating items from the papal collection of antiquities. It amounted to an antique nymphaeum, an oval court with a fountain at its centre flanked by two casinos with loggias in which the pope and his close family and friends could dine in the shade of a green-wood tree cooled by the slightest breeze.[43] The gardens of the Villa Lante also include dining facilities, among them two loggias equipped with stone tables and, more spectacularly, the Fountain of the Table built on the third terrace. This table stretches the full length of the terrace and has water running in a trough through its centre, a feature directly inspired by Pliny's description of floating dinner plates at his Tuscan villa. At Caprarola too, dining venues increased in number. The so-called Barchetto, built in 1584 on a wooded hillside whose approach was by way of a grotto, a *catena d'acqua* and formal gardens, offered a way to dine at a comfortable remove from the pomposities of the state rooms of the palazzo.[44]

A building like the Barchetto catches exactly the mood of mannerist fantasy common among dining locations in the second half of the century, and incidentally leaves us in permanent form what was so often intended only as temporary decor for banquets. Not far away from the Villa Lante is the most bizarre of all mannerist gardens, the Sacro Bosco at Bomarzo. Here one passes through a hell-mouth into a chamber.[45] Outside there is the menace of flaring nostrils and staring mad eyes, with the rather threatening inscription 'Leave every care, you who enter here.' A drawing of this feature dated 1604, however, shows a table inside with a man eating at it while in a corner a musician performs to the lute. It is in fact a dining place, one that must have offered an extraordinary combination of contrasting psychological responses, external horror with internal sensuous delight. There was a similar dining grotto at the Florentine grand ducal villa of Pratolino, created by Bernardo Buontalenti for the Grand Duke Francesco in the 1570s.[46] An octagonal table here has holes in which to place the glasses and bottles in chill spring water bubbling up from beneath. (Alas for the diners, the bubbling did not stop there. While they were being diverted by the performance of a tableau of automata, hidden jets from below made sure they were liberally doused with spring water too.)

Pliny the Elder in his *Historia naturalis* describes the *nidium* or nest of the Emperor Caligula constructed in the branches of a plane tree, which could accommodate fifteen guests and the necessary servants. At the Medici Villa di Castello in the 1540s the architect Niccolò Tribolo duplicated this marvel in an oak tree approached by means of an ivy-clad stairway. The seats inside were made of living foliage. Later, in the 1570s, Buontalenti created another at Pratolino, this time equipped with a double staircase leading to a room with a dining table, benches and 'water jokes'.[47]

Andrea Palladio's villas on the Veneto offer no such fantastic excesses.[48] Rather they reflect an all-pervading preoccupation with hierarchy and rank. This was reflected in the central hall or *sala*, a grand space conceived for entertainments like weddings and banquets. Palladio's villas did not lack loggias, but the dining ambience might take other forms, one of which is most effectively evoked in a canvas by Benedetto Caliari from the 1570s or 1580s. In the foreground there is a landing stage from a canal. From it one lady is about to step into a gondola. Another sits on a bench fishing. The landing stage closes a perspective vista stretching back via a greenery-festooned pergola through a formal garden to a classical villa. The pergola, for dining, is open at the sides to attract the slightest breeze and protected from the heat of the sun's rays by the sylvan ceiling and by a curtain on one side which could be let down or pulled up according to the time of day. A table has been placed there covered with a white linen cloth and a servant is laying it. No other picture sums up so vividly the dining revolution ushered in by the Renaissance villa.

Alas, the story north of the Alps is very different. On the whole, climate was inimical to such alfresco delights. Moreover, in countries such as the Netherlands and France, riven by religious wars during the late sixteenth century, the conditions were hardly conducive to villa life of the Italian kind. French Renaissance châteaux were constructed with a *salle haute* where only those of the same aristocratic rank were allowed to dine, access to which was directly from the outside by a stairway. A servants' hall lay below.[49]

During the sixteenth and early seventeenth centuries, however, those servants who were nobly born – the *maître d'hôtel* and the *écuyers* – increasingly objected to eating in the *salle basse* with the other servants. As a result they were given a table in the *salle haute* or in a separate room. Olivier de Serres in his *Le Théâtre d'agriculture et mesnage des champs* (1601) recommends another arrangement, placing the kitchen on the first floor next to the entrance and then 'a little dining room through which everyone would have to pass on his way to the kitchen; by this means [the master would be] nobly served his food, without mixing with the dregs of his domestics and [would keep] them all at their work'.[50] By the late sixteenth century, many grander families chose to dine in a separate room off their own *chambre* known as a *sallette*; within a few decades this had spread quite far down the social scale, and soon the term 'salle à manger' or 'sallette à manger' begins to appear.

Tudor England, which was not racked by internal war, offers far more interesting material on developments in dining arrangements.[51] During the sixteenth century the hall, although still the dining place of the servants, gave way to a new room, the Great Chamber, or, as it was sometimes called, the Great Dining Chamber. This, like the central *salone* of a Palladian villa, was a multi-functional space, but it retained its position into the early seventeenth century as the setting for the ceremonial dining of the owner. There the lord and his lady sat in state beneath a canopy attended by his sewer (the person in charge of seating guests), carver and cupbearer. Increasingly as the century wore on, however, this took place only on special occasions, though these could be ceremonious indeed. 'At great feasts,' runs a document entitled 'Some Rules and Orders for the Government of the House of an Earl' from the reign of James I, 'when the Earl's service is going to table, they [the musicians] are to play upon Shagbutte, Cornets, Shalms and such other instruments giving with wind. In meal times to play upon viols, violins, or other broken music.'

The food would have been borne in procession through the hall, those there standing as it passed, and up the grand staircase to the Great Chamber.

Yet by the end of the sixteenth century things had moved on. In the 1590s William Cecil, Viscount Wimbledon, ate in his parlour. This room, of which there could be more than one, was situated on the ground floor of the house. It became the family's eating and sitting room and the place where the grandest guests were entertained. By the middle of the sixteenth century beds had disappeared from this family room and the term dining parlour appears. Sir Thomas Lovell's house in London had one as early as 1524. Later in the century there were special parlours for winter, placed next to the kitchen for warmth. At first those who ate there were the family and the upper servants. Later, as the latter increasingly outnumbered the former, the family migrated to its own small private dining chamber. But the movement was not entirely to smaller and more private rooms. In the banqueting house England was to make a remarkable contribution to Renaissance dining architecture. A discussion of this must await our consideration of the country's unique response to a new phenomenon, the sugar banquet.

Convivium revived

WE HAVE ALREADY seen how Platina argued that the sensuous pleasure gained through the consumption of food could, in the right circumstances, be viewed as *honesta*, that is honourable. The humanists – of whom, of course, Platina was one – did much to bring the banquet to centre-stage.[52] The great Florentine humanist Marsilio Ficino actually composed a short treatise on the subject, *De sufficientia*, celebrating it as one of the most complete and balanced forms of human experience, one in which the functions of body and mind were united: 'Only the meal [*convivium*] embraces all the parts of man, for . . . it restores the limbs, renews the humours, revives the mind, refreshes the senses and sustains and sharpens reason.'[53] So dining at table was conceived of as a microcosm of the good society in which social relationships were forged, ideas exchanged in a civilised fashion, and mutual respect established. *Convivium*, humanists would constantly remind the reader, was a word derived from the verb *convivere*, to live together.

Their case for such praise was based naturally on precedents found in a whole range of classical texts. Homer, for instance, provided evidence for the symbolic importance of the Greek banquet in political, social and cultural terms. Plato in his *Laws* assigns the banquet a role as part of any citizen's education. For Athenians it was a means of controlling pleasure, a man at table being seen as occupying a mean between two extremes, reason and delirium. Encouraged by such texts the banquet came to represent a Renaissance philosophical ideal, the balance of opposites.

Michel Jeanneret, who has made the only major study of the part played by the banquet in Renaissance thought, sums it up:

> . . . the feast as a locus of pleasure and plenitude has a multitude of resonances in Renaissance symbolism. Through the feast is expressed the confidence of an age when it was believed, with God's grace, people could grow in harmony with nature while living at the heart of society.[54]

In Renaissance terms the banquet was a model through which society linked men to the gods, demonstrated their place in the natural world and reinforced man's social interdependence. Montaigne cites Plutarch's *The Dinner of the Seven Wise Men*, where it is written that to remove the table from the house is to wreck it, condemning the inmates to solitude, ending hospitality and jeopardising 'the most humane and the first acts of communion between man and man'.[55]

The symbolic resonance of the dining table shifts during the Renaissance. To the Middle Ages the prime reference was always ultimately to the Last Supper and its re-enactment in the sacrifice of the mass. With the Reformation in the sixteenth century came a fierce debate between Protestants and Catholics over the nature of the eucharist.[56] One consequence of this was that there were far fewer visual and symbolic representations of the Last Supper. What takes its place is banquets of the pagan gods or mythological nuptial feasts, like those of Cupid and Psyche or Peleus and Thetis. The nature of the images is very different too, presenting culinary spectacles not of restraint but of abundance, in which a cornucopia of fruit, flowers, splendid tableware and rich food seems to embody every form of sensual pleasure.

Another thing that sets the Renaissance table apart from its medieval predecessor is conversation.[57] In his commentary on Plato's *Symposium* Ficino recalls how, probably in 1478, the revived Platonic Academy at the Medici villa at Careggi had a meal to celebrate the birth and death of Plato on 7 November.[58] During the banquet guests read and acted out Plato's text, which provided classic evidence of the centrality of the meal as an arena for the intellect, and an occasion for learned discourse and discussion. In one scholar's recollection of life at the Villa d'Este, for example, we hear how at dinner, almost certainly in the frescoed ground-floor *salotto*, Cardinal Ippolito d'Este would lead a learned conversation. Afterwards, on very hot days, the *Odes* of Horace would be read 'until the heat would break'.[59] An even earlier instance of the practice comes from the court of the humanist king of Hungary, Matthias Corvinus (*c.* 1443–90):

> There are always disputations going on during his banquets, or speeches held about honourable or enjoyable subjects, or poems sung. There are in fact cythera players [*cithoroedi*] who narrate in their native language the deeds of heroes, singing on the lyre at the dinner-table. This was the custom of the Romans, and has spread from us to the Hungarians.[60]

This new emphasis on the art of conversation inevitably led to the food becoming of secondary importance. The extensive account of classical table manners provided by Plutarch's *Table Talk* and *The Dinner of the Seven Wise Men* emphasised that guests should derive no pleasure from eating and drinking but only from the serious conversation and the actual ceremonial of the feast. In *Table Talk*, for instance, Plutarch concentrates on such topics as 'what kinds of entertainment are most appropriate' for banquets.[61] These antique precedents may explain why accounts of Renaissance feasts rarely if ever describe the food. It is an attitude we can sense as early as 1539 at the nuptial feast of Cosimo I de' Medici to Eleonora of Toledo: 'The courses of the banquet were infinite, with many sorts of food in each course. I do not describe the particulars in order not to lose time for such an unimportant thing . . .'[62]

Renaissance acquaintance with a whole bevy of classical authors, including not only Plutarch but the likes of Cicero and Macrobius, elevated dining from a matter of purely sensual satisfaction to an arena in which reason could be exercised by way of dialogue. Of course this occurred only at the tables of humanists and scholars but it had an impact also on the dining habits of the established and aspiring classes. It ushered in also the cultivation of elegant small-talk. The old medieval heroic chivalrous values were now joined by demands for politeness and good behaviour. The art of speaking as the embodiment of the art of living was central to the humanist educational programme. Informed conversation at table was seen as a vehicle for diffusing differences and dissolving hierarchy by means of light and witty repartee. Rules of conversation emerged. Only subjects to which everyone could contribute should be chosen. The twin vices of the diner were seen to be *garrulitas* and *taciturnitas*, garrulity and silence.[63]

Later in the sixteenth century Montaigne was to write: 'There is no preparation so sweet to me, no sauce so appetizing, as that which is derived from society ... Alcibiades, a connoisseur in making good cheer, banished even music from the table, so that it shouldn't disturb the pleasure of conversation.'[64] Although Montaigne very much spoke for the learned who regarded conversation at table as a means of bringing philosophy down to earth, its equivalent in its courtly guise all too quickly drifted into polite vacuity. In an incident described in the fourth book of Stefano Guazzo's *La civil conversazione* (1574), a handbook on courtly behaviour, provincial nobility gather for a feast in honour of Duke Vespasiano Gonzaga. The food is never referred to, such a reference being seen as far too vulgar. Instead all the attention is lavished on a highly artificial exercise in sophisticated table manners and stylish conversation.

Humanism and the classical revival was also to have a major impact on manners.[65] In terms of behaviour at table the single most important publication was Erasmus' *De civilitate morum puerilium*, a book in which, among other things, the greatest humanist of the Northern Renaissance restated all the dos and don'ts of late medieval table manners, setting them within the broader philosophical perspective of the Renaissance concept of man.[66] Good manners, after all, set civilised human beings above the animal world and the peasantry. Thus they could be seen as a basis of moral rectitude, replacing the chivalrous code of courtesy. Erasmus argued in favour of the new concept of *civilitas*, good manners as an aspect of good citizenship. The exercise of good manners could lift one socially. It is thus easy to see the appeal of *civilitas* to what at that period was a rapidly expanding middle class. Although Erasmus himself had a predilection for food or drink he preached moderation in both, as well as in speech and gesture.

De civilitate morum puerilium was a classic school textbook for three centuries. In the year of its first appearance alone, 1530, it ran into twelve editions. Its all-pervasive European influence can be gauged by the translations: English (1532), German (1536), French and Czech (1537), Netherlandish (1559), Swedish (1620), Dutch (1660) and Finnish (1670). The huge success of this minor work shows how much manners were of urgent concern not only to Erasmus but to contemporary society. Its longest chapter is the one devoted to proper behaviour while eating.

Along with a number of others, Erasmus' book came at a moment that witnessed the dissolution of the old feudal society and its reformation around the absolutist courts.[67] These courts henceforth became the nurseries of good manners. More broadly, the refinement promulgated there was one aspect of the emergence of a new figure, the courtier, and he too was a child of the humanist movement in Italy.[68] The phenomenon of the courtier was institutionalised in one famous book, *The Courtier* (1528) by Castiglione. It lays down the attributes expected of such a person: urbanity, learning, versatility, skill in the art of conversation and an unselfconscious practice of every social grace, including immaculate manners at table. Manners similarly come into the other famous handbook, Giovanni della Casa's *Galateo* (1555). In that book the bishop of Verona is described entertaining a certain Count Ricciardo, 'gentilissime cavaliere e di bellissime maniere', who, alas, proved to be wanting at table. (He smacked his lips too noisily.) The good bishop, anxious to rectify such a social failing, sends Galateo to correct and instruct the count.

Such publications were devoured throughout Europe, for their message was one of self-advancement through the practice of self-fashioning. All of a sudden there is an acute awareness that manners actually mattered. At the same time it became more and more difficult to know what offended, or what to do and what not to do, as the court evolved ever more complex forms of etiquette. We can see such a self-fashioning process at work in an account of Cosimo, the first duke of Florence, eating in public. Seated beneath a canopy at the head of the table, he ate only sparingly, meanwhile exhibiting the most exquisite manners.[69] The Medici were bankers, but in their new guise as the autocratic rulers of Tuscany anxiously cultivated anything that would set them apart from mere mortals.

The Renaissance banquet

B UILDING ON the late medieval Burgundian inheritance, the banquet during the sixteenth century was to be transformed into an event of the highest artifice.[70] Food and taste had no relevance in this show of super-abundance and luxury, the sole indicators of political power and status in the new era of the courts. The duty of the guest was to be actor-spectator in a particular kind of ritual, one governed by specific rules and a single purpose: to glorify the host. Great events like the visit of one ruler to another or a dynastic marriage were marked first by the public spectacle of a state entry and second by the private spectacle of a banquet in the palace, a programme such as still survives in Britain today. Initially, the privacy of the banquet was maintained but gradually, as its full potential to impress became apparent, it became the practice to admit spectators.

In the middle of the seventeenth century Giacomo Colorsi, steward to Cardinal degli Albizi, wrote that 'the man who prepares a banquet has as much to do as he who marshals an army . . .'[71] Practices we have already seen emerging at the Este court spread not only to the other Italian courts but northwards over the Alps. Each court now had to have some kind of master of ceremonies responsible (as Messisbugo was in Ferrara) for every aspect of a feast from the decor to the menu. That officer could vary – he might be the major domo, the *maéstro della casa*, the *scalco* or even the *trinciante*. In any case he was like the conductor of an orchestra, with authority over everyone from suppliers of ingredients to the kitchen staff to those who bore in the dishes – the *scudieri* or *camerieri* aided by the *incontri* and *paggi*. The final event was choreography in the grand manner.

Regardless of what allegorical overlay was superimposed on to a feast, the component parts remained constant. It is now time to consider them. They begin with the selection of a location, and its decoration. Material on that subject is abundant in the archives of the Gonzaga court, which like the Este was anxious to impress.[72] Anyone who has visited the Palazzo Ducale at Mantua will be only too aware that it was never a matter of decorating a single great hall for the occasion; there was a quite extraordinary range of rooms capable of accommodating grand events. The family took intense interest in every detail; it was, after all, through such displays that they presented an image of themselves in the eyes of guests. Francesco II, for example, chose tapestries depicting the story of Troy for the room that staged the nuptial banquet for the marriage of his sister Elisabetta to Guidobaldo di Montefeltro, duke of Urbino. Francesco's wife, Isabella d'Este, who might with some accuracy be dubbed a Renaissance fashion victim, was obsessed with every detail of every feast. For one given in honour of the duchess of Ferrara and Prospero Colonna in 1513, she demanded to see not only a complete description of the decoration but an account of what was played and sung, the exact seating arrangements, and the menu. For the Gonzagas these were prestige occasions, managed in their case by the *maestro della casa*. The greatest of all was the entertainment and banquet given by Marquess Federico in 1530, in the aftermath of his being made duke by Charles V. The Gonzaga classical show palace, the Palazzo del Tè, conceived and built as one great dynastic stage-set, was the scene of opulence so splendid that those who took part were left gasping.

Now, even more than in the late Middle Ages, feasts were occasions for a dazzling array of valuables displayed on what, depending on the country, was called the *credenza*, the buffet or the *dressoir*.[73] Already highly developed at the Burgundian court, the format was to be adopted and recast in terms of its own art by Renaissance Italy. The historian Vasari describes the *credenza* in Giulio Romano's frescoed banquet of Cupid and Pysche in the Palazzo del Tè as laden with 'bizarre vases, basins, jugs, cups . . . fashioned in various forms and fantastic styles'. The painting indeed gives a vivid impression of what one of these buffets would have looked like set up for an alfresco feast. A table with shelves covered in a pure white linen cloth stands framed by an artificial arbour of greenery

A plate-laden alfresco *credenza*.
Detail from a fresco by Giulio Romano,
Palazzo del Tè, Mantua, *c.* 1524–35.

forming the buffet. The items upon it are highly exotic combinations of classical motifs, vegetation and fantastic monsters. That they are not purely imaginary we know, because designs by Giulio Romano for the Gonzaga family survive and they are of exactly this kind.[74]

An extreme instance of such a display was that for the wedding of Marie de'Medici, niece of the grand duke of Tuscany, to Henry IV in 1600. The banquet was staged in the *Sala del Cinquecento* of the old Palazzo Signoria. A vast *credenza* in the form of a jewel-studded lily, a reference both to the lily of the city of Florence and the French fleur de lys, had at its summit a canopy of cloth of silver surmounting a display of some two thousand pieces of gold, silver and silver gilt plate. There were also dishes of *pietre dure* as well as some of the ducal collection of bronzes, in particular Giambologna's set of the Labours of Hercules.[75]

Such displays were never for use, although that fact can be difficult to substantiate. Benvenuto Cellini records in his autobiography a commission by the cardinal of Salamanca for a great ewer, describing it as being of a type used only for decoration on a buffet.[76] The fact that sets of plate were made especially for display, instead of simply showing off disparate arrays of valuables, supports that contention. Two queens of France, Catherine de' Medici in 1549 and Elizabeth of Austria in 1571, had just such sets given them by the City of Paris on the occasion of their state entry. Catherine's consisted of twenty-seven pieces in silver gilt powdered with fleurs de lys.[77] An inventory of the plate of Philip II of Spain made in 1554 draws a clear distinction between pieces for use and those for show.

The tendency towards matched sets of plate for display was echoed in another revolutionary development, the introduction of new and far more luxurious forms of ceramics. These not only radically changed the appearance of the table but also involved the production of services made solely for display. The earliest was commissioned by Isabella d'Este, duchess of Mantua, in 1524, a huge faience service painted by Nicolò da Urbino with her arms and devices as well as other subjects chosen by her.[78] Such a service was far more expensive than plate and was designed to be set out on the buffet in such a way as to be viewed by guests like pictures in a gallery. Most of the subject matter of such sets was pictorial and was generally drawn from classical texts, particularly Ovid's *Metamorphoses*.

Isabella set fashion. As the century progressed a painted service of this kind came to be one of the choicest presents an Italian prince could give to an important foreigner. One service, of which a number of pieces survive, is likely to have been commissioned by Pope Paul III as a gift to Anne de Montmorency in 1553, in gratitude for assistance in the papal election. Decorated with scenes from Ovid's *Metamorphoses*, it included plates, dishes, candlesticks and flasks, and was a major work from the atelier of Guido Durantini of Urbino. Another service from the same studio went to the chancellor of France, Cardinal Antoine Duprat. Later, Philip II was presented with an even grander service adorned with scenes from the life of Julius Caesar designed by the painter Taddeo Zuccaro. By the close of the sixteenth century Bernard Palissy was making elaborate ceramic pieces in France solely for display on the buffet. And similar services were made in glass.

The Italian production of ceramics was to change the appearance of the table, with the plate replacing the trencher as the diner's receptacle for food. This happened first in Italy where, during the fifteenth century, the craft of faience ware, decorated with blue cobalt and metallic lustre, was imported from Spain. The skill had originally been learned from the Arabs during their occupation of the southern Iberian peninsula, and gradually percolated northwards until manufacture began on the island of Majorca (hence the other common term for the ware, maiolica).[79] The Italians were quick to learn to produce it, and by the 1480s they had created a style of their own. This included both the lavishly decorated display services and ceramics for ordinary use. Increased availability in Italy meant that the practice of sharing of vessels at table could gradually cease; Italian travellers north of the Alps now expressed horror when they encountered what they had come to regard as a social barbarity.

Lorenzo de' Medici at the close of the quattrocento had a travelling country service of some forty pieces at his villa of Correggi. In 1518 Clarissa Strozzi ordered a service of forty-eight pieces *alla porcellana*. Both give an indication of the multiplication of vessels for the table. Faenza, which was to become a major centre of production, played a crucial part in the constant elaboration of tableware promoted by the Este court. At one of the 1565 marriage feasts, for example, twelve thousand maiolica plates decorated in the duchess's livery were used.[80] An inventory of Montano Barbaran's Palladian palazzo in 1592 shows that the maiolica collection of this Venetian aristocrat included eighteen candlesticks and a hundred and eighty-one other large and small pieces, all decorated with the Barbaran arms. It was handsome, too – a diarist records dining at the villa 'with many other nobles and officials; the dinner service was of the most beautiful maiolica . . .'[81] These dishes usually had a wide border for the food with a small well at the centre for the sauce. Such services must have done much to give the table a visual unity of a kind unknown to the Middle Ages. Not that the use of maiolica escaped the all-pervading preoccupation with hierarchy. At the grandest events gold and silver plate would continue to be used on the high table, with maiolica given to those below. The multiplication of tableware also meant that each diner had his or her own drinking vessel; there was no longer any question of sharing.

Amidst all this change comes the fork.[82] The Elizabethan traveller Thomas Coryat speaks of these implements in the 1590s with a degree of wonder:

Here I will mention a thing . . . that is not used in any other country that I saw in my travels, neither doe I thinke that any other nation of Christendome doth use it, but only Italy. The Italian and also most strangers that are commorant in Italy, doe alwaies at their meales use a little forke when they cut their meat. For while with their knife which they hold in one hand they cut the meate out of the dish, they fasten their forke which they hold in their other hand upon the same dish, so that whatsoever he be that sitting in the company of any others at meate, should unadvisedly touch the dish of meate with his fingers from which all the table doe cut, he will give occasion of offence unto the company, as having transgressed the lawes of good manners, in so much that for his error he shall at the least be brow-beaten, if not reprehended in wordes. This forme of feeding I understand is generally used in all places in Italy . . . The reason of this their curiosity is, because the Italian cannot by any means indure to have his dish touched with fingers, seeing all mens fingers are not alike cleane. Hereupon I thought my selfe good to imitate the fashion by this forked cutting of meate, not only while I was in Italy, but also in Germany, and oftentimes in England since I came home . . .[83]

Coryat's association of the advent of the fork with a sudden awareness of food hygiene is in fact misleading, for the adoption of the fork was more concerned with hierarchy. It offered yet another opportunity for the upper classes to distinguish themselves from the peasantry. In fact eating with the fingers had always been perfectly hygienic. The diner held the piece of meat intended for himself firmly with the finger of his left hand while he cut it off with the knife in his right. The practicality of the technique explains why it took so long for forks to be adopted north of the Alps. Members of Louis XIV's court were still using their fingers in the 1660s.

The arrival of the fork.
The ladies at the left-hand table are using them for dessert.
Wedding feast from *The Story of Nastagio degli Onesti*, celebrating the marriage
of Giannozzo Pucci to Lucrezia Piero di Giovanni Bini in 1483.
Painting attributed to Sandro Botticelli.

Forks are in fact not much in evidence in Italy during the quattrocento, although we know they existed – in 1492 Lorenzo de' Medici had
eighteen of them.[84] Evidence would suggest that initially they were used
only for special foods like salads and sweetmeats, in particular for fruits

in syrup. Their most spectacular early appearance in a picture is in Botticelli's depiction of a wedding feast, on one of the *cassone* panels painted for the marriage of a relative of the Medici family, Giannozzo Pucci, to Lucrezia Piero di Giovanni Bini in 1483. Based on a story by Boccaccio, the scene shows two tables, one for the ladies and another for the gentlemen. It is the ladies who hold forks elegantly in their fingers. A definite reference to their use comes in 1536 at the great banquet staged to welcome the Emperor Charles V. Each guest, it was recorded, was provided with a knife, spoon *and* fork. Not until 1563 do forks appear again, this time in Veronese's great canvas of *The Marriage at Cana* (in the Louvre). This depicts a great Renaissance princely feast at the dessert stage. To the left, at the angle of the table, a lady sucks on a fork pensively. Already by 1549, however, Messisbugo in his *Banchetti* is taking them for granted. That increase in use may also have something to do with the emergence of pasta as part of Italian cuisine during the cinquecento. Henry III discovered forks while travelling back via Italy from Poland to France in 1574, and introduced them to the French court; they were later to be cited as evidence of Valois decadence.[85]

Another Italian innovation was the silver *cadena*. Michel de Montaigne in his Italian journal describes seeing *cadenas* at a dinner given by Cardinal de Sens in Rome in 1580:

> . . . in front of those to whom they want to do particular honour, who are seated beside or opposite the master, they place big silver squares [i.e. cadenas] on which their salt cellar stands, of the same sort as those they put before the great in France. On top of this there is a napkin folded in four, and on this napkin the bread, knife, fork, and spoon. On top of all of this there is another napkin, which you are to use . . .[86]

As a consequence of this change, that glory of the medieval feast, the nef, was reduced to a mere display object.

Trestle tables remained in use all through the Italian Renaissance.[87] The trestles themselves were shaped like an inverted 'V' at the front, but had only one vertical leg at the back, making it easier to sit on that side. Such tables had the great advantage of flexibility – they could be set up

A lady sucks her fork at the corner of the table during dessert.
Detail from Paolo Veronese's *The Marriage at Cana*, 1562–3.

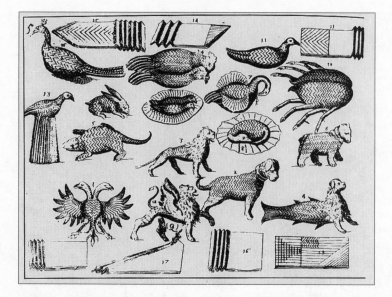

quickly anywhere. As the private dining-room gained currency, however, permanent tables became more common. The first published design for a draw-leaf table appeared in Orléans in 1550, suggesting that the type had been in existence earlier, but whether it was invented in Italy or north of the Alps is unknown.

One of the great set rituals of any major feast was the layering of tablecloths.[88] Platina wrote that the cloths ought to be white. Otherwise, he believed, the appetite would be impaired. Already at the nuptial banquet of Costanzo Sforza to Camilla of Aragon in 1475 the cloth was changed several times at the high table and twice for the other tables. In general, sixteenth-century treatises specify three table coverings: one found on arrival, a second revealed midway and a third for dessert, *colatione*. From Fusoritto's edition of Cervio's *Il trinciante* (1593) we learn that there was a layer of leather between the cloths to prevent any stains seeping through. The changing of cloths is noted in an account of the feast at the wedding of Giulio Thiene, conte di Scandiano: 'Once the upper cloth, which was embroidered with flowers had been lifted, and people had washed their hands, another tablecloth, worked with flowers and little birds was revealed.'[89]

If tablecloths had been made to play a role in the visual spectacle and surprise, even more so had napkins. These now began to be starched

Opposite and above: The art of napkin folding.
Two plates from Mattia Giegher's *Trattato* of 1639
recording a vast repertory of possible shapes.

and stiffened and deployed as an art form akin to paper sculpture. An early reference to this practice comes at a banquet held in Rome in 1513 in honour of Giuliano and Lorenzo de' Medici. Here the napkins were folded so as to enclose a live bird which flew away when the napkin was opened by the guest. Messisbugo is forever referring to napkins being 'divinely made' (*divinamente fatte*) into shapes as varied as flames and birds. Fusoritto describes a banquet for the marriage of Guglielmo Gonzaga, duke of Mantua, and Margherita Farnese in 1581 at which 'the napkins . . . were delightfully sculpted by pleating them into columns, arches and trophies, which made for a very fine sight along with a multitude of flags bearing the arms of all the lords at the feast.'[90] By 1639 Mattia Giegher could publish an illustrated *Trattato* on the art.

In the end napkins became purely decorative and were not used at all, but during the Renaissance they were constantly employed to wipe a spoon or fork or drinking vessel. Gentlemen generally laid the napkin over the left shoulder. A picture now in the National Portrait Gallery in London, celebrating the life of the Elizabethan diplomat Sir Henry

Unton and painted about the time of his death in 1596, shows a feast in progress at which some of the male diners (all wearing hats) have napkins tossed across their left shoulders. There are many other visual sources showing this custom. Nevertheless, both in the Unton picture and the others there is no sign of any napkin for many of the male diners. We must conclude that in such cases the napkin was placed on the lap, as it always was for ladies.

Buffets, tableware, tablecloths, napkins set the scene for the action of the feast. It would not have varied much from court to court, although the Italians would have been in the vanguard of any new display. The ritual was in fact standardised. To illustrate this fact I know of no more informative depictions of court banquets in action than the drawings made on the occasion of the marriage of Alexander, duke of Parma, son of the Emperor Charles V's daughter, Margaret, regent of the Netherlands, to Maria of Portugal.[91] These nuptials were staged in Brussels in November 1565 on a magnificent scale by the regent, whose revival of the splendours of fifteenth-century Burgundy was an attempt to hold the loyalty of an aristocracy uneasy over the repressive policies of Philip II of Spain. It is interesting to see just how far Italian feasting style had percolated north-wards. Most of Margaret of Parma's attendant ladies were Italian and so was one of her three major domos. The staging of the feasts was managed as it might have been in Ferrara, by the steward, the cupbearer and the carver. There were three banquets in all, one on the day of the wedding, a second, the nuptial feast proper, a week later, and a third given by the city of Brussels for the couple at the close of a great tournament in honour of the event. Of these the most splendid was the second, held in the great hall of the palace on 18 November.

We are fortunate that in addition to the drawings, a Bolognese called De Marchi wrote a detailed account of the event. The room was hung with tapestries and at one end the high table stood on a platform approached by three steps. There, beneath a canopy at the centre, sat the bride and groom flanked by the groom's mother, the regent, and, on the other side, the Spanish ambassador representing Philip II. The exalted status of everyone at that table is confirmed by the fact that they are seated on chairs. Three major domos along with thirty gentlemen and many others ministered to the needs of those at the high table.

A great court banquet in action on the occasion of the marriage of
Alexander, duke of Parma to Mary of Portugal.
The setting is the great hall of the royal palace in Brussels on 18 November 1565.
Illumination, Flemish, late sixteenth century.

Below, in the body of the hall at ground level, sat a hundred and twelve
ladies and forty gentlemen. The illustration shows an L-shaped table occupied only by gentlemen, so in that sense its record of the feast must be
considered approximate. But they are shown — accurately one feels — seated
on benches, an indication of their social inferiority. Close to the high table,
to the left, there is an enclosure like a box; here the court musicians have

been placed to provide music during the meal. In the foreground a major domo is shown clutching his staff of office and supervising the entry of a course preceded by trumpeters and drummers. They sweep past a canopied buffet laden with plate.

Our Italian observer noted a number of interesting details not captured in the drawing. One was the presence of what he estimated to be no fewer than two thousand spectators. A second was the fact that the napkins had been folded by 'maestro Giovanni Milanese', evidence of how this Italian elaboration had migrated north. Giovanni had pleated napkins at the high table to make two castles complete with artillery, infantry and artificial fire (the bridegroom was a major military commander), and flaunting the customary heraldry. Finally De Marchi notes that each of the eight courses consisted of food of a particular Low Countries province, such as Flanders or Brabant, giving the meal a political as well as a culinary connotation. Before the guests left the table, there was a masque of eight aristocratic children escorted by musicians and torchbearers. Their performance ended with the presentation of posies of artificial flowers containing sonnets in several languages to the most important personages. Afterwards, the hall was cleared and the customary court ball followed.

In this account we can recognise familiar elements from the fêtes of the Burgundian dukes during the previous century, but they are fused with a new Italianate overlay. There is besides a deliberate emphasis on the internationality of the occasion, in terms of food and the languages used. Spaniards, Italians, Flemings and Portuguese were all on hand. Evident in this banquet is the way fashions in cooking and ceremonial style migrated from court to court, particularly courts directly or indirectly linked to the Habsburgs.

Such banquets were clearly microcosms of society. The ruler and chief guests always sat on an elevated dais. The seat of honour might be at the centre of the high table or at one end (as it was in the picture of the first of the three Brussels feasts), but hierarchy was always observed, both by placement and by changes of level. Sometimes a separate room was involved. A chamber called the *tinello* was employed in Italy to seat those considered too lowly for the main assembly. Consignment to that could be taken as a serious affront. When some of the French accompanying Henry III to Ferrara in 1574 were downgraded to the *tinello*, they complained bitterly. They were forced to eat off coarse earthenware without even knives or forks, together 'with thieving knaves, who jostled and pushed, instead of servants'.[92]

What a guest was given to sit on equally reflected his status. Beginning with the upholstered chair with arms reserved for princes, great lords and, occasionally, ladies, the sequence descended to a chair with a back but no arms, to a stool and, finally, to the lowly bench. Subtleties of seating and gradations of rank became more rather than less complex. Two examples will suffice. Earlier in the sequence of fêtes staged for the great Medici wedding of 1600 in Florence, in which Henry IV was married by proxy to Marie de' Medici, there was a dinner immediately following the ceremony in the Duomo. This niece of the grand duke who, up until then, would never have been accorded a ranking place at table, became queen of France. Like magic, the metamorphosis was immediate. The new queen was escorted to her place at table in the *Sala delle Statue* of the Palazzo Signoria by the French ambassador, who ceremonially presented her with her napkin (an honour which at other courts was to be fought over). She sat alone beneath a canopy at what was still, although grand, essentially a family dinner:

> The Grand Duke [her uncle] sat two arm's lengths from the Queen on her right, with the Grand Duchess opposite; below him was the Duchess of Bracciano, who had a chair, then Signor Don Virginio her husband. Opposite them were the most excellent Signor Giovanni and Signor Antonio de' Medici, uncle and brother respectively of the Queen. But they were seated on stools and served from open dishes [unlike the covered ones for the higher-ups, a protection against contamination] and their goblets lacked *sotto coppe* [the coasters the others had]. As in France, no one drank unless the Queen did so . . .[93]

Almost thirty years on, Charles I's queen Henrietta Maria, one of Marie de' Medici's daughters, celebrated her birthday at her London residence, Somerset House, with a play followed by a supper. The occasion was not in any sense a public one but it was certainly courtly. Here again we can see that everything was done to preserve social distinctions. A separate room served as a *tinello* where 'the inferiour ladyes and maydes of honour'

Banquet given in honour of Christian III, king of Denmark, by Bartolomeo
Colleoni. The king sits alone at the head of the table, his carver administering
to him. Space, in deference to his rank, isolates him from the other diners.
Painting by Marcello Fogolino, 1530s.

ate at a long table along with the servants of the French ambassador. In
the main room the king and queen together with the ambassador all sat
down at the same table along with various lords and ladies. This time
what is striking is the spacing of the guests around the table:

> The kyng and queene in the myddest, and on theyr left hand (with
> the distance of one seat) sat the ambassadour, and on theyr right (wyth

like distance) the lady marquis of Hamilton, and so answerably the
rest of the lordes and ladyes round about the table, except only in the
opposite of theyr majesties (where roome was left) for theyr carver,
sewer, etc.[94]

In this way Charles I and Henrietta Maria were isolated from the rest of
the company in a manner which must have made conversation at the best
awkward.

The emergence of both the *scalco* and the *trinciante* only served to
accentuate every nuance of social gradation. The steward's role was to
keep a sharp eye on what food went where and that its quantity matched
the rank of its recipient. The carver's was to carve and present meat, also

according to rank, the most desirable parts being reserved for those at the high table while items like the giblets filtered downwards.

All of these minutiae of etiquette built on features that were already present in the late Middle Ages. What was new in Renaissance Italy was the change in the actual meal structure. In the quattrocento the sequence followed had been that of Northern Europe, opening with soups with a vegetable or meat base, lasagne, tortellini in broth, all kinds of stewed and stuffed meats served with sauces. Next came the course of roast or baked meats in savoury sauces and then one of fritters, mortadelle, tarts and pies served with the classic white, green and cameline sauces. finally there was dessert consisting of cooked or candied fruit, sweetmeats, dragees, nuts and candied aniseed.[95] During the cinquecento two great changes occurred. The first, as we shall see, was that the last course on any grand occasion detached itself and became a great set piece presented in a separate room.

The other great change involved the actual food and its serving sequence.[96] The Italian Renaissance meal made far greater use of vegetables than before, while the new sequence of courses was related to the *credenza*, the side table on which cold dishes could be arrayed and served. There was a shift to white meat like veal and game, an index of aristocratic status; the guests could imagine themselves a band of noble hunters consuming what they had slain in the chase. The meal structure as it emerged in the cinquecento developed into what became the widely admired 'servizio all'italiana', in which cold dishes – 'servizi di credenza' – were served in varying sequences alternating with hot ones – 'servizio di cucina'. For example, a meal could open with *antipasti* from the *credenza*, items like cold salads and meats, fresh fruit tarts, jellies, melon, grapes and special biscuits which were dipped into malvasia or Trebbiano wine. Then followed one or more courses of roast, fried or stuffed meat (on fast days fish and crustaceans) from the kitchen. This could include rissoles, fricassees, meat pies, *crostate* (a kind of pie), sausages, ravioli, lasagne, macaroni, gnocchi, pappardelle (a form of macaroni), stuffed goose and capon. Within this framework there was the enormous elaboration of cuisine recorded in Bartolomeo Scappi's *Opera*. Often it is almost over-whelming in its richness, with a penchant for things we would find utterly repulsive such as *crostate* of kids' eyes and ears or roasted lambs' testicles. After this came another course from the *credenza* of cooked and raw vegetables, tarts and pastries, cheeses, oysters and milk puddings. Finally (if they were served at table and not elsewhere) *candite confettioni*, sweet things like fruits in syrup and candied seeds. Such a sequence was not immutable. Romoli, 'Il Panunto', for example, does not alternate cold and hot courses but could frame a meal, like one for fish days, with two cold courses sandwiching two hot.

Roughly speaking, what was regarded as *servizio al'italiana* worked on alternating cold and hot courses, cold from the *credenza*, hot from the *cucina*. It is a sequence which is already clear in Platina in the mid-fifteenth century. Even when the courses multiplied, as they did on great occasions, the rhythm was maintained. This can be illustrated with a single example. In May 1583 Pope Clement VII gave a feast in honour of the three sons of William V, duke of Bavaria, in the Castle of St Angelo.[97] In the first place, it incorporates all the food fixations of the Renaissance banquet. Among the dishes we would find repulsive are a second course which had a poussin for each guest accompanied by a pastry shell stuffed with cockscombs, testicles and gooseberries, large pies filled with kids' eyes, ears and testicles, and boned and stuffed calves' heads. The fourth course boasted a dish of capons' testicles and a salad of goats' feet.

Even more typical was the way every ingredient was subjected to display. Quality of ingredients and taste had to give way before the need to show off as part of the never-ending litany of homage to the crown. (The processional presentation of food as a dazzling cavalcade resulted, of course, in its being invariably tepid or cold by the time it reached the table.) The most spectacular display pieces in the case of the papal banquet for the Bavarians included 'white peacocks in their feathers, adorned with pearls, corals, and gold and silver leaf, with earrings in their ears and perfume in their beaks', a marzipan Hercules wielding his club against a pastry Hydra stuffed with chopped veal, hard-boiled egg yolks and pine nuts, and 'lions constituted from hares in large pies'. The finale was a model of the Castle of St Angelo itself, out of which came 'red-billed partridges, harnessed with gold and silver cloth, little hares and white rabbits with collars of little bells round their necks and corals in their perfumed paws'. There was a blackamoor king riding an elephant with a castle on its back full of live birds, a hydra which disgorged red moles and dormice, a horse out of whose mouth flew goldfinches on

silken threads, a flower-bedecked bull which was an automaton and walked up and down the table, and a fully-rigged ship filled with sweetmeats from Bergamo. The cuisine of the feast was international in the Scappi manner. There were Pisan biscuits, English pies, meat cooked in the Florentine and French manner, tortellini stuffed with cheese and ham in the German style, and quince paste from Portugal.

What such a table may have looked like can be seen in two paintings in the Prado by Velvet Brueghel from the opening decades of the seventeenth century. Both are intended to celebrate the senses: one celebrates taste, the other taste, hearing and touch. Brueghel is a brilliant still-life painter who fully communicates the lusciousness of the Renaissance banquet table, its appeal in terms of texture and colour, as well as that of contrasting form. There are pies with a peacock's tail feathers and head arising from the crust and another with swan's wings, head and gold-collared neck. We see lobsters, cascades of oysters, the glistening basted flesh of roasted birds set on pewter and, in one picture, an astonishing compound dish with heraldic pennons fluttering atop a branch of greenery.

The senses of taste, hearing and touch evoked by means of the banquet.
Detail of a painting by Velvet Brueghel, early seventeenth century.

More almost than any other source, apart from Veronese's *Marriage at Cana*, these paintings capture the essence of the Renaissance banquet as spectacle.

In the picture devoted to three of the senses, a lady plays a lute, thus reminding us of an element we have already seen as central to any great banquet at the Este court, music. Ficino regarded music at a banquet as important because of the way it combined opposites, a direct appeal to the senses simultaneously linked to the supernatural harmony of the cosmos.[98] The integration of food and music at Ferrara was emulated by other music-loving European courts. One such was the court of the father of the young Bavarian princes fêted in Rome in 1583, William V of Bavaria. In 1568 the duke had married Renée of Lorraine in Munich. The feast took place in the castle, and was remarkable for the manner in which the dining and the music was integrated. The festivities opened with an hour-long concert of wind instruments. Then the guests began to consume the antipasti to an eight-part composition by the court organist and a six-part motet by Orlando di Lasso played by an ensemble of cornets and trombones:

> Immediately [thereafter] the second course was brought in from the kitchen to the sound of trumpets and timpani . . . The ducal musicians played various six-part compositions . . . During the fourth course was heard an excellent twelve-voiced piece . . . with six stringed instruments, five sackbutts, a cornet and a pleasing positiv [organ] . . . with the fifth course . . . the ensemble accompanied six singers on six violas da gamba sounding a fourth lower than regular ones, [along] with six flutes and a keyboard instrument. With the sixth course . . . those instruments which sounded in a most pleasant manner were a clavicembalo, a sackbutt, a flute, a lute – played masterfully by a virtuoso . . . a bagpipe, a cornet, a viola da gamba, and a fife . . . The seventh course: the ensemble consisted of twelve musicians, who were divided into three choirs, namely four violas da gamba in the first, four large flutes in the second [and] a dulzino, a bagpipe, a fife, and a soft [mute] horn in the third.[99]

It must have been a splendid evening.

Feast into fantasy

ONE OF THE most influential of all Renaissance books appeared in Venice in 1499. Francesco Colonna's *Hypnerotomachia Poliphili* is an allegorical romance with a difference, for the hero seeks his beloved Polia by means of a journey through a humanist classical dreamland. One of the incidents in this phantasmagoria is a seven-course banquet given by a queen.[100] Not only were the cloths changed for every course but the livery of the servants too. Each course was prefaced by the entry of a stupendous buffet on wheels 'with its front made in the form of a boat or drinking cup and the back shaped like a triumphal chariot'. Music accompanied each new stage of the banquet. 'In this way,' runs the text, 'one was always hearing lovely music, listening to gentle harmonies, harkening to delectable melodies, breathing delightful perfumes and receiving the most delicious satisfaction of the appetite.' So, for example, a cloth of purple silk (of which Platina would certainly not have approved) strewn with roses was followed by a yellow cloth sprinkled with lilies of the valley and narcissus. The food ranged from saffron-coloured fritters doused with musk-flavoured water and sugar to peacocks' breasts with sour green sauce. The finale involved five servants in blue silk shot with gold distributing fruit from a bush of coral, followed by a mobile fountain

Buffet in the form of a triumphal chariot from Francesco Colonna's *Hypnerotomachia Poliphili*, 1499.

studded with jewels which revolved and wetted the diners. Finally came a ballet danced by thirty-two dancers dressed as kings and queens.

What Colonna conjures up in his imagination was in fact very little removed from reality. Feasts approaching this level of complexity were a fact of life at the Italian courts by the close of the quattrocento. The *Hypnerotomachia Poliphili* was hugely popular elsewhere, being elegantly translated into French by Jean Martin in 1546 (albeit reduced by a quarter), and into English by Sir Robert Dallington in 1592 (this time stopping short two-fifths of the way through). But the banquet style it described must have struck its Northern European readers as very different from the one they were familiar with. The effect would have been reinforced by the fact that the book was full of illustrations owing much to the labours of Renaissance archaeology and classical scholarship. In the case of the feast, we are once again deep in an imaginative recreation of banqueting in Antiquity. We have already encountered this type of feast, with its concern for scenography and choreography of a highly complex kind, organised by Messisbugo and his successors at the Ferrarese court.

[185]

It is nothing less than the banquet as a unified theatrical production of a kind never achieved in the meandering vaudeville of the Burgundian court, one in which a single theme is fixed and everything from the decor and liveries to the figurative food and entertainment is made subservient to it.

The first banquet with such an elaborate co-ordinated *mise-en-scène* is likely to have been one given to celebrate the marriage of Eleonora of Aragon, daughter of Ferdinand I of Naples, to Ercole I, duke of Ferrara.[101] The festivities which marked this match extended over three months of the summer of 1473. Ercole and the Este court voyaged to Naples to fetch the bride, who then made a triumphal progress to her new domain, stopping along the way in various places, in particular Rome. There a stupendous banquet was given in her honour by one of Pope Sixtus IV's 'nephews' (often a euphemism for illegitimate children), Cardinal Pietro Riario, the driving force in Roman humanist circles behind the revival of ancient theatre and drama. It was staged in front of the cardinal's palace in the Piazza SS Apostoli. A temporary loggia was erected and divided into three rooms hung with tapestries and rich fabrics, and garlanded with greenery and flowers. The piazza itself was shielded from the sun by a fabric ceiling, a *valerium*, while at its centre stood a fountain spouting perfumed water and tended by a youth attired in golden leaves. Two tables seating ten guests each occupied the largest of the three loggia rooms and on a stage opposite the loggia a series of interludes was enacted between the courses of the dinner.

What sets this event apart is that instead of the disparate pageant cars and incidents which could erupt upon diners at a medieval feast, we have for the first time a scenario that embraced the whole event and lasted some seven hours. The four interludes on the stage related to the four courses served at the tables. After each course the tables were cleared and one cloth was lifted to reveal a cloth of another colour beneath, matching the changed liveries of the servants. The cutlery too changed course by course from silver to gold. The food was typically late medieval with a lavish amount of gilding, even on the bread, and the usual parade of reconstituted birds and beasts. Into the momentum of the meal was integrated a series of mythological interludes referring to the bride and groom – Atlanta and Hippomenes, Jason and Medea, Hercules and Deianira, Bacchus and Ariadne. The courtly compliments paid on stage in dialogue, mime and song were echoed on the table in the final dessert course, a sugar banquet featuring three of the Labours of Hercules (in reference to the groom, Ercole) and castles which were broken up and the pieces thrown to the watching crowd. After that a mountain was wheeled in and a man emerged from it to address the onlookers, followed by Venus, goddess of love, in a chariot drawn by two swans. This led on to a re-enactment of the story of Hercules and the dragon in the Garden of the Hesperides. The finale was a dance by eight mythological couples which was rudely interrupted by centaurs carrying shields and maces. This provided an excuse (again in homage to the duke) to stage the battle of Hercules and the centaurs, which of course Hercules won.

This feast seems to have set the style for a whole series of similar ones in the late quattrocento, thus creating what can only be described as a new genre, the allegorical banquet. Two years later, at the marriage of Costanzo Sforza to Camilla of Aragon at Pesaro, the nuptial banquet was supervised by the inhabitants of Olympus, the hot courses being served under the aegis of the sun, Apollo, and the cold under that of the moon, Diana.[102] In 1489, at the marriage of Isabella of Aragon to Gian Galeazzo Sforza, Jason spread his golden fleece on the nuptial table, Mercury presented a calf, and Diana a stag.[103]

A manuscript in the Pierpont Morgan Library in New York, compiled by a Neapolitan cook some time during the last decade of the fifteenth century, records in detail a whole series of banquets. By far the most important was that given by Ascanio Sforza, created a cardinal in 1484, in honour of the prince of Capua.[104] It consisted of eight courses, each of which was served by a different member of the hierarchy of Olympus: Venus, Jove and Juno ushered in the roast course, Diana and her nymphs the game, Neptune on a marine chariot the fish, Jason and three sirens jellies, Pan junkets and curds in golden baskets, and Pomona fruit and sweetmeats with hippocras. Golden brooms swept up what had been thrown to the dogs.

From such highly organised feasts there is a clear line of descent to the kind of supper devised by Messisbugo and his successors with which I opened this chapter. We have traced how that format came to be standard for great occasions throughout the century at the Este court. But such spectacles were not confined to Ferrara alone. Two other instances will show how pervasive the allegorical feast was as a format in the Italian courts as the Renaissance era gave way to the baroque. The first was perhaps the most spectacular of this kind ever given, the banquet of 1600 occasioned by the nuptials of Marie de' Medici and Henry IV.[105] It marked a diplomatic triumph of the highest order, the marriage of a daughter of what, a century before, had been a mere family of bankers to the king of France. A publicity machine always made much of Medici festivals, pouring out commemorative descriptive books and engravings. The year 1600 was no exception. I have already described the gigantic *credenza*, but the *Sala del Cinquecento* had for the occasion superimposed on it an architectural decor. This framed golden statues and contained portraits of the bride and groom as well as their predecessors and prototypes Henry II and Catherine de' Medici. Two grottoes also had their place. The new queen and her family, along with the chief guests, sat elevated at one end of the room while below them three tables, each containing a hundred ladies, were waited on by gentlemen. The food embraced every kind of late mannerist fantasy. On the high table were two oak trees seemingly made of snow with white leaves and silver garlands. Beneath their branches a hunt was in progress. At the ladies' centre table a rampant lion disgorged lilies from his breast while simultaneously metamorphosing into an imperial eagle. At a certain moment in the feast the high table parted in two, drawing aside to be transformed into vases. Meanwhile from beneath the floor arose a table bearing dessert in the form of a winter landscape. A diarist records that at this point the lights were somehow dimmed, dramatically heightening the effect of what happened next. Two clouds slowly propelled themselves from the side grottoes to halt above the diners' heads, opening to reveal the golden and bejewelled chariots of the goddesses Juno and Minerva, who had come to grace this 'superhuman banquet of the gods'. These aerial apparitions then contended over the question of whose presence was more appropriate, at length resolving the issue by hailing the marriage itself, whereupon a vast rainbow was seen to vault the hall. After this the queen and her ladies made their way to the centre table, which again was the subject of a miraculous transformation. By a clever horizontal use of *periaktoi* (turning frames employed vertically on stage for scene change) the surface of the table revolved to reveal first mirrors reflecting the ceiling paintings glorifying the Medici, and then a sugar garden filled with singing birds and other creatures. These the queen presented to her ladies while gentlemen offered them fruit and flowers from the sugar garden.

The feast as theatre.
The duchess of Savoy and her family preside from
a box over an allegorical banquet, 1645.
Illumination, Italian, seventeenth century.

Such a feast drew upon the whole resources of the Medici court. Giovan
Battista Guarino wrote the lyrics for the contention of the goddesses, Emilio
Cavalieri the music. The rest fell to the combined talents of the multi-
faceted architect and designer Bernardo Buontalenti, the painter Jacopo
Ligozzi and the sculptor Giambologna. The latter, assisted by the staff of
his studio, even designed the sugar sculpture for the tables.

The second example comes as late as 1645. On 10 February of that
year, Madame Reali, daughter of Henry IV and duchess of Savoy, celebrated her birthday at the castle of Rivoli with an allegorical banquet.[106]
This event was also charged with political significance; it celebrated

the restoration of political equilibrium to the duchy after years of internal dissension. Like all the festivals at the Savoy court, it was under the direction of one man, a courtier and councillor of state named Filippo d'Aglié, who devised the scenarios for tournaments, ballets and feasts over a period of thirty years. The banquet was given by Duchess Christina's son, the young Duke Charles Emmanuel, in honour of his mother, and was staged in four different rooms, one after another. Each room represented a different province of the duchy, its walls adorned with scenic panoramas and the ceilings with the relevant heraldry. To emphasise the patriotic nature of the feast, as in the case of the wedding feast of Alexander Farnese in Brussels, food associated with the particular province was served in each of the rooms.

We are fortunate in that a remarkable visual record has survived of all Savoy fêtes, painted by a certain Tommaso Borgonio. We need only turn to the picture depicting the province of Savoy to get the full flavour of the event. The duchess, dressed in her widow's weeds, sits flanked by her two daughters, Adelaide and Margherita. They are in an elevated box or pavilion approached by a double staircase and attended by, among others, the duchess's *scalco, trinciante* and *coppiere* (cupbearer). Below them, twenty guests sit at a long table which stretches towards the *credenza* with its display of plate. There are two sets of servants, one in a livery of puce and crimson trimmed in gold, a second in black with red stockings. The former seem to be dealing with the delivery of drink and the latter with the food. Behind the buffet rises a mountainous decor presided over by a statue of Savoy, while on the long side wall is a vista to the fortress of Mommeliano. This is, of course, only the first room; three more rooms followed, dedicated in succession to Turin and Piedmont, Nice, and, finally, Monferrato. After the meal everyone moved on to the *Sala del Balletto* where dancers attired in costumes of the different provinces performed a ballet. In the text accompanying his pictures, Borgonio emphasises the theme of the feast – for those present to rally to the defence of the duchy by arms and arts as well as by devotion of mind and spirit.

Allegorical feasts were in the main a feature of the Italian courts rather than those north of the Alps. Here the traditions of Burgundy continued to be observed throughout the sixteenth century, wherein the feast would be followed by an invasion of masquers like those appearing

A stately masque headed by Mercury and Diana
makes its entrance at a late Elizabethan banquet.
Detail from the *Memorial Picture of Sir Henry Unton, c. 1596.*

at the nuptial feast of Alexander Farnese in 1565. A rare English record of
this type of event in action appears in the memorial portrait of Sir Henry
Unton in the National Portrait Gallery in London. Sir Henry, his wife
and guests sit ranged around a table while in the foreground we can see
the goddess Diana and a train of nymphs advance. Mercury, the messenger
of the gods, seems to be declaiming to Lady Unton at one end of the
table the meaning of the masque. This kind of close conjunction between

feasting and court entertainment was to be broken in the next century when the masque demanded a room of its own and a stage. Food and fête, so closely aligned throughout the Middle Ages, finally parted company.

There is an exception. Hardly surprisingly it was French and staged under the aegis of a Medici, Catherine de' Medici. It took place at Bayonne on the Franco-Spanish border on 24 June 1565[107] as part of a dazzling series of festivities involving members of both courts. This entertainment was the queen's. Guests embarked on a ship constructed like a castle and sailed along the river Adour, encountering various marine deities en route and landing on an island. There they were greeted by two musicians dressed as Linus and Orpheus. Three nymphs sang of peace between the kingdoms while the party made its way along a green alley to an octagonal banqueting house built round an oak tree. At the foot of the tree was a fountain bubbling in a grotto, while within the pavilion eight alcoves each contained a table for eight. An elevated oval table served the royal party. Then followed a feast, exactly in the Italian manner, accompanied by musicians stationed near the service entrances. Five shepherds and ten shepherdesses dressed in cloth of gold and silver bore food to the royal table; more shepherds and shepherdesses served the remainder of the guests. Once the feast was over, musicians masquerading as satyrs struck up music for a ballet danced by nine nymphs.

Catherine's daughter, Marguerite de Valois, the future Henry IV's first wife, describes the occasion in her memoirs. She notes details not recorded elsewhere, for instance the fact that the pastoral waiters were dressed in costumes of the different provinces of France – a political allusion – and that the whole event was washed out by a storm. But for her to mention the occasion at all in her memoirs suggests that she must have thought it very unusual. And indeed it was. Such a tightly co-ordinated manifestation is not typical of the Renaissance in Northern Europe.

Evidence can be found suggesting that not everyone was easily bemused by the dramatic escalation in prodigality of such culinary showpieces. Within the Iberian peninsula there was a strong reaction against the Emperor Charles V's embrace of Burgundian excess and spectacle. The Grand Inquisitor Torquemada, in his *Colloques satiriques* (1553), praises 'antique frugality and Spanish simplicity' as opposed to tables served *à la flamande*. When in Spain, the emperor was careful to curb ostentation.[108]

Giorgio Vasari, in his life of the Florentine sculptor Giovan Francesco Rustico, provides a record of another critical viewpoint.[109] Rustico formed a group which called itself the Company of the Cauldron and staged banquets. Each member was allowed to bring four guests and was expected to supply one dish. The result sounds like a deliberate parody of the decor and the food of a grand Medici court banquet. At one of these gatherings, the diners were placed around what seemed to be an enormous cauldron in such a way that they appeared to stand in boiling water. The dishes were outrageous versions of court figurative food:

> In his turn the present of Rustico was a cauldron made of pastry, in which Ulysses was roasting his father to rejuvenate him, the two figures being capons shaped like men . . . Andrea del Sarto [the painter] presented an octagonal church like S. Giovanni, but resting on columns. The pavement was formed of jelly, resembling a variously coloured mosaic; the columns, which looked like porphyry, were large sausages; the bases and capitals parmesan cheese; the cornices were made of pastry and sugar, and the quarters of marchpane. In the middle was a choir desk made of cold veal, with a book made of pastry, the letters and notes being formed of peppercorns. The singers were roast thrushes with open beaks, wearing surplices of tender pig's caul, and behind these were two large pigeons for the bases, with six larks for sopranos . . .

Rustico was member of another company, that of the Trowel, which also staged feasts of this kind during the second decade of the cinquecento. Each dinner had a theme. One was architectural, with the guests, dressed as builders and labourers, ordered to construct a building from food which was in the end torn apart and eaten. The Trowel's most memorable dinner was a precisely inverted version of the allegorical feast typical of the Italian courts at the end of the quattrocento. The theme was Ceres seeking her daughter Proserpine in the Underworld, and although Pluto disdains to give her up, he invites everyone to the nuptial feast. The guests enter through a door disguised as a serpent's mouth:

. . . and find themselves in a round room illuminated by one small light in the middle, so that they scarcely recognise each other. They are shown into their places at the black-draped table by a hideous devil holding a fork, and Pluto commands that the pains of hell shall cease so long as they remain there, in honour of the wedding. The holes of the damned were all painted, and their torments, and on a light being applied flames sprang up which showed the nature of the torment. The viands were all animals of the most repulsive appearance but with delicate meats of various kinds underneath. The exteriors were serpents, toads, lizards, newts, spiders, frogs, scorpions, bats, and such things, with the most delicious viands inside. These were placed before each guest with a fire-shovel, and a devil poured choice wines from an ugly glass horn . . . Instead of fruits, dead men's bones followed . . . but they were of sugar . . .

And so it proceeded until at a certain moment all of this was swept away, 'lights were brought and a regal scene took its place, decent servants bringing the remainder of a magnificent banquet'. It is difficult not to believe that the artists responsible for these travesties were the same as those who created the wonderful court events being parodied. Could they have been entirely ignorant at whose expense they were having such amusing evenings?

The collation and banquet

W HAT I HAVE not yet touched upon are the consequences of the introduction of one single ingredient, sugar. Sugar was to give birth to a distinctive genre of its own, the collation of sweet and sugared things forming a separate part of the grand meal. The all-consuming passion for sugar which swept through society changed the composition of food and gave new impetus to the practice of reshaping natural ingredients into figurative forms. Nothing was to eclipse sugar in its ability to do precisely that.

Sugar was in fact little known or used in Ancient Greece and Rome.[110] In the sixth century it was brought from India to the Middle East by the

Arabs and thence penetrated the Mediterranean via Cyprus, Crete, Sicily and Spain. In the late Middle Ages sugar came into Northern Europe from the East by way of Venice, but was still a relatively rare commodity. All of this was suddenly to change in the mid-fifteenth century, when the cultivation of sugar cane moved from Spain and Sicily under the aegis of the Portuguese to Madeira and the Canaries, in whose climates it thrived. In the following century it was introduced into the New World, to Brazil and the Caribbean islands, with the result that Europe had a super-abundance. The key ports for the trade were initially Genoa and Venice, the former developing candied fruits as a speciality, the latter all manner of confectionery and pastrywork, including sugar sculpture. But Genoa and Venice were quickly eclipsed by Lisbon and Antwerp. Sugar's conquest of Renaissance courtly society was aided by what were then understood to be its valuable medicinal properties. Considered 'warm' in the first degree, it was supposed, among other properties, to be helpful to the stomach, to cure cold diseases and soothe lung complaints.

We have already encountered sugar sculptures, first at the feast given in 1457 by Gaston de Foix and later at the two marriages of Ercole I d'Este in 1473 and 1491. In each case, carried in procession, they brought the feast to a close. Their purpose was not only to provide spectacle but to pay tribute to both hosts and guests through the flattery of symbolism. Such pieces were made in two ways. Sugar could be rendered malleable like wax and modelled or, in a melted state, could be cast in moulds and worked with the chisel afterwards. Hence the involvement of the major sculptors of the Renaissance. The sugar itself would be brown, because it wasn't refined, and the objects made out of it – known as *trionfi* – were often painted and gilded.

The precedent set at the Este court was quickly imitated.[111] At the marriage of Costanzo Sforza to Camilla of Aragon at Pesaro in 1488, sugar castles were presented to the ambassadors. In the same year, at the wedding of Guidobaldo da Montefeltro to Elisabetta Gonzaga at Urbino, the sugar sculptures included not only castles but cities, fountains, birds and animals, as well as ten life-size trees. At the nuptials of Cosimo I, duke of Florence, in 1539 the feast ended with flora attended by five nymphs bearing gifts for the guests which 'were made of sugar and were dyed a natural colour. Also of sugar were the plates, basins, and other

The sugar banquet in the 'salle enchantée' at Binche, 1549.
Drawing, mid-sixteenth century.

containers holding presents. Each was coloured silver or gold or another hue, as was appropriate.'[112]

Gradually the sugar collation detached itself and became a separate event, one staged in a separate room to which guests were led after the banquet and a ball. There is a remarkable record of one of these, part of the great suite of fêtes staged by Mary of Hungary, regent of the Netherlands, in 1549 at Binche.[113] The festivities welcomed the future Philip II to the Netherlands as heir to his father Charles V, who was also present along with the queen of France. At midnight, following a court ball, the regent conducted the royal party to what was called 'la salle enchantée', a chamber whose ceiling was an artificial heaven across which clouds moved in the wind to reveal stars in the form of lamps burning perfumed oil. To one side of the room a rock spouted different kinds of wine while in the centre rose four massive jasper pillars. In a surviving drawing of the scene the three courses of the collation can be seen descending between the pillars simultaneously. In fact they came down one at a time, and as one course sank into the ground the next was lowered. Each time this happened there was thunder and lightning with a fall of hail and perfumed rain. The hail was 'dragées délicieuses' – pieces of sugar candy. The first table to descend was porcelain and on it was every kind of conserve, 'tous les fruits imaginables'. What was not consumed was pillaged by the onlookers once the royal party had taken its pick. The next table was crystal and glass, containing different-coloured sweets and a hundred kinds of conserve, all white. The last table to arrive was arrayed in nothing but sugar sculpture: a deer, a boar, birds and fish and, in the middle, a rock of red sugar surmounted by five laurel trees with gold and silver leaves bearing sugar fruits. These were decked with the arms of the states of the old Burgundian inheritance and to them was attached a squirrel by a silver chain.

Sixteen years later, at the marriage of Alexander Farnese, there were two such collations after the nuptial banquet.[114] The first, part of the court's celebration, offered every conceivable form of sweetmeat and (as in Florence in 1539) was further remarkable for the fact that not only all the plates, dishes and glasses were of sugar but so, too, were the knives, forks, candlesticks and even the bread. Only the tablecloth was real. Guests were said to have toured the table pointing things out and laughing. That, however, was but a preliminary skirmish for the main sugary event, a gift of the city of Antwerp. The Italian observer, Marchi, writes that he had only once before seen sugar sculptures to equal it (at the marriage of Alessandro de' Medici in 1536 in Naples). No fewer than three thousand pieces depicted the journey of the bride from Lisbon to the Netherlands and her reception there. The voyage was shown as beset by storms, whales and marine monsters, with an effigy of Alessandro awaiting his bride's disembarkation at Middelburg. The tableau went on to record her triumphal progress through several cities before arriving in Brussels. We are told that guests each took away a piece of sculpture as a souvenir.

One more instance must suffice. In 1571 the city of Paris gave a banquet followed by a sugar show on the occasion of the entry of Elizabeth of Austria.[115] The feast was held in the hall of the Palais Épiscopal amidst an extraordinarily esoteric decor devised by the humanist Jean Dorat and executed by the painter Niccolo dell'Abate. Dorat was also credited with the conception of the six major sugar sculptures, which were designed by the court sculptor Germain Pilon. These took pride of place amid some three hundred smaller sugar pieces imitating Venetian glassware. Described as 'grandes pièces de relief . . . du sucre dorée et enrichy', the major sculptures had as their subject the history of the goddess Minerva, equated with the formidable figure of the queen mother, Catherine de' Medici, and were related directly to what Elizabeth of Austria would have seen on the triumphal arches which bestrode the streets of the city in her honour. These wishfully prophesied a mighty eastern empire for her husband, Charles IX.

The only picture which survives showing one of these late sixteenth-century sugar collations is an engraving of one staged for the marriage of Johann Wilhelm, heir to the duke of Jülich-Cleve, to Jakobaea of Baden in 1587. It is somewhat misleading as to scale; the figures strolling in the foreground suggest that the items on the table were enormous. The plates laid along the table's edge give a truer guide. But the display is nevertheless grand and imposing – the trees, the heraldic animals, an elephant with a castle on its back, a unicorn, a bear, a peacock, a camel, a giraffe, a huntsman, a pelican in her piety and, in the middle of it all, the ducal castle with flags flying and a ducal figure within.

Sugar collation on the occasion of the marriage of Johann Wilhelm,
heir to the duke of Jülich-Cleve, 1587. The people in the foreground have
been shrunk to the size of pygmies. Engraving, late sixteenth century.

The sugar collation represents one instance in dining history where
something new and unique was devised in England for the first time.[116]
There the late medieval practice of withdrawing to another room after
dinner to be regaled with wine and spices evolved into something more
complicated. During the sixteenth century, as we have seen, servants ate in
the great hall and the family and their guests in either the great chamber
on formal occasions or a dining parlour on less formal ones. Further
withdrawal to another setting was customary for the delights of what
in England came to be called the banquet. And this precipitated the
invention of the banqueting house.[117]

Between the years 1549 and 1553, Sir William Sharington built a tower with two banqueting rooms, each with a stone table seating seven, at Lacock Abbey in Wiltshire. Not far away at Longleat House, during the early Elizabethan period, Sir John Thynne dotted the roof of his mansion with little rooms like pepperpots. Here guests could combine enjoyment of the banquet itself with enjoyment of fresh air and the prospects of the countryside.

During the reign of Elizabeth such architectural features settled into two types: prospect rooms such as those built into Hardwick Hall, Derbyshire, by the countess of Shrewsbury in the 1590s or completely separate buildings in the grounds of the estate, like the banqueting house designed by Robert Lyminge for Blickling Hall, Norfolk, during the Jacobean period. Francis Bacon, philosopher and lord chancellor, had 'a curious banquetting-house of Roman architecture, paved with black and white marble' on an island. As a familiar adjunct to great mansions such banqueting houses were to last until the landscape movement of the eighteenth century swept them away.

The word 'banquet' in England came into use in the 1530s for the very purpose of differentiating it from the word 'feast'.[118] There is also a link to the humanist yearning to revive the art of conversation. In 1539 Sir Thomas Elyot published *The Bankette of Sapience*, a compendium of witty sayings and aphorisms associating the Tudor form of banquet with a revived art of discourse. As for the comestibles, although the banquet may have started out with imported items such as preserved citrus peels, marmalades of quinces and conserves of soft fruits, it was to add, as was typical of Northern Europe with its dairy produce, things like syllabubs, milk and cream jellies and rosewater and cream cheeses. These were served with Southern European sweet wines and an elaborate range of biscuits. Gervase Markham in his *The English Huswife* (1615) tells how to set forth one of these displays with 'a dish for shew only' of a figurative kind and all the other dishes arranged around it.

The fullest account of an Elizabethan sugar banquet rivalling those of the Italian courts describes the entertainment given Queen Elizabeth I at Elvetham in 1591 by the earl of Hertford, who was anxious to curry favour with her.[119] While the queen and her train, ensconced in a temporary gallery on a hillside, looked down upon an artificial lake ablaze with a firework display, two hundred gentlemen escorted by a hundred torchbearers slowly made their way in procession up the slope bearing the banquet. The procession was headed by the arms of the queen and the nobility, followed by an array of objects associated with warfare – castles, guns and soldiers. (The English were at that very time fighting in France.) Then came 'beastes', 'all that can flie', 'all kind of wormes' and 'all sorts of fishes'. Marchpane came in every shape and, finally, fresh fruit and an array of jellies, preserves, leches, comfits and suckets.

During the Jacobean period the banquet became a standard element in an evening on which a court masque was performed.[120] After supper and the masque, King James I would lead the audience through to a room in Whitehall Palace for the banquet. What happened next was not always edifying. In 1605 the assault on the tables was so ferocious that they collapsed under the onslaught. In 1613, on the occasion of the marriage of the king's only daughter, Elizabeth, to the Elector Palatine, there were 'long tables laden with comfits and thousands of mottoes'. None the less they were 'in a moment rapaciously swept away'.

Ben Jonson wrote more than one scenario framing banquets for his patron William Cavendish, earl of Devonshire and later duke of Newcastle.[121] The most delightful is that connected with the two events staged at Bolsover Castle on 30 July 1633, in the presence of King Charles I and Henrietta Maria on their journey south after the coronation in Scotland. Jonson's elegant scenario celebrated the nuptial bliss of the royal couple, linking it to the harmony of the kingdom and the cosmos:

> When were the senses in such order
>   plac'd?
> The Sight, the Hearing, the Smell,
>   Touching, Taste,
> All at one Banquet.

The answer to this was that Love had set forth this banquet: 'Love will feast Love!' in a true banquet of the senses, recalling the pictures by Velvet Brueghel that evoked the opulence of Renaissance food. Then, the first banquet over, the king and queen retired to be further entertained by a witty dialogue satirising the court architect, Inigo Jones, as Colonel Vitruvius and a dance of mechanics. Next came the second banquet, a far more ambitious affair, for it was 'set downe before them from Cloudes by two Loves'.

Meals and the mystery of monarchy

L oue's welcome to Bolsover uses a meal as a vehicle to celebrate the divinity of royalty in an age which believed in the Divine Right of Kings. Throughout the Middle Ages and the Renaissance monarchs seldom made public appearances and rarely ate in public. When they did, for example at a coronation banquet, it was a great event for those privileged enough to be admitted, akin to being allowed to witness some esoteric liturgy, although far rarer. All over Europe during the sixteenth century, the cult of dynasties dictated a move towards absolutism. This inevitably had a major impact on the inherited tradition of royal eating, serving to increase rituals emphasising the divinity of he who wears the crown.[122] During a state banquet at the papal court, for instance, the pope ate alone seated on a quadrangular dais a few inches high in the middle of the hall. If the emperor was present, he too ate alone, on a separate dais situated to one side. From here he descended to minister to the pope for the hand-washing, as an outward symbol of the subordination of *regnum* to *sacerdotium*. During this ritual everyone present knelt. Each time the pope drank everyone also had to kneel, as if honouring the elevated chalice at mass.[123]

There is no study of the development of this phenomenon, but it is clear that the frequency with which rulers dined in public varied from court to court, and that the custom spread during the sixteenth century. By the 1560s it had reached the Bavarian courts and by the 1580s the Tuscan, where it took a heavily religious turn. Its introduction in fact marches hand in hand with the growing tendency of the court to take up a fixed location in a palace, thus sharpening its definition as a world apart, a sacred precinct in which rules both preserved and enhanced social distance.

The connection between royal eating in public and the action of the mass, already highly developed at the Burgundian court, was built upon by that court's lineal descendants, the Habsburg emperors and kings. Initially, the Emperor Charles V observed the Burgundian ceremonial only when he dined in public. He would make a processional entry, the knives on the table would be arranged in the form of a Burgundian cross, the hand-washing would take place while the dishes were uncovered for selection. After the highest prelate present had blessed the meal, the emperor would sit down alone at a table with a canopy suspended above him. This spectacle was enacted only four times a year, at the four great liturgical feasts of Christmas, Easter, Pentecost and All Saints.

In 1548 all of this changed, when Charles V introduced the full Burgundian etiquette into the household of his son, the future Philip II.[124] The household staff was as a consequence doubled in size and, after weeks of rehearsal, with the full panoply of the old Burgundian court, Philip ate in public in a style which was to continue until the end of Habsburg rule. As before, this happened only four times a year, but Epiphany, the feast of the kings, replaced All Saints. In his *Etiquetas de corte* (1561) the Spanish courtier Sebastian Gutierrez de Parrega describes the new ceremony. It began with the table beneath the canopy being laid by the *ugier de sala* in the antechamber of the Throne Room. The table itself was raised on a dais so that spectators could get a clearer view. A major domo, a great aristocrat, directed the proceedings; his most jealously guarded privilege was to present the napkin to the king. Philip's major domo major was the great soldier, the duke of Alva. When Philip came to England in 1554 to marry Mary Tudor, the English hastily cobbled together a Burgundian-type household, but made the mistake of allowing someone else to present the king's napkin. Alva was mortally affronted. The flasks of wine and water assumed a particular meaning in the Spanish ceremony. The cupbearer had to genuflect every time he poured liquid into the king's cup.

The parallels with the mass are vivid enough here. Viewed in the context of post-Reformation England, where ecclesiastical ceremonial had been all but abolished, they are even sharper.[125] The etiquette set in place by Henry VIII for royal dining survived into the eighteenth century. In Henry's reign, any form of public eating took place in the Presence

Henry VIII dining in the Privy Chamber.
Drawing attributed to Hans Holbein, *c.* 1540.

Chamber, also known as the dining chamber or the chamber of estate. The king normally ate in his Privy Chamber, where the ceremonial was also elaborate. At the close of a meal, for instance, the king stood to allow a kneeling usher to remove any crumbs from the skirts of his coat (he was of course dining alone on a dais beneath a canopy). Then a sewer and a gentleman brought a linen surnap and a towel from the ewery table and positioned it at the table's end to the king's right. An usher inserted a rod into it and unfolded it across the table, reverencing the king as he passed him. A sewer at the other end on his knees pulled it tight. More along the same lines followed until they reverenced and withdrew, making way for the two nobles carrying the ewer and basin to advance for the king to wash. The same motions by the sewer and the usher were gone through in reverse, continuing by removing everything – including the table – and leaving the king standing beneath the canopy. We can get a pretty accurate impression of this sequence from a late sixteenth-century drawing in which Henry sits alone with a throng of servants attending to his needs and a buffet to one side.

All of this becomes even more interesting in the reign of his daughter Elizabeth. Although she never ate in public, the ritual of dining in public was re-enacted every day as if she were. Visitors from abroad witnessed and described the event. Paul Hentzner, for example, provides an account in 1598 of what was an almost surreal happening:

A gentleman entered the room bearing a rod, and along with him another who had a table-cloth, which, after they had kneeled three times with the utmost veneration, he spread upon the table, and, kneeling again, they both retired. Then came two others, one with the rod again, the other with a salt-cellar, a plate, and bread; when they had kneeled as the others had done, and placed what was brought upon the table, they too retired with the same ceremonies performed by the first. At last came an unmarried lady (we were told she was a countess), and along with her a married one, bearing a tasting-knife; the former was dressed in white silk, who, when she had prostrated herself three times in the most graceful manner, approached the table and rubbed the plates with bread and salt with as much awe as if the Queen had been present. When they had waited there a little while, the yeomen of the guards entered, bare-headed, clothed in scarlet, with a golden rose upon their backs, bringing in at each turn a course of twenty-four dishes, served in plate, most of it gilt; these dishes were uncovered by a gentleman in the same order they were brought and placed upon the table, while the lady taster gave to each of the guard a mouthful to eat of the particular dish he had brought, for fear of poison. During the time that this guard . . . were bringing dinner, twelve trumpets and two kettled drums made the hall ring for half an hour together.[126]

At the end of all this two maids of honour appeared who ceremoniously lifted the dishes off the table and carried them in to the queen in the Privy Chamber, 'where, after she had chosen for herself, the rest goes to the ladies of the Court'. This extraordinary display has to be considered in the context of a country where there were no longer altars nor Christ's presence in the bread and wine. The altar in a sense had become the royal table and the mass the royal dinner.

James I, who openly proclaimed the divinity of kings, returned to

Charles I and his family dining in public.
Painting by Gerrit Houckgeest, 1635.

eating in public weekly, and there is also a picture of Charles I doing so.[127]
The setting is an imaginary classical room of a kind he would have loved
to possess. From an elevated balustraded colonnade people look down on
the scene. The royal table is set before a fireplace as in the Middle Ages
but with no canopy (presumably artistic licence); the table has a cloth

fringed with gold and is covered with dishes. At it sit Charles and Henrietta Maria and the young prince of Wales. Opposite the royal couple their carver, napkin on shoulder, is at work while a sewer places a plate before the king. Behind the royal group stand an assembly of bareheaded courtiers and household officials. Two buffets – one for food, the other (including a wine cooler) for drink – flank an arch opposite, through which covered containers of food are carried in procession. A cupbearer with a flask of wine is in the foreground.

If the relationship of these proceedings to pre-Reformation liturgy needs further reinforcement, we need only move forward a little in time to the 1660s and Wenceslas Hollar's engraving of the Grand Feast of the Order of the Garter in St George's Hall, Windsor. There the church-like arrangements are emphasised by a draped partition resembling a communion rail, creating what is in effect a 'sanctuary' with an 'altar' behind which the king is seated, dining. His holiness is manifest in the kneeling figure proffering him wine.

A similar ritual existed at the French court, as an engraving of 1633 by Abraham Bosse of the feast of the Order of the Holy Spirit at Fontainebleau bears testimony. But in France the serving of dinner to the Rex Christianissimus was to take a far weirder turn than anywhere else. There, by the mid-sixteenth century, meals had become an integral part of the royal funeral rites, with service to the deceased body and effigy of the king.[128] The roots of this extraordinary practice reach back into the Middle Ages. It was customary on the death of a monk in a monastery to continue to serve him his food for thirty days at his customary place at table, after which it was given to the poor. Something akin to this had been done at papal funerals in the early fifteenth century, during which a meal was served and the food distributed to penitents. But the funeral rites for the French monarchy were to develop into something much more particular.

The first certain reference to the custom comes in 1498 on the death of Charles VIII, when a meal was served 'even as hitherto by the king in his lifetime'. In 1547, on the demise of Francis I, the arrangement was elaborated under the influence of humanist ideas looking back to imperial Roman funeral rites. Herodian's description of the rites for the Emperor Septimius Severus told how the ruler's effigy was exhibited and attended as if he were still alive. This continued until, at a certain moment, a physician declared him dead. The funeral ceremonies for Francis I began immediately after his death with the service of a meal to the coffin. Meanwhile, a wax effigy of the king was made. This was not in itself anything new – effigies had commonly been made and placed atop the coffin in the funeral procession during the Middle Ages. But what happened in 1547 was very different. The effigy was made with joints and displayed seated upright in a *salle d'honneur* hung with tapestries, to be ritually served with meals as if alive. Then, quite suddenly, all this was swept away and the meals ceased. The king's coffin, sans effigy, appeared on exhibit in a *salle de deuil* hung in black.

When Charles IX died in 1574, the service of food to the effigy went on for forty days: 'at the hour of dinner and supper the forms and fashions of service were observed and guarded just as was customary in the lifetime of the king . . .' But the practice did not last. Its final observation came in 1610 during the rites for the assassinated Henry IV. After that date only a vestige remained. The coffin stood in the choir of the royal church of Saint-Denis. Meanwhile, in an adjoining room where the *garde du corps* had their dining table, a vacant seat of honour was kept for the king. At meal-times a herald proclaimed thrice 'Le roi est servi!' followed by a silence and then 'Le roi est mort!'. That practice was to continue throughout the *ancien régime*, only to vanish along with much else at the Revolution. Between then and that event, however, was to come the ultimate in the alliance between eating and power, the reign of *le Roi-Soleil*.

CHAPTER FIVE

From Court to Cabinet

L OUIS XV'S THREE main passions were food, hunting and women. In the figure of Jeanne Antoinette Poisson, marquise de Pompadour, he found a mistress in whom all three coincided. Educated, accomplished and beautiful, she was endowed not only with intelligence but with supremely good taste. She was thus able to create and sustain around the king a private world in which the pursuits of the chase and those of love could flourish, and also one in which his penchant for delectable food found fulfilment in a new form of meal, the *souper intime*.[1]

The memoirs of the duc de Croÿ vividly describe a number of these meals, which were usually held after the king had been out hunting. Any of the courtiers accompanying him might apply for an invitation, although there was no guarantee that the applicant would be admitted. Those who applied were required to wait nervously in a group outside the king's apartments until an usher arrived bearing a list with a tick against the names of those gentlemen the king wished to see. Those not favoured simply had to bear the humiliation. De Croÿ was often disappointed, but on the evening of 30 January 1747 he was one of the fortunate ones bidden to ascend the stairs at Versailles to 'les petits cabinets'.[2]

These were the king's private apartments, quite separate from the state rooms once occupied by his great-grandfather, Louis XIV, in which the public ritual of royal dining continued to be maintained. The guests assembled in the *Galerie des Chasses*, pausing there before entering the dining-room. To de Croÿ, all 'was delightful and the supper extremely pleasant and easy going'. The king appeared once his guests had gathered,

Opposite: The aristocratic classes discover the joys of informality.
The Oyster Dinner by Jean François de Troy, 1735.

[211]

bringing with him the ladies, this time four; they were always fewer in number than the men. The Pompadour was one of them. De Croÿ notes that the king was 'fort amoureux' with her. Eighteen in all squashed around the circular table, but the king, in spite of the unconstrained atmosphere, preserved his 'grandeur', placing the Pompadour on his right and her great friend, the comtesse d'Estrades, on his left. The rest found places anywhere they could, pell-mell, without any thought of precedence. There were no more than two or three servants, and these withdrew after serving, allowing even greater freedom of conversation.

> We were two hours at supper, free and easy but without any excess. Then the King went into the *petit salon*, where he made the coffee and poured it out; there were no servants and we helped ourselves. He made up a table of *Comète* [a game] . . . the King rather enjoyed that sort of little game, but Madame de Pompadour seemed to hate gambling and to be trying to put him off it . . . finally, at two o'clock, he got up and said, half under his breath to her, I thought, very gaily – 'come on then, let's go to bed.' The women curtseyed and went out, he bowed and went into his *petits cabinets*. The rest of us left by Madame de Pompadour's staircase and came round through the state rooms to his public *coucher* which took place at once.

De Croÿ's account makes plain that we have moved worlds away from the allegory and choreography of the Renaissance banquet. This still represented the meal as an exercise in social discrimination, but of a very different kind. To have one's name ticked by the king marked a height of social aspiration, enabling one to step into another world and leave those not so bidden to look on in envy and, quite possibly, not a little resentment.

But to step into another world presupposes an existing world. That the public realm remained intact and functioning we gather from learning that after supper the king went to his state bedroom to take part in the public ritual of the *coucher*. The *grands appartements* were not replaced by the suite known as the *petits cabinets* or *petits appartements*, where the *soupers intimes* were usually held; on the contrary, the latter were deliberately constructed so that the king could escape the rigid protocol of life in public. He had moved into them in 1738. The format of the informal suppers had originated three years earlier under the aegis of Cardinal Fleury, the king's minister, who intended them to help the king overcome his shyness, although they owed much to similar suppers given by Louis's uncle, Philippe, duc d'Orléans, at the Palais Royal in Paris. In this case their objective had been heavily in the direction of gourmandising (Orléans had learned to cook in Spain) and seduction (aphrodisiacs appeared). Seduction became part of Louis XV's scenario as well when two of his cousins, Mlle de Charolais and the comtesse de Toulouse, initiated 'petits soupers' to which ladies were invited. It was at one of these that the king encountered his first mistress, Mme de Mailly, a liaison which directly precipitated not only the creation of the *petits appartements* but the *petits voyages* which he began to make away from Versailles to the châteaux of La Muette and Choisy, both settings for the new informal dining. There he could revel in the hunt and afterwards enjoy intimate supper parties with his cronies of the chase and a select group of women headed by the Pompadour.

These *soupers intimes* were like nothing else we have encountered so far. They are in fact the archetypal eighteenth-century meal, one that sought to banish ritual and which was devoid of symbolic messages. Their atmosphere was one of high fashion, flirtation, wit and gossip. The use of a round table absolved diners from the complications of precedence. The absence of servants for much of the meal meant not only uninhibited conversation but also the free flow of wine; it was placed along with glasses right on the table. Jean François de Troy's *The Oyster Dinner* (1735), which was painted for the *première salle à manger* at Versailles, although devoid of the frisson of female company, suggests the convivial ambience of these gatherings. There is the round table covered with a white cloth. On it we can see the little Chinese or Japanese *seaux* or bowls filled with water in which glasses are upturned for washing. A guest leans out to grab a bottle of wine. There are huge napkins draped across the laps of the diners. In the foreground there is a wine cooler with bottles on ice and with shelves containing plates. Everyone is having a splendid time.

At Choisy privacy was taken even further. Servants could be virtually eliminated, because a special mechanism allowed the centre of the dining table to sink to the level of the floor below, then reascend bearing the new course.[3] In the room itself four buffets made plates and glasses readily available, and also contained pen, ink and paper for guests to write down what they wanted to drink. The ringing of a tiny bell produced the miraculous changes.

The drive towards privacy precipitated another innovation, the menu, a written description of the courses and dishes to be served. The only eighteenth-century menus to survive relate to suppers staged at Choisy, sixty-seven in all, thirty-one from 1751 and thirty-five from 1757.[4] Some of the menus are rectangular, others are round, and the fact that duplicates of one exist may indicate that several copies were placed on the table. They describe food for between thirty-one and thirty-six guests, of a very different sort from that of the typical Italian Renaissance table. In the first place, the courses are far fewer, just four plus dessert. Yet it is strikingly clear that these menus mark an intense interest of a different kind on the part of the guests in what they are actually eating. The age of the gourmet is at hand.

The meal opens with soups and ragouts or 'oilles', moves on next to a huge range of entrées and then to roasts and finally to 'Petits Entremets'. Within that structure there is a new progression from savoury to sweet. Also, notably, there are dishes attributed to or named after certain people, like 'Dindon du mareschal de Richelieu' or 'Pâté de Madame la Marquise de Pompadour'. What does this mean? Did these grandees actually cook these dishes, or were they the *spécialité de la maison* of these individuals? What we can certainly see is that they reflect a cuisine of a hitherto unknown complexity.

An extraordinary journey has been made since the opening years of the seventeenth century. We have arrived at meals where rank is put aside, where guests help themselves, where the focus is on relaxed and elegant social interplay and discourse, where the art of cuisine has become of such central interest that the guests wish to know in writing what is to be served to them. We seem to be within easy reach of our own experience at table. How did this happen? That it happened at all suggests that it was simply a sharp reaction to the suffocating old style of upper-class eating by those imprisoned within its formalities. But in fact the change is a far more complex phenomenon than that. Louis XV's *soupers intimes* could never have happened without several wider developments. One was the loss of faith in the old Renaissance cosmology of correspondences. Another was the emergence of the new social ideals of the *philosophes* of the

Enlightenment. And yet another was the eclipse of innocent belief in the truth of what one sees, the principle behind the idea of the table as vehicle for ceremonial and allegory.

All of this did not happen overnight, nor simultaneously in all the countries of Western Europe. It was necessary that the ceremonial manner of eating reach a height of such crushing grandeur that escape was imperative. In stylistic terms the journey is one from the baroque to the rococo. But we must begin with the baroque. And even that has its ironies, for at precisely the time when a new cuisine was emerging in France, the apparatus of the banquet in Italy in its baroque phase was developing a unique aesthetic aberration: the art of figurative food, first orchestrated at the Este court at Ferrara in the quattrocento, and now culminating in the culinary sculpture of the Rome of Bernini.

The triumph of illusion

IN JANUARY 1687, Roger Palmer, earl of Castlemaine, ambassador of King James II to the Holy See, staged a spectacular banquet in the Palazzo Pamphili in Rome in honour of some eighty cardinals and other ecclesiastical dignitaries.[5] We fortunately know a good deal about this magnificent event; the earl's chamberlain, the painter John Michael Wright, who had trained in Rome, wrote a detailed description published in both Italian and English editions. The latter appeared only a month before James II was forced to flee his kingdom, and as a consequence few copies exist. Most were destroyed because the lavishly illustrated folio volume recorded what Protestant England regarded as a mortal affront to the realm – an embassy sent to pay homage to the pope.

It was a hugely costly embassy. Although it arrived in Rome by Easter 1686, it was months before Castlemaine made his official ceremonial entry into the city and paid his homage to the pope. Both that and the feast which followed in January were done in the Italian manner, Castlemaine utilising the services on both occasions of two of the leading exponents of the baroque style, Ciro Ferri and his amanuensis Lenardi. On the evening of the feast the guests ascended the stairs to the *piano nobile* of the palace to find themselves in the first of a suite of three rooms. In this room, the *Sala dei Palafrenieri*, there were two tables running the length of the chamber on which the desserts had been arranged, 'wonderful quantities of Fruit, Sweetmeats, Parmegian cheese, and other delicacies . . .' On the other two walls, again facing each other, there were two canopied *credenze*, one banked with silver plate, the other with precious vessels in glass. Members of the Swiss papal guard and twenty footmen stood protecting them.

The banquet itself was staged in the third room, a glorious gallery with frescoes by Pietro da Cortona adorning the ceiling. Below that the walls had been enriched with tapestries brought from England, another *credenza*, this time with a display of English plate and, halfway along the table beneath a canopy, a full-length portrait of James II enthroned. Eighty gilt chairs were arranged around the table in groups of four, and a waiter and a *trinciante* served each group. Twenty-one dishes were served before dessert was carried in from the first room. What is most striking in the long engraving that records the appearance of the table is its decoration. Along the edge are napkins folded in the form of rocks, and within the central enclosure a scattering of heraldic animals, lions and unicorns from the royal arms, made out of sugar. All of these creatures were subsidiary to the massive tableau running down the table's spine, eleven major sugar sculptures. Wright's published account includes engravings of these sculptures or *trionfi*, which were impressive indeed. Four depicted the elements in mythological guise, four more were of groups representing regal virtues, two sported palm trees (in reference to Castlemaine's family name of Palmer), and, finally, the tallest – no less than six feet high – allegorised the return of England to the Catholic fold. Above an aureole the figure of Holy Church is seen presiding over Time unveiling Truth, while a winged hero vanquishes Fraud, Discord and a hydra 'denoting Rebellion supprest' (the rebellion in question being the duke of Monmouth's). Intriguingly, the book tells us that the whole display was set up and open for the public to view for two days before the event, 'that curiosity might have some share in the Entertainment'. After the feast these handsome transitory masterpieces of the art of the Roman baroque were presented to some of the great ladies of Rome.

There is nothing quite like the *seicento* Italian state banquet, a culinary dead-end in which the innovatory cuisine of Scappi was run into the ground in favour of anything that ravished the eye and evoked opulence and excess in the grand manner.[6] The achievements of the Renaissance cook were subordinated to those of the *scalco* and *trinciante*. Where Scappi at the close of the sixteenth century had maintained the integrity of each dish, the cookery books written by his successors are given over to every form of visual effect which could be achieved by the manipulation of food. This overriding desire to turn everything edible into something else reached its climax in Antonio Latini's *Lo scalco moderna* (1692), with a vast section given over to *trionfi* of the type encountered at the Castle-

Britain returns to the Catholic faith. Trionfo at the banquet staged by Lord Castlemaine, 1687. Engraving, 1688.

maine banquet. This included folding napkins into ever more complex shapes, butter sculpture, and architectural and figurative compositions made of marzipan, pastry and sugar. Yet despite its perversity, the form reached a certain aesthetic level. At no other time in the history of the table has food been able to take its place, for better or worse, alongside the major decorative arts of an age, in particular small sculptural compositions in bronze and silver.[7] Contemporaries were well aware of the fact; one of the criticisms levelled against Bernini's great equestrian statue of the Emperor Constantine was that 'the whole horse seems a *trionfo* of marzipan and meringue'. Such a charge is understandable when we realise that the Vatican kitchen complex included a room called the *stanza dei trionfi* dedicated to nothing else but the manufacture of such pieces. Moreover, they might well be designed by the leading artists of the day. We know for a certainty that the great Giovanni Lorenzo Bernini himself

Feast on Holy Thursday at the Vatican with figurative *trionfi*.
Drawing by Pierre Paul Sevin, 1668.

designed a series of *trionfi* for a banquet given by Princess Aldobrandini in honour of Cardinal de' Medici in 1668.

In addition to the Castlemaine engravings, there are two sets of drawings by Pierre Paul Sevin, a pensioner of the French Academy, of such banquet tables in Rome at the close of the 1660s.[8] One group records the extraordinary Maundy Thursday tableau customary each year, when the pope washed the feet of twelve poor priests in imitation of Christ. After this ritual it was customary to give the priests a dinner which in 1675, in the words of one account, included '*trionfi*, and sugar sculptures, and elegantly folded napkins'.[9] What to modern eyes is so bizarre is to see dining tables exhibiting food sculptures in the form of Christ carrying the Cross, the Agony in the garden of Gethsemane and angels clasping the instruments of the Passion. Interwoven among these are vases of flowers, trees bearing fruit and such features as a *tempietto* supporting the family arms of the reigning pope. Creations like these might be unsettling, but they should not be lightly dismissed; in them leading artists essayed subject matter never commissioned in more permanent form.

Sevin's drawings go on to record the remarkable appearance of a number of more secular feasts. One, in particular, provides an unmatched aerial view of such an occasion in progress. The feast has not been identified, but it must date like the others from the late 1660s. The host is a cardinal and the figure to his left is likely to be Queen Christina of Sweden in her notoriously mannish attire. At one end of the room the host and the chief guests sit at a semicircular table on a raised dais, at each end of which there is a *trinciante* busy carving while a waiter, bearing a dish, approaches the centre. Behind the chairs of the guests stand what are likely to be personal attendants. Below, in the main body of the hall, other guests are seated at long tables facing each other while down the centre run a series of *credenze*, one for servicing the head table, two others, with perfume-burners on them to disguise the smell of food, for the rest. On them there is an array of silver and edibles. In the foreground a course is being borne in procession headed by a *scalco* or the *maestro della casa* holding a wand of office. Other waiters carry away dishes from previous courses on stretchers while, to the left, a small group of onlookers, including a woman, observe the spectacle. What we do not see must be on the missing wall, some kind of *bottigliera* for dispensing drink.

The likely presence of Queen Christina of Sweden is a reminder that in her honour in 1655 were staged some of the most complex of all the Italian baroque banquets, as she made her way from the north through Italy to Rome on her conversion.[10] The closer she came to the city the more elaborate were the confections to celebrate the event. Such importance was attached to them that the most famous confectioner of the era, Luigi Fedele, who had learned his craft at the Gonzaga court at Mantua before being summoned to Rome by Innocent X, travelled as part of her train. At Forli the *trionfi* were so amazing that they were greeted with a burst of applause equal to that accorded the queen. At Imola the decor for the feast included, among other marvels, a marzipan Religion trampling on Heresy, Pallas Athene in her chariot, and angels supporting a crown over the queen's arms. At Mantua on 27 November she saw 'Mount Olympus with the altar of faith. At the summit two putti held up a royal crown above the coat of arms of Her Majesty.' Around this were

grouped four silver vases from which grew orange trees made of gelatine and arcaded galleries in which warriors and virtuous men stood interspersed with fabulous beasts. That Christina had never seen the like before can be gathered from the fact that at Assisi she requested that all the *trionfi* should be brought to her room so that she could study them. This occasioned a great to-do because one had already been given away and had to be retrieved.

But even *trionfi* could not eclipse the almost grotesque arrangements precipitated by Alexander VII's decision to bestow the honour on the queen of dining with her in public. This event took place on 26 December, the day after he had confirmed her, and provides a startling example of the complexities of protocol that could arise from a feast in the seventeenth century. The pope was, of course, the earthly embodiment of spiritual power. He always ate alone and never in the presence of a woman. A further complication was the queen's status; she had abdicated, so she was no longer a sovereign ruler. This meant that she did not qualify for a chair with arms. Bernini was commissioned to design a chair devoid of arms which at the same time appeared to have them. The creator of the sugar sculptures was the single most influential designer for the decorative arts in baroque Rome, Giovanni Paul Schor. Two sketches by him survive for the *trionfi*, one with a phoenix, an emblem of Christina's. These were cast in sugar and then painted and gilded. Other craftsmen, the accounts reveal, were also involved, including a certain Niccolò Perretti, who made 'a triumphal car of citron [crystallised] representing Aurora and the horse Licaseo' and 'a tree of marzipan and its pedestal of carved wood'. To gain some idea of what this looked like we must move on thirteen years to a second dinner given in honour of Christina, this time by Clement IX on 9 December 1668. It was staged in the Quirinale Palace and to all intents and purposes must have been a rerun of the previous occasion. Sevin made a drawing, and from it we gain a vivid impression of the splendour. The two tables are laden with *trionfi*, including one on the queen's table of a crown in the midst of ears of corn, an allusion to the Vasa arms. The two tables and dais are placed at different levels, both somehow embraced by

Opposite: Banquet staged for Queen Christina of Sweden.
Drawing by Pierre Paul Sevin, late 1660s.

Queen Christina dines with Pope Clement IX.
Drawing by Pierre Paul Sevin, 1668.

a gigantic canopy suspended above. The spectators, all male, are held back
by a balustrade, and though women were present they are hidden behind
the tapestries along the walls and peep through any chink they can find.
Every movement was choreographed. The pope entered at one door, the
queen at another. The major domo proffered the pope his napkin, to have

it taken from him by the queen who herself handed it to the pope. When the pope toasted the queen everyone knelt. Conversation was carried on through a *monsignore* placed between them. When the main course had been cleared the *trionfi* were removed and returned filled with sweetmeats.

Such spectacles continued in Italy into the eighteenth century, but not for long.[11] The advent of hard-paste porcelain spelled the end of sugar *trionfi*, but more important was the change of mood. The election of the puritanical Clement XI in 1700 brought the golden age of baroque Rome to an end, inaugurating what became known as the 'long Roman Lent'. Already by then La Varenne's revolutionary *Le Cuisinier françois* (1651) had appeared in Italy, published under the title *Il cuoco francese* in 1682. By that date table style was beginning to be set by the court of the Sun King.

A culinary revolution

THE SEVENTEENTH CENTURY was one of major gastronomic change, reflected in the arrival of new foods and shifts in taste, but above all a revolution in cooking itself.[12] For France this was *le grand siècle*, and that country, which had contributed so little to the development of cuisine for nearly two centuries, was suddenly responsible for radical developments in both cooking style and the structure and presentation of meals. The latter came to be known as *service à la française*. No country in Western Europe was to be left untouched by these developments, which took place between 1650 and 1670 – precisely the period when French court civilisation as enacted at Versailles became the universal model.

Taste in food altered. The consumption of exotic birds like peacock and swan, crane and heron went out of fashion along with lampreys and whale. Pork henceforth figured only in the form of sucking-pig or ham, otherwise being relegated, in the guise of mince, to stuffings and the provision of lard. The preferred meats now were beef, veal and mutton (lamb was considered insipid), and, in the case of fowl, chicken in all its varieties plus duck, ortolans, teal, pigeons and game birds. Game in general, until the French Revolution, remained the prerogative of the aristocracy and therefore continued to be a status symbol. Turkey was served only at feasts. Fish was still consumed in huge quantities – in Catholic countries, the old fast days remained in place – but it was freshwater fish like salmon and trout that were now preferred. (Sea fish such as sole, plaice and whiting achieved fashionable status in the eighteenth century.)

This was the era of the horticultural triumphs at Versailles of Louis XIV's great gardener Jean de la Quintinie. There was an enormous multiplication in the varieties of fruit and vegetables grown and, thanks to the development of hotbeds, such delicacies as asparagus and strawberries could be produced in the depths of winter. Mushrooms of every kind, truffles, cardoons, artichokes, lettuces and especially peas moved to the culinary forefront. Recipes and menus indicate that vegetables occupied a star place as *entremets*. Salads, epitomised in John Evelyn's essay *Acetaria* (1699), were hugely popular served simply with a vinaigrette dressing, a sprinkling of aromatic herbs, and sometimes violets and borage.

As for wine, during the last quarter of the seventeenth century the *méthode champenoise* was invented and the consumption of champagne took off. By 1784 1,735 bottles of it were being provided annually for Louis XVI along with 5,230 bottles of Burgundy. Champagne and Burgundy were the preferred wines of the aristocratic classes, designated *vins de table*. (Those consumed by the lower orders were called *vins de suite*.) In the seventeenth century all kinds of liqueurs, perfumed waters and iced drinks also came into fashion.

To these we can add three novelties of an even greater significance: chocolate, tea and coffee.[13] Chocolate came from South America and was already a popular drink in sixteenth-century Spain. That popularity spread in the next century, arriving at the French court together with Louis XIV's Spanish bride, who brought along a maid whose prime task was to brew the queen's chocolate. Chocolate was adapted for European taste by adding a sweetener, honey or sugar, plus vanilla, cinnamon and, sometimes, black pepper to enhance the flavour. In the 1670s chocolate cultivation was introduced to the French colony of Martinique. This brought the price down, and in 1682 the *Mercure galant* records that chocolate was served at all the great fêtes at Versailles.

But chocolate never had the social impact of coffee, which engendered a new social venue for the emergent polite society, the coffee house. It was the Dutch who first initiated the commercial exploitation of coffee, the earliest shipment arriving in 1637. By 1660 there was a large trade in coffee beans. Like tea it caught on initially because it was believed to have medicinal properties. In terms of high fashion the seal was set at Versailles by the embassy of the Turkish Sultan Muhammad IV, who served to the court coffee in the oriental manner. The fact that by the middle of the following century Louis XV, as we have seen, actually brewed it himself says much about its status.

Tea, which first came into Europe again by way of the Dutch in 1610, was never to attain the popularity in France that it did in England. Although by the 1650s it was being drunk in London, and by the 1680s its wide acceptance had led to the manufacture of special tables, it was to be in the eighteenth century that tea drinking became an upper-class ritual. In the new genre of the conversation piece, tea came to symbolise elegant sociability, family and friends grouped around a table replete with silver teapot and caddy with porcelain dishes for drinking.

All of these developments were significant, but they were cast in the shade by what amounted to the reinvention of culinary method in France during the 1650s.[14] The roots of the change probably stretched back much further, but by the middle of the century there suddenly appeared an array of French cookbooks presenting a new system of cooking, one which incorporated an integrated repertory of techniques making use of certain basic mixtures and raw materials subject to what were in fact a series of rules. This concern for systematising even the art of the kitchen was yet another expression of a society obsessed with discovering and imposing order in every sphere of human activity. (The same phenomenon may be seen at work in the foundation, in 1635, of the Académie Française, intended to govern and purify the language.) The new cooking incidentally called for a high degree of literacy, with no fewer than two hundred and thirty editions of French cookbooks being published between 1651 and 1789.

What were the factors which converged to precipitate this sea change? Some were mundane, others were more complex. Among the former the simple replacement of the medieval bread trencher with solid ceramic, pewter or silver plates meant that liquid mixtures could be served. More, such vessels provided a firm surface upon which a knife could cut and, latterly, a fork could press its prongs. Cutlery among the upper classes began to be commonplace. Guests no longer arrived bringing their knives with them – the table was already fully equipped. The increased variety and quality of produce must certainly have been a contributory factor, inspiring cooks to experiment. Added to that were improvements in the mechanics of the kitchen itself with the development of ever more sophisticated means of controlling heat.

But there were also sociological reasons. The fact that the new cuisine was spread by way of books indicates that any important cook would be expected to be able to read. The number of books also reflects a new interest in cooking and food among the upper classes – the most likely literate segment of society. Yet even this interest was complicated by social considerations. A new cuisine can only take hold if it fulfils a deep need, and in the case of France that need was to establish rank during a period of acute social division. The aristocracy sought a cooking style which set them apart from the lower orders, because even as the condition of the peasants spiralled ever downwards, a growing body of bourgeois was pushing upwards. Thanks to expanding commerce and industry and the rise of the professions, the bourgeoisie found themselves within reach of the aristocracy, and were determined to imitate them. The response of the aristocracy was, inevitably, to elaborate their cooking style and again close ranks against the interlopers.

But what made the break with medieval and Renaissance cuisine so decisive was the abandonment of the cosmological context. For centuries food had been inextricably linked to astrology, alchemy and medicine. The seventeenth century witnessed the piecemeal dissolution of the old occult universe in favour of a mechanistic version. Released from this context, cooking gradually became more of an art. That process must have begun in France quite early. Although the mania for colouring dishes gold – with its astrological and alchemical associations – persisted in England till 1700 and lasted even longer in Italy, Spain and Germany, it had already vanished in France during the sixteenth century. The move towards the mechanistic universe in the second half of the seventeenth century, moreover, was bolstered by the appeal to its adherents of the atomism of Epicurus, a philosopher for whom food was firmly one aspect of voluptuous living. Hence the term epicure. This is not to say that Renaissance cuisine was devoid of sensual overtones, but they were firmly held in check while the old spiritual ones remained in place. Once these were gone, cuisine was free to be not only sensual but secular, with the primary aim of stimulating desire.

The new style took the salt–acid side of Renaissance cookery and adapted it, fusing the various contributory ingredients to make a whole. In the new scheme of things, salt rose to major prominence. By the middle of the eighteenth century it was being added to virtually all dishes. Simultaneously sweetness – principally gained by adding sugar, and once a feature of almost every course in a meal – was by 1700 confined in France to the dessert course. In countries like England, noted even today for its predilection for sugar, the old system prevailed far longer. Thus by the middle of the eighteenth century the classic progression from the savoury to the sweet, still fundamental to Western European cuisine, was in place.

Of course sugar was still consumed at a great and increasing rate. Indeed it led to a split in household departments between the *cuisine*, which prepared the main courses of the meal, and the *office*, whose responsibility was an ever-expanding empire of complex dessert dishes and ices, and also included the preservation of fruit and flowers. Its activities also embraced the elaborate decoration of tables with sugar sculpture.[15]

Another great change was a shift of primary focus from pleasing first the eye to pleasing first the palate. Figurative food gradually disappeared. At the most it found a residual life in the form of game, fish and vegetable shapes used to decorate the new silver and porcelain containers in which food was served. The food itself looked and tasted very different. This was partly due to the use of new techniques, such as marination, and the reinvention of older ones, such as braising and larding meat. It also came from the lavish use of the dairy products typical of Northern Europe, butter and cream. At the heart of the new culinary system were basic bouillons which, along with certain liaisons, stuffing, herbs and spice mixtures, were applied to whatever seasonal ingredients happened to be available. Medieval and Renaissance cooking had depended upon the lavish use of a whole range of exotic spices, as a way of indicating rank. These were now abandoned in favour of aromatic herbs, garlic, onion, parsley, mint, sorrel and rosemary. Of course such herbs had all been known and used in the Middle Ages, but never with such prominence. Now they took their place in a cuisine whose use of such seemingly simple ingredients was so sophisticated as to make it inaccessible outside a narrow spectrum of society. Other herbs like chervil, tarragon, basil, thyme, bay, chives and spring onions came into the mix, aimed at the subtle enhancement of flavour. Overall the move was from quantity to quality as the new expression of hierarchy.

The landmark publication was François Pierre La Varenne's *Le Cuisinier françois* (1651). This was the first cookbook to represent a definitive break with the Middle Ages, opening with recipes for the bouillon, meat and fish stocks that served as bases or *fonds* for the repertory of dishes which followed, and were the foundations of the new system. This publication was complemented by a second book generally accepted as being by La Varenne, *Le Pâtissier françois* (1654), covering pastry and egg recipes – for tarts, wafers, waffles, pies, cheesecakes, omelettes and biscuits. A third volume entitled *Le Parfaict confiturier* (1667) dealt with the work of the *office*.

Le Cuisinier françois continued to be printed into the eighteenth century, but it was followed in the 1660s by other books by Nicolas Bonnefons, 'premier valet du roi', Pierre de Lune and a number of other anonymous writers, all of whom built on La Varenne. The drive was always towards greater complexity. After a lull came a book by the unidentified L. S. R., *L'Art de bien traiter, ouvrage nouveau, curieus et fort galant* (1674), which was specifically aimed at the aristocracy. Inspired by the magnificent fêtes at Versailles, in which food played a major role, it instructed the reader how to cater for 'colations d'hyver' for balls, for 'assemblées et galanteries de Carnival', for 'sociétés et régales' and more. Decor is discussed at length along with 'the exquisite choice' of dishes and their elegant presentation to guests.

La Varenne was finally replaced in 1691 by François Massialot's *Le Cuisinier roial et bourgeois* (although there was little about the latter except dismissive phrases). This was a book written for the cooks of the aristocracy, and the first to arrange recipes alphabetically. It was reissued in a new two-volume edition in 1712 and again in 1714, whereupon it became the great cookery classic of the eighteenth century. All of these books aimed to create a cuisine for the aristocracy which placed them in another world in terms of decor, ambience and service, and encouraged sheer extravagance in food.

As the century progressed, however, such prodigality went against the grain of the Enlightenment and led to a reaction. We can see this in the attitude of Émile in Rousseau's eponymous book. He, we are told, had no taste for dishes like the costly ragouts but 'il aime les bons fruits, les bons légumes, la bonne crème et les bonnes gens [he loved good fruit, good vegetables, good cream and good people]'. Yet though the *nouvelle cuisine* pleaded austerity, the truth was rather different. The book that sums up contemporary reality was François Marin's *Les Dons de Comus ou les délices de la table* (1739 and 1740), which differentiated between *la cuisine moderne* and *la cuisine ancienne*. For Marin modern cooking was akin to chemistry, but a chemistry which could involve, for example, using four to five pounds of veal, a quarter of a ham plus a fowl, beef marrow, onions and parsnips, not to mention the labour of many cooks, in order to produce precisely one quart of quintessence. This was hardly simplicity.

It is not surprising therefore that when a book finally appeared that responded to the desire for simplicity it was an instant success. Menon's *La Cuisinière bourgeoise* (1746) was precisely what its title states, a cookery book for the bourgeois housewife. Its recipes avoided aristocratic excess on the one hand and, on the other, bypassed coarse peasant vulgarity. One of its guiding principles was to be economical. Indeed the 1774 edition states that it was intended for those 'd'une condition ou d'une fortune médiocre'. Thus it was that by 1789 the twin strands central to classic French cooking were firmly in place: *haute cuisine* and *cuisine bourgeoise*.

Just as during the Renaissance it was Italian cooks and cookery books that spread a new style, so in the late seventeenth and eighteenth centuries it was the turn of the French.[16] In England, which had a cuisine based on the country and not the court, the medieval tradition lingered on. La Varenne was translated into English in 1653 and other translations followed, but they were balanced by a steady stream of domestically produced volumes. These started with Robert May's *The Accomplisht Cook, or the Art and Mystery of Cooking* (1660), which resolutely took 'good plain English country fare' well into the eighteenth century. (It was still being served at the court of George II in 1740.) The English writers vigorously refused to cave in to the French but only assimilated what was considered appropriate. Indeed the existence of such strong anti-French culinary sentiment suggests that there was considerable interest in the new cuisine in some upper-class quarters. Why else Hannah Glasse's famous diatribe in her *The Art of Cookery Made Plain and Easy* (1747): 'so much is the blind Folly of this Age, that they would rather be imposed on by a *French* Booby, than give Encouragement to a good English Cook!'?

In England, unlike in France, cooking style was not the expression of a caste but one shared by the aristocracy, gentry and middle classes alike, and based on ingredients which the average country estate produced. But French culinary ideas gained ground nevertheless. William Verrall, who was trained by the duke of Newcastle's French cook, 'Monsieur de St Clouet', grounds his *A Complete System of Cookery* (1759) on French principles.

Verrall's book is indicative of what happened in other countries where French cuisine was modified and introduced into the existing scheme of things. French cooks travelled everywhere. They are recorded as working at the courts of Hanover, Prussia and Saxony in Germany and also in Italy, where the new cuisine was taken up by the aristocracy and middle classes in the eighteenth century. In 1724 Massialot's book appeared as *Il cuoco reale e cittadino*; Menon's famous volume was translated in the year of its first publication as *Cuoco piemontese perfezionato a Parigi* and had run into twenty-two editions by the early nineteenth century. No kitchen in Europe quite escaped what had occurred in France, nor equally was anyone to escape the change it brought about in the arrangement of the table and the presentation of food.

Service à la française and tablescapes

ONE OF THE consequences of the revolution in cuisine was a new sequence and method of serving food at table known as *service à la française*.[17] It reflected the seventeenth century's concern for order, balance, good taste and elegance. The number of dishes for each course was calculated on a fixed ratio of dishes to diners. A four-course meal for twenty-five, for example, meant a hundred dishes. One could multiply up or divide down from that. Increasing the number of diners did not mean, as it would today, merely producing a greater quantity of the same dishes. On the contrary, it demanded more different dishes. The result was that although large robust dishes like roasts maintained their place they tended to serve as anchors on a table, surrounded by a myriad of smaller ones.

Service à la française.
Engraving in Vincent La Chapelle, *Le Cuisinier moderne*, 1742.

Meals came in services — two, three or four, although in the case of
supper there might be only one plus dessert. The production of any meal
called upon two quite separate departments in a household, the *cuisine* for
the majority of the courses, the *office* for dessert. La Chapelle provides
both a table plan and the menu for a two-course supper in the 1742
edition of his *La Cuisinier moderne*; an examination of these will enable us to
get our bearings.[18] Sixteen silver plates are arranged around a rectangular
table and all the containers for the food are also of silver. (By the 1770s

these would all have been porcelain.) In the centre there is an oval platter for a quarter of veal flanked by a pair of soups in splendid tureens and a pair of terrines. In the four corners of the table are four *entrées* of poultry, while between them, again symmetrically arranged, are six more dishes, two small and four large with various *hors d'oeuvres*, mutton chops with chicory, a dish of chicken breast, and glazed eels with an Italian sauce. During this course the two tureens would have been removed and replaced by two *relevés*, a turbot and a salmon, in exactly the same positions in order to maintain the balance of the composition. The second course repeats this pattern, but with new dishes which included a ham as the centre-piece and cakes where previously the salmon and the turbot had been. The table would then have been cleared for the course prepared by the *office*, always a great spectacle, an elaborate tableau which could include cheeses, fresh, preserved and stewed fruit, ice creams, sorbets and puddings attendant upon an elaborate focal point, perhaps of sugar sculpture and flowers.

Illustrated cookery books by 1700 are full of these table plans for meals, without exception symmetrical. In an aristocratic house, the pattern of presentation was the task of the *maestro della casa*, *maître d'hôtel* or butler, but whatever the permutation, the new system represented a definite break with the medieval and Renaissance practice of making the placement and choice of food accord with the rank of the diner. To an extent the new equality was illusory, because different parts of the household now ate in different places. But wherever one ate, everyone now ate exactly the same thing.

That this way of arranging food could achieve great elegance may be seen in a detail from a picture by Martin van Meytens of a banquet held in 1764 at Frankfurt on the occasion of the crowning of Archduke Joseph as king of the Romans.[19] The table in question, already set with the first course, was intended for the subsidiary Electors. Each of the twelve places has a silver plate flanked by another novelty – an abundance of cutlery. To the right of each plate is a knife, to the left two forks, one with two prongs, the other with three. In front of each plate there is a spoon, the bowl turned downwards. Every plate has a carefully folded napkin concealing the bread. The centrepiece is formed by a *surtout*, a handsome rococo object containing, at its lower level, sugar castors and bottles of oil

The elegance of *service à la française*.
Detail from Martin van Meytens, *Feast on the Occasion of the Coronation of
the King of the Romans*, Frankfurt, 3 April 1764.

and vinegar, and above, a bowl filled with fruit and flowers. Around the
surtout on the white damask cloth we can see three sets of matching silver
containers, all arranged in mirror-image order. The four largest are tureens,
pots à oilles, the four smaller *terrines*, and there are four salts. There is also
one large serving spoon visible, for the guests to help themselves.

We can take this basic arrangement further in a second picture,
this time of a supper, 'un repas nocturne' by candlelight given by Prince
Nicolas-Léopold de Salm-Salm about 1770.[20] Seventeen people in all are
ranged around this table, with the host in the traditional medieval place of
honour with his back to the fire, although it is summer. The guests include
two ladies, but otherwise the rest are either clerics or officers. Vast napkins

are tucked into their cravats or a buttonhole by the men and into the décolletage by the ladies, falling in ample folds on to the lap. The meal is already in progress; the roasts have just been placed upon the table. By this period, we note, silver has given way to porcelain. Knives and forks are in action (the spoons were presumably removed along with the first course of soups and *oilles*). Once again everything is laid out in a careful pattern, with two candelabra acting as anchors throughout. The focal point of the current course is a sucking-pig flanked by a cruet and a sauceboat, four salts and four more dishes, two of game and two of vegetables, one of which is certainly a salad. The *maître d'hôtel* stands by the chimney in his supervisory role and the waiters are busy serving drink. No glasses appeared on seventeenth- or eighteenth-century tables. When a diner wanted to drink he summoned a waiter (as we see here), who brought a salver bearing a glass of wine, together with a decanter of water should there be a desire to thin the wine. Porcelain wine coolers are at the feet of certain of the guests and there is a larger one containing six bottles in the foreground. To the left there is a serving table with piles of plates and an array of glasses. The dessert, still to come, stands on another table, ready to be moved over at the appropriate moment; it includes an extraordinary floral temple centrepiece in the manner of the master pastrycook, Joseph Gilliers.

The men in attendance here are clearly servants, and this marks another change. During the Middle Ages and into the Renaissance many of these menial roles were filled by men of good birth, anxious to secure a place with access to a prince or noble lord. By 1700 in France not only had that practice ended but households had contracted by 50 per cent.[21] The average staff of an eighteenth-century French château was fifteen to twenty, supervised by either the *maître d'hôtel* or the *cuisinier*. Almost exactly the same thing happened across the Channel.[22] There the old processional ritual vanished almost entirely. Where it was kept going, as at the duke of Chandos's house at Cannons in the 1720s, it was enacted only on Sunday, when each course entered headed by the gentleman usher of the hall bearing his wand of office. Virtually everywhere else, service by gentlemen and yeomen had ceased: the job was considered too demeaning. The eighteenth century saw their replacement by a new type of servant, the footman. Initially a footman was a servant whose duty was to run alongside the master or mistress's horse or coach, but gradually he migrated to serving

at table. By the later decades of the eighteenth century the great spectacle
to impress guests was that of a butler and under-butler heading a small
army of immaculately liveried footmen.

At its most refined, the effect of *service à la française* must have been
almost balletic. As dishes did not stay on the table much longer than about
fifteen minutes, there was a constantly shifting panorama as old dishes were
taken away, new ones arrived, and used plates were replaced by clean ones.
The impact was further enhanced by that other introduction of *service à la
française*, the dinner service – the array of vessels created to carry the food
to the table. As with the symmetrical table placement, there was a steady
progression towards an ever-greater unity of effect through the use of
matching containers for the various dishes.[23] It began in France during the
1670s with the advent of a new vessel, the *pot-à-ouille* or oval tureen. These
major pieces of the silversmith's art came either singly, and acted as
centrepieces, or in pairs, and were set at each end of a table. Gradually such
innovatory pieces multiplied. The earliest reference to a *terrine* occurs in
1719, while many more new pieces were called for as dessert became increasingly elaborate. Inventories make it clear that Louis XIV had services for
each and every occasion, most of them made at the end of the seventeenth
century in the late baroque style, although the decoration on each piece
varied instead of comprising matched sets. But it is clear that items like
'Vaisselle qui sert dans les offices de la maison du Roy' or 'Vaisselle faite
pour le service du Roy à Versailles et Marly' must have been sets.

What Versailles set as fashion, the rest of the world soon followed.
Other courts either ordered their services direct from the royal silver-
smiths or copied French models. Almost all dinner services at the close of
the seventeenth and the opening of the eighteenth centuries were made
either in France or England. But it was France under the aegis of Louis
XV that produced the services exported to the courts of Russia, Austria,
Spain and Portugal. The French royal silver itself vanished, either melted
down to pay for expensive wars or during the Revolution. But we can gain
an accurate idea of its magnificence from the services which have survived
in other countries by Germain, Ballin, Durand and Auguste.

Opposite: A candlelit dinner given by the Prince de Salm.
Painting, *c.* 1770.

The style set by the court was soon copied by the upper classes. The arrival of the silver dinner service marked a fundamental change in the use of the dining table. Hitherto the tiered buffet had been the location for an ostentatious display of plate. Now this display migrated to the dining table, and we see commentators measuring the splendour of a meal by the quantity of silver spread out there. In England, for example, whereas in the 1720s the accent was on great displays of baroque silver gilt and silver plate on a side buffet with a wine cooler below, within a decade pieces used at table included tureens, sauceboats, sugar castors, salts, *épergnes* and the *surtout*. By the 1740s whole services were being commissioned by the aristocracy and the gentry. The aspiring classes followed this lead, building up their table silver piece by piece over a period of time as and when they could afford it.

Next to the tureen the most striking novelty was the *surtout*. This splendid object first appeared in 1692 during the fêtes for the marriage of the duc de Chartres at the Palais Royal, where it was noticed as 'a great silver gilt piece of a new invention'.[24] At first it served to incorporate in one place items that until then had been scattered across the table – candleholders, containers for sugar, mustard, oil and vinegar, even (as we have seen) a bowl that could be filled with fruit and flowers. The innovation caught on, reaching England by 1715, and became a commonplace of the European table during the eighteenth century. Gradually practicality gave way to sheer decorative excess. Particularly during the rococo phase of the 1740s and 1750s, the *surtout* as decorative centrepiece became *de rigueur*; this was the era that produced such confections as the marine service for Frederick, prince of Wales, with its *surtout* crowned by a recumbent Neptune celebrating British sea power. Simultaneously, those arrangements of metalwork baskets for fruit and sweetmeats known as *épergnes* made their appearance.

This explosion of silver gilt and silver was for the rich. For the rest there was either pewter or ceramics in the form of delftware, faience and, later, porcelain.[25] What is significant here is the gradual ascent of these ceramics on to the tables of the aristocracy. Economic necessity played a role. In Spain, for example, the shortage of silver led Philip III in 1601 to restrict its use. As a result, table services of Talavera pottery were commissioned by the Spanish nobility. In France, even more strikingly, the ruinous cost of Louis XIV's wars brought edicts in 1689 and 1709 ordering all vessels of gold and silver to be melted down. Saint-Simon in his memoirs wrote: 'Every man of any status or consequence turned within a week to faience.' New manufactories met the demand for banqueting services with armorial bearings for princely tables. At the same period a craze for Chinese export porcelain swept Europe, to be followed, when Europeans had mastered the technique, by a plethora of new porcelain works headed by Meissen (1710) and Sèvres (1756). The latter had the prestige of the French monarchy behind it, and soon large porcelain dinner services, either sent as gifts or specially commissioned, began making their way to the courts of Vienna, Stockholm, Copenhagen and St Petersburg.

Yet when it came to the emergence of the fully-fledged ceramic dinner service, it was not France that led the way but Germany, thanks to the Meissen factory patronised by Augustus the Strong of Saxony. In 1710 Augustus charged his court silversmith to 'render possible the production of sometimes exceedingly large and sometimes other kinds of neat and artistic tableware'. The choice of a silversmith for the job links the porcelain 'service' with its antecedents. The term 'service' itself, as applied to a matching set of items for the table, originally came into use in seventeenth-century France, and referred to a group of silver serving bowls and dishes placed upon the table and uncovered simultaneously. As Augustus' order suggests, the early porcelain dinner service shapes derive from their silver forerunners. It was not until the 1730s, however, that Meissen actually began producing the great services. One made for Count Brühl ran to two thousand two hundred pieces. After 1750 other factories began following suit, with variants produced in different countries. The English, for example, had a taste for containers in the shape of vegetables or – for the hunt dinner – game.[26]

Both silver and ceramics are immense fields of study in their own right. Suffice it to say that these changing fashions in tableware served to change the experience of eating for the average diner. The visual impact of a meal was completely different in 1750 from what it had been a century before.[27] We can trace a series of tablescapes as these changes took place, dependent successively for visual effect on the food, on the silver, and finally on the porcelain. Related to this was the increasing importance of the *office*, with its highly skilled pastrycooks. It was the staff of the *office* who dressed the tables.

In the middle of the seventeenth century the great problem of table design was how to create vertical effects – apart from candelabra – rising from the flat surface of the table. The solution was *service en pyramide*, which became the most distinctive form of food presentation down to the close of the first quarter of the eighteenth century. The arrangement was particularly used for presenting dessert, which was usually set up in a different room, although it could stand at the centre of a table through-out a meal. Complex arrangements of preserved fruit with artificial flowers and leaves were piled in diminishing tiers with what were called *porcelaines* between them, dishes of silver, pewter or tin, often disguised with leaves, to keep the composition from collapsing. The numerous engravings of grand meals at the court of Louis XIV show endless variations on *service en pyramide*.

The pyramidal presentation was succeeded by layouts of the kind seen in the pictures of the Frankfurt banquet, symmetrical compositions of silver set around a tureen or *surtout*. But by the mid-eighteenth century, particularly on grand occasions, dessert stood in place all through a meal in the form of a vast parterre stretching down the middle of the table. In these astonishing creations a complex marriage of the arts of the silver-smith, the potter and the pastrycook took place. The latter used sugar pastes, biscuit dough, wax, cardboard, silk chenille trimming and coloured sugar to make temples and arbours, box hedges and statuary, often set upon mirror glass to increase the light through reflection. Joseph Gilliers, pastrycook to King Stanislas of Poland, wrote the definitive book on the subject, providing a complete guide to the construction of these toytown rococo dreamworlds. *Le Canneméliste français* (1751) is filled with engravings of every kind of effect, including whole tables arranged as rococo parterres complete with statues and vases. In other circumstances they could pass for the design of actual gardens. By the third quarter of the century, how-ever, the sugar creations of the pastrycook were succeeded by permanent versions made of porcelain. In 1790 the Danish court possessed no fewer than eight hundred and fifty pieces of porcelain and biscuit in shapes ranging from cascades and rocks to warships and pavilions, not to mention the ubiquitous vases and statues.[28]

The dining table as a parterre.
Engraving from Joseph Gilliers, *Le Canneméliste français*, 1751.

In this context let the provincial English diarist Parson Woodforde have the last word. In 1782 he went to a grand dinner given by the bishop of Norwich. He describes what to him at that date was still a novelty: 'a most beautifull Artificial Garden . . . which remained at Dinner and afterwards, it was one of the prettiest things I ever saw, about a Yard long, and about 18 Inches wide, in the middle of which was a high round Temple supported on round Pillars, the Pillars were wreathed around with artificial flowers – on one side was a Shepherdess on the other a Shepherd, several handsome Urns decorated with artificial flowers also etc etc'.[29] It had taken thirty years for the Frenchified dessert parterre to reach the fastnesses of Georgian East Anglia.

The *salle à manger* and eating rooms

THE EARLIEST APPEARANCE of the term *salle à manger* appears on a plan for a house in a French architectural book published in 1647.[30] The creation of a separate room for dining was a direct outgrowth of what had been occurring in the grand Parisian town houses of the aristocracy during the preceding decades. To the old basic sequence of a shared reception room, the *salle*, followed by a series of apartments consisting of an antechamber and a bedroom, new rooms were added, arranged *en enfilade* to provide an elegant interior vista through a series of double doors. Introduced between the *salle* and the apartment were the *salle à manger*, for eating, and the *salon*, for conversation. As the seventeenth century progressed this sequence of aligned rooms developed still further, opening with the vestibule, then an antechamber, where servants waited, a second antechamber in which people could assemble and which was also the *salle à manger*, then the *salon* for receiving those deemed of quality (but also used for dining on grand occasions), and, finally, the bedroom.

What is striking is the way separate rooms have been devoted to the two functions of eating and conversation. That division sprang from the form of social life initiated by the *précieuses*, a group of highly educated ladies led by Catherine de Vivonne, marquise de Rambouillet, who refurbished the Hôtel de Rambouillet in 1619. The *précieuses* were responsible for pioneering a new social sensibility in which intellectual conversation intermingled with gallantry and the cult of platonic love. Not for them the great dinners characteristic of medieval and Renaissance entertaining, followed by dancing. Rather, they were engrossed by interaction of minds in the form of cultivated conversation, with guests presided over by another new phenomenon, the hostess. Hence the emergence of the *salon*, yet another step towards investing areas of private space with a specific meaning and function.

By the 1640s the *salon* had embarked on its long heyday. Its ever-increasing importance is reflected in the fact that the architect Le Vau in the 1650s was to move it from the *piano nobile* to the ground floor and make it the most important of the sequence of rooms on the axis of any château. In this capacity it was to become the chief reception room, place of parade and, on grand occasions, the setting for large dinners. In effect, this served to downgrade the role of the meal in social life. Where in previous eras the apogee of entertainment had been a handsome dinner, by the middle of the eighteenth century a host's best offering to his guests was enshrined in the new room, the *salon*, and its activities – conversation, music-making and games. The *salle à manger* became a relatively small room off the *salon*, and the meal incidental to the events in the more important location. The new arrangements admirably reflected the ideals of Enlightenment society.

The *salle à manger*, of which many survive, was usually equipped with a handsome marble buffet for service and the display of plate, and often with a 'fontaine' for washing glasses and a porcelain stove for heating. All of this was a far cry from earlier centuries. Even by the middle of the 1650s the tiered buffet had gone out of fashion, and elaborate buffets for the display of plate became rare; for special occasions they might have to be specially constructed.[31] The buffet or sideboard was for practical use and perhaps also the display of dessert. We have encountered this already in the picture of Prince de Salm-Salm's grand dinner; two temporary buffets have been erected in what must be the *salon*, one for service including drink and the other for exhibiting dessert. Another distinctive feature of the *salle à manger* was the wine-cooler or *refraîchissoir* filled with ice, if available, or, if not, with water to which camphor or saltpetre was added to assist refrigeration.

The French established what was to become the standard for social occasions on the mainland of Europe. English practice was slightly different. There, although the concept of the dining-room had emerged by the 1630s, the actual use of the room was to remain uncertain until well into the eighteenth century. The main development was the multiplication of rooms where people ate in differing circumstances. Lord Craven's house at Hamstead Marshall in the 1660s had a 'Little Parlour or Ordinary Roome to Eat in', leading on to the 'Withdrawing Roome or Roome for the Lord to Eat In' and then to the 'Great Parlour'. On the opposite side of the entrance hall there was a 'Roome for the Gentlemen to eat in' and a 'Roome for the Servants to eat in'.

The last-mentioned 'roome' provides the clue to the disappearance by 1700 of the gentleman servant.[32] Now that servants were employees, a different eating dispensation was needed. In France the family would eat with any secretaries, governesses and tutors at their table, the upper servants, *valets* and *femmes de chambre*, presided over by the *maître d'hôtel*, at a second, and the lower servants, everyone from the kitchen staff to the maid of all work, presided over by the *cuisinier*, at a third, all three of which would be in a different location. By 1700 more or less the same thing had happened in England, where there was a similar contraction in the size of households. By 1700, a separate servants' hall was the norm there. In a large establishment more than one might well be necessary. In the 1720s at Cannons, the great country house of the duke of Chandos, the upper servants ate in the chaplain's room, the lesser in the gentleman-of-the-horse's room, and the remaining lower servants in either the kitchen or the servants' hall. Henceforward, only on great occasions like a marriage, a coming-of-age or Christmas did the hall resume its medieval function. In this way architectural space was used to separate and define the pecking order of a stratified society.

In England the term 'dining-room' first officially appears in 1755 in Dr Johnson's dictionary, although in fact it goes back a century earlier.[33] In his *Graphice* (1658), William Sanderson refers to the 'Dyning-Roome' in his discussion of picture-hanging, recommending that portraits of the king and queen should preside there, along with those of two or three members of the family and chief nobility, 'to waite upon their princely Persons'.[34] Nearly thirty years before Johnson's dictionary, Narford Hall already had 'a fine dining room, painted white and gilt'. But it was the architect Robert Adam who highlighted the fundamental difference between the French and English over dining-rooms. In France everyone got up at the end of a meal and went into the *salon* for conversation. In England by 1700, the men were remaining behind to talk and drink, and, if they liked once the ladies had departed, to make use of a discreetly installed chamber-pot.[35] This convenience was sometimes kept in a small closet, but sideboards in the Sheraton style of the 1790s and later included a small cupboard at the side to accommodate it.[36] In 1773 Adam wrote that dining-rooms are therefore 'considered the apartments of conversation, in which we are to pass a great deal of our time. This renders it desirable to have them fitted up with elegance and splendour, but in a style different from that of the apartments. Instead of being hung with damask, tapestry, etc., they are always furnished with stucco, and adorned with statues and paintings, that they may not retain the smell of the victuals.'[37] Working from that premise Adam argued that it was essential for the architect to have total control over the whole *mise-en-scène*, down to the curtains and the silver.

What is easily forgotten today when visiting an eighteenth-century country house is that dinner was, by the latter half of the century, eaten at four or five o'clock; it was still daylight, which explains the choice of a decoration light in tone.[38] It was only in the next century, when dining hours moved later and later, that dark colours became fashionable. At the same time that Adam was writing, women's magazines were busy developing the notion that certain areas of a house related to one sex or the other. The dining-room, because of the English custom of the ladies withdrawing, was deemed masculine.[39]

Even though a special room for eating was an established feature by the start of the eighteenth century, it does not follow that the room had a table permanently set up in it.[40] That only happened in England after 1780, with the invention of tables with leaves to drop in or remove according to the number of diners. The chairs stood against the wall and were brought forward for the meal. Earlier there had been long solid tables in the hall of the kind which still survive from the late sixteenth or early seventeenth century at places like Hatfield House or Hardwick Hall. Heavy draw-leaf tables were used for dining by the family in parlours. More generally, however, servants carried drop-leaf tables into whatever room was chosen for the dinner to take place.

The popularity of round and oval tables with hinged flaps and swinging gate-legs at the close of the seventeenth century reflected a new desire for greater informality. Developments in seating echoed this move.[41] Until about 1675 the commonest form of seat was a farthingale chair, basically a stool with a back. Originally such a chair stood midway in a descending sequence of importance, starting at the top with a chair with arms, next one without and then down to stools with no back, which could even be of slightly different heights depending on a guest's social standing. After that date, sets of cane-seated chairs, identical except for the carver, became the norm both in France and England. The fact that those of the same rank ate all at the same table but in separate rooms meant that there was no longer a need for a hierarchy of chairs.

Manners into etiquette

UNTIL THE CATACLYSM OF 1789, manners related to the rules observed at courts.[42] What began in the Renaissance as a system of behaviour drawing men of different social classes into a shared pattern of social interchange became, in the seventeenth and eighteenth centuries, a means whereby caste could be maintained. Manners were no longer a vehicle for inclusion but exclusion. The aristocracy, of course, was perpetually under pressure from the ever-expanding commercial and professional classes with access to a stream of books describing the intricacies of court behaviour. Most of these books were already in the fifteenth century little more than courtesy treatises, long lists of dos and don'ts, such as remembering to sit upright and to keep one's elbows off the table. But embedded in them are nuances pointing up changes in dining *mores* arising from the new cuisine as well as the multiplication of cutlery and the increasingly universal use of the fork. The greatest practical change was the individualisation of eating. Each diner for the first time formed his own unit with his own plate, napkin and cutlery; he no longer had to share. But we can sense a still greater though less tangible change: the emergence of taste as a new index of social status. What defined taste was intellectual and aesthetic discernment, and this in turn was regarded as an innate attribute finding expression in an increasingly consumer-oriented society. Taste, moreover, embraced judgement about food.

Antoine de Courtin's *Nouveau traité de la civilité* (1671), next to Erasmus the most influential guide to manners ever written, and one which went through numerous editions, is an index to these changes. From it we learn that by the late seventeenth century actions such as ceremonial hand-washing before meals now involved only the chief guests; that spitting was no longer acceptable; that a man took his hat off while grace was said and also doffed it when he helped serve a lady of rank or when a superior toasted him. Forks began to be taken for granted: 'You should cut the meat on your plate, and then carry it to your mouth with the fork. I say with the fork, because it is . . . very indecent to touch something greasy, or with a sauce, or in a syrup, etc., with the fingers; and further-more it obliges you to commit two or three other indecencies.' These included wiping one's fingers on the napkin, making it 'like a kitchen towel', or on the bread or, worse still, actually licking one's fingers 'which is the ultimate impropriety'.

But what the book says should be done and what actually happened were two quite different things. Louis XIV continued to use his fingers to eat meat. As late as 1737 a Flemish manners book, *De hoofsche Welleventheid*, incorporates what Courtin writes on table manners but replaces Courtin's references to the knife and fork with 'a knife, spoon or other'. A study has revealed that in the area of Ghent in Flanders forks were used even by the *petite bourgeoisie* by the mid-eighteenth century, even if only on a Sunday, but their omission in the translation is an indication that they were not to be taken for granted.[43] Knives and forks were apparently the norm for the upper classes, but among the middle classes forks remained prestige pieces kept with the silver to be brought out and used only on particular occasions. It is clear that their adoption was a slow process all over Europe, only gradually drifting down the social scale, and even then no further than the middle classes. Their prevalence as the eighteenth century proceeded, how-ever, meant a decline in the number of napkins; it was no longer necessary to soil the fingers. The statement by Jean-Baptiste de la Salle in his *Les Règles de la bien-séance et de la société chrestienne* (1729) therefore that 'It is completely contrary to good manners to touch meat and even more "potage" with the fingers' may have made sense in court society but not far outside it.

There were, of course, variations in practice between countries, and what was considered good form in one place might be rude in another. Jean Gailhard in *The Compleat Gentleman* (1678) notes some differences between France and England:

> In England the manner is for the master of the house to go before a Stranger. This would pass for very great incivility in France: so here the Lady or Mistress of the House uses to sit at the upper end of the Table, which in France is given to Strangers; so if we be many in a company, we make no scruple to drink all out of a Glass, or Tankard, which they are not used to do: and if a servant would offer to give them a glass before it was washed every time they drink, they would be angry at it.

Other sources fill out what happened at the English dinner table.[44] In Mrs Alice Smith's rare book *Art of Cookery* (1758) we find a reluctance to accept French table habits as strong as the resistance to their cookery. She writes approvingly of the 'good old English custom' of the hostess herself carving and helping her guests to the dishes on the table, all of which they are meant to sample. The newer practice, where 'everyone helps himself as he likes' and eats only what he chooses, she regards as lamentable.

The evolution of manners before 1789 may be described as a perpetual reinvention. No sooner did the upwardly aspiring learn to ape their social superiors than the latter promptly moved the goalposts. The standard eating techniques familiar to us today were in place, taking for granted the use of a napkin, knife, fork and spoon, although the use of a full *couvert* with an abundance of tableware and cutlery must have been the prerogative of relatively few. Peasant eating went on much as it always had done, unchanged since the Middle Ages.

A social divide opened up over times of meals.[45] In the Middle Ages everyone ate dinner, the main meal of the day, at the same time regardless of class. Now the dinnertime of the social elite moved later and later, in this way setting them apart from the commercial and labouring classes. The same shift occurred in concurrence with the emergence of a leisured urban class; dinner was always served later in the city than in the country. In 1740 at Bulstrode, the duchess of Portland's house in the country, dinner was at two, tea at eight and supper at ten. In sharp contrast, by the

1770s dinner in London had moved to four-thirty or five. The country still lagged behind, but by that date dinner there was being served at three or four. The same happened in France. Following the fashion set by elegant Parisian society, Marie-Antoinette and her circle would dine as late as four or five when she was at the Petit Trianon.[46] Each Sunday, still bound by the formal etiquette of Versailles, she would then have to return to the palace and sit through the formalities of public dining *au grand couvert*, not eating or even bothering to unfold her napkin.

Once in place, manners became etiquette. The first book to use that word was the anonymous *The True Gentleman's Etiquette* published in 1776. But with etiquette we anticipate the bourgeois era to come. Until the French Revolution, the history of eating and the table continues to revolve around courts, and one court in particular, Versailles. It is to that extraordinary phenomenon we must now turn our attention.

Messieurs, au couvert du Roi!

EATING WAS LOCKED into the very structure of the absolutist courts of the seventeenth and eighteenth centuries. The era witnessed an intensive elaboration of ceremony, manners, taste and conversation, all of which originated with the court and were deployed to one end – to impress upon everyone the existence of an immutable power structure. This was achieved through the creation of a complex system governing degrees of admittance to the monarch's presence.[47] Versailles, as it evolved under the aegis of *le Roi-Soleil* from the 1660s onwards, presented to the outside world a spectacle of unparalleled magnificence, one in which regal public eating came to be a central ritual enacted daily by the wearer of the crown.[48]

At Versailles between three and five thousand were fed daily by means of a hierarchy of tables.[49] The entire operation was the responsibility of the so-called *Maison-Bouche*, which embraced seven different departments with a staff of some five hundred, plus a hundred and sixty *garçons*. These all came under the *Grand Maistre de France*, an office hereditarily held by a member of the House of Condé. The other medieval officers connected with royal eating, the *Grand Panetier* and the *Grand Échanson*, had by this time become ceremonial sinecures, but the princes of Condé presided over the *Maison-Bouche* until the downfall of the monarchy. Beneath the *Maistre* came the *Premier maître d'hôtel* with a deputy and a staff which served on a rota basis. This organisation was responsible for the tables of the king and the princes of the blood, together with those of any visiting sovereign or ambassador.

The production side of the *Maison-Bouche* was headed by the *Contrôleur Général*, who was in control of finance and who met with the other officers three times a week to review expenditure. Of the seven departments only two, *le Gobelet* and *la Cuisine*, actually provided for the royal table. Of the five others, three catered for court officials. *Le Gobelet* was itself subdivided into two sections, each with its own chef plus twelve assistant chefs. One of those sections dealt with bread, salt, linen and fruit, the other with wine, water, liqueurs, coffee, ices and similar refreshments. *La cuisine-bouche*, which cooked solely for the royal family, had a rotating staff of fifty-five. To this section also pertained all tableware, both that of silver and gold, and, later, porcelain.

To begin with, Louis XIV ate both dinner and supper in public, an action encapsulated in the term *au grand couvert*. Then, in the 1690s, dinner at midday ceased to be a public event except for such great feast days as Easter, Pentecost, New Year's Day and certain Sundays. Dinner began to be eaten privately, *au petit couvert*. This in turn was modified further into other distinctive forms, *le très petit couvert* and *les jours de médecine. Le petit couvert* meant that the king ate alone at a table set up in his state bedroom.[50] After the queen's death he sometimes ate in the antechamber of the dauphine's suite but, when she too died, he returned to his own room. The king, whose appetite, like that of all the Bourbons, was large, ordered what he wished to eat earlier in the day at the *petit lever*. When the time came to dine, he was summoned to the meal by the first Gentleman of the Chamber, who also served him in the absence of the Grand Chamberlain. Being alone at table did not mean that the king was literally alone; in addition to the servants, a group of high-ranking nobles and court officials would always stand at a respectful distance looking on.

Nor was there anything informal about the meal. No fewer than fifteen persons were required to carry the king's meat in procession all the way from the *Grand Commun*, where the food was cooked, to the king's room.

'Two guards entered first. Then followed the usher of the room, the major domo with his stick, the gentleman-in-waiting of the king's buttery, the *Contrôleur Général*, his office clerk, then the officers carrying the meat, the kitchen equerry and the keeper of the king's china. Behind them two more royal guards ended the procession.' The very word *couvert* means that the dishes were covered in an attempt to keep them warm. The word lives on today to designate a place set at a meal table.

Should the king wish for a drink, the gentleman acting as cupbearer cried 'À boire pour le Roi!', bowing and going to the buffet, where the chief cupbearer handed him a gold tray carrying two crystal decanters, one filled with wine the other with water, and a glass covered with a napkin. The chief cupbearer, his attendant, and the gentleman cupbearer then went to the royal table and bowed low before assaying the contents of the decanters, using silver-gilt cups. Bowing again, the gentleman cupbearer proffered the tray and lifted the napkin from the glass; the king poured a mixture of wine and water, for he never drank wine undiluted. Bowing yet again, the gentleman cupbearer handed the tray back to the chief cupbearer, who took it back to the buffet.

Supper was always *au grand couvert* at ten o'clock.[51] Early in Louis XIV's reign it followed the ritual first drawn up for Henry III, in which the hereditary officers acted out their ceremonial roles under the direction of the *maître d'hôtel*, and the great nef was placed on the table.[52] In 1674 the ritual changed. The hereditary officers gave way to waiting by gentlemen, and the nef — by then it had acquired an almost mystical status as a symbol of sovereignty — vanished from the table. Henceforward, when not placed on one of the buffets erected in the guardroom, the nef was consigned to a glass-fronted cupboard. Anyone passing had to genuflect.

Until the death of the Dauphine-Bavière in 1690, supper *au grand couvert* took place in the antechamber to the queen's apartment. After that date it moved to the king's antechamber, and until 1789 was staged in one or other of those two rooms. To this meal came not only the king but also the queen and other princes and princesses of the royal family. Which kitchen supplied the food depended on where the meal took place. If it was in the king's antechamber the food came from the *Bouche du roi*. If in the queen's, the king and his guests sat on one side of the table, the queen and hers opposite, and each side was served with food from its own *Bouche*.

This was also an occasion governed by exact protocol. Like everything else at Versailles it was regulated down to the last detail by the king himself, who decided exactly who was of high enough rank to sit with him. In March 1710 the diarist Saint-Simon records that the king had decreed that 'Princesses of the Blood should not eat at the *Grand Couvert*. After supper, they do not follow the King into his closet: such an honour is only for the sons and daughters, grandsons and grand-daughters of France. They are only invited on special occasions, wedding feasts in the royal family or other exceptional events.'[53] At Versailles gradations of rank were assiduously studied down to the last hair's breadth.

In order to understand such a matter it is crucial to grasp the room sequence which shaped the existence of the French monarchy until its collapse.[54] The system allowed for no privacy. As Versailles was originally built in the 1670s, the progression of royal rooms ran as follows: an approach up the *Escalier des Ambassadeurs*, then through two reception rooms (the *Salons de Vénus* and *de Diane*), the guard chamber (the *Salon de Mars*), the antechamber or throne room (the *Salon de Mercure*), the state bedchamber (the *Salon d'Apollon*), the great closet and council chamber (the *Grand Cabinet*) and, finally, the king's private bedchamber with some minor closets off it. Meals *au grand couvert* took place in the *Salon de Mercure*. This changed towards the end of the seventeenth century when the king moved to the opposite wing of the palace, and the approach was now by way of the queen's staircase. That led straight to the king's guard chamber and into what was called the *Antichambre du Grand Couvert* and then the *Antichambre de l'Oeil de Boeuf* which, until 1701, comprised the king's state bedchamber, where he actually slept, and a smaller antechamber.

The ceremonial of eating *au grand couvert* began with two ushers of the antechamber crying 'Messieurs, au couvert du Roi!' and striking on the door of the guard chamber asking for a guard officer to descend with the two ushers to *le Gobelet*. From the latter a procession was formed bearing the items needed for setting up the royal table. This included a torchbearer and the head of the *Paneterie-bouche* bearing the royal nef flanked by bodyguards. Hats were doffed as the nef passed. On reaching the guard room two tables were set up, one the small *buffet du gobelet*, which had on it the ewer and basin needed for hand-washing, carafes of wine and water, glasses and napkins. The other larger table, the *table du prêt*, had the nef set upon it and was used for cutting bread and applying finishing touches to dishes before they were carried in. When the king dined *au grand couvert* in the queen's antechamber the number of buffets was doubled for king and queen.

After the guard chamber had been arranged, the royal table was erected in the neighbouring antechamber. It was sited in the same way as in the Middle Ages, with the king's back to the fire. The table was in fact quite small and the cloth was spread on it by a gentleman usher and the *Chef de la Paneterie*. Then two gentlemen laid the table. A diagram dated 1702 shows exactly how the table might be laid.[55] On this occasion the king sat alone on one side with six other members of the royal family facing each other to his right and his left. Two candelabra flanked by two salts are placed at the centre, framing the person of the king. On the table itself the first course is arranged in a symmetrical pattern in the manner of *service à la française*. The princes and princesses have merely a plate shown in front of them, presumably with the addition of cutlery and bread folded into a napkin. In the case of the king the arrangements are more complex. Immediately in front of him there is 'the royal napkin' with, to his left, two other plates, one labelled 'the King's porcelain in which he dips his bread in his soup' and the other 'the King's special small plate'. To his right there is a rectangular object labelled 'Cadenas'.

We have already encountered the cadenas on the table of the cardinal archbishop of Sens in Rome in the 1580s.[56] These objects seem to have been a specifically French development, an additional means to frustrate the poisoner. They replaced the nef, for they combined a rectangular area on which the royal knife and spoon, in Louis XIV's case, were placed, with a casket containing salt and pepper. The caskets must originally have been locked to prevent any poisonous substance being added to the contents (the word 'cadenas' now means 'padlock' in French), and the earliest mention in France of such a piece occurs in the reign of Henry II. The cadenas was not so exclusive an attribute as the nef, because in the seventeenth century not only the king and queen had them but also princes of the blood and dukes.

When the table was laid the usher would knock upon the guard chamber door once more and cry: 'Messieurs, à la viande du Roi!' He then descended accompanied by three guards to the *office-bouche* where he found the *maître d'hôtel* of the day and the controller awaiting him with the first course already assayed. Another procession was formed (it was a quarter of a mile from the kitchen to the royal table) headed by an usher bearing a torch, then the *maître d'hôtel* holding his baton of office, then two *gardes du Corps* with rifles on their shoulders, then two carrying the food and finally two more guards. On reaching the guard chamber the food was placed on the *table du prêt* and assayed a second time. Then it was borne into the antechamber and placed on the royal table. This ritual was repeated for each of the courses.

As soon as the first course was set in place the king was informed by the *maître d'hôtel* while a gentleman usher went to summon the princes and princesses. Depending on his location, it could take up to a quarter of an hour to get the king to the table. Already an hour before, at nine o'clock, those who had been formally recognised or with the correct form of recommendation had begun to assemble in hopes of admission to the chamber. It was in fact not difficult to get in; accounts exist expressing some shock at the make-up of the audience. The princesses, duchesses and other ladies entitled to the *tabouret* sat in a semicircle while behind them stood other ladies, lords and gentlemen. Women had to wear full court dress with a train. Precedence was strictly observed even at the royal table, the king having a chair with arms while the princes and princesses sat on *tabourets*.

Behind the king to his right stood the first Gentleman of the Chamber, while to his left there was the Captain of the Guard or his deputy, the *Premier maître d'hôtel*. An almoner, a doctor and a surgeon were also in attendance. Service was under the direction of one of the quarterly *maîtres d'hôtel*. The meal began with grace said by the almoner followed by hand-washing. Then the *Chef de la Paneterie* entered bearing the royal napkin on a gold plate. This was proffered to the king by the *maître d'hôtel*, but if there was a prince of the blood or some other great person present, the task was assigned to him. Under Louis XV it became the custom for the dauphin and the eldest daughter to present the napkin to the king and queen respectively.

Three courses were served and then dessert. Each course was served by five or six gentlemen who placed the dishes on the table, uncovered them and removed them. When the king required a drink the gentleman assigned the role of butler cried 'À boire pour le Roi!' and the procedure already described for *le petit couvert* was enacted, this time involving the gentleman butler, the *Chef d'Echansonnerie* and the *Aide du Gobelet*.

During the meal the princes and princesses talked in pairs while the king and queen, while she was alive, chatted to any distinguished person serving. It is extraordinary that this crippling performance went on virtually unchanged until 1789. Music must have added a lighter touch, for Louis XIV had the 'petits violons de son Cabinet' play pieces by Lully and Lalande.[57] Music vanished under Louis XV, to be revived by Marie-Antoinette. Louis XV relegated the assay of drink to the buffet and Marie-Antoinette's revival of music put an end to the cry of 'À boire'. But these were minor modifications. The ritual lasted all told about an hour, ending – one expects with relief for all – by eleven.

Saint-Simon in 1710 gives an exact description of what happened afterwards:

> When the King left the table he was accustomed to stand for less than half a quarter of an hour with his back to the balustrade in his bedroom, where all the ladies who had attended him at supper stood waiting in a semi-circle; all, that is, except those who had tabourets. The tabouret-ladies followed him from the supper room behind the princes and princesses of the blood [who would have been at table with the king], stepped forward one by one to drop a very low curtsey, and then completed the half-circle of standing ladies with the men standing behind them. The King amused himself for a little while admiring the dresses, faces, and graceful curtseys; said a word or two to the princes and princesses, and then, bowing right and left to the other ladies, repeating this gesture once or twice with unexampled majesty, moved towards his outer study. He stayed there a moment to give his orders and then continued into his inner study. There, with all the doors left wide open, he seated himself in an armchair . . .[58]

There, seated on either side of him and slightly behind, were the female members of his family on *tabourets* and the male members, including bastards, standing. All the doors were left wide open so that everyone could hear everything that was said. After this family gathering the king went to his public *coucher*.

No other ruler was subject to such exposure. In other areas of mainland Europe the Burgundian-Spanish system preserved a monarch's privacy, drawing a sharp distinction between his private as against his public life. Eating in public was restricted to certain days in the year. In the main, rulers ate in the bedchamber or cabinet privately. At the imperial and Bavarian courts eating in public was staged in the *Ritterstube* or ceremonial hall of the palace four times a year, when the emperor dined with the Knights of the Golden Fleece at Christmas, Easter, Pentecost and on the feast of St Andrew.[59] In addition, on Sundays, gala days and certain feast days, he dined with the empress alone in the *Ratstube* in the presence of his courtiers. In Spain, the king ate once a week in the presence of his courtiers.[60] But only on certain great religious festivals did he and the queen eat in public, seated beneath a canopy at a table raised on a dais, with heralds arrayed in their tabards standing at each corner. In Munich the Elector of Bavaria normally ate in private, but again on certain holidays and galas the ducal family would eat at one table, with their courtiers at another, in public. It was the rule to watch in silence.[61]

As the eighteenth century progressed, this kind of ritual became increasingly anachronistic and uncomfortably demanding on those who took part. In some countries it fell into disuse. England is a case in point.[62] Charles II, after his restoration in 1660, revived the practice. John Evelyn noted in his diary on 17 August 1667: 'Now did his Majestie dine in the Presence in antient State with Music and all the Court ceremonies which had been interrupted since the late War.' But the revival was short-lived, falling again into abeyance during the reign of Charles's niece, Queen Anne, who in the aftermath of the death of her husband, Prince George of Denmark, withdrew from the public gaze. The incoming Hanoverian George I resolutely opposed it until his son, the future George II, attempted to reinstate dining in public as a deliberate bid for popularity. George I, as usual at loggerheads with the prince, was briefly forced to revive the practice for himself. This too did not last. It would find no favour with what was now a constitutional monarchy. George III and Queen Charlotte, noted for their frugality, dined alone.

More or less the same thing happened in Denmark, where there was for a brief period an attempt to institute royal public dining in the aftermath of a visit to Versailles by Christian VII.[63] On his return in 1769 the shape of the royal table was changed to rectangular, a display of confectionery in the manner of Gilliers installed in its centre, and the food carried in in procession. But this was over by 1771, after which royal dining became purely personal.

The Danish royal family supping in public on New Year's Day, 1779.
Painting by Pehr Hilleström, 1779.

One picture more than any other evokes what royal dining in the high public style must have looked like, albeit at a minor court, that of Gustavus III of Sweden.[64] The occasion recorded is supper *au grand couvert* on New Year's Day 1779. Although far removed from the grandeur of Versailles it captures the mysterious and somewhat hallucinatory quality of such events during the age of the courts. Behind a long rectangular table, the king sits with his two brothers to his right and the queen mother, his queen and sister to his left. Silver in the latest neo-classical style (some of which still survives) is arranged along with porcelain figures on a sheet of mirror glass known as a *chemin de table*. The handsome candelabra and single candles, not to mention the wall sconces and the five rococo chandeliers above, bestow a flickering beauty on the scene. Before each royal person there is a *couvert* consisting of a gold plate, a knife, fork, spoon and bread. The moment recorded is some way into the first course, for the most important pieces on the table are two magnificent tureens symmetrically sited, one of which has its lid removed with the handle of a serving spoon protruding. In the centre is the court marshal in charge of service, with a figure which is likely to be the seneschal to the right accompanied by three esquires of the *Bouche*. To the left a squire of the *Bouche* advances carrying a plate. It would be reasonable to conclude that the onlooking courtiers have been rearranged, for they would normally be standing where the painter is. Everyone is attired in court livery, with certain ladies who were accorded the privilege of the *tabouret*, the wives of councillors and ambassadors, seated. It is difficult to believe that the French Revolution lies just a decade away.

Food and festival at Versailles

E VERY SO OFTEN during the first half of the reign of Louis XIV, Versailles would be set ablaze by festival. With such displays the king was reviving the traditions of the Valois court, where festivals were staged in sets called 'magnificences'. The allegorical banquet arranged by Catherine de' Medici at Bayonne in 1565 was just such an event. The aim was to impress not only the court and the nation but the rest of Europe with the richness and cultural sophistication of the French crown. Thus during the decade 1664–74 Louis XIV staged three fêtes whose splendour he made sure was known, for each was the subject of a handsome tome illustrated with engravings recording the proceedings in the minutest detail. And on each occasion food played an integral part in the celebrations.

In May 1664 Le Nôtre's spectacular gardens at Versailles, recently laid out and still in the process of formation, were inaugurated by the festival dubbed *Les Plaisirs de l'Île Enchantée*.[65] The event celebrated the treaty of Aix-la-Chapelle and was ostensibly dedicated to the queen mother and the queen, although in reality the true heroine of *Les Plaisirs* was the king's new mistress, Louise de la Vallière. *Les Plaisirs* extended over a fortnight and included carrousels (tournaments), ballets, firework displays, and plays by Molière. In addition there was a revival of the allegorical banquet. It followed the opening carrousel, in which the king appeared in the guise of Roger from Ariosto's *Orlando furioso* (the source of much of the scenario for the fêtes). The feast, staged in the same enclosure as the tournament, was introduced by a grand procession of allegorical pageant cars headed by Apollo, with figures like the seasons and signs of the zodiac in attendance. The feast itself followed, borne in by four groups of twelve attired to represent the seasons: gardeners bearing green and silver baskets, harvesters red ones, grape-pickers sylvan baskets and, finally, fur-shrouded old men carrying baskets made to resemble ice. One of the engravings shows some of these waiters moving across the foreground with huge dishes on their heads piled high *en pyramide*. A huge semicircular table curves around half the arena, while the knights who had fought there a short time before continue to stand by, their fancy dress and towering plumed helmets adding splendour to the scene.

By the time the dinner took place night had fallen, but a small forest of chandeliers painted silver and green, together with two hundred masked men clasping torches, resulted in 'a clarity almost as bright as day'. The feast itself was of a 'sumptuosity which surpassed anything one could describe, as much for its abundance as for the delicacy of the things which were served'. The *Mercure de France* reported that 'It seemed that this was a banquet of the gods and the park of Versailles was transformed into their Olympus.'

The *Mercure*'s comment was astute; it neatly summed up the artistic aim of such fêtes, which was to transform the setting in such a way that no one knew where reality ended and fantasy began. Four years later another festive series was held to celebrate the conquest of Flanders, but this time it was contained in the course of one night, 18 July, beginning at six in the evening and continuing until morning.[66] Once again a team of artists and craftsmen transformed the gardens into a series of temporary venues devoted to a succession of spectacles. The evening opened with the king and his party viewing the new fountains and water parterre, after which refreshments were served in a pentagonal room of greenery at the apex of five *allées*. The engraving shows the enclosure with a *jet d'eau* spouting thirty feet high in the centre. Around it two of the five tables are visible, 'laden with all sorts of items which make up a magnificent collation'. This was figurative food of the extreme Italian variety: one buffet table supported a mountain with grottoes filled with cold meats and another had the façade of a palace made of marzipan and sugar paste. There were huge pyramids of preserved fruits and all sorts of liqueurs. After the king, the queen and the ladies had eaten what they wished 'the king abandoned the tables to the pillage of the people who followed'.

After this the royal party made its way to the central axis of the gardens. Here a temporary theatre had been erected and the ballet *Les Fêtes de l'Amour et Bacchus* with music by Lully was performed, followed by a play by Molière. Then came the supper, served in an octagonal pavilion designed by Henri Gissey. Several designs for the pavilion survive. It was fifty feet high, with a ceiling of treillage from which garlands of silver gauze and flowers looped downwards. Its eight sides were arched, and two of the facing arches were made into buffets for a massive tiered display of silver plate. Between the arches there were fountains and torchères; the frieze, lit by luminous crystal bowls, depicted the seasons and the times of day in a reference to the sun god Apollo, Louis XIV's mythological counterpart. *Le Roi-Soleil* was further apotheosised in the decoration at the centre of the pavilion, which depicted Apollo attended by the nine Muses on Mount Helicon with the horse Pegasus at the top and a stream trickling downwards. The supper table was set out around this, laden with a collection of plate that included the king's nef, and vases of flowers and other decoration. The supper consisted of five courses, each one of fifty-six dishes, carried in by members of the Swiss Guard. The dessert included sixteen vast pyramids of preserved fruit. What the engraving does not show are the other tables within the octagon and outside, which accommodated the rest of the diners. The evening concluded with a ball and the illumination of the palace as the king and his suite made their way back.

The supper pavilion for the fêtes at Versailles, 1668.
Engraving, 1678.

The last great set of fêtes celebrated the conquest of Franche-Comté.[67] This time the various events were scattered through the months of July and August 1674, and included the usual mixture of opera, plays, firework displays, trips in gondolas on the canal and several collations. Of these, easily the most extraordinary was a supper of a kind called a *media-noche*, which took place in the *Cour de Marbre*, the small courtyard of the original château built by Louis XIII, on 28 July after a revival performance of Lully's *Les Fêtes de l'Amour et Bacchus*. The guests made their way to the courtyard to find that its central fountain, though still playing, had been encased in a vast structure which ascended from an octagonal buffet table to consoles of imitation lapis lazuli supporting figures playing musical instruments which, in their turn, were surmounted by an eighteen-foot Tuscan column crowned with a vase. The entire arrangement was dotted with hundreds of candles. The engraving by Le Pautre shows the windows thronged with onlookers and a crush of spectators below being held back by the guard. On the buffet table there is what amounts to a sugar collation, huge pyramids of preserved fruits interspersed with flowers, vases of ice and pyramids of iced sweets.

Perhaps the most delightful of all these garden collations took place at Chantilly in August 1688 when the prince de Condé entertained the dauphin, known as Monseigneur.[68] The designer, Jean Bérain, created a parterre of fruit in the middle of a labyrinth. Architectural walls of greenery formed a background to the usual pair of buffets facing each other, this time banked with melons and porcelain dishes, with further lesser buffets in the corners in tiers with silver and porcelain containers full of flowers. In the centre was a table on which lay a symmetrical parterre built of silver baskets filled with fruit, an orange tree covered with flowers and fruit, and small vases of flowers. The absence of any form of lighting indicates that this delectable refreshment was consumed during daylight hours.

By 1688 the oppressive routine of Versailles was beginning to take its toll even on Louis XIV, who first sought escape from it at the Trianon de Porcelaine. More significant for the history of the table, however, was to be Marly.

The quest for informality

IN 1678 THE KING, then at the height of his power and popularity, reacted suddenly against the very world he had created and desired instead a small secluded place where he could escape from the ceremony and grandeur of Versailles. The place he choose was Marly, a small château flanked by small pavilions for his guests, ten each side looking down upon terraces which descended to a *pièce d'eau* with fountains. Marly from the outset was private and exclusive. To be invited was the ultimate sign of favour, one eagerly sought. There formality dissolved amidst a constant round of hunting parties, concerts, picnics and other divertissements. From 1685 until his death in 1715 Marly was Louis XIV's obsession.

Royal eating there was so unlike the patterns followed at Versailles that the baroque ritual was bound ultimately to be undermined and destroyed.[69] Supper was served at two oval tables, each of which could take two courses at a time. At one table sat the king, at the other Monseigneur. The rest of the diners were all women, thus preserving one ancient hierarchical principle – that the king never sat at the same table with a man except a member of his own family. The king and Monseigneur would choose which princesses and other titled ladies they wished to have sit near them, while the rest filled the vacant places as best they could. All the guests sat on *tabourets* and the dress code was less formal than at Versailles. There was some gradation in the quality of the plate, the king being served on silver gilt, the princesses on silver and the rest on old palace plate. But neither the nef nor cadenas were anywhere to be seen. Virtually all of the ritual observed in the *petit couvert* or the *grand couvert* was abandoned. The *Premier maître d'hôtel* served the king, the controller general and the controller in ordinary, aided by officers of *le Gobelet*, the rest. These suppers were roistering affairs. The king threw bread at the ladies, who in their turn threw theirs back at him. Apples and oranges flew across the table, and on one occasion a female guest propelled a dish of dressed salad in the direction of the king. At the suggestion of the duchess of Burgundy, wife of the king's grandson, who was well aware of new developments in the fashionable salons of early eighteenth-century Paris, a table stacked with plates, glasses, wine and water was introduced, making it possible to dispense almost entirely with servants during the course of the meal.

Here we see the court no longer setting style but following it. By the opening decades of the eighteenth century there was a widespread desire for a new informality. Already in the *hôtels* of Paris a new refinement and lightness of touch went hand in hand with an affectation of simplicity. Convention was deliberately flouted by ignoring the rules of hierarchy in seating guests at table, although such departures never moved beyond the superficial. Meals were increasingly seen as vehicles of amorous dalliance. The line of descent to the scene that opened this chapter – Louis XV and his mistress, the marquise de Pompadour, presiding over a *souper intime* in the king's private apartments – is complete, and we have only to glance at Jean-Michel Moreau le Jeune's engraving, *The Elegant Supper*, published in Paris in 1781, to see how vast was the change from a century before. Supper has reached its close, and it is not difficult to imagine how the evening is destined to end. No servants are present and two small occasional tables have bottles of wine, an ice bucket, a *rafraîchissoir*, glasses and plates within reach. In the centre of the table a biscuit group of the Graces supports a pineapple. Little vases of flowers surround it. A bouquet of flowers and a letter lie on the floor beside a bow that could only have been plucked from a woman's corsage. The atmosphere is of a frank sensuality, calling to mind the alliance of food and love-making that we find recorded in Casanova's memoirs.[70]

Everywhere we look as we advance through the century, the ceremonial eating of the baroque age becomes more and more of an anachronism, to be enacted only on certain state occasions. In the 1720s at the Bavarian court the Elector and the ladies would take the places assigned to them, but the other diners sat anywhere or cast lots for places. Often when the Elector ate privately he would sit down at the same table as his suite. In 1774, the Elector Maximilian III Joseph extended the principle of free choice to members of his own family.[71] Even at Versailles, Marie-Antoinette attempted to change things; her *soupers de société* enabled her and the princesses for the first time to sit side by side with men who were not members of the royal family.[72]

The old ritual of *le grand couvert* at Versailles had already crumbled substantially by then.[73] As long as the Sun King was alive it was maintained. His grandson, the duke of Burgundy, likewise dined in public with his mother from the age of four. But things changed with Louis XV. During the Regency he lived in Paris; although he re-established the old ceremonial when he returned to Versailles in 1722 at the age of twelve, and even multiplied it after his marriage in 1725, with the advent of mistresses – especially Madame de Pompadour – this move was reversed. *Le grand couvert* was now enacted only twice a week, on Tuesdays and Sundays.

Opposite: The Elegant Supper.
Engraving by Jean-Michel Moreau le Jeune, 1781.

13. Informality *à la chasse*. The hunt picnic.
Detail from a painting by Carel van Loo, 1737.

It was left to the queen and the dauphin to keep the ritual alive. Under Louis XVI and Marie-Antoinette the performance took place only once a week; the custom of eating in public on Sundays and feast days was reduced to the royal couple eating alone, with the ceremonial greatly simplified.

The yearning for a new and more relaxed style of eating is caught sharply in the numerous eighteenth-century canvases depicting picnics, usually at the hunt, by artists such as Nicolas Lancret, Carel van Loo and Jean-François de Troy. De Troy's hunt breakfast (1737), for example, is in a series commissioned to decorate Louis XV's dining-room in the *petits appartements*. There men and women jostle around a table eating and drinking in happy informality. In Van Loo's canvas of a hunt picnic the gentlemen wait on the ladies and the couples are seated on the ground around a cloth scattered with plates of ham and game and bottles of wine. A man and a woman gaze into each other's eyes. The mood is overtly amatory, untroubled, sensuous, a world away from eating as an expression of power.

The high Victorian dinner party. A short-sighted guest searches for her place.
Engraving, *c.* 1870.

CHAPTER SIX

Dinner is Served

OAKLY PARK IS a handsome neo-classical house just north of Ludlow in Shropshire on the borders of England and Wales.[1] In 1852 it was the seat of Robert Henry Clive, a direct descendant of the famous Clive of India, and his wife, Lady Harriet Windsor, younger daughter of the earl of Plymouth. On New Year's Day 1852 they gave a dinner for an American family who had leased the nearby estate of Moor Park. One of that family was an observant young woman of twenty-three, Anna Maria Fay, who in letters home wrote graphic descriptions of her experiences of living in this mid-Victorian county society. Her account of the dinner is perhaps unique, if only because she was describing the customs of one country to correspondents abroad.

Anna Maria approached the event with some trepidation. She had heard that Lady Harriet was 'a great personage, very tall, dignified, and as frigid as the Arctic ocean . . .' But let the young lady speak for herself:

> . . . Therefore it was with beating heart I found myself at the hall door. Two footmen in red plush breeches and blue coats and silver buttons, and the groom of the chambers in black, received us in the vestibule, where we took off our cloaks. The dignitary in black preceded us through the hall and throwing open the door announced us as Mr. and Mrs. Fay, and the Miss Fays, and Mr Fay. We found ourselves in a large and beautiful library, and an elegant circle of ladies and gentlemen rose to meet us. Lady Harriet received us with great dignity, and though no one was introduced every one spoke to us. It was not until the end of the evening that we knew who composed the party, and I will tell you here, that you may know in what distinguished company we dined. When dinner was announced Mr. Clive rose and offered his arm to the

Dowager Countess of Powis, a fine-looking woman . . . Of course her rank gave her precedence over Aunt Catherine, whom Lady Harriet requested Mr. Robert Clive, the heir of the house, to take in to dinner . . . Then uncle Richard followed with Lady Lucy Herbert . . . She preceded Lady Harriet Herbert and a Mr. Clive . . . They are daughters of the Countess of Powis and sisters of the Earl of Powis. After these, Maria followed with the Honorable Mr. Herbert . . . Lady Harriet requested the Honorable William Herbert to take me in; then Miss Clive and Mr. Longworth, the Vicar of Bromfield [the local village]; and Richard and Miss Mary Clive followed; and finally Lady Harriet and the Earl of Powis . . .

We found ourselves in a large dining-room hung with pictures . . . Seated at a beautiful table, we found ourselves in a family circle, which made the compliment all the greater. At the head of the table, which was long and broad, sat Mr. Clive and Lady Powis. On his right was Aunt Catherine, and next to her Mr. Robert Clive; then Maria and Mr. Herbert; next Mr. Clive and Lady Harriet Herbert; then Richard and Miss Mary Clive. At the foot of the table were the Earl of Powis and Lady Harriet. Uncle Richard was to Lady Harriet's left, and beside him Lady Lucy Herbert; then a shy young man whose name I do not know; then a young son of the Clives, the Honorable William and myself. Miss Clive sat next to me and Mr. Longworth on the left of the Countess. Thus you have us seated at the table after grace by Mr. Longworth.

Now I must describe the arrangement of the hospitable board. In the centre of the table was a gilt plateau on which stood two immense candelabra with ornaments of china figures. At each end of the table were two candelabra on stands similar though smaller than the plateau. The effect produced by these four candelabra filled with wax candles, and the becoming light thrown upon every one was very fine. The portly butler in white vest and cravat and black coat, and the groom of the chambers, and a half-dozen or more footmen in red plush and blue coats gave great elegance to the whole effect. I cannot tell you how many kinds of soup there were. Suffice it, that mine was most delicious. Then followed several varieties of fish. The turbot was placed before Mr. Clive. After that came little entrées, delicious pâtés, and mutton chops,

The dining table laid at Attingham Park, Shropshire.
Watercolour by Lady Hester Leeke, between 1848 and 1861.

well served. On the side table were every variety of meat – turkeys, chickens, anything you could wish. These courses over, the game followed. I should have told you that the vegetables were cucumbers and asparagus. The service was entirely of silver. The dessert service was of pretty china, but nothing remarkable. The ices and jellies and other most beautifully arranged and delicious dishes were placed on the table. The dessert was composed of fruit, oranges, pears, grapes, etc . . .

Sitting a little while after dessert, Lady Harriet gave the signal to rise and we left the room, Lady Powis preceding on her side of the table and Aunt Catherine on the other. Passing through the hall . . . we entered the large and elegant drawing-room. Coffee was brought in, and some of the ladies sat down to their beautiful worsted work, while others disposed themselves around the room . . . I told Miss Clive how much I had heard of her drawings and how anxious I was to see them, and she in a very kind manner brought in her portfolio . . .

When the gentlemen came in, Lady Harriet Herbert played a beautiful piece by Blumenthal . . . Maria and Richard sang some German songs. After these, what do you think was asked for in this aristocratic circle – Negro Melodies!!!! . . .

I forgot to mention the ceremony of passing the loving-cup around to the gentlemen at the end of the dinner. A large cup with handles on each side filled with toasted ale is brought in, and the gentleman to whom it is given first takes a long draught, after which the footman passes it to the next gentleman, and so on.[2]

More than a century has passed since Louis XV's *souper intime* with his mistress and cronies, with its disregard of rank, and such informality that the king even made coffee. What is striking is that developments seem to have gone in reverse. Though this dinner at a lesser country house occurs at the heart of the bourgeois age, indeed is almost contemporaneous with that apotheosis of Victorian life the Great Exhibition, it has a formality and panoply that take us back to the baroque age. Rank determines everything. The diners, controlled by the host and hostess, are marshalled in strict hierarchical order into the dining-room, where they are seated in terms of rank. Everything is designed to impress on the guests the splendour, magnificence and status of the hosts, from the liveried servants on arrival, on through the dining table laden with silver, the huge flaming candelabra, the elegance of the food (which includes things like asparagus, cucumbers and grapes, quite out of season in January) to the parade of footmen in livery.

Anna Maria's account is peppered with rarely recorded details: how no one was introduced on arrival, how the women left the room, how the old custom of the loving cup has survived, how grace was still said (although perhaps only because a cleric was present) and how the dinner was served *à la française* in the fashionable style introduced in the 1820s among the upper classes. And yet in essence – and this is what impressed Anna Maria – it was a family dinner despite all the pomp and circumstance. This is the era of the house as the shrine of the domestic virtues. Although the hosts and the setting are aristocratic, the ethic is bourgeois. We have arrived at a period in which the highest compliment that could be paid any stranger was admission to the family table. By the 1850s the dinner party had become an expression of class solidarity, a demonstration that the person invited was accepted to be of the same social status as the host and hostess. Given this understanding it is hardly surprising that the Fays were bowled over at finding themselves on easy terms with a group from the closed ranks making up what was now defined as Society.

But that is to anticipate. There are questions to be answered first. Why did the dinner party, a culinary institution that is still alive and well in the twenty-first century, come to take centre stage? What governed its form and etiquette? England, until now on the fringe of innovations in developments in feasting, was to play a key role, even if the main focus of culinary innovation remained firmly on the other side of the Channel. But why England?

One key fact is this: it was England which first experienced the full impact of the industrialisation and urbanisation that are the hallmarks of nineteenth-century Europe. Nowhere else did the mass exodus from country to town take place on such a stupendous scale, at so early a date. When cities like London, Birmingham, Manchester and Liverpool exploded in size, for the first time there emerged a market economy totally replacing the old subsistence economy. Families ceased to be self-sufficient and relied for what they ate on the food trade. The same thing happened in Paris too. New transport systems meant that diet ceased to be regionally based, and by 1900, thanks to the emergence of the processing industry, canning and refrigeration, food became international. These tremendous changes affected everybody, and radically altered the nature of cuisine. But what propelled the dinner party to the dizzy social heights from which it has never since been dislodged was something far more profound – the huge and continuing expansion of the middle classes, a peculiarly British phenomenon.

All over Europe in the nineteenth century, new fortunes were being made. In the aftermath of the French Revolution and the Napoleonic Wars, the old aristocratic and established classes were perpetually under siege from below. Their mechanism for survival was the creation of a new set of criteria for admittance to their ranks. Next to cleanliness and modesty, table manners became a major test. Aspirants to higher standing learned to distance themselves from the kitchen and anything to do with the processes of cooking (apart from deciding the menu). One needed to have a separate dining-room for meals. And above all it was necessary to be able to stage dinner parties in which the choice of guests, like the paraphernalia and provision of food, supported one's claim to be a member of Society.

All of this was established by the 1850s, but no one caught up in the cataclysmic events of 1789 and after could have predicted it. The long-term effect of the French Revolution on table customs might have suggested quite another result. No event in modern history, not even the Russian Revolution of 1917, had such repercussions as the revolution that took place in France. It set out to redefine every human act and aspiration, including that of eating. Indeed during the heady days when revolutionary fervour was at its peak, anything remotely resembling a dinner party of the kind described by Anna Maria would have been viewed as wholly unacceptable and counter-revolutionary. In the dawning age of liberty, fraternity and equality, a meal was to be something completely different from the ritual pretentiousness that had gone before.

From revolution to the return of ritual

IN JULY 1789, only a few days after the storming of the Bastille, the Marquis Charles de Villette proposed that the new ideal of fraternity could be achieved by common dining in the streets. 'The rich and poor could be united, and all ranks would mix . . . the capital, from one end to the other, would be one immense family, and you would see a million people all seated at the same table . . .' And then, standing on its head the *ancien régime* tradition of the royal family dining *au grand couvert*, Villette goes on to add: 'On that day, the nation will hold its *grand couvert*.' Ironically, of course, the proposal would have represented just as much a manipulation of the meal in service of the state as anything ever staged at Versailles.[3]

That flirtation with the communal meal as emblematic of a new age of equality and fraternity was to continue to ebb and flow through the early, more extreme, years of the Revolution. On 14 July 1790, the first anniversary of the fall of the Bastille, a Festival of Federation was staged, prefaced the previous day by two thousand spectators watching members of the National Assembly share an open-air 'patriotic meal' in the circus of the Palais Royal. On the day itself General Lafayette invited provincial participants in the festival to feast at one of the 'endless tables' which had been set up beneath the trees of the Parc de la Muette. The left-overs from this fraternal repast were distributed afterwards to the poor.

Three years were to elapse before such communal feasting resurfaced again.[4] On 10 August 1793 the painter David staged one of the most spectacular of the French Revolutionary fêtes on the anniversary of the overthrow of the monarchy. A huge procession wound its way to the Place de la Révolution, upon which a vast statue of Liberty had been erected. Part of the ceremonial was a ritual meal, echoing the mass, during which a 'cup of regneration' was shared. A 'frugal repast' on the ground of the Champ de Mars followed.

Villette's notion of the fraternal banquet gained official currency. No expression of civic solidarity was deemed more acceptable than for high and low to be seen eating and drinking together at the same 'gamelle politique', a meal consumed in the open, or at least by the door. Any passer-by was supposed to be invited to join in. By July 1794 communal meals at tables set up in the streets of Paris had become mandatory. They remained so until Bertrand Barère, a prominent radical, denounced them as shams, superficial exhibitions that gave even unreconstructed aristocrats a chance to claim 'fraternity' merely by shouting 'Vive la république'. Barère called instead for gatherings of a few families to share in a frugal meal, not what he regarded as this saturnalia of the streets with the sexes wantonly mingling. Classical texts supported the appeal for restraint and frugality, which also by its very nature represented the antithesis of the prodigality of pre-revolutionary French aristocratic cuisine.

All of this was to be as dust within a few years, yet what occurred in the period after 1789 fundamentally shaped developments around the table down to our own day. A primary effect was to dissolve the equation of cuisine and class. Henceforward cuisine of a kind seen as the prerogative of royalty and the nobility would be available to anyone who could afford to pay for it. That profound shift was to be visibly epitomised in a new institution, the restaurant, to which I shall come shortly. Another effect, less obvious, was the relationship between the public and the private. Revolutionary policy, evidenced in the case of the meal around the classless communal table in the street, was the deliberate erasure of the division between the public and private spheres of life. But the attack on privacy – viewed as the prerogative of the rich and driven on by the intervention of the state between the years 1789 and 1794 – in the long run produced a reaction in the opposite direction. The eventual consequence was the creation of private domestic space, the essence of the bourgeois age to come. Similarly, revolutionary hopes of emancipating women by overturning the existing 'natural' sexual order also backfired; reaction saw them recast as domestic goddesses in the newly fashioned private sphere of life. And central to that sphere was the dinner party over which these goddesses were to preside.

So the effect of the Revolution on the classes dislodged in France and threatened elsewhere was for them to set in motion a revival of all the Revolution had set out to destroy. The desire by pre-revolutionary monarchs and aristocrats to behave and live as ordinary gentlemen gave way to new impulses towards hierarchy and splendour. In France, for example, we see Napoleon progressing from first consul to an emperor presiding over the revival of the court. His *grand maître des cérémonies* was Louis-Philippe, comte de Ségur, a man well equipped to put the clock back for, besides worshipping both the emperor and etiquette, he had known Versailles in all its pre-1789 glory. In this role Ségur promulgated the *Étiquette du palais impérial*, a document that reinstated a Napoleonic version of the *grand couvert*.[5]

Although Napoleon himself ate his dinner in ten minutes flat from a pedestal table over which a napkin had been thrown, he revived public dining for great occasions. These occasions numbered only eight. Later, in exile on Elba, he was to regret that he had not fully revived the *grand couvert* as practised by Louis XVI which, on account of its free admittance to the royal presence of anyone respectably attired, would have given people access to the emperor and thus built up a wider circle of allegiance to the imperial cause.

The greatest of these events took place on 2 April 1810, when Napoleon married Marie-Louise of Habsburg. Only members of the court or those with a ticket were admitted. The imperial family sat *en tableau* at a horseshoe table raised on a dais. The table itself was covered with a cloth fringed with gold and embroidered with Ns and eagles. On its surface there was a *chemin de table* of mirror glass on which stood neo-classical biscuit figures along with two urns of artificial flowers interspersed with silver-gilt candelabra. At each end there was a little table displaying that icon of the French monarchy, the nef. The painter Casanova captures exactly the almost hallucinatory quality of this return to the world everyone thought had gone. At the sides of the picture there are bejewelled members of the court leaning forward from what resemble boxes in a theatre to catch a glimpse of the ritual. Ségur's *Étiquette* describes in detail every single action appropriate to such an event, from the ceremonial hand-washing under the auspices of the Grand Chamberlain to the requirement that each napkin, once used, was tossed on the ground. Behind the imperial table stand in serried ranks all the court officers needed to serve the meal. It is astounding to realise that twenty years on from the French Revolution we are witnessing a living version of something invented at the Burgundian court in the fifteenth century. Moreover, every place in Europe where Napoleon established a state with a member of his family as its ruler saw the same ritual enacted.

With the restoration of the Bourbon monarchy in the aftermath of the fall of Napoleon in 1815, the French court entered one of its great periods.[6] It lasted until 1830, and during this time Charles X also occasionally staged the *grand couvert*. Unlike Napoleon, however, Charles allowed a walkway permitting members of the public to file by and peer at him, flanked by the dauphin and his wife. On either side ladies of the court sat looking on while musicians played. Only with the advent of the Citizen King, Louis-Philippe, did the *grand couvert* finally fall into abeyance. But by then it had already had a three-hundred-year life.

Overleaf: Banquet at the Tuileries on the occasion of Napoleon's
marriage to Marie-Louise, 1810.
Painting by Dufay called Casanova, 1812.

The story does not quite end there, for the world of the courts under-went a remarkable revival during the nineteenth century, especially during the decades preceding the outbreak of the First World War. Louis-Philippe, stingy as he was, might have abandoned the *grand couvert* but, equally, he was aware of the value of an invitation to a meal at the palace.[7] In fact his entertainments set the scene for what is still with us today. On 30 May 1830, on the occasion of the marriage of the duke of Orléans, a banquet for five hundred was given in the *Galerie des Glaces* at Versailles. Present at it were all ranks of society, and this was the great change. Instead of staring at the royal family from afar, members of the old established classes, ministers, politicians and representatives of the emergent *nouveaux riches* could find themselves seated at the royal table. The state banquet as a format is still alive and well today. It has survived the abolition of monarchies and the advent of republics. It has proved an infinitely flexible manifestation of food and power in countries as politically disparate as China and the United States. In countries with surviving monarchies these stately parades – as splendid as if the world had not changed – revisit the past and wed it to the present. Such is the power of pageantry in maintaining an outward expression of the unity of society.

The century of Carême

ONE EVENING IN July 1829 Lady Morgan, novelist, inveterate traveller and society hostess, was invited to dine in Paris by baron de Rothschild at his Château de Boulogne. 'Dinners in France,' she writes, 'have two objects; sociality and gastronomy . . .'[8] The dinner was served in a marble pavilion set in a grove of orange trees and she was seated in the place of honour on her host's right. The table itself was adorned 'with the beautiful and picturesque dessert', among which the baron drew her attention to what was called a *pièce montée*: 'a column of the most ingenious confectionery architecture, in which my name was inscribed in spun sugar . . . With less genius than went into the composition of this dinner, men have written epic poems . . .' It was a surprising effusion for an age when it is difficult to find any written response to food.

Lady Morgan was keenly aware that she was a guest at a gastronomic event of the first order, and here is how she records it:

> To do justice to the science and research of a dinner so served, would require a knowledge of the art equal to that which produced it. Its character, however, was, that it was in season, that it was up to its time, that it was in the spirit of the age, that there was no *perruque* in its composition, no trace of the wisdom of our ancestors in a single dish; no high-spiced sauces, no dark-brown gravies, no flavour of cayenne and allspice, no tincture of catsup and walnut pickle, no visible agency of those vulgar elements in cooking, of the good old times, fire and water. Distillations of the most delicate viands, extracted in 'silver dews', with chemical precision, 'on tepid clouds of rising steam', formed the *fond* of all. Every meat presented its own natural aroma; every vegetable its own shade of verdure.[9]

The man who evoked that eulogy was Antonin de Carême.

Carême is one of those people in the history of cuisine, like Taillevent, Scappi or La Varenne, after whom nothing will be quite the same again.[10] Until the arrival of *nouvelle cuisine* in the 1960s, he was to be the fount of the cooking that dominated Europe, *cuisine classique*. Born in 1783, the abandoned son of a Parisian workman, Carême was apprenticed to one of the finest pastrycooks of the day, Sylvain Bailly. By 1803 he had set himself up as a specialist pastrycook for great events, and after that his career was one long dazzling progress, working for such luminaries as Talleyrand, George IV and the tsar of Russia.

Although he described his culinary style as new, and denounced eighteenth-century aristocratic cuisine as old-fashioned, in many ways he is better seen as the last in the line of aristocratic practitioners stretching all the way back to La Varenne. What Carême did was to transmit a version of the traditional style to the *nouveaux riches*. He was a man who cast gastronomy as a synthesis of both the arts – including architecture, sculpture, painting, literature and poetry – and the sciences, including physics, chemistry, political economy and commerce. While in the service of Talleyrand he established an unrivalled reputation as a master stylist. He would control every aspect of a great culinary event, not only the choice of dish and visual appearance of the food, but also how the table was laid and the room decorated and lit.

The return of figurative food.
Engraving from Carême, *Livre de pâtisserie*, 1854.

His pride and joy were his *pièces montées* of the kind Lady Morgan describes, the result of time spent studying architectural prints in the Bibliothèque Nationale. These were displayed as part of the tableau of dessert which ran down the centre of the table and remained there for the entire meal. Known as the 'Palladio de pâtisserie', Carême peopled the table with miniature follies from a *jardin anglo-chinois* of the second half of the eighteenth century: ruins, classical temples, colonnades and other structures in a whole range of styles, Greek, Roman, Moorish, Indian and Chinese. For a banquet for George IV as regent given on 15 January 1817, his creations included the ruins of Antioch, a Syrian hermitage, the ruins of a Turkish mosque and a Chinese hermitage. To construct them he used everything from lumps of lard to spun sugar. They transformed the land-scape of the table.

What these display pieces also represented was a return to figurative food, a journey backward in time to an earlier age similarly obsessed by transforming every ingredient into some recognisable shape. Exactly as in the ages of mannerism and the baroque, food at grand dinners in the nineteenth century was to bear little relationship to how it began as a raw ingredient. It was always being processed into some architectural or sculptural shape further enlivened by the addition of colouring, pattern and paper decoration.[11] In this eternal swing of the pendulum from simplicity to complexity the appearance of food mirrors cycles in the history of style as rococo gives way to neo-classicism or art nouveau to modernism.

Carême was of major importance not only because he lifted the profession of chef to new heights, being courted by both royalty and the new rich, but also because of a long stream of illustrated books that put into print the first detailed account of *cuisine classique*. The most important of these was the five-volume *L'Art de la cuisine française au dix-neuvième siècle* (1833), the last two volumes of which (1843–4) were by a pupil, Plumerey, chef to the comte de Pahler. Among other things Carême reformed sauce-making, establishing three basic sauces as foundations for any number of others. These volumes were to be the gospel of *cuisine classique* until replaced by the work of Escoffier at the opening of the twentieth century.

In the kitchen this was a century of huge technical change and advance. Already at the close of the eighteenth century stoves had developed so that temperature could be controlled, a matter of central importance to the use of the *sauté* pan, the making of soufflés and complicated sauces. In the 1840s gas became available for use in places like restaurants and clubs and the grander houses, although most of the population continued using solid-fuel ranges with all the problems they entailed. By 1900 the earliest refrigerators were beginning to proliferate. All of these developments, however, should not disguise the fact that the kitchen scarcely benefited from the rapid mechanisation seen in so many other areas of society. There was no real imperative to save labour in the kitchen when labour was so cheap.

Thanks to Carême, French cooking, even more than in the previous century, was to dominate the European scene. It spread both through a steady stream of cookery books, the most important of which were translated, and the migration of French cooks to the palaces and great houses of Europe.[12] The first great book on *cuisine classique* was A. Viard's *Le Cuisinier impérial* (1806) which, like the works of Carême, continued to be reprinted all through the century. As a genre, however, what is new about the cookbooks of this century is that they begin to divide between those aimed at the professional chef and those designed for the vast new bourgeois audience born of industrialisation and the expansion of towns and cities. The split is reflected in the title of Louis Eustache Audot's *La Cuisinière de la campagne et de la ville* (1818), a work which also went through numerous editions and ended the century three times as thick as it had begun. For chefs the key works were Urbain Dubois and Emile Bernard's *La Cuisine classique* (1856) and Jules Gouffé's *Livre de la cuisine* (1867). The pillar of bourgeois home cooking was Antoine Gogue's *Les Secrets de la cuisine* (1856), a book which actually faced up to a major preoccupation for cooks in a bourgeois society – what to do with left-overs. (This issue, born of urbanisation, came to be of obsessive interest and eventually led to books dealing exclusively with how to rehash the surplus from other meals.)

If Carême was the towering figure in cuisine for the whole of the nineteenth century, Georges Auguste Escoffier was to dominate the twentieth, right up to the advent of *nouvelle cuisine* in the 1960s. His *Guide culinaire* (1903) was for decades the main text used in the training of chefs. Chef at the Ritz Hotel in Paris and later at the Savoy in London, Escoffier's cuisine was still within the classical tradition, but it was a response to a new quest for luxury and novelty on the part of the international rich of the 1880s and 1890s. This was food for the restaurants in the new, opulent hotels and exclusive establishments colonised by the *beau monde* in the decades before 1914 (places, for instance, where for the first time upper-class women could be seen dining in public). Escoffier also responded to something else then in the air – speed. We have entered the age of the motor car and the telephone. In response to that acceleration of life Escoffier dissolved the centuries-old division of the *cuisine* and the *office*, going on to abolish also their old subsections. As a result the ancient craft distinctions vanished, with the result that dishes for a meal structured in several courses could be produced much more speedily, and delivered without delay.

Everywhere one finds the influence of France. In Italy, Viard's work appeared as *La cuciniera della città e di campagna* (1845) and went into sixty-five editions.[13] Italian cookery books, whether written by one of the chefs to the many Italian courts or by a cook with the middle classes in mind, all looked north of the Alps. This changed with the unification of the country, when the quest for a new collective identity affected even cooking. Pellegrino Artusi's *La scienza in cucina e l'arte di mangiar bene* (1891) is a landmark publication in which what were essentially a series of regional cuisines were assembled in a single publication. Artusi could never have foreseen that a century on Italian cuisine, aided by its accordance with modern dietary discoveries, was to challenge the dominance of France.

In Britain the story was very different.[14] Political unity of the island had been achieved as early as 1707, so there was no need to amalgamate an indigenous native cuisine. In fact the one that existed in the eighteenth century went into radical decline during the nineteenth, for two reasons. One was urbanisation, during which people lost their direct connection with the soil and with it a culinary tradition that had been an expression of the country estate. The other reason, equally if not more powerful, was the fact that the upper classes adopted French cooking. The century opened with the English tradition still intact in publications like Maria Rundall's *A New System of Domestic Cookery* (1806) and Dr William Kitchiner's *The Cook's Oracle* (1817). But already by 1813 the English had been introduced to the cuisine of the court of Louis XVI in Louis Eustache Ude's *The French Cook*. Ude had been a chef at Versailles, became chief cook to the earl of Sefton, and later presided over the kitchens of Crockford's, the gambling club in St James's. In 1835, the gourmet Abraham Howard could recite a long list of French cooks in aristocratic service in England. By 1850 their hegemony over both royal and upper-class tables was complete, with Charles Esmé Francatelli being in the service of no less a personage than Queen Victoria herself. Francatelli's *The Modern Cook* (1845) instructed the upper classes in how to dine elegantly in the French manner. French dominance was equally illustrated by the career of Alexis Soyer, a showman chef in the Carême tradition working in London, who specialised in banquets. He was to produce a steady stream of books including *The Gastronomic Regenerator* (1846), 'suited to the income of all classes', and, a reflection of the reforming zeal of the age, *A Shilling Cookery Book for the People* (1854).

Soyer's books are dull and pedestrian, emblematic of the sad state of English cookery. Here cuisine became emphatically equated with class, the top echelons of society being a class apart on account of their employment of French cooks. Even the menus on the table were in French. The vast majority of the middle and lower middle classes practised a debased version of the native tradition. The books which catered to this vast and expanding section of society reveal palates which were not only unsophisticated but ignorant. They also reveal an obsession with economy, the basic cuisine revolving around a roast joint and a week of recycled left-overs. By 1900 the English had totally forgotten that they had ever had a cooking tradition, accepting that when it came to the culinary arts, they were inferior.

Although Eliza Acton's *Modern Cooking for Private Families* (1845), in which she explored dishes both of the English regions and of the globe, gained widespread currency, no publication quite eclipsed Isabella Beeton's thousand-page *The Book of Household Management* (1861). Its success relied more than anything else on the fact that its point of departure was a description of the woman of the house as 'the commander of an army', with attributes that defined her status as a lady in mid-Victorian terms. That sense of social aspiration and keeping up appearances is vividly caught in the gap between Mrs Beeton's menus for dinner parties – the major index of a family's social position – and the frugality of the family meals based on the inevitable left-overs. French dishes were excluded from the book, and the recipes cannot be said to be anything other than dreary and uninspired. They are redeemed only by the novelty of exact measurements for the ingredients, the time a dish would take to cook, and how many it would serve. It may be anachronistic to observe that the book was devoid of nutritional knowledge and any concern at all with the importance of fresh fruit, vegetables and salads.

Mrs Beeton's colour plates, which offer a vivid record of the figurative form that even her dull dishes could take, must have been a draw. For this was a century during which cookery books poured from the presses, aided by the new techniques of mass printing and new ways of illustration. In them we witness the transmission of the various culinary traditions passing finally out of the oral form into the written.

✳   ✳   ✳

The nineteenth century saw the birth of a new public space for eating, the restaurant.[15] Although inns and cookshops had existed for centuries, the food they provided offered no choice of fare. The restaurant was to be a wholly different experience, breaking the monopoly of the elite on fine eating, opening it to anyone who could afford it. The first of them appeared before 1789 as places where people of sensibility, responding to the Enlightenment's new awareness of the importance of diet, went to drink a restorative broth in the interest of their health. Gradually restaurants extended their range of dishes to create something quite new. The inventor of the earliest kind of 'health' restaurant was Mathurin Roze de Chantoiseau in 1766, but the first great restaurateur in the modern sense was Antoine Beauvilliers, who opened his establishment in the Palais Royal in 1790. The Revolution accelerated the development by putting many former chefs of the fallen aristocracy out of work. Beauvilliers himself had previously been employed in the kitchens of both the comte de Provence and the prince de Condé. His menu, listing a hundred and sixty-eight different items including thirty-two different dishes for poultry and game, reflected this aristocratic background. Another encouragement for the efflorescence of restaurants was the demise of the trade guilds which, with all their old restrictive practices, had been swept away by the Revolution. But restaurants were to remain a specifically Parisian phenomenon, and it was not until the 1850s that they began to be a feature of urban life in other cities and towns of Western Europe.

The restaurant was to change the way people perceived food. It made those who had never given it a thought conscious for the first time of the art of cooking. Confronted by a restaurant menu they could not help but be made aware of the dozens of different ways of preparing a single ingredient. Such variety had of course existed in the past, but only in sharply restricted circles. The average consumer would have had no knowledge of it and had probably never seen a cookery book. To select from a menu meant knowing, for instance, what *poulet à la Marengo* was – or in any case, finding out. Thus eating in a restaurant became a learning process, and, what's more, a means of gaining and exercising an attribute much prized by the Enlightenment, taste.

Restaurants also contributed greatly to making 'the art of good eating', gastronomy, an arena for critical aesthetic debate.[16] Alexandre-Balthazar-Laurent Grimod de la Reynière was the world's first food critic, inventor of the restaurant review in his famous *Almanach des gourmands*, which appeared between 1803 and 1812. His *Le Manuel des amphitryons* (1808) was equally celebrated. Such publications served to open up the elite knowledge of food to anyone who was literate, thus democratising taste and keeping up the pressure on restaurants to be innovative and preserve standards or else lose their clients. The restaurant was also home ground for a new character, the gourmet, a person who prided himself on his knowledge of fine food and wine. The greatest of these was without doubt Jean-Anthelme Brillat-Savarin, whose *La Physiologie du goût* (1826) became the gourmet's gospel.

What collectively all these developments reflected was a general retreat from the initial thrust of French revolutionary politics, which had intruded upon the minutest details of private life – including eating. In the Napoleonic era such interference ceased, and the arts of the table became finally separated from politics and the state. Eating became a private matter. The archetypal meal of the nineteenth century was to be the private family dinner party, a focal point of social acceptance and respectability in an era of rapid change.

The proliferation of the dining-room and shifting mealtimes

As we have seen, virtually nothing, not even eating, was spared in the attempt by the French revolutionaries to overturn the accepted order of things, to obliterate rank and deference and question the centuries-old roles of the sexes. Much of what happened as a result was precisely a reaction to that attempt. In the case of women, the Revolution simply accelerated a process that had begun before 1789 – relegation to the private sphere, to the home, in contrast to men's role in the public world.

Nowhere was this new scheme of things more evident than in England. Industrialisation and urbanisation created new tiers of classes that replaced for ever the old dual division of society.[17] To the old middle-class professions, such as lawyers and doctors, was now added a string of new ones – industrialists, bankers and brokers, insurers, shippers, engineers and designers, and more. They had pushed their way upwards during the 1830s and 1840s in the aftermath of the extension of the franchise in 1832, and, by the 1850s, formed so large a group that the middle class began to form tiers within itself.

That profound change in the structure of society went hand in hand with the exaltation of the domestic virtues enshrined in private life and the discovery of happiness within the family. The orchestrator of this new scheme of things was the mistress of the house, a definition of whose role and duties was to produce a European literature typified by Mme Pariset's *Manuel de la maîtresse de la maison* (1821) and Mrs Beeton's opus. In this new pattern of daily existence the family meal and the dinner party were to be quintessential expressions not only of domestic bliss but also social status. Nineteenth-century painting, typified by the work of the Impressionists, for example, celebrates time and again the centrality of the dining table.

The new significance attached to family meals clearly accounts for the rapid spread through a large swathe of society (which had previously not been over-concerned where it ate) of a separate room for dining. Even among the upper classes in the eighteenth century, a room devoted solely to eating was still something of a novelty. Indeed this is shown by the fact that the table was normally still set up for each meal and taken down afterwards, with the dining chairs pushed back against the walls of the room to stare out on the empty space at the centre. By 1850, however, anyone with a claim to social cachet had to have a dining-room. Thus architectural books aimed at the aspiring classes describe these rooms in lush detail – and in doing so provide us with a wealth of information lacking for the earlier periods.

In England John Claudius Loudon in his *The Suburban Gardener and Villa Companion* (1838) states that the dining-room 'ought to be . . . of masculine importance' with a sideboard for the display of plate to honour guests, chairs upholstered in crimson leather, a square, round or expanding table, crimson flock wallpaper and scarlet or geranium curtains. By that date the table had become a permanent fixture in the middle of the room; Loudon refers to the new fashion 'to place the chairs, or a portion of them, when not in use, not against the walls, but around the table'.[18] Already by 1820 gas was replacing the Argand oil lamp, and by 1830 gas chandeliers had appeared, affording more and more light after dark. Candles never vanished, but the ability to light a room handsomely at night gradually ceased to be the prerogative of the rich. Significantly too, it made possible a later and later dinner hour.

By the 1850s the number of rooms for eating multiplied still further, a process which had begun in the later eighteenth century. Robert Kerr's *The Gentleman's House* (1864) lists a dining-room, a breakfast or luncheon room and even a state dining-room. Dining-rooms, he writes, should face north or north-east, be 'spacious and always comparatively stately' with a handsome sideboard and side tables, with doors both for the guests and for the servants. Indeed the choreography of the dinner party by that date had become a major preoccupation for architects, who were conscious of the necessity to create a processional route from the drawing-room to the dining-room which did not cross paths with the servants.[19] As the century moved to its close there was a reaction to the dark mid-Victorian pomposity with a turn towards the newly fashionable cult of 'sweetness and light'.[20] But even that did not affect the basic ground-planning.

In France, the emphasis was always on the *salon* rather than the *salle à manger*, but there too dining-rooms proliferated as part of the new *mise-en-scène* essential to the status of the bourgeoisie. Anastase Garnier in his *Tapissier décorateur* (1830) describes a Parisian dining-room equipped with a round table, which could be taken down, chairs with rush or horsehair seats, a stove, side tables called 'servantes', a sideboard buffet, a clock and bell with which to summon the servants.[21] In Germany the idea of a separate dining-room came to the middle classes from England and France in the 1850s. There again it was to be north-facing, and its accoutrements were to include a draw-leaf rectangular table, a side buffet and lighting from petroleum lamps and, later, a gas chandelier.[22]

The dining-room was a clear symbol of class distinction, an embodiment of the separation of the owners and the family from the servants and the practicalities of cooking. It was a room of display and would continue to reign in suburban middle-class houses until the third quarter of the twentieth century, at which point changes in eating habits and reductions in living space pointed up the absurdity of devoting a whole room to only a few hours' use a day. But in the nineteenth century the dining-room had all the excitement of a new phenemonon. Eating had finally ceased to be migratory and come at last to rest in a special room assigned to it.

That development was not the only one that set the nineteenth century apart. Times of eating also changed dramatically. The main meal of the day moved later and later. Until then there had always been a sharp difference in mealtimes between the leisured classes and those who worked for a living. That difference gradually began to dissolve as a result of urbanisation and the emergence of fixed office hours. By 1914 even upper-class eating times reflected the new work pattern.[23]

In eighteenth-century England, breakfast had been eaten between ten and eleven as a light meal in the aftermath of work already done. Gradually, in the 1820s and 1830s, it began to move back, first to nine and then, by 1860, to eight or eight fifteen. It also changed its nature, taking the form of a purely working meal before setting off to the office – tea, muffins, a hot dish. At the same time, in the 1830s, a new meal emerged: luncheon. The word itself was new, although Samuel Johnson had spoken of 'Nunchin: A piece of victuals eaten between meals' in his *Dictionary* (1755). Luncheon began as an informal cold meal eaten by the lady of the house and whoever happened to be there. In 1859 we find a reference to 'a luncheon party'. That form of entertainment customarily took place in town at 2 p.m. and in the country at 1.30 p.m. Ladies kept their hats on at table (a practice that persisted into the post-Second World War period) and gentlemen carried their hats into the drawing-room. An 1885 book of etiquette describes luncheon as 'an unceremonious, an inconsequent meal'. Tea, as a separate repast, arrived during the 1840s and forty years later took on a life of its own, particularly in the great houses in the country, where it was served at 5 p.m.

But the meal of the day *par excellence* was dinner. In society, Mrs Beeton noted, supper vanished 'as people now generally dine at an hour which precludes the possibility of requiring supper'. Dinner in the later eighteenth century had been eaten somewhere between three and five in the afternoon; hosts and guests changed from the undress of the earlier part of the day into something more formal. By the 1820s and 1830s, how-ever, the timing of dinner was in a state of flux to match the rapidly changing pattern of the average day. Some people stuck to the earlier time while others delayed. Finally, with the business day in the 1850s fixed to run from 9 a.m. to 5.30 p.m., the time for dinner fell between seven and eight o'clock. By 1900 invitations for a quiet informal dinner would indicate 7.30 p.m. for 7.45 p.m. and, for something grander, 7.45 p.m. for 8 p.m. In the twentieth century in fashionable circles the time has drifted later, but not markedly, generally being 8 for 8.30 p.m.

In France roughly the same shift of dinnertime occurred. Breakfast in the English sense never developed, the *premier déjeuner* being taken on waking and consisting of milk, coffee, tea or chocolate, a *flûte* (a long thin loaf) or toast. What was called the *deuxième déjeuner* or *déjeuner à la fourchette* was eaten at ten or noon, a family meal with the food, virtually all cold, placed on the table together, to which everyone helped themselves. But dinner made the same stately progress from 5 p.m. in the first decade, with guests invited to arrive at 7.30 p.m. by 1900.

But now it is time to turn our attention to a detailed consideration of the dinner party itself.

The dinner party

IT WAS BRILLAT-SAVARIN who composed what still remains the most celebrated definition of the ideal dinner party, in his *La Physiologie du goût*. His criteria are worth quoting in full to remind ourselves of such agreeable perfection before the parade and pretence of nineteenth-century dining engulfs us:

> That the number of guests does not exceed a dozen, so that conversation can constantly be general.
>
> That they should be most carefully chosen, that their professions be different but their tastes similar and with such points of contact that one will not have to resort to the odious formality of presentations . . .
>
> That the dining-room be luxuriously lit, the cloth be of the utmost cleanliness and the temperature from 13 to 16 degrees by the Réaumur thermometer [61–66°F].

That the men be witty without pretensions and the women charming without being too coquettish.

That the choice of dishes should be exquisite but restricted in number and the wines of the first quality, each the best of its kind.

That the order, for the former, should be from the most substantial to the lightest and, for the latter, from the lightest to those with greatest bouquet.

That the speed of the eating should be moderate, dinner being the last affair of the day, and that the guests behave like travellers who aim to arrive at the same destination together . . .

That the guests be held by the pleasure of the company and stirred by the hope that the evening will not pass without some further entertainment.[24]

So much for dinner in an ideal world! What of course Brillat-Savarin does not record is what happened in reality, or at any rate what became reality. For the dinner party would be one of the great prestige symbols of the era, an index of a family's taste, discrimination, bank balance and connections.[25] It was an occasion for a host to display his wife and daughters to advantage, especially the marriageable ones. It was an exercise in public relations, an exhibition of a family's degree of refinement and elegance of manners. The decor, the clothes, the number and quality of the servants, the decoration of the table, the choice of guests and food, all were indexes of how to impress. The dinner party was also a place in the new age of commerce for combining pleasure and profit – when the ladies left the room, the host could talk politics and business with his male guests. Meanwhile in the drawing-room the ladies could chatter about fashion and turn their attention to matchmaking. Giving a dinner was a visible act of middle-class status. For that class once a month was the norm. For the upper classes, once a week was more usual.

The struggle to make one's way into that league is caught vividly in a book by J. E. Panton entitled *From Kitchen to Garret* (1888). It was written especially for 'little people' with incomes of between three and five hundred a year (£15,000 to £25,000 today) and only one maid. Panton describes how, with a little economy, such a couple might just, very occasionally, be able to stage a dinner party for six at a cost of £1 1s. 4d.

(the equivalent today of about £55). In this we catch the preoccupation spreading down through the lower middle classes.

That the socially ambitious became obsessed by the dinner party is hardly surprising. To give one successfully was an emblem of being admitted to membership in a cohesive bourgeois class. Dinner in the eighteenth century never had such a role, being more often than not the prelude to some other entertainment. Now the dinner itself became that entertainment, functioning as a gate of admission through which the aspiring had to pass both as guest and as host and hostess.

The novelist William Makepeace Thackeray in *The Book of Snobs* (1847) vividly illustrates how important the dinner party had become by the late 1840s, wickedly pointing a finger at those who hope to leg it up with hired servants and bought-in food:

> Suppose you get in cheap-made dishes from the pastry cook's, and hire a couple of greengrocers, or carpet-beaters, to figure as footmen, dismissing honest Molly, who waits on common days, and bedizening your table (ordinarily ornamented with willow-pattern crockery) with twopenny-halfpenny Birmingham plate. Suppose you pretend to be richer and grander than you ought to be – you are a Dinner-giving Snob.[26]

By the second half of the century the dinner party enters its apotheosis. A flood of books on etiquette and household management all instruct the upwardly mobile how to ape the class they wished to enter. 'Dining is the privilege of civilisation . . .' Mrs Beeton proudly writes in 1861. 'The nation which knows how to dine has learnt the leading lesson of progress.'[27] Etiquette books spell out the social advantages. Dinner-giving is 'a *direct* road to obtaining a footing in society . . . there is no better or surer passport to good society than having a reputation for giving good dinners'. Thus *Manners and Tone of Good Society and Solecisms to be Avoided, by a Member of the Aristocracy* (1885).[28] Or, to quote Mrs Humphry, the ubiquitous 'Madge' of the magazine *Truth*: 'The hostess who gives good dinners is pretty sure to succeed in social life, and will be almost certain to marry her daughters well.'[29] The motives for dinner parties are barely concealed or, if we turn to *Etiquette for Ladies* (1894), not concealed at all.

The author writes that to receive an invitation to dinner is 'an unequivocal acknowledgement that you belong to the same class as your entertainers. Every country has some particular test of this kind, and in England the invitation to dinner is the hall-mark of social equality.'[30]

If the dinner party at the middle-class level was a means by which the private world of the family and home was opened up to strangers deemed as of equal standing, for the upper classes it was much more. By the close of the century, as a consequence of social pressures from below, the established classes had closed ranks to form what was known as Society. Hugely enlarged over the course of the century, in England it now consisted of some four thousand families. (In Germany its equivalent made up about one and a half per cent of the population.) This was a new social body created and fenced in by its own tremendous wealth. It was competitive, snobbish, parvenu, purse-proud, earnest and, at times, vulgar. Once admitted to its exclusive precincts, a member's task was to maintain vigilance over the selection of further candidates. That involved creating – by means of ritual, points of style, manners and taste – a series of hurdles every aspirant had to cross. An invitation to a dinner party was as much a hurdle as the giving of one. It still is.

Service à la française to service à la russe

B Y THE CLOSE of the eighteenth century the traditional service of meals in the French manner, as it had evolved in the baroque age, was already under strain.[31] It had begun reasonably enough. A set of dishes was placed on the table from which people either helped themselves or were assisted by the servants. Everything was arranged in perfect symmetry, and when one course ended the dishes were cleared and replaced by the next, equally symmetrical, course. The rule that dishes were multiplied in dozens according to the number of guests meant that a table could end up with as many as a hundred dishes on it at a time, mainly of only two types, tureens and oval or round pot d'oille. By 1800, however, the range of containers and other tableware had increased hugely, so that the festive board resembled a forest of wine coolers, glass coolers, sauceboats, vinegar and oil sets, mustard, cream and sugar pots, sugar spoons, ice cream vases, bread baskets, *entremets* dishes, *réchauds* and spice boxes, not to mention the multiplication of cutlery. And all of this was orchestrated to form a matching service. The consequence was that a vast amount of food went uneaten and, worse still for the diners, it was inevitably cold or, at best, lukewarm.

This was eating in the grand manner, but on a far more modest scale the system was the same. An amateur watercolourist named Ellen Mary Best recorded the first course of a dinner as it awaited the entry of the guests at a surgeon's house in York in 1838.[32] All the food is already placed on the table. This was for a version of the French system known as *service à l'anglaise*, in which the hostess served the soup and the host carved the joint at table. The soup tureen can be seen at one end with a stack of plates next to it. The hostess would serve the soup, which was then delivered to a diner by a servant. When the soup had been consumed, the cloche covering the roast at the opposite end of the table would be removed so that the host could proceed with carving. At this point, the lids would have been simultaneously lifted from the various other tureens. Here again, the servants assisted with the serving. Warm plates may have been brought in from the kitchen or fetched from a plate-warmer by the fire. The hot dishes can be seen to be standing on placemats to prevent scorching the table's surface and each *couvert* has bread and a napkin flanked by a knife and fork only (the spoon for soup is oddly missing, as are any side plates). We are one year into the reign of Queen Victoria.

At more elaborate dinners a fish would be placed on the table together with the soup, and a 'remove' of roasted or baked meat would come in as a second course. For each subsequent course the table would be cleared until, finally, the cloth was taken off and dessert brought on. When a diner had finished what he wanted of a particular dish he would place his knife and fork on the plate in a parallel position (as is still done today, although on the Continent the cutlery is crossed) and a servant would remove it and provide him with fresh cutlery.

This sort of provincial Sunday dinner would have already been regarded as old-fashioned among the upper classes, who were eagerly adopting changes which had their origins in France.[33] In June 1810 at a reception in Clichy, near Paris, the Russian diplomat Prince Borisovitch

Dinner at a house in York.
Watercolour by Mary Ellen Best, 1838.

Kourakine served his guests in an entirely novel manner. Instead of entering and finding the food *en tableau*, there was no food on the table at all. The centre was on the contrary adorned with a galleried *chemin de table* on which stood candelabra, vases and *étagères* along with displays of artificial flowers (until about 1850 the smell of real flowers was thought to detract from the food) and the fruit and sweetmeats which would later be served for dessert. Then, once the guests were seated, a still greater surprise. Each diner was presented by a footman with an already-filled plate from which to help themselves, with the food prepared to be eaten, filleted or cut into slices and combined with the appropriate sauce, garniture or side dish. A series of courses were served in this way, each arriving from the kitchens ready dressed or, in the case of larger dishes, to be carved quickly by the servants at side tables. The food arrived, of course, far hotter and everyone for the first time had a chance to sample some of everything. The new form of service came to be known as *service à la russe*. It gradually spread through Western Europe, although it took the whole century to do so.

That the new service, with the opportunities it presented for ostentatious display, began to gain acceptance can be seen from the fact that the great goldsmith Pierre-Philippe Thomire was already making *surtouts à la russe* in 1810. Carême, however, did not favour *service à la russe* and the traditional method *à la française* lingered on until the 1850s. For Carême it was 'plus élégant et plus somptueux' with its dazzling symmetrical display of dishes around his legendary *pièces montées*. That initial display included soup, *hors d'oeuvre*, *entrées* and *relevés*. The importance of any dinner was in fact measured by the number of *entrées*. All of it was then cleared and the table relaid with the roast and *entremets* and, finally, cleared yet again for the service of ices, bonbons, *petits fours*, fruit and cheese.

In France it was to take until the last decade of the nineteenth century for *service à la russe* to become the norm. Even then for state dinners and great occasions *service à la française* was retained for its spectacular effect and *service à la russe* deployed mainly on the occasion of meetings that were more or less professional and where the aim was unimpeded conversation. Only when *service à la russe* was finally universal could Escoffier establish the sequence of courses that remains familiar to this day: *hors d'oeuvre* or soup, fish, meat with vegetables, sweet, savoury and dessert.

In England the move to the new method of service was equally slow. *Service à la française* continued into the 1870s and 1880s, with the usual two great courses followed by dessert. The vast majority of Mrs Beeton's 'Bills of fare' are intended for this system, but she also takes note of the new one:

> In a dinner à la Russe, the dishes are cut up on the sideboard, and handed round to the guests, and each dish may be considered a course. The table for a dinner à la Russe should be laid with flowers [real ones

by 1861] and plants in fancy flower pots down the middle, together with some of the dessert dishes. A *menu* or bill of fare should be laid by the side of each guest.[34]

The effect of *à la russe*, apart from the hot food, was to multiply the courses, but the result was a welcome contraction of the time spent at table. Under the old system a meal could last for hours. A dinner *à la russe* lasted an hour and a half at the most. The sequence in England in the 1870s and 1880s ran as follows: *hors d'oeuvre* on the table on entering, two soups, one clear and one thick, fish, the *entrée*, the joint or *pièce de résistance*, a sorbet, roast and a salad, vegetables, a hot sweet, ice cream, dessert, coffee and liqueurs. That added up to twelve courses, but already by the 1890s, in response to new ideas about diet, the number had contracted to eight.

Like everything else to do with the nineteenth-century dinner party the style of service offered a point to be scored. 'Dinners à la Russe,' writes Mrs Beeton, 'are scarcely suitable for small establishments; a large number of servants being required to carve, and to help the guests.' It also called for a plenitude of cutlery and porcelain. *The Habits of Good Society*, undated but belonging probably to the 1850s, refers to it as 'a foreign custom lately introduced into this country . . .'[35] Its triumph is also connected with the emergence of an extremely rich new middle class. The opportunity for lavish display and the need for a small army of servants effectively marked *service à la russe* as the choice only for those who could afford it. Moreover, by employing domestics to carve and serve it clarified social distinctions – no one at table need have anything remotely practical to do with handling the food. It also gave scope for a renaissance in the art of table-laying and decoration, or rather a return to the glories of the centuries-old buffet. As before, it was all about display – showing off an owner's riches in such *objets* as silver centrepieces and candelabra, exquisite flower arrangements, fruit and sweetmeats arranged as a still life . . . exercises, in short, in wealth and taste.

The ritual and etiquette of dinner

THE NINETEENTH CENTURY witnesses a shift in behaviour as fundamental as that which had precipitated Erasmus' discourse on manners three centuries before.[36] The new urban society thrown up by industrialisation demanded a fresh framework of etiquette. In England, in the aftermath of the extension of the franchise in 1832, the customs of the old aristocratic era finally evolved into what we call manners, a class-bound set of rules, one of whose primary aims was to preserve the caste of those admitted and keep out those who were not. Manners spoke an elaborate language and imposed a discipline that had to be learned by anyone wishing to gain admittance to a higher level of society. Those already within the charmed circle ruthlessly deployed manners as a means of exclusion, either ossifying behavioural codes to indicate their own superiority or wilfully changing them to make it harder for the *nouveaux* to catch up.

A dinner party was one long essay in manners. Thanks to that fact it gave birth to a plethora of books designed to provide the unknowing with a detailed guide to every nuance and formality demanded on such an occasion. These handbooks of etiquette, because of their huge detail, provide us with more information about the table than we have for any earlier period. What we do not know is how accurately they record reality. It was England, where the social pressure from below was most powerful, that led the way in the genre, and English books that were influential abroad, especially in Germany. Viewed overall they are inevitably repetitive, so let us synthesise their comments in order to get a picture of what it was like to be a guest at a dinner party between about 1850 and the outbreak of war in 1914. The scenario would run roughly as follows.[37]

Invitations would be sent out between a fortnight and three weeks in advance, printed on proper cards. (In the case of a major guest of honour, advance notice might be as much as six weeks.) All dinner parties started with a consideration as to the number and type of guest. Six, eight or ten was deemed the ideal number, as it facilitated general conversation both around and across the table. However, it was recognised that the party might include as many as twenty. Those asked should be of the same social standing, with shared views and a similarity of lifestyle. Writing in the 1850s, one book specifically lists the various professions, including medicine, the army and the navy, as being acceptable presences at dinner tables along with artists, architects and sculptors, 'but not always their families'. What this indicates is that the man might be invited without his wife, if she were deemed socially unacceptable. The invitations had to be delivered not by post but by hand, via a servant.

Women were always more elaborately dressed in the evening, but the codification of evening dress for men as it survives today was fixed only at the close of the 1860s.[38] *Cassell's Household Management*, published in that decade, notes: 'The style of dress worn at dinner-parties is for a gentleman, strictly that of a black dress suit, with an open waistcoat and white neckerchief.' Up until the 1830s there is no sign of a separate dress code for the evening, but gradually pantaloons made of black knitted silk or wool and buttoned at the ankle, which gave a more shapely look to the leg, became the norm. The move towards what we now designate as 'white tie' must have been piecemeal but all the elements were firmly in place by the 1870s: the black dress coat, the white vest, wing collar, white tie, stiffened and starched shirt front, the top hat, cape and carnation. This ensemble has survived virtually unchanged for great formal occasions like a state dinner at Buckingham Palace or the Royal Academy. The only blip in the history of men's evening dress occurred in the 1890s when black was adopted by menservants as evening livery. It was no doubt out of a desire to avoid confusion that the more usual semi-formal black tie dinner jacket emerged which, give or take a bit, is still worn today.

The time of arrival for guests was, as we have already seen, 7.45 p.m. for 8 p.m. or 8 p.m. for 8.15 p.m. On arrival a servant took the guests' cloaks and hats. Women wore gloves. The guests either singly or in couples or groups were then escorted to the drawing-room by the butler or another manservant and announced on entering the room. A lady would always enter ahead of a gentleman and the couple would shake hands with the hosts. It was then customary for the ladies to sit and the gentlemen to stand. Introductions were effected, men bowing but not shaking hands. The host would tell each gentleman which lady he was to escort into dinner.

Going in to dinner.
From George du Maurier's *English Society at Home*, 1880.

The drawing-room gathering was not a prolonged one. Drinks were
not served, although in France an aperitif came to be offered. When
the butler announced dinner a procession was formed. John Trusler, in
his *Honours of the Table* (1788), records as a risqué novelty the placement
of the sexes alternately around the table; that arrangement soon became
the norm, and would have demanded some kind of pairing. So what
had been a somewhat pell-mell arrival in the dining-room (of a kind
which continued in France) evolved into a stately procession headed by
the host with the most important lady on his arm followed, in order of

rank, by a series of pairs ending with the hostess on the arm of the chief male guest.

The concern with precedence continued at table. The host and hostess generally sat at opposite ends or, if there were many diners, in the middle flanked by their chief guests on their right (in France on the left). Either the hosts directed guests to their seats or there were place cards. Use of the latter ebbed and flowed with fashion. 'Madge' observed that 'It is distressing, in these days of short sight and small rooms, to see several couples wandering about endeavouring to decipher the names on the small cards.'

Gwen Raverat, in her account of her childhood in late Victorian Cambridge, provides a vivid account of the stultifying formality of dinner parties governed by precedence:

> The regular and formal dinner parties were very important in Cambridge. In our house parties were generally of 12 or 14 people, and everybody of dinner party status was invited strictly in turn. The guests were seated according to protocol, the Heads of Colleges ranking by the dates of the foundation of their colleges, except that the Vice-Chancellor would come first of all. After the Masters came the Regius Professors in the order of their subjects, Divinity first; and the other Professors according to the dates of their chairs, and so on down all the steps of the hierarchy.[39]

The table itself was a monument to opulence, especially if the dinner was being served à la russe. Table decoration was for the hostess a challenge. By the 1850s what in earlier ages had been rare and unusual was now, thanks to mass manufacture, available in quantity for anyone with the means to purchase it: cutlery, vases, artificial flowers, épergnes, and every kind of table centre in silver or silver-plate, anything indeed which could be pressed into service to adorn a table. Status could therefore no longer be registered merely by the exhibition of an abundance of expensive paraphernalia. The new criteria were much less obvious and more difficult to satisfy – taste and style. And, although the dining-room remained resolutely a masculine domain, the table was feminine.

So table decoration was inevitably a quagmire as fashion fluctuated.

One book rages against 'slippers as flower-vases on a dinner table. The association of shoes and food is not an agreeable idea.'[40] Another, published in 1904 and devoted to the arts of the home, denounces as bad taste: 'wired flowers twisted into all kinds of impossible positions, with leaves tortured into loops and bows – garnished with stuffed birds and sham butterflies, and served up with china stiles and bridges and owls with candles stuck in their heads . . .'[41] In the case of *service à la russe* these bizarre *objets* had of course to incorporate the food destined to be eaten as dessert. Time and again the books harp on the necessity of seeing the guests on the opposite side of the table instead of obscuring them by a hedge of ferns and flowers. After about 1850, when real flowers replaced artificial, it is hardly surprising that table decoration became a constant problem. The shifting sands of fashion were entirely likely to become quicksands in which an aspiring but unobservant hostess could sink.

As for lighting, candles gave way to gas and finally, by 1900, to electricity. When each new method became commonplace, the aspiring classes moved on, coming, by the close of the period, back to where they had started: to dining by candlelight. A century on that still pertains.

Attempts to categorise people by their taste never ceased. Mrs Loftie, an apostle of the 'House Beautiful', wrote a book called *The Dining-Room* (1878) dispensing what she called 'information for the ignorant and aid for the advancing'. In it she throws up her hands in horror at flowers which in any way resembled mid-Victorian bedding-out, preferring old-fashioned blooms in sweet disarray on the table. Equally censured were the 'frightful nightmares of the china manufacturers . . . So long,' she writes, 'as people enjoy having sprawling red lobsters as large as life, butterflies, snails, cater-pillars, or cockatoos, on their plates they will be satisfied.'[42] Taste on the table was a minefield.

A great array of cutlery, glass and napery welcomed the guest. On the white damask tablecloth, which still remained an irreplaceable feature, stiff and starched and admirable for its reflective qualities, was laid a battery of cutlery.[43] A typical setting consisted of two large knives, a silver knife and fork for fish, a tablespoon for soup, and three large forks. In the eighteenth century cutlery had not been so plentiful; the custom then was for it to be taken away, washed and reset as the dishes changed during dinner. Now every piece required for the whole meal – except for the dessert course –

lay ready for use at the start. The diner worked from the outside in. Whether blades of knives faced in or out or the tines of the forks up or down could vary. Special types of cutlery appeared, such as fish knives; previously the fish course had been eaten with the fork alone, assisted by a piece of bread. The acid in fruits was viewed as likely to corrode steel cutlery; this led to special services of dessert cutlery in silver, silver gilt and gold. Everything was multiplied and categorised, an exercise typical of the Victorian love of the classification of things.

By 1900, as a consequence of mass production, merely to possess a range of cutlery was no longer sufficient to distinguish one as upper class. Instead those in fashion adopted new methods of using it. The knife, for instance, developed a rounded and no longer a pointed blade. That was because food could now be pinned down on the plate with the ubiquitous fork. 'Madge' in the 1890s wrote that the safest rule was never to use a spoon or knife when a fork would do. Thus we have at last come full circle, from the time when the fork was regarded as little more than a peripheral ostentation to its role as the single most important tool for carrying food to the mouth. Its triumph has been so complete that today we live in the age of the fork lunch.

But care must be taken. Eating could be treacherous to one's social standing. The indefatigable 'Madge' writes again, for instance, that cheese was now cut in small pieces and placed on a piece of bread or biscuit and then taken to the mouth: 'Very few persons continue to eat it in the old-fashioned way by carrying it to the mouth with the knife.' (She thus affords us a glimpse of an earlier wholly acceptable way of consuming cheese.) Eating anything with the knife was declared 'glaringly vulgar' in Charles Day's *Etiquette and Usages of Society* (1840). Knives should be used for cutlets, poultry and game, a knife and fork for asparagus, all made dishes should be eaten with a fork, all sweets with a fork except fruit tarts, for which it was permissible to use a spoon in addition. What emerges is that it was only in this century that holding and using a knife and fork jointly in both hands finally became a fully acceptable norm of eating. (Not universally, however, for in America the knife is put down while the food is carried to the mouth by the fork.)

There were further refinements in table usage as the repugnance barrier continued to rise. Washing the mouth out at table was already in

England in 1840 regarded as a 'filthy custom'.[44] It was still acceptable in France at that date, and in Germany it so continued into the 1860s. By 1900, that practice, along with toothpicks, had been banished from the polite table in all three countries. Customs also changed. In England, for example, the old custom of a host or guest taking wine with another diner, in a kind of mutual toast, fell into desuetude in the 1850s.

As if the cutlery were not enough to cope with, to his left the inexperienced diner found a side plate on which rested a napkin enfolding a roll or piece of bread, and to his right a small army of glasses. Ahead there would be the menu and near to hand a salt. Dealing with most of this was straightforward except, perhaps, for the glasses.[45] There would generally be three, one for sherry, a second for hock (as German white wine was generally called) and a third for champagne. Tumblers for water were on the sideboard and would be brought on request by a servant. Glasses would not have been found on the table in the eighteenth century; they would then have been brought to it by a servant and taken away, after drinking, to be washed. Now glass was available so readily that it too could be added to the fittings of the dinner table. That was already happening in Regency England by about 1800 and became usual in France in the 1820s. As the century progressed glasses developed their own particular size and shape for each form of drink. In some cases – hock, for example – coloured glass was permissible.

The number of servants needed to minister to a dinner party inevitably depended on its size. A dinner for ten might call for a butler and two footmen. The servants must be male; maidservants at table were viewed as totally déclassé. Those short of staff might thus be forced to dress up the gardeners or even (as Thackeray suggested) hire in the local greengrocer. The service itself worked up and down the table, starting with the persons seated to the right of the host and hostess. Ladies had already, while seating themselves, removed their gloves.

Conversation was seen to be the essence of the dinner party. This worked on the swing principle, starting with the host talking to the lady on his left. One topic was utterly forbidden: any comment whatsoever on the food was considered beyond the pale. But the importance of being a good conversationalist was vital, and is dwelt upon at length by all the etiquette books. Indeed the dinner party gave birth to a new figure, the conversationalist. The poet Robert Browning, for example, was noted as being 'one of the most entertaining and instructive conversationalists at dinner in London'. The cult of the dinner party therefore opened a whole new arena of social competition, in which success depended on recruiting the best talkers – guests educated, informed and witty, yet dependable enough to avoid bringing up anything, like religion or Darwinism, that might prove divisive.[46]

The diner worked his way through the courses and a succession of wines in a fixed and predictable manner: sherry after the soup, hock with the fish and champagne after the first *entrée* (and on until dessert). At that stage the table was cleared and a dessert plate placed before each diner. (If an ice was to be served then an ice plate would be included.) On the plate (or plates) stood a finger-bowl on a doily together with a gold or silver spoon for the ice and a dessert knife and fork. The cutlery was removed by the diner and placed on either side of the plates, and the finger-bowl on its doily directly in front of him. At the same time glasses for sherry and claret were laid and a claret jug and two decanters of sherry were placed before the host. The displays of fruit were then brought forward from the middle of the table.

Dessert ended, the hostess caught the eye of the chief lady guest and the ladies rose, donning their gloves again, and left the room. On the Continent male and female guests left together, but in England the separation of the sexes continued, indeed the custom spread by 1850 to the middle classes. The ladies gone, the men pulled their chairs closer together around the table to drink claret and puff on cigars and cigarettes. The conversation took on a more robust, masculine, character and, after a period of time ranging from a quarter to three-quarters of an hour, the men rose and joined the ladies in the drawing-room.

Meanwhile in the drawing-room the ladies had been served with their coffee, after which it was taken into the dining-room to the gentlemen. When they finally emerged, tea might be served, general conversation ensued and perhaps someone would play or sing. All of this lasted at the most an hour, bringing the event to an end at 10.30 p.m.; at that time the host would escort the principal female guests to their carriages. Earlier in the century it had been a custom for the servants to line up for a tip, but by mid-century this was deemed 'extremely vulgar and ill judged'. There was one small finale to come: within a week of the entertainment guests were expected to call on their hosts. But by then the hosts would doubtless be deeply involved in planning the next party and the whole process would be starting all over again.

The way we live now

WHERE DO WE find ourselves as Europe stood on the verge of an engulfing and devastating war? Placed within the perspective of the centuries through which we have travelled, the dinner party still represents compromise, a curious amalgam of pre-1789 hierarchy and post-1789 equality. Everybody now sits down together at the same table in a way that the revolutionaries envisaged, yet the diners are disposed in order of precedence. If an accident of birth no longer determines whether or not one shall be admitted, there are still tests — some subtle, some obvious — to be passed before entry can be gained. On the other hand such inequalities as the high table (except in places where it survives as an archaism), separate tables for women and different food according to rank have all vanished. Class snobbery and social division are all still firmly in place, but tempered by the possibility of Everyman gaining admittance. We may still be a long way from the street democracy of the French Revolution where anyone could roll up to the common table and join in, but we have arrived, give or take a bit, at the table of our own age. After the invention of the dinner party, everything since in the history of feasting, I think it might accurately be said, is little more than a footnote.

The Eclipse of the Table?

E DWARD VII'S CORONATION banquet in August 1902 may be taken as the end of an era. All over Europe in the two decades before 1914 the ritual splendour of the European courts had been enhanced to counter the emergence of socialism. The royal chef Gabriel Tschumi, writing in 1954, realised the significance of the occasion as he looked back on it:

> It is unlikely that such a banquet will ever be held again, and by present standards [post-Second World War food rationing] it seems very extravagant and wasteful. The sole which featured in the fish course was poached in chablis and garnished with oysters, prawns and other types of sea food. We allowed one quail per person, and a third of a very plump roasting chicken, not to mention the asparagus with Hollandaise sauce, the roast beef, and the snipe cutlets which went to make up the menu. A banquet like this should always end with a savoury such as the *Soufflé parmesan* served in 1902. We allowed forty egg-yolks for two hundred and fifty guests, 2 lb. of flour and 1 lb. of grated cheese, adding the whites well whipped separately. There is no more attractive coronation dessert, either, than the *Caisses de fraises Miramare* [a straw-berry dish that Tschumi described earlier, which took the confectioners who made the baskets of sugar holding the dessert and the cooks who made the jellied strawberries and vanilla cream mix-ture a full three days to prepare] . . . Many of the decorations on the table were also made from sugar. There were sugar ribbons and flowers, and the confectioners made a large sugar plaque bearing the royal crest which King Edward used during his reign. Each guest received a small sugar souvenir in the form of a crown at that banquet.[1]

Surely this is closer in spirit to the feasts of the Renaissance and the baroque than to any aspect of twentieth-century living. But the outbreak of the First World War and the advent of universal food rationing effectively spelled the end of *cuisine classique* and of the grand tradition of court catering.

The end of the war and the abolition of the monarchy in Germany, Austria and Russia merely accentuated the change. The centuries-old tradition of grandeur and opulence had already disappeared in France. Britain was the exception, but even there we can trace its sad decline. In 1914 Queen Mary, wife of George V, had reduced the household breakfast from eight to two courses. After 1918 dinner contracted from fourteen to ten courses. In 1932, with the collapse of the gold standard, a vast swathe of the royal kitchen staff was made redundant. By 1947, in the aftermath of another world war — which left Britain in economic ruin — the wedding breakfast of the present queen was just four modest courses: *filet de sole Mountbatten, perdreau en casserole* with *haricots verts, pommes noisettes* and *salade royale* followed by *Bombe Glacée Princesse Elizabeth* and dessert. Within half a century a great history had been virtually terminated.[2]

Other developments were also to erode the patterns of upper- and middle-class eating.[3] Servants after 1918 gradually became a thing of the past. After 1945 they almost ceased to exist. One major benefit ensued, however: the mechanisation of the kitchen. The ever-wider advance of the refrigerator by the third quarter of the twentieth century was joined by the gas and electric cooker, the dishwasher, and a wide variety of appliances which shredded, blended, chopped or stirred ingredients. To these can be added the deep-freeze and the microwave. Simultaneously we enter the era of commercial food preservation, with everything from a single ingredient to a complete meal being canned, dried or frozen. New modes of inter-national trade and transportation made available the most exotic fruits in the depths of winter. The seasons were banished, strawberries and asparagus could be had as freely in December as in June. Eating out became an option for every class of society as restaurants opened and chains sprang up, first national and then international. Cuisine which in the past had been purely local now became global, with Indian, Chinese, Malaysian, Libyan, Japanese and other restaurants springing up in every major city.

The twentieth century was an age of vast culinary variety (if not cacophony), but also one of culinary fear. Already by 1900 nutrition had begun to emerge as a matter of interest, to be taken seriously in the 1920s, and from then onwards obsessively. The connection between diet and health continued to be a fixation, not to mention the obsession with slimming, which has become an industry. The century closed with dietary disorders like obesity and anorexia exercising us in a way that would have astonished our ancestors.

The story of twentieth-century eating is untidy and diffuse, lacking the clarity of earlier centuries and perhaps too close to us for any degree of objectivity. The very expression 'feasting' no longer seems pertinent. The table, that icon we have traced over two thousand years of history, retains only a much-diminished meaning. In the ritual of the mass and holy communion of the Christian Churches, it can still claim its centrality as the re-enactment of a first-century supper. In religious communities we can still catch echoes of a way of eating which goes back to late Antiquity and the Dark Ages. Secular communities, like city companies and ancient universities, still retain the structure of medieval dining with a high table in place, massive displays of plate on the buffet and rituals such as the passage of a dish filled with rosewater for ablutions. And at any great state banquet we witness still the ritual of processional entry in order of precedence and relive much of the ceremonial of the absolutist courts.

But all of these are survivals from other ages, living uncertainly on in what I would now categorise as a post-table society. In the 1980s the number of occasions when two or more people sat at table together for a meal declined sharply. By the 1990s we had entered the era of grazing and of the snack. Everything points to the fact that for the vast majority of the population the idea of at least one meal in the day being a shared experience has gone for ever. The table no longer plays the crucial socio-cultural role it once did in the evolution of Western society. The meal rituals of centuries have to all intents and purposes been deconstructed and replaced by the spectacle of a solitary figure munching before a television screen. At least among the educated classes the private dinner party lives on. For that we should be grateful.

But, as often as not, that now takes place in a restaurant, removing from the hosts all the burdens of entertaining at home. The dinner in the private house, the touchstone of social acceptability throughout the nineteenth and most of the twentieth centuries, has, in effect, been replaced by a different kind of social filtering, that exercised by the restaurant. Such restaurants determine who shall and who shall not be allowed to book a table at gatherings which will include those whom they deem the glitterati of the age. And so we see meritocracy replace aristocracy, a gathering of those born of the media age, stars of stage and screen, pop idols, fashion designers and footballers. To be seen dining in such ambience is yet another milestone in the long history of admittance to the table. So, in a sense, transported from the palace, the aristocratic house and the bourgeois mansion, the shared table continues to exert, even today, its power as an index of social aspiration, privilege and acceptance.

CHAPTER ONE

CONVIVIUM: WHEN IN ROME

1. Quotations are from Petronius, *Satyricon*, trans. and ed. P. G. Walsh, Clarendon, Oxford, 1993, pp. 12–66. For discussions on the text and feast see ibid., introduction; Eugenia Salza Prina Ricotti, *L'arte del convito nella Roma antica*, Bretschneider, 1983, pp. 117–50; Antoinetta Dosi and François Schnell, *A tavola con i Romani antichi*, Edizioni Quasar, 1984, pp. 275–80; same authors' *I Romani in cucina*, Vita e Costumi dei Romani Antichi, Museo della Civiltà Romana, 1992, pp. 85–90; Andrew Dalby and Sally Grainger, *The Classical Cookbook*, British Museum Press, 1996, pp. 97–100.

2. Ricotti, pp. 11–18; Heleen Sancisi-Weerdenburg, 'Persian Food. Stereotypes and Political Identity', in *Food in Antiquity*, ed. John Willeins, David Harley and Mike Dobson, University of Exeter Press, 1993, pp. 286–302; Francis Joannes, 'The Social Function of Banquets in the Earliest Civilisations', in *Food. A Culinary History*, ed. Jean-Louis Flandrin and Massimo Montanari, Columbia UP, 1999, pp. 32–45.

3. Homer, *The Odyssey*, trans. A.T. Murray, Loeb Classical Library, 1919, I, p. 303.

4. The most important survey of food and wine in Ancient Greece, to which this account is much indebted, is Andrew Dalby, *Siren Feasts. A History of Food and Gastronomy in Greece*, Routledge, 1996. See also Massimo Montanari, 'Food Systems and Models of Civilisation', in Flandrin and Montanari (ed.), pp. 69–78; Marie-Claire Amouretti, 'Urban and Rural Diets in Greece', ibid., pp. 79–89; James Davidson, *Courtesans and Fishcakes. The Consuming Passions of Classical Athens*, Fontana Press, 1997, pp. 3–35; Gianni Race, *La cucina nel mondo classico*, Edizioni Scientifiche Italiane, 1999, Part 1; and the articles in Willeins, Harley and Dobson (ed.).

5. Dalby and Grainger, pp. 19–21; Dosi and Schnell, *I Romani in cucina*, pp. 22–5.

6. Elizabeth Craik, 'Hippokratic Diaita', in Willeins, Harley and Dobson (ed.), pp. 343–50; Vivian Nutton, 'Galen and the Travellers', ibid., pp. 359–70; Innocenzo Mazzini, 'Diet and Medicine in the Ancient World', in Flandrin and Montanari (ed.), pp. 141–52; Mark Grant, *Galen on Food and Diet*, Routledge, 2000.

7. Andrew Dalby, 'The Banquet of Philoxenus: A New Translation with

Culinary Notes', *Petits propos culinaires*, 26, 1987, pp. 28–36; Dalby and Grainger, pp. 42–55.

8. Andrew Dalby, 'The Wedding Feast of Caranus the Macedonian', *Petits propos culinaires*, 29, 1988, pp. 37–45.

9. Dalby and Grainger, pp. 11–13.

10. The definitive work on the civic banquet is Pauline Schmitt Pantel, *La Cité au banquet. Histoire des repas publics dans les cités grecques*, École Françaises de Rome, 1992. See also Louise Bruit, 'The Meal at the Hyakinthjia: Ritual Consumption and Offering', in *Sympotica. A Symposium on the Symposion*, ed. Oswyn Murray, Oxford, 1994, pp. 162–74; Pauline Schmitt Pantel, 'A Civic Ritual', in Flandrin and Montanari (ed.), pp. 90–5; same author's 'Sacrificial Meal and the Symposion: Two Models of Civic Institutions in the Archaic City?', in Murray (ed.), pp. 14–33; same author's 'Symposion: banquets, orgies et transgressions. Introductions au débat sur l'Antiquité', in *La Sociabilité à table. Commensalité et convivialité à travers les ages*, Actes du Colloque de Rouen, ed. Martin Aurell, Olivier Dumoulin and François Thélamon, Publications de l'Université de Rouen, no. 178, 1990, pp. 49–53; Peter Garnsey, *Food and Society in Classical Antiquity*, CUP, 1999, pp. 131–6.

11. Euripides, *Ion*, trans. Gilbert Murray, Allen & Unwin, 1954, pp. 85–6.

12. The account of the *symposion* I draw from Oswyn Murray, 'Sympotic History', in Murray (ed.), pp. 3–13; Birgitta Bergquist, 'Sympotic Space: A Functional Aspect of Greek Dining-Rooms', ibid., pp. 37–65; Frederick Cooper and Sarah Morris, 'Dining in Round Buildings', ibid., pp. 66–85; R. A. Tomlinson, 'The Chronology of the Perachora *Hestiatorium* and its Significance', ibid., pp. 95–101; John Boardman, 'Symposion Furniture', ibid., pp. 122–31; Jan N. Bremmer, 'Adolescents, Symposion, and Pederasty', ibid., pp. 135–48; Ezio Pellizer, 'Outlines of a Morphology of Sympotic Entertainment', ibid., pp. 177–84; Burkhard Fehr, 'Entertainers at the Symposion', ibid., pp. 185–95; François Lassarague, 'Around the *Krater*: An Aspect of Banquet Imagery', ibid., pp. 196–209; the same author's *The Aesthetics of the Greek Banquet. Images of Wine and Ritual*, Princeton UP, 1990, esp. pp. 3–18, 123–39; Massimo Vetta, 'The Culture of the Symposion', in Flandrin and Montanari (ed.), pp. 96–105; Oswyn Murray, 'Les Règles du *Symposion* ou comment problématiser le plaisir', in *La Sociabilité à table*, pp. 65–9; Davidson, pp. 43–9.

13. Xenophon, *Anabasis . . . and Symposium and Apology*, trans. O. J. Todd, Loeb Classical Library, 1922, pp. 373 ff.

14. The fundamental work is Jacques André, *L'Alimentation et la cuisine à Rome*, Les Belles Lettres, Paris, 1981. See also Ricotti, pp. 219–34; Dosi and Schnell, *A tavola con i Romani antichi*, pp. 18 ff.; same authors' *I Romani in cucina*; Garnsey, pp. 122 ff.

15. *The Attic Nights of Aulus Gellius*, trans. John C. Rolfe, Loeb Classical Library, 1927, II, pp. 65–7.

16. Race, pp. 172–3.

17. J. P. V. D. Balsdon, *Life and Leisure in Ancient Rome*, The Bodley Head, 1969, p. 44.

18. Florence Dupont, 'La Consommation du pourri et la sociabilité alimentaire à Rome', in Aurell, Dumoulin and Thélamon (ed.), pp. 29–32.

19. Balsdon, pp. 39–40; Ugo Enrico Paoli, *Rome. Its People, Life and Customs*, trans. R. D. Macnaughten, Longmans, 1963, p. 97; Apicius, *Cookery and Dining in Imperial*

Rome, ed. and trans. Joseph Dommers Vehling, Dover, 1977, pp. 24–6; Dosi and Schnell, *A tavola con i Romani antichi*, pp. 291–6; same authors, *I Romani in cucina*, pp. 32 ff.

20. For editions of Apicius see Barbara Flower and Elisabeth Rosenbaum, *The Roman Cookery Book*, Harrap, 1958; John Edwards, *The Roman Cookery of Apicius*, Rider Books, 1988; Apicius, *Cookery and Dining in Imperial Rome*. For studies see Race, pp. 191–220; Ricotti, pp. 207–18; Carol A. Dery, 'The Art of Apicius', in *Cooks and Other People*, Proceedings of the Oxford Symposium on Food and Cookery, 1995, Prospect Books, 1996, pp. 11–17; Dalby and Grainger, pp. 13–16; Jon Solomon, 'The Apician Sauce: Ius Apicianum', in Willeins, Harley and Dobson (ed.), pp. 115–31.

21. On the meal structure of the Roman day see Paoli, pp. 92–6.

22. On frugality see Emily Gowers, *The Loaded Table. Representations of Food in Roman Literature*, Clarendon, 1993, pp. 16–19.

23. Cicero, *Two Essays on Old Age and Friendship*, trans. E. S. Shuckburgh, Macmillan & Co., London, 1927, p. 69.

24. Dupont, in Aurell, Dumoulin and Thélamon (ed.), pp. 29–32. Generally on the *convivium* see *A History of Private Life*, I, *From Pagan Rome to Byzantium*, ed. Paul Veyne, Harvard UP, 1987, pp. 186–9.

25. On the origin and development see Annette Rathje, 'The Adoption of the Homeric Banquet in Central Italy in the Orientalising Period', in Murray (ed.), pp. 279–88; Garnsey, pp. 136–8.

26. Lilian M. Wilson, *The Clothing of the Ancient Romans*, Johns Hopkins UP, Baltimore, 1938, pp. 78–83, 169.

27. Martial, *Epigrams*, ed. and trans. D. R. Shackleton Bailey, Loeb Classical Library, 1993, I, p. 423(7).

28. *The Roman History of Ammianus Marcellinus*, trans. C. D. Yonge, Bohn's Classical Library, 1894, p. 489.

29. Pliny the Younger, *Letters and Panegyricus*, trans. Betty Radice, Loeb Classical Library, 1969, I, p. 97.

30. Quoted Gowers, p. 26.

31. See John d'Arms, 'The Roman Convivium and the Idea of Equality', in Murray (ed.), pp. 308–20.

32. On food hierarchy see Mireille Corbier, 'The Broad Bean and the Moray: Social Hierarchies in Food in Rome', in Flandrin and Montanari (ed.), pp. 128–40.

33. Cicero, *Letters to Atticus*, trans. E. O. Winstedt, Loeb Classical Library, 1918, III, p. 214.

34. Pliny, *Letters and Panegyricus*, ed. cit., I, pp. 96–7.

35. Martial, *Epigrams*, ed. cit., I, p. 245.

36. John d'Arms, 'Slaves at Roman Convivia', in *Dining in a Classical Context*, ed. W. J. Slater, Ann Arbor, 1991, pp. 171–83.

37. On the *triclinium* see Race, pp. 151–4; Paoli, pp. 64–5; Dosi and Schnell, *A tavola con i Romani antichi*, pp. 48–9; Katherine M. D. Dunhabin, 'Triclinium and Stibadium', in Slater (ed.), pp. 121–48.

38. Dosi and Schnell, *A tavola con i Romani antichi*, pp. 314–22.

39. Suetonius, *The Twelve Caesars*, trans. Robert Graves, Penguin, 1957, p. 229.

40. J. Carcopino, *Daily Life in Ancient Rome*, trans. Henry T. Rowell, Routledge, 1941, pp. 272–3.
41. Ibid.
42. Alan Booth, 'The Age for Reclining and its Attendant Perils', in Slater (ed.), pp. 105–20.
43. For *cena* see W. Warde Flower, *Social Life in Rome in the Age of Cicero*, Macmillan, London, 1909, pp. 276–82; Carcopino, pp. 263–76; Race, pp. 170–2; Ricotti, pp. 18–25; Paoli, pp. 92–6; Florence Dupont, 'The Grammar of Roman Dining', in Flandrin and Montanari (ed.), pp. 113–27; Gowers, ch. 1; Andrew Dalby, *Empire of Pleasures: Luxury and Indulgence in the Roman World*, Routledge, 2000, pp. 243–57; Dosi and Schnell, *A tavola con i Romani antichi*, pp. 43–7, 52–69; Balsdon, pp. 632–41.
44. Macrobius, *The Saturnalia*, trans. Percival Vaughan Davies, Columbia UP, 1969, p. 229, p. 248.
45. Ibid., p. 55.
46. Cicero, *De officiis*, trans. Walter Miller, Loeb Classical Library, 1913, pp. 135–41.
47. Pliny, *Letters*, ed. cit., I, p. 473.
48. Cicero, *Letters to Friends*, trans. D. R. Shackleton Bailey, Loeb Classical Library, 2001, III, pp. 196–7.
49. *The Attic Nights of Aulus Gellius*, ed. cit., I, p. 99.
50. Martial, *Epigrams*, ed. cit., I, p. 237 (50).
51. Generally see Balsdon, pp. 46–7: Richard C. Beacham, *Spectacle Entertainments of Early Imperial Rome*, Yale UP, 1990, pp. 197 ff.
52. Christopher P. Jones, 'Dinner Theater', in Slater (ed.), pp. 185–98.
53. Dosi and Schnell, *A tavola con i Romani antichi*, pp. 299–328; Paul Veyne, *Bread and Circuses. Historical Sociology and Political Pluralism*, trans. Brian Pearce, Penguin, 1990, pp. 220–1.
54. Stanislaus Mrozek, 'Caractère hiérarchique des repas officiels dans les villes romaines du Haut-Empire', in Aurell, Dumoulin and Thélamon (ed.), pp. 181–5.
55. Race, pp. 393 ff.
56. Suetonius, trans. Graves, pp. 273–4.
57. Beacham, pp. 221–2; Tacitus, *The Annals of Imperial Rome*, trans. Michael Grant, Penguin, 1959, p. 351; *Dio's Roman History*, trans. Earnest Cary, Loeb Classical Library, 1961, VIII, pp. 109–10.
58. Ibid., VIII, pp. 335–6; Phyllis P. Brober, 'The Black or Hell Banquet', in *Fasting and Feasting*, Oxford Symposium on Food and Cookery, 1990, Prospect Books, 1990, pp. 55–7.
59. Jeremy Rossiter, '*Convivium* and Villa in Late Antiquity', in Slater (ed.), pp. 199–214. For texts see Sidonius, *Poems and Letters*, trans. W. B. Anderson, Loeb Classical Library, 1936, I, pp. 427, 453–7.
60. Anthimus, *On the Observance of Foods*, trans. and ed. Mark Grant, Prospect Books, 1996.
61. *The Works of Luitprand of Cremona*, trans. T. A. Wright, Routledge, 1930, pp. 241, 247, 254; for the Byzantine tradition see Ewald Kislinger, 'Christians of the East. Rules and Realities of the Byzantine Diet', in Flandrin and Montanari (ed.), pp. 194–206.
62. Quoted Andrew Dalby, 'Christmas Dinner in Byzantium', in *Food on the Move*,

Proceedings of the Oxford Symposium on Food and Cookery, 1996, Prospect Books, 1997, ed. Harlan Walker, pp. 75–83.

63. Ibid., p. 80.

CHAPTER TWO

INTERLUDE: FAST AND FEAST

1. *The Autobiography of Giraldus Cambrensis*, ed. and trans. H. E. Butler, Cape, 1937, pp. 70–2.
2. Ibid., p. 72.
3. Massimo Montanari, 'Romans, Barbarians, Christians. The Dawn of European Food Culture', in *Food. A Culinary History*, ed. Jean-Louis Flandrin and Massimo Montanari, Columbia UP, 1999, pp. 165–7.
4. Same author's 'Production Structures and Food Systems in the Early Middle Ages', 'Peasants, Warriors, Priests. Images of Society and Styles of Diet' and 'Toward a New Dietary Balance', in ibid., pp. 168–75, 178–85, 247–50. Also Antoni Riera-Melis, 'Society, Food and Feudalism', in ibid., pp. 251–60.
5. T. Sarah Peterson, *Acquired Taste. The French Origins of Modern Cooking*, Cornell UP, 1994, ch. 1.
6. For what follows see Robin Lane Fox, *Pagans and Christians*, Viking, 1986, pp. 395–6 and especially Veronika E. Grimm, *From Feasting to Fasting. The Evolution of a Sin. Attitudes to Food in Late Antiquity*, Routledge, 1996; also Bridget Henisch, *Fast and Feast. Food in Medieval Society*, Pennsylvania State UP, 1976, ch. 1 *passim*.
7. *The Rule of St Benedict*, trans. Cardinal Casquet, Chatto & Windus, 1925. For monasticism and the emergence of manners see Leo Moulin, *Les Liturgies de la table. Une histoire culturelle du manger et du boire*, Fonds Mercator, Albin Michel, 1989, pp. 187–90.
8. Wolfgang Braunfels, *Monasteries of Western Europe. The Architecture of the Orders*, Thames & Hudson, 1972, pp. 12–19, 147–51.
9. See Riera-Melis, 'Society, Food and Feudalism', in Flandrin and Montanari (ed.), pp. 260 ff.; *A History of Private Life*, ed. Philippe Ariès and Georges Duby, II, *Revelations of the Medieval World*, ed. Georges Duby, Harvard UP, 1988, pp. 44–55.
10. John Goodall, 'How the Monks of Fountains Sat Down to Eat', *Country Life*, 29 November 2001, pp. 58–61.
11. Henisch, ch. 1.
12. Marjorie A. Brown, 'The Feast-Hall in Anglo-Saxon Society', in *Food and Eating in Medieval Europe*, ed. Martha Carlin and Joel T. Rosenthal, The Hambledon Press, 1998, pp. 1–13.
13. Régis Boyer, '"Dans Upsal ou les Jarls boivent la bonne bière": Rites de boisson chez les Vikings', in *La Sociabilité à table. Commensalité et convivialité à travers les âges*, Actes du Colloque de Rouen, ed. Martin Aurell, Olivier Moulin and François Thélemon, Publications de l'Université de Rouen no. 178, 1994, pp. 83–9.
14. P. E. Schramm, *A History of the English Coronation*, trans. L. Wickham Legg,

Clarendon, 1937, pp. 3, 62–3; Zeer Gourarier, 'Modèles de cour et usages de table: les origines', in *Versailles et les tables royales en Europe XVIIe–XIXe siècle*, Musée National des Châteaux de Versailles et de Trianon, exhibition catalogue, 1993–4, pp. 16–17.

15. See Elisa Acanfora, 'La tavola', in *Rituale, ceremoniale, etichetta*, ed. Sergio Bertelli and Giuliano Crifo, Bompiani, 1985, pp. 53–66.

16. Gerd Althoff, 'Obbligatorio mangiare: pranzi, banchetti e feste nella vita sociale del Medioevo', in *Storia dell'alimentazione*, ed. Jean-Louis Flandrin and Massimo Montanari, Laterza, 1997, pp. 234–42.

17. *Early Lives of Charlemagne by Einhard and the Monk of St Gall*, ed. Prof. A. J. Grant, De la More Press, 1905, p. 39.

18. Janet L. Nelson, 'The Lord's Anointed and the People's Choice: Carolingian Royal Ritual', in *Rituals of Royalty. Power and Ceremonial in Traditional Societies*, ed. David Cannadine and Simon Price, CUP, 1987, pp. 172–5; M. Rouche, 'Le Repas de fête à l'époque Carolingienne', in *Manger et boire au Moyen Age*, ed. Denis Menjot, Actes du Colloque de Nice, 1982, Publications de la Faculté des Lettres et Sciences Humaines de Nice, no. 27, 1st series, Les Belles Lettres, 1984, I, pp. 265–96.

19. Ariès and Duby (ed.), II, pp. 71–5.

20. Elizabeth Lamond, *Walter of Henley's Husbandry*, Longmans, Green and Co., 1890, pp. 121 ff.

21. William Michael Rossetti, *Italian Courtesy-Books*, EETS, 1869.

22. Ibid., p. 112.

23. Ibid., pp. 144–5.

24. Jacques le Goff, 'Saint Louis à table: entre commensalité royale et humilité alimentaire', in Aurell, Dumoulin and Thélemon (ed.), pp. 133–44.

25. *The Life of St Louis by John of Joinville*, trans. René Hague, ed. Natalis de Wailly, Sheed & Ward, 1955, pp. 47–8.

26. Ibid., pp. 196–7.

CHAPTER THREE

IN THE EYE OF THE BEHOLDER

1. The text is printed both in the original Catalan and in translation in *Plaisirs et manières de table aux XIVe et XVe siècles*, exhibition catalogue, Musée des Augustins, Toulouse, 1992, pp. 308–9.

2. On the emergence of cookery books see Stephen Mennell, *All Manners of Food. Eating and Taste in England and France from the Middle Ages to the Present*, Basil Blackwell, 1986, pp. 49–54; Bruno Laurioux, *Le Moyen Age à table*, Adam Biro, Paris, 1989, pp. 110–12; the same author's 'Entre savoires et pratiques: le livre de cuisine à la fin du Moyen Age', *Médiévales*, XIV, 1988, pp. 60–9; *Du Manuscrit à la Table*, ed. Carole Lambert, University of Montreal Press, 1992; Odile Redon, Françoise Sabban and Silvano Serventi, *A tavola nel medioevo con 150 ricette dalla Francia e dall'Italia*, Editori Laterza, 1995, pp. 7–11; Terence Scully, *The Art of*

Cookery in the Middle Ages, Boydell Press, Woodbridge, 1995, pp. 4–6. For the Italian contribution see *Arte della cucina. Libri di Ricette. Testi sopra lo scalco Il Trinciante e i vini*, ed. Emilio Faccioli, Il Polifilo, Milan, 1966.

3. *The Viandier of Taillevent. An Edition of all Extant Manuscripts*, ed. Terence Scully, University of Ottawa Press, 1988; *Plaisirs et manières de table*, pp. 13–15; Terence Scully, *The Viandier. A Critical Edition with English Translation*, Prospect Books, 1997; Bruno Laurioux, *Le Règne de Taillevent. Livres et pratiques culinaires à la fin du Moyen Age*, Publications de la Sorbonne, 1997; A. S. Weber, 'Queu du Roi, Roi des Queux: Taillevent and the Profession of Medieval Cooking', in *Food and Eating in Medieval Europe*, ed. Martha Carlin and Joel T. Rosenthal, Hambledon Press, 1998, pp. 145–6.

4. Eileen Power, *The Goodman of Paris (Le Ménagier de Paris)*, George Routledge & Sons, 1928; *Le Ménagier de Paris*, ed. Georgina Brereton and Janet Ferrier, Clarendon, 1981; *Plaisirs et manières de table*, pp. 9–11; Nicole Grossley-Holland, *Living and Dining in Medieval Paris*, University of Wales Press, Cardiff, 1996; Alan Davidson, *The Oxford Companion to Food*, OUP, 1999, s. v. Menagier de Paris.

5. *Curye on Inglysche. English Culinary Manuscripts of the Fourteenth Century*, ed. Constance B. Hieatt and Sharon Butler, EETS, 1985, pp. 20–1. See also Lorna Sass, *To the King's Taste. Richard II's Book of Feasts and Recipes Adapted for Modern Cooking*, John Murray, 1976. For English late medieval cookery manuscripts see Constance B. Hieatt, 'Listing and Analysing the Medieval English Culinary Recipe Collections: A Project and its Problems', in *Du Manuscrit à la table*, pp. 15–26; *Two Fifteenth-Century Cookery Books*, ed. Thomas Austin, EETS, 1888, and Constance B. Hieatt, *An Ordinance of Pottage*, Prospect Books, 1988.

6. *Chiquart's 'On Cookery'. A Fifteenth-Century Savoyard Culinary Treatise*, ed. and trans. Terence Scully, American University Studies, series, IX, History, 22, Peter Lang, 1986.

7. Ibid., pp. xviii-xxv; *The Viandier of Taillevent*, 1988, ed. Scully, pp. 20–4; Scully, *Art of Cookery*, pp. 40 ff.

8. What follows on medieval food and drink is a distillation of what is already a considerable literature, of which the following are the most pertinent: *Plaisirs et manières de table*; Redon, Sabban and Serventi; Scully, *Art of Cookery*; Laurioux, *Le Moyen Age à table*, pp. 35–50; Laurioux, 'Les Menus de banquet dans les livres de cuisine de la fin du Moyen Age', in *La Sociabilité à table. Commensalité et convivialité à travers les âges*, Actes du Colloque de Rouen, ed. Martin Aurell, Olivier Dumoulin and Françoise Thélemon, Publications de l'Université de Rouen, 1990, pp. 273–9; Laurioux, 'Cucine medievali (secoli XIV e XV)', in *Storia dell'alimentazione*, ed. Jean-Louis Flandrin and Massimo Montanari, Editori Laterza, Rome-Bari, 1996, pp. 356–70; P. W. Hammond, *Food and Feast in Medieval England*, Alan Sutton, 1993; Barbara Ketcham Wheaton, *Savoring the Past. The French Kitchen and Table from 1300 to 1789*, Simon & Schuster, 1996, pp. 1–26; Claudio Benporat, *Storia della gastronomia italiana*, Mursia, Milan, 1990, pp. 13–81; Bruno Laurioux, *Le Règne de Taillevent*, Publications de la Sorbonne, 1997; D. Eleanor Scully and Terence Scully, *Early French Cookery. Sources, History, Original Recipes and Adaptations*, Ann Arbor, 1995; Jean-Louis Flandrin and Carol Lambert, *Fêtes gourmandes au Moyen Age*, Imprimerie Nationale, Paris, 1998; Phyllis Bray Bober, *Art, Culture and Cuisine*, University of Chicago Press, 1999, pp. 230–7.

9. *Plaisirs et manières de table*, pp. 21–5.
10. Ibid., pp. 27–31.
11. Scully, *Art of Cookery*, pp. 207–17. See also Constance B. Hieatt, 'Sorting Through the Titles of Medieval Dishes: What Is, or Is Not, a "Blanc Manger"', in *Food in the Middle Ages. A Book of Essays*, ed. Melitta Weiss Adamson, Garland Publishing, 1995, pp. 25–43.
12. Scully, *Art of Cookery*, ch. 6; Redon, Sabban and Serventi, pp. 22–4.
13. Hieatt, *An Ordinance of Pottage*, pp. 15–16.
14. Weber, in Carlin and Rosenthal (ed.), p. 156.
15. Johann Maria van Winter, 'Interregional Influences in Medieval Cooking', in Adamson (ed.), pp. 45–59.
16. Hall's *Chronicle* as quoted in William Edward Mead, *The English Medieval Feast*, Allen & Unwin, London, 1967 ed., p. 203.
17. Benporat, pp. 56–9.
18. Barbara Santich, 'The Evolution of Culinary Technique in the Medieval Era', in Adamson (ed.), pp. 61–81.
19. Laurioux, 'Cucine medievali', in Flandrin and Montanari (ed.), pp. 36–61; *Plaisirs et manières de table*, pp. 63–5; Scully, *Art of Cookery*, pp. 28 ff.
20. *Forme of Cury*, ed. Hieatt and Butler, pp. 10–12; Laurioux, 'Cucine medievali', p. 362; Jocelyn Gledhill Russell, *The Field of the Cloth of Gold*, Barnes & Noble Inc., New York, 1969, p. 146.
21. Brenda S. Rose, 'Aspects of Visual Art in the Gastronomy of Fifteenth-Century France', in *Look and Feel. Studies in Texture, Appearance and Incidental Characteristics of Food*, Proceedings of the Oxford Symposium on Food and Cookery, 1993, ed. Harlan Walker, Prospect Books, 1994, pp. 174–80; Mireille Vincent-Cassy, 'La Vue et les mangeurs: couleurs et simulacres dans la cuisine médiévales', in *Banquets et manières de table au Moyen Age*, Centre Universitaire d'Études et de Recherches Médiévales d'Aix, Sénéfiance no. 38, 1996, pp. 161–72; see also on colour *Plaisirs et manières de table*, pp. 67–8; Scully, *Art of Cookery*, pp. 104–5.
22. C. Anne Wilson, 'Ritual, Form and Colour in the Medieval Food Tradition', in *The Appetite and the Eye*, Food and Society, no. 2, University of Edinburgh Press, 1991, pp. 16–26; T. Sarah Peterson, *Acquired Taste: The French Origins of Modern Cooking*, Cornell UP, 1994, ch. 1 and 2.
23. See the account from Corio's *L'historia di Milano* (1557) printed in Benporat, pp. 39–40.
24. R. Fabyan, *The New Chronicles of England . . .*, London, 1811, pp. 599–601; Austin (ed.), p. xiv.
25. George Cavendish, *Thomas Wolsey, late Cardinal, his Life and Death*, ed. Roger Lockyer, Folio Society, London, 1962, pp. 102–3.
26. What is covered in this section and the next is dealt with in a general way in the following: Bridget Ann Henisch, *Fast and Feast. Food in Medieval Society*, Pennsylvania State UP, 1976, ch. 6; Madeleine Pelner Cosman, *Fabulous Feasts. Medieval Cookery and Ceremony*, George Braziller, New York, 1976, pp. 12–17; Mark Girouard, *Life in the English Country House*, Yale UP, 1978, pp. 22 ff.; Laurioux, *Le Moyen Age à table*, pp. 95–105, 119–40; Redon, Sabban and Serventi, pp. 19 ff.; C. Anne Wilson, 'From Medieval Great Hall to Country-House Dining Room', in *The Appetite and the Eye*, pp. 28–37; Zeev Gouranier, 'Le "banquet" médiéval (XIVe–XVIe siècles)', in *Les*

Français et la table, exhibition catalogue, Musée national des arts et traditions populaires, 1985–86, pp. 149–61.

27. *Plaisirs et manières de table*, pp. 52–3.
28. Scully, *Art of Cookery*, p. 66.
29. Hammond, pp. 120–2.
30. Scully (ed. and trans.), *Chiquart's 'On Cookery'*, pp. 1–6.
31. *Plaisirs et manières de table*, p. 277. Other instances where food quantities are listed in detail are those for the feast given in 1467 on the occasion of the installation of George Neville as archbishop of York, J. Leland, *Collectanea*, ed. T. Hearne, 1744, VI, pp. 2 ff.; Richard Warner, *Antiquitates Culinariae . . .*, London, 1791, pp. 93–101; Mead, p. 33; the feast for the enthronement of William Warham as archbishop of Canterbury, Warner, *Antiquitates*, pp. 107–24; the Lord Mayor's Banquet of 1505, *The Babees Boke . . . The Bokes of Nurture of Hugh Rhodes and John Russell . . .*, ed. Frederick Furnivall, EETS, London, 1868, pp. 378–80.
32. Scully, *Art of Cookery*, pp. 236 ff.
33. Cavendish, pp. 46–8.
34. *The Babees Boke*, pp. 310 ff.
35. For which see Olivier de La Marche, *L'Estat de la maison de duc Charles de Bourgogne, dit le Hardy (1474)* in *Nouvelles collections des mémoires pour servir à l'histoire de France*, ed. Richard and Poujoulat, 1st series, III, Paris and Lyon, 1850.
36. *The Babees Boke*, pp. 61–73; also see John Russell's *The Bokes of Nurture*, pp. 129–30, and Wynken de Worde's *The Boke of Kervynge*, p. 266. See also *A Fifteenth-Century Courtesy Book*, ed. R. W. Chambers, EETS, 1914, p. 11.
37. Piers Langland, *Piers Plowman*, Text B, Passus X, 97–101.
38. Mark Girouard, *Life in the French Country House*, Cassell, 2000, pp. 53 ff.
39. Leland, *Collectanea*, VI, pp. 2 ff.
40. Russell, pp. 160–3.
41. R. Vaughan, *Philip the Good*, Longmans, 1970, pp. 56–7.
42. Ibid., pp. 49–50.
43. For the evolution of the *dressoir* see R. W. Lightbown, *Secular Goldsmith's Work in Medieval France: A History*, Reports of the Research Committee of the Society of Antiquaries of London, no. xxxvi, 1978, pp. 16–17, 39 ff.
44. Ibid., p. 40.
45. *Mémoires d'Olivier de La Marche* in *Nouvelles collections des mémoires pour servir à l'histoire de France*, ed. Richard and Poujoulat, 1st series, III, Paris and Lyon, 1850, p. 521.
46. Lightbown, p. 40.
47. Sydney Anglo, *Spectacle, Pageantry and Early Tudor Policy*, Clarendon Press, 1969, p. 130.
48. For what follows on plate see Charles Oman, *English Domestic Silver*, A. & C. Black, 1934, pp. 18 ff; Françoise Robin, 'Le Luxe de la table dans les Cour Princières (1360–1480)', *Gazette des Beaux-Arts*, 86 (1975), pp. 1–16; *Les Fastes du Gothique. Le siècle de Charles V*, exhibition catalogue, Grand Palais, Paris, 1981–2, pp. 204–6, 220–4; Lightbown, *passim*; *Plaisirs et manières de table*, pp. 216–21.
49. Lightbown, p. 37.
50. Ibid., pp. 78 ff.
51. Lightbown, p. 19.

52. See Charles Oman, *Medieval Silver Nefs*, Victoria & Albert Museum, HMSO, 1963.
53. Oman, *Domestic Silver*, pp. 29–32; Lightbown, p. 29.
54. Ibid., pp. 11, 43–5; *Les Fastes du Gothique*, p. 236.
55. *Plaisirs et manières de table*, pp. 103–9, 181–3, 199.
56. Russell, p. 161.
57. Generally for aspects covered in this section see Cosman, pp. 39–74; Redon, Sabban and Serventi, pp. 24–35; on visual sources M. Closson, 'Us et coutumes de table du XIIe siècle au XVe siècle à travers les miniatures', in *Manger et boire au Moyen Age*, Actes du Colloque de Nice (15–17 October 1982), ed. Denis Menjot, Publications de la Faculté des Lettres et Sciences Humaines de Nice, no. 27, 1st series, Les Belles Lettres, 1984, II, pp. 21–32.
58. Weber, in Carlin and Rosenthal (ed.), p. 147.
59. See Flandrin and Montanari (ed.), between pp. 240–1.
60. On the development of hierarchy see *The Household Book of Edward IV. The Black Book and the Ordinance of 1478*, ed. A. R. Myers, Manchester UP, 1959, p. 24; A. Planché, 'La Table comme signe de la classe. Le témoignage du roman du comte d'Anjou (1316)', in *Manger et boire*, I, pp. 239–60.
61. Austin (ed.), pp. xi–xii, 55–8; Janet Lawrence, 'Royal Feasts', in *Feasting and Fasting*, Proceedings of the Oxford Symposium on Food and Cookery, 1990, Prospect Books, 1990, pp. 138–42.
62. Giovanna Bonardi, 'Manger à Rome. La *Mensa* pontificale à la fin du Moyen Age. Entre Cérémonial et alimentation', in *Banquets et manières de table*, pp. 440–2.
63. *William Gregory's Chronicle of London* in *The Historical Collections of a Citizen of London*, ed. James Gairdner, Camden Society, n.s., 17, 1879, pp. 22–3.
64. Daniele Alexandre-Bidon, 'Banchetto d'immagini e "antipasti miniati"', in Flandrin and Montanari (ed.), pp. 417–23.
65. Bruno Laurioux, 'Table et hiérarchie sociale à la fin du Moyen Age', in *Du manuscrit à table*, ed. Carole Lambert, University of Montreal, 1992, pp. 87–108; Allen J. Grieco, 'Food and Social Classes in Late Medieval and Renaissance Italy', in *Food. A Culinary History*, ed. Jean-Louis Flandrin and Massimo Montanari, Columbia University Press, 1999, pp. 302–12.
66. A. Rucquoi, 'Alimentation des riches, alimentation des pauvres dans un ville castillane au XVe siècle', in *Manger et boire*, I, pp. 297–312.
67. *The Regulations and establishment of the household of Henry Algernon Percy, the 5th Earl of Northumberland, 1512*, London, 1770.
68. Frances E. Baldwin, *Sumptuary Legislation and Personal Regulation in England*, Johns Hopkins Press, Baltimore, 1926, p. 47.
69. Raphaela Averkorn, 'L'Organisation et le déroule des banquets dans les villes du Nord de l'Allemagne au Bas Moyen Age', in *Banquets et manières de table*, pp. 13–34.
70. Hieatt, *Ordinance of Pottage*, p. 18.
71. *William Gregory's Chronicle of London*, in Gairdner (ed.), pp. 113–14.
72. Baldwin, p. 167.
73. Hammond, pp. 103–5.
74. *The Babees Boke*, pp. lxxx–lxxxvi.
75. See accounts in ibid., pp. 132–3, 322–3.

76. Ibid., pp. 196, 322, 324–5.
77. Lightbown, p. 30.
78. Maria José Palla, 'Manger et boire au Portugal à la fin du Moyen Age – textes et images', in *Banquets et manières de table*, pp. 105–6.
79. Russell, p. 160.
80. *The Babees Boke*, pp. 140–52, 374–5.
81. Scully, *Art of Cookery*, p. 171; *The Babees Boke*, p. 120.
82. Hammond, pp. 131–4.
83. On this topic see Scully, *Art of Cookery*, pp. 126 ff.; *Plaisirs et manières de table*, p. 276; Cosman, pp. 20 ff.; *Cury on Inglysch*, pp. 4–5; Redon, Sabban and Serventi, pp. 17–19; Jean-Louis Flandrin, 'Structure des menus français et anglais au XIVe et XVe siècle' in *Du manuscrit à la table*, pp. 173–92. The debate about meal sequence is to be the subject of a forthcoming book by Prof. Ken Albala to whom I am grateful.
84. Hieatt and Butler (ed.), pp. 40–1, also with an invaluable glossary.
85. For what follows see Alfred Franklin, *La Vie privée d'autrefois*, Paris, 1889, pp. 168–87; same author's *La Civilité, l'étiquette, la mode, le bon ton du XIIe au XIXe siècle*, Paris, 1908, I, *passim*; William Michael Rossetti, *Italian Courtesy-Books*, EETS, 1869, pp. 8–32; Norbert Elias, *The Civilising Process. The History of Manners*, Blackwell, Oxford, 1978, pp. 60–70; Henisch, ch. 7; Scully, *Art of Cookery*, pp. 174 ff.; Hammond, pp. 103–4; Jean La Croix, 'Un Art des belles manières de table en Lombardie au XIIIe siècle: *De quinquaginta curialitatibus ad mensam* (1288) de Bonvesin de la Riva', in *Banquets et manières de table*, pp. 71–91; Marie-Geneviève Grossel, 'La Table comme pierre de touche de la courtoisie: à propos de quelques *Chastoiements, ensenhamen* et autres *contenances* de table', in ibid., pp. 181–95; Daniela Romagnoli, '"Guardano sil vilan". Le buone maniere a tavola', in Flandrin and Montanari (ed.), pp. 396–408; Jonathan Nicholls, *The Matter of Courtesy. Medieval Courtesy Books and the Gawain Poet*, D. S. Brewer, 1998, p. 7.
86. Ffiona Swabey, 'The Household of Alice de Breyne, 1412–13', in Carlin and Rosenthal (ed.), pp. 33–44.
87. *The Babees Boke*, p. 6.
88. Quoted in Redon, Sabban and Serventi, p. 9.
89. *Le livre du fais et bonnes meurs du sage roy Charles* quoted in Franklin, *La Civilité*, p. 306.
90. Quoted Henisch, *Fast and Feast*, p. 217.
91. *The Babees Boke*, p. 373.
92. H. Aliquot, 'Les Épices à la table des papes d'Avignon au XIVe siècle', in *Manger et boire*, I, pp. 132–44.
93. Lightbown, pp. 18–19.
94. Mireille Vincent-Cassy, 'La *Gula Curiale* ou les débordements des banquets au début du règne de Charles VI', in Aurell, Dumoulin and Thélemon (ed.), pp. 91–102.
95. Mennell, pp. 41–2; Benporat, p. 37.
96. For what follows on the development of the *entremets* see Benporat, pp. 38–9; Cosman, pp. 31–5; Henisch, ch. 8; Agathe Lafortune-Martel, *Fête noble en Bourgogne au XVe siècle. Le Banquet du Faisan (1454): Aspects publiques, sociaux et culturels*, Institut d'Études Médiévales, University of Montreal, 1984, pp. 25–54;

same author's 'De l'entremets culinaire aux pièces montées d'un menu de propagande', in *Du Manuscrit à table*, pp. 121–9; Terence Scully, 'The Medieval French *Entremets*', *Petits propos culinaires*, 17, 1984, pp. 44–56; Danielle Queruel, 'Des Entremets aux intermèdes dans les banquets bourguignons', in *Banquets et manières de table*, pp. 143–57; Scully, *Art of Cookery*, pp. 104–9; Wilson, 'Ritual, Form and Colour in the Medieval Food Tradition', pp. 13–16.

97. Lightbown, p. 44.
98. Lafortune-Martel, pp. 45 ff.
99. Vaughan, pp. 111–12.
100. *Chiquart's 'On Cookery'*, pp. 30–7.
101. Vaughan, p. 143.
102. *Mémoires d'Olivier de La Marche*, pp. 526 ff.
103. Ibid., pp. 548–9. See also 'Account of the Ceremonial of the Marriage of the Princess Margaret, Sister of King Edward the Fourth to Charles, Duke of Burgundy . . .', *Archaeologia*, 31, 1846, pp. 336–7.
104. On subtleties see *Two Fifteenth-Century Cookery Books*, pp. 67–9; Hammond, pp. 142–3; Glynne Wickham, *Early English Stages 1300–1660*, I, *1300 to 1576*, Routledge & Kegan Paul, 1980, pp. 211, 381.
105. Robert Fabyan, *The New Chronicles of England and France*, London, 1811, p. 586.
106. See Bertram Wolffe, *Henry VI*, Eyre Methuen, 1981, pp. 50–1; *The Minor Poems of John Lydgate*, ed. H. N. MacCracken, EETS, 1934, II, pp. 623–4. For subtleties for the enthronement of George Neville, 1465, and of William Warham, 1504, see Warner, *Antiquitates*, pp. 97–8, 113 ff.
107. *The Babees Boke*, pp. 376–7.
108. Hammond, pp. 144–8.
109. Reinhard Strohm, *The Rise of European Music 1380–1500*, CUP, 1993, pp. 7–13, 313–19; same author's *Music in Late Medieval Bruges*, Clarendon Press, 1985, pp. 92–101.
110. Wickham, I, p. 213.
111. *The Chronicles of Froissart translated . . . by . . . Lord Berners*, David Nott, London, 1902, pp. 281–2.
112. Palla, 'Manger et boire au Portugal', pp. 107–8.
113. Vaughan, p. 143.
114. *Minor Poems of John Lydgate*, II, pp. 668–701.
115. Anglo, pp. 101–3; Gordon Kipling, *The Triumph of Honour. Burgundian Origins of the Elizabethan Renaissance*, Sir Thomas Browne Institute, University of Leiden, 1977, pp. 102 ff.
116. For the Feast of the Pheasant see *Mémoires d'Olivier de La Marche*, pp. 478–88; Lafortune-Martel; F. Alberto Gallo, *Music of the Middle Ages*, II, trans. Karen Eales, CUP, 1985, pp. 102–7; M. Santucci, 'Nourritures et symboles dans le Banquet du Faisan et dans Jehan de Sainté', in *Manger et boire*, I, pp. 429–40.
117. Vaughan, pp. 144–5.
118. Ibid., p. 178.
119. G. Hyvernat-Pou, 'Un repas princière à la fin du XVe siècle d'après le Roman de Jehan de Paris', in *Manger et boire*, I, pp. 261–4.
120. R. Vaughan, *Charles the Bold, the Last Valois Duke of Burgundy*, Longmans, 1973, p. 179.
121. Lafortune-Martel, pp. 72 ff.

CHAPTER FOUR
RENAISSANCE RITUAL

1. Cristoforo Messisbugo, *Banchetti, composizioni di vivende e apparecchio*, ed. Fernando Bandini, Neri Pozza, Venice, 1960, pp. 31–42; Adriano Cavicchi, 'Nel Parnasso dei sensi tra spettaculo, simbolo e storia', in *A tavola con il principe*, ed. Jadranka Bentini, Alessandra Chiappini, Giovanni Battista Panatta and Anna Maria Visser Travagli, exhibition catalogue, Castello Estense, Ferrara, Gabriele Gorbo, 1988–9, pp. 387–400; Michel Jeanneret, *A Feast of Words. Banquets and Table Talk in the Renaissance*, Polity Press, 1991, pp. 52–4. For the Cardinal Ippolito d'Este see Mary Hollingsworth, 'Ippolito d'Este: A Cardinal and his Household', *The Court Historian*, 5, 2 (2000), pp. 105–26.
2. One of the most oft-cited is the feast given on the occasion of the first performance of Ariosto's *La Cassaria* on 24 January 1529, for which see Susan Weiss, 'Medieval and Renaissance Weddings and Other Feasts', in *Food and Eating in Medieval Europe*, ed. Martha Carlin and Joel T. Rosenthal, Hambledon Press, 1998, p. 172.
3. This account of Ferrara is based on Werner L. Gundersheimer, *Ferrara. The Style of a Despotism*, Princeton UP, 1973; Sergio Bertelli, Franco Cardini and Elvira Garbero Zorzi, *Italian Renaissance Courts*, Sidgwick & Jackson, 1986, pp. 65–73; *Le muse e il principe. Arte di corte nel Rinascimento padano*, exhibition catalogue, Franco Cosimo Panini, 1991. On the culinary and feasting aspects of Ferrarese Renaissance culture see Luigi Alberto Gandini, *Tavola, cantina e cucina della corte di Ferrara nel quattrocento*, Modena, 1889; Angelo Solerti, *Ferrara e la corte estense*, Citta di Castello, 1891, pp. lxxix–lxxxi; Emilio Faccioli, 'Scenita dei banchetti estensi', in *Il Rinascimento nelle corti padane. Società e cultura*, De Donato, 1977, pp. 597–606; Giuseppe Montovano, 'Il banchetto rinascimentale: arte, magnificenza, potere', in *A tavola con il principe*, pp. 46–63; Jadranka Bentini, 'Per ricostruzione del banchetti del principe. Documenti figurativi e fonti manuscritti e a stampa', in ibid., pp. 269–82; Anna Maria Fioravanti Baraldi, 'Gli "apparamenti" del banchetto', in ibid., pp. 321–32.
4. Quoted Gundersheimer, p. 188.
5. Thomas Tuohy, *Herculean Ferrara. Ercole d'Este, 1471–1505, and the Invention of a Ducal Capital*, CUP, 1996, p. 272, note 215.
6. Ibid., p. 273, note 219.
7. On whom see Messisbugo, *Banchetti*, ed. Gandini; Luciano Chiappini, *La corte estense alla meta del cinquecento. I compendi di Cristoforo di Messisbugo*, Belriguardo, 1984, pp. 39–80; Giovanni Battista Panatta, 'La mensa del principe', in *A tavola con il principe*, pp. 89–91; Luciano Chiappini, 'Lo scalco ideale: Cristoforo da Messisbugo', in ibid., pp. 311–13; Claudio Benporat, *Storia della gastronomia italiana*, Mursia, 1990, pp. 113–20; 'Les banquets princiers de Christoforo di Messisbugo', in *La Table et ses dessous. Culture, alimentation et convivialité en Italie (XIVe–XVIe siècles)*, ed. Adelin Charles Fiorato and Anna Fontes Baratto, Cahiers de la Renaissance Italienne, 4, Presses Sorbonne Nouvelle, 1999, pp. 223–37.
8. Giacomo Grana, *Descrizione del banchetto nuziale per Alfonso II duca di Ferrara e Barbara principessa d'Austria . . .*, Domenico Taddei, Ferrara, 1869.

9. Benporat, pp. 124–31.

10. F. Sabban and S. Serventi, *A tavola nel Rinascimento*, Laterza, 1991, p. 7; June de Schino, 'The Triumph of Sugar Sculpture in Italy, 1500–1700', in *Look and Feel. Studies in Texture, Appearance and Incidental Characteristics of Food*, Proceedings of the Oxford Symposium on Food and Cookery, ed. Harlan Walker, Prospect Books, 1994, p. 205.

11. For what follows see *Gastronomia del Rinascimento*, ed. Luigi Firpo, Unione Tipografico, Turin, 1974; Jeanneret, pp. 78–88; Benporat, pp. 53–148; *The Splendours of the Table. The Art and Pleasure of the Renaissance Banquet*, Seville Universal Exhib., Ragione Lazio, 1992, pp. 15–24, 31–8; T. Sarah Peterson, *Acquired Taste: The French Origins of Modern Cooking*, Cornell University Press, 1994, chs 3–8; Bruno Laurioux, 'Les Livres de cuisine italiens à la fin du XVe et au début du XVIe siècle: expressions d'un syncrétisme culinaire méditerranéen', in *La Mediterrania area de convergencia de systemes alimentari (sigees V–XVIII)*, XIV, *Journades d'Estudis Historics Locals*, Palma, 1996, pp. 73–8; Sabban and Serventi.

12. On whom see Benporat, pp. 56–60; also same author's *Cucina italiana del quattrocento*, Leo S. Olschi, 1996; Maestro Martino, *Libro de arte coquinaria*, ed. Luigi Ballerini and Jeremy Parzen, Guido Tommasi, Milan, 2001.

13. On whom see ibid., pp. 60–4; Gillian Riley, 'Platina, Martino and their Circle', in *Cooks and Other People*, Proceedings of the Oxford Symposium on Food and Cookery 1995, Prospect Books, 1996, pp. 214–19; Platina, *On Right Pleasure and Good Health*, trans. and ed., Mary Ella Milham, *Medieval and Renaissance Texts and Studies*, 168, Tempe, Arizona, 1998.

14. See note 8.

15. For which see Sabban and Serventi, p. 8.

16. See K. T. Butler, 'An Italian's Message to England in 1614: Eat More Fruit and Vegetables', *Italian Studies*, II, 1938, pp. 1–18; Firpo (ed.), pp. 32–3, 131–76; Giacomo Castelvetro, *The Fruit, Herbs and Vegetables of Italy*, trans. Gillian Riley, Viking, B.M. Natural History, 1989.

17. Sabban and Serventi, pp. 42–4.

18. For these idiosyncrasies see ibid., pp. 22–8; Benporat, pp. 89 ff.

19. On whom see Firpo, pp. 21–6, 39–92; Bartolomeo Scappi, *Opera [dell'arte del cucinare]*, ed. Giancarlo Roversi, Arnoldo Forni Editori, Testi Antichi di Gastronomia, 12, 1981; Benporat, pp. 93–106; Sabban and Serventi, pp. 28–32.

20. Benporat, pp. 120–3.

21. On whom see *Arte della cucina*, ed. Emilio Faccioli, Il Polifilo, Milan, 1975, pp. 345 ff.; Benporat, pp. 120–3. On the whole evolution of the carver see Cristiano Grottanelli, 'Cibo, istinti, divieti', in *Rituale, ceremoniale, etichetta*, ed. Sergio Bertelli and Giuliano Crifo, Bompiani, 1985, pp. 37–40; Giuseppe Montovano, 'Il banchetto rinascimentale: arte, magnificenza, potere', in *A tavola con il principe*, pp. 48–50; Benporat, pp. 133 ff.

22. Benporat, p. 33.

23. Firpo, pp. 26–9, 98–129; Benporat, pp. 133–6.

24. Barbara Ketcham Wheaton, *Savoring the Past. The French Kitchen and Table from 1300 to 1789*, Simon & Schuster, 1996, pp. 27–34; Alain Girard, 'Du manuscrit à l'imprime: le livre de cuisine en Europe aux XVe et XVIe siècles', in *Pratiques et discours alimentaires à la Renaissance*, ed. Jean-Claude Margolin and Robert Sauzet,

Actes du Colloque de Tours, March 1979, Centre d'Études Supérieures de la Renaissance, pp. 197–27.

25. Philip Hyman and Mary Hyman, 'Printing the Kitchen: French Cookbooks, 1480–1800', in *Food: A Culinary History*, ed. Jean-Louis Flandrin and Massimo Montanari, Columbia UP, 1999, pp. 394–6; Jacqueline Boucher, 'L'alimentation en milieu de cour sous les derniers Valois', in Margolin and Sauzet (ed.), pp. 161–76.

26. Launcelot de Casteau, *Overture de cuisine*, De Schutter, Antwerp/Brussels, 1983 (reprint).

27. *The Letters of Pliny the Consul*, trans. William Melmoth, London, 1810, pp. 85–95.

28. Ibid., pp. 210–24.

29. Vitruvius, *The Ten Books on Architecture*, trans. Morris Hicky Morgan, Dover Pub., NY, n.d., pp. 179, 181, 209.

30. Peter Thornton, *The Italian Renaissance Interior, 1400–1600*, Weidenfeld & Nicolson, 1991, pp. 285 ff.

31. Leon Battista Alberti, *On the Art of Building in Ten Books*, trans. Joseph Rykwert, Neil Leach and Robert Taverner, MIT Press, Cambridge, Mass., 1988, p. 147.

32. Platina, *On Right Pleasure and Good Health*, p. 115.

33. Margherita Azzi Visentini, *La villa in Italia. Quattrocento e cinquecento*, Electa, 1995, pp. 71–2.

34. Sebastiano Serlio, *The Five Books of Architecture*, trans. Robert Peake, Dover Pub., NY, 1982, f. 70v–71.

35. There is a vast literature on villas. For the present purpose I have used Visentini, pp. 74 ff., and David Coffin, *The Villa in the Life of Renaissance Rome*, Princeton UP, 1974, pp. 73 ff.

36. Vitruvius, trans. Morgan, p. 211; Alberti, trans. Rykwert *et al.*, p. 299.

37. Coffin, p. 83.

38. Ibid., pp. 87 ff.; Visentini, pp. 87–92.

39. Coffin, pp. 150–74, 244–56; Visentini, pp. 95 ff., 116 ff., 159 ff.

40. Coffin, pp. 281 ff.; Visentini, pp. 185 ff.

41. Coffin, pp. 340 ff.; Visentini, pp. 195 ff.; Claudia Lazzaro, *The Italian Renaissance Garden*, Yale UP, 1990, pp. 243 ff.

42. Coffin, pp. 311 ff.; Visentini, pp. 173 ff.; Lazzaro, pp. 215 ff.

43. Coffin, pp. 267 ff.; Lazzaro, pp. 106–8.

44. Ibid., p. 142 and fig. 137.

45. Ibid., p. 137 and fig. 128.

46. Ibid., p. 137.

47. Ibid., pp. 55–6.

48. For Palladio's villas I have used Donata Battilotti, *The Villas of Palladio*, Electa, 1990, and Paul Holberton, *Palladio's Villas. Life in the Renaissance Countryside*, John Murray, 1990.

49. Mark Girouard, *Life in the French Country House*, Cassell, 2000, pp. 92–101.

50. Quoted Wheaton, pp. 64–7.

51. For Tudor England see Mark Girouard, *Life in the English Country House*, Yale UP, 1978, pp. 88, 103; Nicholas Cooper, *Houses of the Gentry 1480–1680*, Yale UP, 1999, pp. 289–93; Sara Paston-Williams, *The Art of Dining. A History of Cooking and Eating*, National Trust, 1993, pp. 123 ff.

52. What follows is indebted to Michel Jeanneret, *A Feast of Words. Banquets and Table Talk in the Renaissance*, Polity Press, 1991.
53. Quoted ibid., p. 20.
54. Ibid., p. 15.
55. *Plutarch's Moralia*, trans. Frank Cole Babbitt, Loeb Classical Library, 1928, II, p. 417.
56. For a discussion of the representation of tables, see Hélène Albani, 'Repas sacrés, repas profanes dans la peinture italienne du XVIe siècle', in *La Table et ses dessous, culture, alimentation et convivialité en Italie (XIVe–XVIe siècles)*, ed. Adelin Charles Fiorato and Anna Fontes, Cahiers de la Renaissance Italienne, 4, Barotto, Presses de la Sorbonne Nouvelle, 1999, pp. 279–95. Another consequence of the religious divide was the Protestant attack on feasts, followed later in the century by a Counter-Reformation Catholic attack. See Marc Vennard, 'La Fraternité des banquets', in *Pratiques et discours*, pp. 137–45.
57. Jeanneret, *passim*.
58. Ibid., p. 21.
59. Coffin, p. 335.
60. Reinhard Strohm, *The Rise of European Music 1380–1500*, CUP, 1993, pp. 315–16.
61. *Plutarch's Moralia*, trans. Edwin L. Minar, Jr, F. H. Sandbach and W. C. Helmhold, Loeb Classical Library, 1961, IX, p. 77.
62. Andrew C. Minor and Bonner Mitchell, *A Renaissance Entertainment. Festivities for the Marriage of Cosimo I, Duke of Florence, in 1539*, University of Missouri Press, 1968, p. 36.
63. Jeanneret, pp. 91–197.
64. *The Complete Works of Montaigne*, trans. Donald M. Frame, Hamish Hamilton, 1958, pp. 846, 849.
65. Generally see Esther B. Aresty, *The Best Behavior*, Simon & Schuster, NY, 1970, pp. 63–9; Norbert Elias, *The Civilising Process. The History of Manners*, Blackwell, Oxford, 1978, pp. 533 ff.; Bertelli, Cardini and Zorzi, pp. 190 ff.; Jeanneret, pp. 40 ff.
66. *De civilitate morum puerilium (On good manners for boys)*, in *Collected Works of Erasmus*, ed. J. K. Sowards, University of Toronto Press, 1985, XXV, pp. 269 ff. and pp. 280–6 on table manners. See also Franz Bierlaine, 'Erasme, la table et les manières', in *Pratiques et discours*, pp. 147–60.
67. James W. Holme, 'Italian Courtesy Books of the Sixteenth Century', *Modern Language Review*, V, no. 2, 1910, pp. 145–66.
68. Sydney Anglo, 'The Courtier. The Renaissance and Changing Ideals', in *The Courts of Europe. Politics, Patronage and Royalty 1400–1800*, ed. A. G. Dickens, Thames & Hudson, 1977, pp. 33–53.
69. Elisa Aconfora, 'La Tavola', in Bertelli and Crifò (ed.), pp. 53–66.
70. Generally see Bertelli, Cardini and Zorzi, pp. 164–6, 194–201; Jacques Heers, *La vita quotidiana nella Roma pontifica ai tempi dei Borgia e dei Medici 1420–1520*, Rizzoli, 1986, pp. 108–11; Benporat, pp. 137–43; Jeanne Allard, 'Les Grands Banquets à la cour de Charles Quint', in *La Sociabilité à table. Commensalité et convivialité à travers les âges*, Actes du Colloque de Rouen, ed. Martin Aurell, Olivier Dumoulin and Françoise Thélemon, 1990, Publications de l'Universite de Rouen, no. 178, 1990, pp. 145–53; *The Splendours of the Table. The Art and Pleasure of the Renaissance Banquet,*

Seville Universal Exhibition, Regione, Lazio, 1992; Giovanni Attolini, *Teatro e spettaculo nel Rinascimento*, Editori Laterza, 1997, pp. 180–4.

71. Quoted Bertelli, Cardini and Zorzi, p. 28.
72. Giancarlo Malacarne, *Sulla mensa del principe. Alimentazione e banchetti alle corti dei Gonzaga*, Il Bulino, Edizione d'Arte, 2000, pp. 51–89, 164–8.
73. For the Renaissance phase of the buffet see *Le Dressoir du prince. Service d'apparat à la Renaissance*, exhibition catalogue, Musée Nationale de la Renaissance, Château d'Écouen, 1995.
74. *Splendours of the Gonzaga*, ed. David Chambers and Jane Martineau, exhibition catalogue, V & A Museum, 1982, nos 188–93.
75. *Il luogo teatrale a Firenze*, ed. L. Zorzi, M. Fabbri, E. Garbero Zorzi and A. M. Tofani, exhibition catalogue, Florence, Tofani, Electa, Milan, 1975, pp. 102–3.
76. *Autobiography of Benvenuto Cellini*, Everyman ed., 1907, pp. 29–30.
77. I. D. McFarlane, *The Entry of Henri II into Paris 16 June 1549*, Medieval and Renaissance Texts and Studies, 7, Binghamton, 1982, in the text of *L'Entrée de la royne à Paris*, p. 35; Victor E. Graham and W. McAllister Johnson, *The Paris Entries of Charles IX and Elisabeth of Austria 1571*, U. of Toronto, 1971, pp. 83–5.
78. *Splendours of the Gonzaga*, pp. 175–8.
79. On maiolica see Timothy Wilson, *Ceramic Art of the Italian Renaissance*, B.M. Pubs, 1987; *Le dressoir du prince*, pp. 23–4.
80. See Elena Corradini, 'I servizi nell' "apparecchio della tavola" del principe', in *A tavola con il principe*, pp. 345–54.
81. Howard Burns, *Andrea Palladio 1508–1580*, exhibition catalogue, Arts Council, 1975, p. 49.
82. For the fork see Pasquale Marchese, *L'invenzione della forchetta*, Rubbettino Editore, 1989, pp. 72 ff.
83. Thomas Coryat, *Coryat's Crudities . . .*, Maclehose & Sons, Glasgow, 1905, I, pp. 236–7.
84. Malacarne, pp. 59–66.
85. Wheaton, pp. 52–6, citing Thomas Artus' *Description de l'isle des Hermaphrodites*.
86. *The Complete Works of Montaigne*, p. 940.
87. Thornton, pp. 205–6.
88. For the tablecloth ritual see Elvira Gerbero Zorzi, 'Ceremoniale e spettacolita. Il tovagliolo sulla tavola del principe', in Bertelli and Crifò (ed.), pp. 6–83.
89. Burns, *Andrea Palladio*, p. 51.
90. The text is printed in Benporat, p. 140.
91. For which see Giuseppe Bertini, *Le nozze di Alessandro Farnese. Feste alle corti Lisboa e Bruxelles*, Skira, 1997. For Marchi's account see pp. 106–8.
92. Bertelli, Cardini and Zorzi, *Italian Renaissance Courts*, p. 196.
93. Quoted ibid., pp. 197–8.
94. *Ceremonies of Charles I. The Note Books of John Finet 1628–41*, ed. Albert J. Loomie, Fordham UP, 1987, p. 75.
95. Benporat, p. 73.
96. Ibid., pp. 102–3; Sabban and Serventi, p. 46.
97. For which see *The Splendours of the Table*, pp. 7–14, where the account is given in translation of Fusoritto's text.
98. Jeanneret, p. 20.

99. Edmund A. Bowles, *Musical Ensembles in Festival Books 1500–1800. An Iconographical & Documentary Survey*, UMI Research Press, Ann Arbor, 1989, pp. 59–61.

100. *Hypnerotomachia Poliphili*, trans. Jocelyn Godwin, Thames & Hudson, 1999, pp. 106–19.

101. Fabrizio Cruciani, *Teatro nel Rinascimento. Roma 1450–1550*, Bulzoni Editore, 1983, pp. 151–64; Benporat, pp. 74–8.

102. Bertelli, Cardini and Zorzi, p. 166.

103. The description is printed in *L'ordine de la imbandisone se hanno a dare a cena*, Il Collizionista, Milan, 1983.

104. Benporat, pp. 64–8.

105. Angelo Solerti, *Musica, ballo e drammatica alla corte medicea dal 1600 al 1637*, Florence, 1905, pp. 235–8; A. M. Nagler, *Theater Festivals of the Medici*, Yale UP, 1964, p. 94; *Feste e apparati medicei da Cosimo I a Cosimo II*, exhibition catalogue, by Giovanna Gaeta Bertela and Annamaria Petrioli Tofani, Leo S. Olschki, Florence, 1969, pp. 96 ff.: *Il luogo teatrale a Firenze*, pp. 102–3; Sara Marmone, 'Feste e spettacoli a firenze e in Francia per le nozze di Maria de' Medici e Enrico IV', in *Il teatro dei Medici*, Quaderni di Teatro, II, no. 7, 1980, pp. 206–28.

106. Mercedes Viale Ferrero, *Feste delle Madame Reali di Savoia*, Istituto Bancario San Paolo di Torino, 1965, pl. VI and VII with text.

107. Victor E. Graham and W. McAllister Johnson, *The Royal Tour of France by Charles IX and Catherine de' Medici. Festivals and Entries 1564–66*, University of Toronto Press, 1979, pp. 44, 317–18, 378–9.

108. Jeanne Allard, 'Les Grands Banquets à la cour de Charles Quint', in *La sociabilité à table*, pp. 145–53.

109. The quotations which follow are from Giorgio Vasari, *The Lives of the Painters, Sculptors and Architects*, ed. William Gaunt, Everyman ed., 1963, II, pp. 32–7.

110. For sugar see Alan Davidson, *The Oxford Companion to Food*, OUP, 1999, s.v. sugar; J. Materne, 'Anvers comme centre de distribution et d'affinage d'épices et de sucre depuis la fin du XVème jusqu'au XVIIème siècle', in *L'Europe à table*, exhibition catalogue, Antwerp, 1993, pp. 49–60.

111. The best general account of these is in Katharine J. Watson, 'Sugar Sculpture for Grand Ducal Weddings from the Giambologna Workshop', *Connoisseur*, CIC, 1978, pp. 20–6. See also Tuohy, p. 274.

112. Bowles, pp. 23–5.

113. A. van de Put, 'Two Drawings of the Fêtes at Binche for Charles V and Philip (II)', *Journal of the Warburg and Courtauld Institutes*, III, 1939–40, pp. 49–55; Calvete de Estrella, *Le très-Heureux Voyage fait par très-haut et très-puissant prince Don Philippe*, Brussels, Olivier, 1883, IV, pp. 151–3.

114. Bertini, *Le nozze di Alessandro Farnese*, pp. 110–12.

115. Graham and McAllister Johnson, pp. 83–5, 391–5; Frances A. Yates, *Astraea. The Imperial Theme in the Sixteenth Century*, Routledge & Kegan Paul, 1975, pp. 140–4; Wheaton, pp. 51–2.

116. C. Anne Wilson, 'The Evolution of the Banquet Course: Some Medicinal, Culinary and Social Aspects', in *'Banquetting Stuffe'. The Fare and Social Background of the Tudor and Stuart Banquet*, ed. C. Anne Wilson, Edinburgh UP, 1986, pp. 9–35.

117. See Girouard, *Life in the English Country House*, pp. 104–16.

118. See Jennifer Stead, 'Bowers of Bliss: The Banquet Setting', in Wilson (ed.), pp.

115–57; Peter Brears, 'Rare Conceites and Strange Delightes: The Practical Aspects of Culinary Sculpture', in ibid., pp. 60–114; Lynette Hunter, '"Sweet Secrets" from Occasional Receipts to Specialised Books: the Growth of a Genre', in ibid., pp. 36–59. There is also a confused account, in which feast and banquet are not always differentiated, in Alison Sim, *Food and Feast in Tudor England*, St Martin's Press, NY 1997, pp. 134–57.

119. Jean Wilson, *Entertainments for Elizabeth I*, D. S. Brewer, 1980, pp. 114–15, 165.

120. E. K. Chambers, *The Elizabethan Stage*, Clarendon Press, 1923, I, pp. 206–7, III, p. 235.

121. *Ben Jonson*, ed. C. H. Herford, Percy and Evelyn Simpson, Clarendon Press, 1941, VII, pp. 805–14.

122. Werner Paravicini, 'The Court of the Dukes of Burgundy: A Model for Europe', in *Princes, Patronage and Nobility. The Court at the Beginning of the Modern Age c. 1450–1650*, ed. Ronald Asch and Adolf Birke, OUP, 1991, pp. 69–102.

123. Bertelli, Cardini and Zorzi, pp. 21–2, 28–30; Sergio Bertelli, *Il corpo del re. Sacralità nell'Europa medievale e moderna*, Ponte alle Grazie, 1995, pp. 167–88; Sergio Bertelli, 'Rex et sacerdos: The Holiness of the King in European Civilisation', in *Iconography, Propaganda and Legitimation*, ed. Alan Ellenius, European Science Foundation, Clarendon Press, 1998, p. 141.

124. Bertelli, 'Rex et sacerdos', p. 141; *The Princely Courts of Europe. Ritual, Politics and Culture under the Ancien Regime 1500–1750*, ed. John Adamson, Weidenfeld & Nicolson, 1999, pp. 46–7.

125. Simon Thurley, *The Royal Palaces of Tudor England. Architecture and Court Life 1460–1547*, Yale UP, 1993, pp. 122–5; Peter Brears, *All the King's Cooks. The Tudor Kitchens of King Henry VIII at Hampton Court Palace*, Souvenir Press, 1999, pp. 163 ff.; Adamson (ed.), pp. 104–5.

126. Paul Hentzner, *Travels in England during the Reign of Queen Elizabeth*, Cassell & Son, 1899, pp. 49–51; see also accounts in *Thomas Platter's Travels in England*, ed. Clare Williams, Cape, 1937, pp. 193–4; G. W. Roos, *The Diary of Baron Waldstein. A Traveller in Elizabethan England*, Thames & Hudson, 1981, pp. 80–1.

127. *Eat, Drink and Be Merry. The British at Table 1600–2000*, Philip Wilson, 2000, pp. 52–3, fig. 34.

128. Ralph E. Giesey, *The Royal Funeral Ceremony in Renaissance France*, Travaux d'Humanisme et Renaissance, XXXVII, Librairie E. Droz, Geneva, 1960, pp. 145–6, 164–74; same author's *Le Roi ne meurt jamais*, Flammarion, 1987, pp. 240–3, 254–6.

CHAPTER FIVE

FROM COURT TO CABINET

1. For the emergence of the *souper intime* see Béatrix Saule, 'Tables à Versailles 1682–1789', in *Versailles et les tables royales en Europe XVIIème–XIXème siècle*, Musée National des Châteaux de Versailles et de Trianon, exhibition catalogue, 1993–4, pp. 58–60.

2. See *Journal inédit du duc de Croÿ (1718–1784)*, ed. De Grouchy and Paul Cottin, Flammarion, 1906, I, pp. 71–2. See also Jacques Levron, *Daily Life at Versailles in the Seventeenth and Eighteenth Centuries*, trans. C. E. Engel, Allen & Unwin, London, 1968, pp. 157–61; Nancy Mitford, *Madame de Pompadour*, Hamish Hamilton, London, 1968, p. 109.

3. Saule, in *Versailles et les tables royales*, p. 60.

4. For the emergence of the menu see Zeer Gouranier, 'L'Histoire du menu', in *La Sociabilité à table. Commensalité et convivialité à travers les âges*, Actes du Colloque de Rouen, ed. Martin Murell, Olivier Dumoulin and Françoise Thélamon, Publications de l'Université de Rouen, 1992, pp. 307–13; *Versailles et les tables royales*, pp. 272–3 (nos 54–5).

5. For the Castlemaine embassy see: Margery Corbett, 'John Michael Wright: An Account of His Excellence Roger Earl of Castlemain's Embassy . . .', *Antiquaries Journal*, 70, 1990, pp. 117–20; Alain Gruber, 'Le festin offert par Roger earl of Castlemaine', *Gazette des beaux-arts*, ser. 6, 126, 1995, pp. 99–110; Roberto Valeriani, 'Fasto nobiliare. Il gusto e l'etichetta', in *La festa a Roma dal Rinascimento al 1870*, ed. Marcello Fagiolo, exhibition catalogue, Umberto Allemani & Co., 1997, pp. 120–3, 228–9; Timothy Clifford, *Designs of Desire. Architectural and Ornamental Prints and Drawings 1500–1850*, exhibition catalogue, National Gallery of Scotland, 1999, pp. 170–3 (nos. 76–7); *Life and the Arts in the Baroque Palaces of Rome*, ed. Stefanie Walker and Frederick Hammond, exhibition catalogue, Yale UP, 1999, pp. 224–5 (nos. 81–2); for an account of another banquet of this type but earlier in date (1638), see Peter Bietberger, 'Prince Eckenbergh comes to dinner: Food and Political Propaganda in the Seventeenth Century', *Petits propos culinaires*, 15, 1983, pp. 45–54.

6. For this period in Italy see Claudio Benporat, *Storia della gastronomia italiana*, Mursia, 1990, pp. 163–244.

7. On which see Katherine J. Watson, 'Sugar Sculpture for Grand Ducal Weddings from the Giambologna Workshop', *Connoisseur*, CIC, 1978, p. 20; Maurizio Fagiolo Dell'Arco and Silvia Carandini, *L'effimero barocco. Strutture della festa nella Roma del '600*, exhibition catalogue, Bulzoni, Rome, 1977–8, II, pl. 195–7; Jennifer Montagu, *Roman Baroque Sculpture. The Industry of Art*, Yale UP, 1989, pp. 190 ff.; Peter Brown and Ivan Day, *Pleasures of the Table. Ritual and Display in the European Dining Room 1600–1900*, exhibition catalogue, Fairfax House, York, 1997, pp. 10–12.

8. For the Sevin drawings see *Christina, Queen of Sweden*, exhibition catalogue, Nationalmuseum, Stockholm, 1966, pp. 310–16 (nos 710–17); Per Bjurström, *Feast and Theatre in Queen Christina's Rome*, Stockholm, 1966, p. 142 (nos 56–7), 143 (nos 62–7); Georgina Masson, 'Food as Fine Art in the Seventeenth Century', *Apollo*, 83, 1966, pp. 338–41; Giulia Fusconi, *Disegni decorativi del barocco romano*, exhibition catalogue, Gabinetto dei Disegni e delle Stampe, Villa La Farnesina alla Lungara, Rome, 1986, pp. 29–36 (nos. 1–7); Peter Fuhring, *Design into Art. Drawings for Architecture and Ornament. The Lodewijk Houthakker Collection*, Philip Wilson, 1989, II, pp. 678–89 (nos 1006, 1008, 1009, 1014, 1016, 1019).

9. Montagu, p. 22 note 100.

10. On the banquets for Christina see Georgina Masson, 'Papal Gifts and Roman Entertainments in Honour of Queen Christina's Arrival', in *Queen Christina of*

Sweden. Documents and Studies, ed. J. Magnus von Platen, Analecta Reginensa, I, 1966, pp. 244–61; Bjurström, pp. 47–69; Fagiolo Dell'Arco and Carandini, II, pp. 207 ff.; June di Schino, 'The Triumph of Sugar Sculpture in Italy 1500–1700', in *Look and Feel. Studies in Texture, Appearance and Incidental Characteristics of Food*, Proceedings of the Oxford Symposium on Food and Cookery, 1993, ed. Harlan Walker, Prospect Books, 1994, pp. 204–5; same author's 'Queen Christina and the Triumph of the Baroque Banquet in Italy', in *Food on the Move*, Proceedings of the Oxford Symposium on Food and Cookery, ed. Harlan Walker, Prospect Books, 1997, pp. 97–101; Valeriani, 'Fasto nobiliare', in Fagiolo (ed.), pp. 224–6.

11. See, for instance, Edward J. Olszewski, 'Decorating the Palace: Cardinal Pietro Ottoboni (1667–1740) in the Cancelleria', in *Life and the Arts in the Baroque Palaces of Rome*, pp. 93–111.

12. For what follows see Marie-France Noël-Waldteuffel, 'Manger à la cour: alimentation et gastronomie aux XVIIe et XVIIIe siècles', in *Versailles et les tables royales*, pp. 69–71; Benporat, pp. 167–73.

13. Gunther Schiedlausky, *Tee, Kaffee, Schokolade*, Prestel Verlag, Munich, 1961; Barbara Ketcham Wheaton, *Savoring the Past: The French Kitchen Table from 1300 to 1789*, Simon & Schuster, 1996, pp. 87–94; Frédéric Mauro, *Histoire du café*, Éditions Desjonquères, Paris, 1991; L. Swaelen, 'Le chocolat: une histoire culinaire', in *L'Europe à table*, exhibition catalogue, Antwerp, 1993, pp. 61–73; Alain Huetz de Lemps, 'Colonial Beverages and the Consumption of Sugar', in *Food. A Culinary History from Antiquity to the Present*, ed. Jean-Louis Flandrin and Massimo Montanari, Columbia, UP, 1999, pp. 383–93.

14. Esther B. Aresty, *The Delectable Past*, Allen & Unwin, 1965, chs 6 and 7; Alain Girard, 'Le Triomphe de "La Cuisinière Bourgeoise". Livres culinaires, cuisine et société en France aux XVIIe et XVIIIe siècles', *Revue d'histoire moderne et contemporaine*, XXIV, 1977, pp. 497–523; Philip and Mary Hyman, 'La Chapelle and Massialot: an 18th Century Feud', *Petits propos culinaires*, 2, 1979, pp. 44–54; same authors, 'Vincent La Chapelle', ibid., 8, 1981, pp. 35–40; Stephen Mennell, *All Manners of Food. Eating and Taste in England and France from the Middle Ages to the Present*, Basil Blackwell, 1986, pp. 64–82; T. Sarah Peterson, *Acquired Taste. The French Origins of Modern Cookery*, Cornell UP, 1994, pp. 163 ff., 183 ff.; La Varenne, *Le Cuisinier français*, ed. Jean-Louis Flandrin and Philip and Mary Hyman, Montalba, Paris, 1995, pp. 12–99; Wheaton, chs 6 and 8; Jean-Louis Flandrin, 'Dietary Choices and Culinary Technique 1500–1800', in Flandrin and Montanari (ed.), pp. 403–17; same author, 'The Early Modern Period', in ibid., pp. 349–73; Philip and Mary Hyman, 'Printing the Kitchen. French Cookbooks 1480–1800', in ibid., pp. 394–402.

15. On this and the development of ices and confectionery see Wheaton, pp. 180–5, 192–3.

16. For the dissemination of and resistance to the French style see ibid., pp. 160–6; Mennell, pp. 83–133; Benporat, pp. 184–9, 248–54; Stephen Mennell, 'Food at the Late Stuart and Early Hanoverian Courts', *Petits propos culinaires*, 17, 1984, pp. 22–9; Sara Paston-Williams, *The Art of Dining. A History of Cooking and Eating*, National Trust, 1993, pp. 163 ff., 231–2.

17. For *service à la française* see Wheaton, pp. 138–48; Noël-Waldteuffel, in *Versailles*

et les tables royales, pp. 74–6; Claudine Marenco, *Manières de table. Modèles de moeurs 17ème–20ème siècle*, Éditions de L'E.N.S. Cachan, 1992, pp. 41–56; Peter Brears, 'À la française . . .,' in *Luncheon, Nuncheon and Other Meals*, ed. C. Anne Wilson, Alan Sutton, Stroud, 1994, pp. 91–116; Alan Davidson, *Oxford Companion to Food*, OUP, 1999, s.v. *service à la française*.

18. Wheaton, p. 140.

19. Alain Gruber, 'Le Cérémonial de table dans les cours européennes', in *Versailles et les tables royales*, pp. 150 and 300 (no. 141).

20. Ibid., pp. 300–1 (no. 140).

21. Mark Girouard, *Life in the French Country House*, Cassell, 2000, p. 248.

22. Same author's *Life in the English Country House*, Yale UP, 1978, pp. 136–48.

23. The history of silver is a subject on its own. What follows is merely items I found of use for the synthesis I give: Carl Hernmarck, *The Art of the European Silversmith 1430–1830*, Sotheby Parke Bernet, New York and London, 1977, I, pp. 176 ff.; James Lomax, 'Silver for the English Dining Room 1700–1800', in *A King's Feast. The Goldsmith's Art and Royal Banqueting in the 18th Century*, exhibition catalogue, Kensington Palace, 1991, pp. 118–33; Gerard Mabille, 'Germain, Duran, Auguste: The Art of the French Gold- and Silversmith in the Age of the Enlightenment', ibid., pp. 78–91; same author's 'Orfèvrerie de table royale sous Louis XIV et Louis XV', in *Versailles et les tables royales*, pp. 94–105; Yves Cartier, 'L'Orfèvrerie de table de Louis XVI', ibid., pp. 106–9; Léonor d'Orey, 'L'Histoire des services d'orfèvrerie francaise à la cour du Portugal', ibid., pp. 165–70.

24. For the *surtout* see Hernmarck, I, pp. 182–5; Brown and Day, pp. 15–25.

25. The history of ceramics, like that of silver, is a vast one and outside the scope of the present book. In the context of the great porcelain dinner services made fashionable by the French kings: David Peters, 'Les Services de porcelaine de Louis XV et Louis XVI', in *Versailles et les tables royales*, pp. 110–23; Dorothée Guillème Brulon, 'Les Services de porcelaine de Sèvres, présents des rois Louis XV et Louis XVI aux souverains étrangers', ibid., pp. 184–7.

26. Peter Wilhelm Meister and Horst Reber, *European Porcelain of the 18th Century*, trans. Ewald Osers, Phaidon, Oxford, 1993, pp. 101–11.

27. For the evolution of table decoration see Georgiana Reynolds Smith, *Table Decoration Yesterday, Today & Tomorrow*, Charles E. Tuttle Co., 1968; Stefan Burrsche, *Tafelzier des Barock*, Editions Schneider, Munich, 1974; Alain Charles Gruber, 'Le Décor de table éphémère aux XVIIe et XVIIIe siècles', *Gazette des beaux-arts*, 73, 1974, pp. 285–300; Brown and Day, pp. 26–35; Joop Witteveen, 'Of Sugar and Porcelain. Table Decoration in the Netherlands in the 18th Century', in *Feasting and Fasting*, Proceedings of the Oxford Symposium on Food and Cookery, 1990, Prospect Books, 1990, pp. 212–21.

28. Ibid., pp. 30–1; Oleg Villumsen Krog, 'Usages et objets de table à la cour du Danemarck', *Versailles et les tables royales*, p. 173; Meister and Reber, pp. 111–13.

29. James Woodforde, *The Diary of a Country Parson 1758–1802*, OUP, 1972 ed., p. 212.

30. For the development of the dining-room in France see Peter Thornton, *Seventeenth-Century Interior Decoration in England, France and Holland*, Yale UP, 1978, pp. 282–93; same author's *Authentic Decor. The Domestic Interior 1620–1920*,

Weidenfeld & Nicolson, 1984, pp. 18–25, 50–60, 93–4; Jean-Pierre Babelon, *Demeures parisiennes sous Henri IV et Louis XIII*, Hazan, 1991, pp. 199–200; Girouard, *Life in the French Country House*, pp. 92–101, 120–44, 191 ff.

31. Thornton, *Seventeenth-Century Interior Decoration*, pp. 238–43.

32. Girouard, *Life in the English Country House*, pp. 136 ff.; same author's *Life in the French Country House*, p. 250.

33. For the dining-room in England see Charles Saumarez Smith, *Eighteenth-Century Decoration. Design and the Domestic Interior in England*, Harry N. Abrams Inc., 1993, pp. 39 ff., 76, 215 ff.

34. William Sanderson, *Graphice*, London, 1658, pp. 26–7. I am indebted to Ann Buddle for this reference.

35. Girouard, *Life in the English Country House*, pp. 204–5.

36. Thornton, *Authentic Decor*, p. 39 and note 29.

37. Robert Adam, *Works*, I, pl. V, quoted John Fowler and John Cornforth, *English Decoration in the 18th Century*, Barrie & Jenkins, 1974, p. 67.

38. Fowler and Cornforth, pp. 66–8.

39. Saumarez Smith, p. 234.

40. For tables see Thornton, *Seventeenth-Century Interior Decoration*, pp. 226–30; Fowler and Cornforth, p. 68.

41. Thornton, *Seventeenth-Century Interior Decoration*, pp. 183, 187.

42. For what follows on manners see Alfred Franklin, *La Vie privée d'autrefois*, Paris, 1889, pp. 214–83 (for texts); Esther B. Aresty, *The Best Behavior*, Simon & Schuster, NY, 1970, pp. 101 ff.; Norbert Elias, *The Civilising Process. The History of Manners*, trans. Edmund Jephcott, Basil Blackwell, Oxford, 1978, pp. 92–7 (for texts); Jean-Louis Flandrin, 'Distinction through Taste', in *A History of Private Life*, ed. Philippe Ariès and Georges Duby, III, *Passions of the Renaissance*, ed. Roger Chartier, Harvard UP, 1989, pp. 265–307; Zeer Gouranier, 'Modèles de cour et usages de table: les origines', in *Versailles et les tables royales*, pp. 28–9; Marenco, pp. 31–9.

43. C. Terryn, 'Simplicité et délicatesse: norme et réalité des bonnes manières à la table gantoise du XVIIIème siècle', in *L'Europe à table*, pp. 75–82.

44. '"The John Trot Fault": An English Dinner Table in the 1750s', *Petits propos culinaires*, 15, 1983, pp. 55–9; *The Art of Carving excerpted from a work entitled The Honours of the Table* (1788), Cambridge University Press, 1932, pp. 1–8.

45. Fowler and Cornforth, p. 67.

46. Beatrix Saule, 'Tables royales à Versailles 1682–1789', in *Versailles et les tables royales*, pp. 60–1.

47. See John Adamson, 'The Making of the Ancien-Regime Court 1500–1700', in *The Princely Courts of Europe. Ritual, Politics and Culture Under the Ancien Regime 1500–1750*, ed. John Adamson, Weidenfeld & Nicolson, 1999, pp. 7–41.

48. For the French court see Jacques Levron, *Daily Life at Versailles in the Seventeenth and Eighteenth Centuries*, trans. Claire Eliane Engel, Allen & Unwin, 1968; Olivier Chaline, 'The Valois and Bourbon Courts', in Adamson (ed.), pp. 67–93.

49. Saule, 'Tables royales à Versailles', pp. 41–6.

50. Levron, pp. 46–8.

51. For *le grand couvert* see Wheaton, pp. 135–7; Saule, 'Tables royales à Versailles', pp. 47–52; *Versailles et les tables royales*, pp. 255 ff. (nos. 13–15); Samuel John

Klingensmith, *The Utility of Splendor. Ceremony, Social Life, and Architecture at the Court of Bavaria 1600–1800*, University of Chicago Press, 1993, pp. 122–5.

52. See Hernmarck, *The Art of the European Silversmith*, I, pp. 172–3; *Versailles et les tables royales*, p. 97.

53. Quoted Levron, p. 39.

54. For room sequence see Hugh Murray Baillie, 'Etiquette and the Planning of the State Apartments of Baroque Palaces', *Archaeologia*, CI, 1967, pp. 169–99; Klingensmith, pp. 11–12, 115 ff., 125–44.

55. *Les Tables royales en Europe*, p. 255 (no. 14).

56. For the cadenas see Hernmarck, *The Art of the European Silversmith*, pp. 173–4; *Versailles et les tables royales*, pp. 257 (nos 18–20), 262 (no. 30), 269–70 (nos 44–5), 289 (no. 94).

57. Jérôme La Gorge, 'Musiques de table à Versailles', in *Versailles et les tables royales*, pp. 91–3, 255 (no. 13).

58. Saint-Simon, *Memoirs*, II, 1710–1715, ed. and trans. Lucy Norton, Prion Books, 2000, p. 40.

59. For the imperial court see Jeroen Duindam, 'The Court of the Austrian Habsburgs *c.* 1500–1750', in Adamson (ed.), pp. 165–87.

60. For Spain see Maria del Carmen Sinon, 'La Théâtricalité des repas royaux dans l'Espagne des XVIe et XVIIe siècles', in Aurell, Dumoulin and Thélamon (ed.), pp. 159–68; Glyn Redworth and Fernando Chesa, 'The Courts of the Spanish Habsburgs 1500–1700', in Adamson (ed.), pp. 43–65.

61. Klingensmith, pp. 159–69.

62. For England see John M. Beattie, *The English Court in the Reign of George I*, CUP, 1967, pp. 26 ff.; Philippa Glanville, 'Dining at Court, from George I to George IV', in *A King's Feast: The Goldsmith's Art and Royal Banqueting in the Eighteenth Century*, exhibition catalogue, Kensington Palace, 1991, pp. 106–17; same author's 'Protocole et usages de table à la cour d'Angleterre', in *Versailles et les tables royales*, pp. 159–69; John Adamson, 'The Tudor and Stuart Courts 1509–1714', in Adamson (ed.), pp. 95–117.

63. For Denmark see Ole Villumzsen Krog, 'The Royal Table in the 18th Century', in *A King's Feast*, pp. 134–44; same author's 'Usages et objets de table à la cour du Danemarck', in *Versailles et les tables royales*, pp. 171–9.

64. For Sweden, see Gruber, in *Versailles et les tables royales*, p. 150; Bo Vahlne, 'La Table du Palais Royal de Stockholm', in ibid., pp. 180–7 and 301 (no. 142).

65. For the 1664 festival see Wheaton, pp. 129–32; Sabine du Crest, *Les Fêtes à Versailles. Les divertissements de Louis XIV*, Aux Amateurs de Livres, 1990, pp. 4–21; *Versailles et les tables royales*, p. 250 (1).

66. For 1668 see Bursches, pp. 66–9 (for the text); du Crest, pp. 22–37; *Versailles et les tables royales*, pp. 250–1 (nos 2–4).

67. For 1674 see Bursches, pp. 69–71 (for the text); *Versailles et les tables royales*, p. 251 (no. 5).

68. *Versailles et les tables royales*, p. 352 (no. 8).

69. Saule, 'Manger à la cour', pp. 60–1.

70. Thornton, *Authentic Decor*, p. 171 (215); Maria Attilia Fabbri All'Oglio and Alessandro Fortis, *Il gastronomio errante Giacomo Casanova*, Ricciardi & Associati, 1998.

71. Klingensmith, pp. 165–6.
72. Saule, 'Tables royales à Versailles', pp. 60–1.
73. Ibid., pp. 35–40.

CHAPTER SIX
DINNER IS SERVED

1. Christopher Hussey, 'Oakly Park, Shropshire', *Country Life*, 1 March 1956, pp. 380–3, 426–9; John Cornforth, *English Interiors 1790–1848*, Barrie & Jenkins, 1978, p. 20.
2. Anna Maria Fay, *Victorian Days in England. Letters of an American Girl 1851–1852*, Houghton Mifflin, Riverside Press, Cambridge, 1923, pp. 79–84.
3. See Emmett Kennedy, *A Cultural History of the French Revolution*, Yale UP, 1989, p. 336; Marcel David, *Fraternité et la Révolution française 1789–1799*, Aubier, 1987, pp. 157–9.
4. Rebecca Spang, *The Invention of the Restaurant. Paris and Modern Gastronomic Culture*, Harvard UP, 2000, pp. 94–105.
5. For Napoleon see Philip Mansel, *The Eagle in Splendour. Napoleon I and his Court*, George Philip, 1987, pp. 50, 59; same author's *The Court of France 1789–1830*, CUP, 1988, pp. 67–8; Jean-Pierre Samoyault, 'La Table impériale', in *Versailles et les tables royales en Europe aux XVIIe–XIXe siècles*, Musée National des Châteaux de Versailles et de Trianon, exhibition catalogue, 1993, pp. 199–206; same author's 'L'Orfèvrerie de table de la couronne sous le Premier Empire', in ibid., pp. 207–15.
6. Mansel, *The Court of France*, pp. 150 ff.
7. Daniel Meyer, 'La Table royale sous le règne de Louis-Philippe', in *Versailles et les tables royales*, pp. 225–9.
8. *Lady Morgan in France*, ed. Elizabeth Suddaby and P. J. Yarrow, Oriel Press, 1971, pp. 228–39.
9. Ibid., p. 237.
10. For Carême see *L'Art culinaire au XIXe siècle. Antonin Carême*, Délégation à l'Action Artistique de la Ville de Paris, 1784–1984, Mairie du IIIe Arrondissement, Orangerie de Bagatelle, 1984; Stephen Mennell, *All Manners of Food. Eating and Taste in England and France from the Middle Ages to the Present*, Basil Blackwell, 1986, pp. 144–9; Barbara Ketcham Wheaton, 'Antonin Carême: The Food, the Bad, the Useful', in *Cooks and Other People*, ed. Harlan Walker, Proceedings of the Oxford Symposium on Food and Cookery, 1995, Prospect Books, 1996, pp. 290–5.
11. For the effect of this return on Victorian food, see Valerie Mars, 'Kitsch Culinary Icons: The Cultural Roots of Changes in Nineteenth-Century Dinner Cuisine', in *Look and Feel. Studies in Texture, Appearance and Incidental Characteristics of Food*, Proceedings of the Oxford Symposium on Food and Cookery, 1993, ed. Harlan Walker, Prospect Books, 1994, pp. 108–18.
12. Esther B. Aresty, *The Delectable Past*, Allen & Unwin, 1965, pp. 126–59; *L'Art culinaire au XIXe siècle*, pp. 71 ff.; Mennell, pp. 149–77.

13. Claudio Benporat, *Storia della gastronomia italiana*, Mursia, 1990, pp. 319 ff.
14. Aresty, pp. 160–80; Mennell, pp. 150–6, 213 ff.; Sarah Freeman, *Mutton and Oysters. The Victorians and Their Food*, Victor Gollancz, 1989, pp. 110–77; Dena Attar, 'Keeping up Appearances: The Genteel Art of Dining in Middle-Class Victorian Britain', in *'The Apetoite and the Eye.' Visual Aspects of Food and Its Presentation within Their Historic Context*, ed. C. Anne Wilson, Edinburgh UP, 1991, pp. 12–40; Peter Brears, Maggie Black, Gill Corbishley, Jane Renfrew and Jennifer Stead, *A Taste of History. 10,000 Years of Food in Britain*, English Heritage, 1993, pp. 263 ff. For Francatelli see *Chef to Queen Victoria. The Recipes of Charles Esmé Francatelli*, ed. Ann M. Currah, William Kimber, 1973. For Isabella Beeton, Sarah Freeman, *Isabella and Sam. The Story of Mrs Beeton*, Victor Gollancz, 1977, pp. 186–217; for Alexis Soyer, *Memoirs of Alexis Soyer*, ed. F. Volant and J. R. Warren, Cooks Books, Rottingdean, 1985; Helen Morris, *Portrait of a Chef. The Life of Alexis Soyer*, CUP, 1938; Elizabeth Ray, *Alexis Soyer. Cook Extraordinary*, Southover Press, 1991.
15. For the emergence of the restaurant and its consequences see Pierre Andrieu, *Fine Bouche. A History of the Restaurant in France*, translated by Arthur L. Hayward, Cassell, 1956; *L'Art culinaire au XIXe siècle*, pp. 38–9, 47–54; Mennell, pp. 135–44; Jean-Robert Pitte, 'The Rise of the Restaurant', in Jean-Louis Flandrin and Massimo Montanari, *Food. A Culinary History from Antiquity to the Present Day*, Columbia UP, 1999, pp. 471–80; and especially Spang.
16. Mennell, pp. 266–90; Giles MacDonogh, *Brillat-Savarin. The Judge and His Stomach*, John Murray, 1992.
17. Anne Martin-Fugier, 'Bourgeois Rituals', in *A History of Private Life*, ed. Philippe Ariès and Georges Duby, IV, *From the Fires of Revolution to the Great War*, ed. Michelle Pivrot, Harvard UP, 1990, pp. 261–337.
18. J. C. Loudon, *The Suburban Gardener and Villa Companion*, London, 1838, pp. 86–95.
19. Robert Kerr, *The Gentleman's House*, London, 1864, pp. 101–18, 201–2.
20. Mrs Loftie, *The Dining-Room*, London, Macmillan, 1878.
21. Peter Thornton, *Authentic Decor. The Domestic Interior 1620–1920*, Weidenfeld & Nicolson, London, 1985, pp. 145, 151, 157, 210 ff.
22. Hans-Jurgen Teuteberg, 'The German Bourgeois Family at the Dining Table: Structural Changes of Meal Manners, 1880–1930', in *Food and Material Culture*, 4th Symposium on Food History, Prospect Books, 1991, pp. 133–70.
23. For mealtimes see Jean-Paul Aron, *Le Mangeur du XIXe siècle*, Éditions Robert Laffont, Paris, 1973, pp. 207–16; Arnold Palmer, *Moveable Feasts. Changes in English Eating Habits*, OUP, 1984; Freeman, pp. 178 ff.; John Bennett, 'Time, Place and Content: The Changing Structure of Meals in Britain in the Nineteenth and Twentieth Centuries', in *Food and Material Culture*, pp. 116–31.
24. Brillat-Savarin, *La Physiologie du goût*, Pierre Waleffe, Paris, 1967, pp. 149–50.
25. See John Burnett, *Plenty and Want. A Social History of Diet in England from 1815 to the Present Day*, Thomas Nelson & Sons, 1966, pp. 186–7; Claudine Marenco, *Manières de table, modèles de moeurs 17ème–20ème siècle*, Éditions de l'E.N.S.-Cachan, 1992, pp. 106–38.
26. W. M. Thackeray, *The Book of Snobs* (1847), in *Works*, Smith, Elder & Co., London, 1889, XIX, p. 79.
27. *Mrs Beeton's Book of Household Management*, London, 1861, Chancellor Press Reprint, 1986, p. 904.

28. *Manners and Tone of Good Society and Solecisms to be Avoided, by a Member of the Aristocracy*, 12th ed., Frederick Warne & Co., 1885, pp. 77–103.

29. Mrs Humphry ('Madge' of *Truth*), *Manners for Women*, n.d., Pryor Publications, 1993, p. 71.

30. Quoted Valerie Mars, 'À la Russe: The New Way of Dining', in *Luncheon, Nuncheon and Other Meals*, 7th Symposium on Food History, Prospect Books, 1994 pp. 117–44.

31. Hans Ottomeyer, '*Service à la française* and *Service à la russe*: or the Evolution of the table in the Eighteenth and Nineteenth Centuries', in *Food and Material Culture*, 4th Symposium on Food History, 1991, pp. 107–83; Peter Brears, '*À la française*: The Waning of a Long Dining Tradition', in *Luncheon, Nuncheon and Other Meals*, pp. 91–116.

32. Caroline Davidson, *The World of Mary Ellen Best*, Chatto & Windus, London, 1985, p. 107 (no. 103).

33. For the whole subject of the transfer over to *à la russe* see *L'Art culinaire au XIXe siècle*, pp. 59–60; Mars, in *Luncheon, Nuncheon and Other Meals*; Burnett, pp. 176 ff.; D. J. Oddy, 'Food, Drink and Nutrition', in *The Cambridge Social History of Britain 1750–1950*, 2, *People and their Environment*, ed. F. M. L. Thompson, CUP, 1990, pp. 258–9; Freeman, pp. 184 ff.

34. *Mrs Beeton's Book of Household Management*, p. 954.

35. *The Habits of Good Society* (1850s), p. 220.

36. Esther B. Aresty, *The Best Behavior*, Simon & Schuster, NY, 1970, pp. 129 ff.; Mennell, pp. 206–11; Leonore Davidoff and Catherine Hall, *Family Fortunes. Men and Women of the English Middle Class 1780–1850*, Hutchinson, 1987, pp. 399–400; Teuteberg, in *Food and Material Culture*; Leonore Davidoff, *The Best Circles. Society, Etiquette and the Season*, Croom Helm, London, 1973, pp. 13 ff.; Andrew St George, *The Descent of Manners. Etiquette, Rules and the Victorians*, Chatto & Windus, London, 1993, chs 1 and 2.

37. The selection used here is: *The Habits of Good Society: A Handbook of Etiquette for Ladies and Gentlemen*, James Hogg & Sons, London (n.d. but 1850s), pp. 300 ff.; *Cassell's Household Guide*, Cassell (1860s), III, pp. 243 ff.; 1911 ed., Waverley Press, London, II, pp. 447–51; *Manners and Tone of Good Society*, ch. v; Mrs Humphry ('Madge' of *Truth*), *Manners for Men*, James Bowden, 1897, reprint, Pryor Publications, 1994, pp. 55–82; same author's *Manners for Women*, Pryor Publications reprint, 1993, pp. 71 ff.; *Etiquette of Good Society*, edited and revised by Lady Colin Campbell, Cornell & Co. Ltd, 1902, ch. XI (first edition 1872). See also Freeman, pp. 184 ff.; Sara Paston-Williams, *The Art of Dining. A History of Cooking and Eating*, National Trust, 1993, pp. 244 ff.

38. See Davidoff, p. 107 and note 54; Farid Chenoune, *A History of Men's Fashion*, Flammarion, 1993, pp. 95, 109–12.

39. Gwen Raverat, *Period Piece. A Cambridge Childhood*, Faber & Faber, n.d., p. 78.

40. Humphry, *Manners for Women*, p. 80.

41. *The Book of the Home*, ed. H. C. Davidson, Gresham Publishing Co., London, 1904, VI, pp. 251 ff.

42. Loftie, pp. 84 ff.

43. Thomas Shurrmann, 'Cutlery at the fine Table: Innovations and Use in the Nineteenth Century', in *Food and Material Culture*, pp. 171–83.

44. Aresty, *The Best Behavior*, pp. 174–8.
45. Fabienne de Sèze and Dany Sautot, 'Du verre au cristal: une noblesse acquise', in *Versailles et les tables royales*, pp. 230–1.
46. St George, p. 49.

POSTSCRIPT

1. Gabriel Tschumi, *Royal Chef. Recollections of Life in Royal Households from Queen Victoria to Queen Mary*, William Kimber, 1954, p. 97.
2. Ibid., ch. VIII.
3. Generally for the twentieth century see Jean-Louis Flandrin and Massimo Montanari, *Food. A Culinary History from Antiquity to the Present*, Columbia UP, 1999, pp. 435 ff.; Hans-Jürgen Teyteberg, 'The German Bourgeois Family at the Dining Table: Structural Changes of Meal Manners, 1880–1930', in *Food and Material Culture*, 4th Symposium on Food History, 1991, pp. 13–70; Claudine Marenco, *Manières de table, modèles de moeurs 17ème–20ème siècle*, Éditions l'E.N.S.-Cachan, 1992, pp. 139 ff.

INDEX

Page numbers in *italic* indicate illustrations and captions